Stone and Dung,
Oil and Spit

Stone and Dung, Oil and Spit

Jewish Daily Life in the Time of Jesus

Jodi Magness

WILLIAM B. EERDMANS PUBLISHING COMPANY

GRAND RAPIDS, MICHIGAN / CAMBRIDGE, U.K.

Published 2011 by
Wm. B. Eerdmans Publishing Co.
2140 Oak Industrial Drive N.E., Grand Rapids, Michigan 49505 /
P.O. Box 163, Cambridge CB3 9PU U.K.

Printed in the United States of America

17 16 15 14 13 12 11   7 6 5 4 3 2 1

Library of Congress Cataloging-in-Publication Data

Magness, Jodi.
Stone and dung, oil and spit: Jewish daily life in the time of Jesus / Jodi Magness.
        p.   cm.
Includes bibliographical references.
ISBN 978-0-8028-6558-8 (pbk.: alk. paper)
1. Jews — Social life and customs — To 70 A.D.
2. Jews — History — 586 B.C.–70 A.D.
3. Judaism — History — Post-exilic period, 586 B.C.–210 A.D.   I. Title.

DS112.M2325   2011
933′.05 — dc22

2010046336

www.eerdmans.com

Contents

v

CONTENTS

Figures

(following page 96)

Preface

My interest in the subject matter of this book evolved out of my work on the archaeology of Qumran. Originally I hoped to write a book on the archaeology of purity, correlating the literary and archaeological evidence for the purity practices of the major Jewish groups and sects of the late Second Temple period. In light of comments that I received on a first draft of the manuscript, I revised the title and focus to aspects of Jewish daily life in late Second Temple period Palestine, which more accurately reflects the contents.

Numerous colleagues helped me grapple with the textual evidence — especially rabbinic literature and the New Testament — by offering advice and comments on drafts of this manuscript. I owe special thanks to Yonatan Adler, Nahum Ben-Yehuda, Hannan Birenboim, Stephen Goranson, Hannah Harrington, Joel Marcus, Joan Taylor, Cecilia Wassen, and an anonymous outside reviewer. Of course, I am responsible for the content and any errors that remain. My research on the topics covered in this book has long been enriched by conversations with my friends Hanan Eshel z"l, Andrea Berlin, Magen Broshi, and David Amit. I also wish to thank Sidnie White Crawford, Paula Fredriksen, Lee Levine, and Eric Meyers for their support in writing letters of recommendation for sabbatical fellowships.

The original draft of this manuscript was completed at the end of a sabbatical in 2007-2008. My leave was supported by funding from the following sources, which I gratefully acknowledge: the University of North Carolina at Chapel Hill (and especially the faculty and staff of the Department of Religious Studies); a fellowship from the Hetty Goldman Membership Fund and membership in the School for Historical Studies at the Institute for Advanced Study at Princeton, NJ (Spring 2008), and a visiting professorship (the Morgan Chair of Architectural Design) in the Department of Visual Arts at the University of Louisville, KY (Fall 2007). During my sabbatical I benefited from the friendship and hospitality of many colleagues. I owe a special debt of gratitude to Karen Britt at the University of Louisville and her husband Barry Walker, who welcomed me into their lives and shared with me their home. My stay at the Institute for Advanced Study was enriched particularly by conversations with Patricia Crone, the late Oleg Grabar, Avishai Margalit, Lloyd Moote, and Heinrich von Staden. I also wish to thank the faculty and staff in the Department of Visual Arts at the University of Louisville and the Institute for Advanced Study at Princeton for making the time I spent in Kentucky and New Jersey as enjoyable as it was productive.

I am fortunate to have a loving family, including my parents Herbert and Marlene Magness and my nephew Mike Miller, who has enriched our lives by joining us in North Carolina. I am especially grateful for the unconditional love and support of my husband Jim Haberman, who quietly and patiently keeps the home fires burning (and cats fed) whenever I am away. Jim also gets the credit and my thanks for scanning and preparing the illustrations for this book.

In memory of

my dear friend and colleague,

Hanan Eshel z"l

NOTE: *unless otherwise indicated, all translated passages are from the following sources:*

Dead Sea Scrolls except the Temple Scroll: García Martínez and Tigchelaar, *The Dead Sea Scrolls Study Edition.*
The Temple Scroll: Yadin, *The Temple Scroll,* vol. 2.
Josephus's *War:* Vermes and Goodman, *The Essenes According to the Classical Sources.* Josephus's other works: Whiston, online at http://pace.mcmaster.ca/york/york/texts.htm.
Philo, Pliny, and Eusebius: Loeb edition.
Greek and Roman authors except Josephus, Philo, Pliny, and Petronius: Stern, *Greek and Latin Authors on Jews and Judaism.*
Mishnah: Neusner, *The Mishnah.*
Tosefta: Neusner, *The Tosefta.*

The Palestinian Talmud: Neusner, *The Talmud of the Land of Israel.*
The Babylonian Talmud: Soncino Talmud.
Tractate Semahot: Zlotnick, *The Tractate "Mourning."*
Bible (Hebrew Bible + New Testament + Apocrypha): NRSV.

Acknowledgments

The author thanks the following organizations and individuals for kindly granting permission to reproduce illustrations:

Israel Exploration Society (Figs. 1-3, 7-19, 32-34, 37-38)
Israel Antiquities Authority (Figs. 35, 44-46)
The British Academy (Figs. 24-29)
Jane Cahill (Fig. 41)
Emanuel Damati (Fig. 20)
Hanan Eshel z"l (Fig. 36)

Abbreviations

AASOR	Annual of the American Schools of Oriental Research
AB	Anchor Bible
ABD	*Anchor Bible Dictionary,* ed. David Noel Freedman
ABRL	Anchor Bible Reference Library
AGJU	Arbeiten zur Geschichte des Spätjudentums und Urchristentums
AJA	*American Journal of Archaeology*
ALGHJ	Arbeiten zur Literatur und Geschichte des hellenistischen Judentums
APOT	*The Apocrypha and Pseudepigrapha of the Old Testament in English,* ed. R. H. Charles
AuOr	*Aula Orientalis*
BA	*Biblical Archaeologist*
BAR	*Biblical Archaeology Review*
BASOR	*Bulletin of the American Schools of Oriental Research*
BETL	Bibliotheca ephemeridum theologicarum lovaniensium
BibOr	Biblica et orientalia
BJS	Brown Judaic Studies
BRS	Biblical Resource Series
BZNW	Beihefte zur Zeitschrift für die neutestamentliche Wissenschaft
CBQ	*Catholic Biblical Quarterly*
CHANE	Culture and History of the Ancient Near East
CIL	*Corpus inscriptionum latinarum*
CJ	*Classical Journal*
ConBNT	Coniectanea biblica: New Testament Series
CP	*Classical Philology*
CRINT	Compendia rerum iudaicarum ad Novum Testamentum
DJD	Discoveries in the Judaean Desert
DSD	*Dead Sea Discoveries*

EDB	*Eerdmans Dictionary of the Bible*, ed. David Noel Freedman, Allen C. Myers, and Astrid B. Beck
ErIsr	*Eretz-Israel*
ESA	Eastern [Terra] Sigillata A
ETL	*Ephemerides theologicae lovanienses*
HTR	*Harvard Theological Review*
HUCA	*Hebrew Union College Annual*
IEJ	*Israel Exploration Journal*
IOS	*Israel Oriental Studies*
JAOS	*Journal of the American Oriental Society*
JBL	*Journal of Biblical Literature*
JJS	*Journal of Jewish Studies*
JNES	*Journal of Near Eastern Studies*
JQR	*Jewish Quarterly Review*
JRA	*Journal of Roman Archaeology*
JSJ	*Journal for the Study of Judaism*
JSJSup	Journal for the Study of Judaism: Supplement Series
JSNTSup	Journal for the Study of the New Testament: Supplement Series
JSOTSup	Journal for the Study of the Old Testament: Supplement Series
JSPSup	Journal for the Study of the Pseudepigrapha: Supplement Series
JTS	*Journal of Theological Studies*
LSTS	Library of Second Temple Studies
MT	Masoretic Text
NEA	*Near Eastern Archaeology*
NEAEHL	*The New Encyclopedia of Archaeological Excavations in the Holy Land*, ed. E. Stern
NovTSup	Novum Testamentum Supplements
NTOA SA	Novum Testamentum et Orbis Antiquus Series Archaeologica
NTS	*New Testament Studies*
PEQ	*Palestine Exploration Quarterly*
Pillar	Pillar New Testament Commentary
PTSDSSP	Princeton Theological Seminary Dead Sea Scrolls Project
Qad	*Qadmoniot*
RB	*Revue biblique*
RBL	*Review of Biblical Literature*
RevQ	*Revue de Qumrân*
SBFCM	Studium Biblicum Franciscanum Collectio maior
SBLDS	Society of Biblical Literature Dissertation Series
SBLEJL	Society of Biblical Literature Early Judaism and Its Literature
SBLSymS	Society of Biblical Literature Symposium Series
SDSSRL	Studies in the Dead Sea Scrolls and Related Literature
SHR	Studies in the History of Religions
SJLA	Studies in Judaism in Late Antiquity
SNTSMS	Society for New Testament Studies Monograph Series

Abbreviations

STDJ	Studies on the Texts of the Desert of Judah
StPB	Studia post-biblica
TRENT	Traditions of the Rabbis from the Era of the New Testament
TSAJ	Texte und Studien zum antiken Judentum
VC	*Vigiliae christianae*
VTSup	Supplements to Vetus Testamentum
WUNT	Wissenschaftliche Untersuchungen zum Neuen Testament
ZDPV	*Zeitschrift des Deutschen Palästina-Vereins*

CHAPTER 1

Footprints in Archaeology and Text

It was the best of times, it was the worst of times, it was the age of
wisdom, it was the age of foolishness, it was the epoch of belief, it
was the epoch of incredulity, it was the season of Light, it was the
season of Darkness.

Charles Dickens, A Tale of Two Cities

Introduction

Perhaps no epoch in the history of humankind has been the subject of greater fascination and more intensive study than the late Second Temple period in Palestine — that is, the first century B.C.E. and first century C.E. — for this was the world of Jesus. We are fortunate to have a relative abundance of literary sources that inform us about this period, including the writings of the ancient Jewish historian Flavius Josephus, the literature of the Qumran sect (the Dead Sea Scrolls), and the books of the New Testament. Archaeology too has yielded a wealth of information, with excavated sites throughout the country including Jerusalem, Jericho, Masada, Herodium, Caesarea Maritima, Qumran, Sepphoris, and Gamla, to name just a few. And yet, paradoxically, there are many aspects of the late Second Temple period in Palestine that remain obscure or poorly understood. These gaps in our knowledge continue to fuel old debates and controversies and spawn new ones, with many spilling over from the ivory tower of academia into the public arena.

1

To be sure, this is a fascinating era to study. The late Second Temple period in Palestine was an unusually turbulent time, encompassing the collapse of the Hasmonean (Maccabean) state and its annexation to Rome, the brutal reign of the client king Herod the Great (40-4 B.C.E.), and the breakdown of Roman rule under Herod's sons and a series of ineffective and insensitive Roman administrators. Smoldering tensions occasionally erupted into open fighting, pitting Jews against Gentiles, Jews against Romans, Jews against Samaritans, rich against poor, and rural populations against town and city dwellers. Urban terrorists called Sicarii — literally, "dagger men" — openly assassinated their opponents. Escalating cycles of violence culminated with the outbreak of a Jewish revolt against Rome in 66 C.E., which ended disastrously for the Jews four years later when Jerusalem fell and the second temple was destroyed (70 C.E.).

What do we know about the everyday life of Jews in Palestine during this turbulent era? That is the question this book addresses, focusing especially on the mid-first century B.C.E. (end of the Hasmonean period and beginning of the reign of Herod the Great) to 70 C.E. The subjects of this study are the ancient inhabitants of Judea as well as the Judaized populations of other parts of Palestine (Galilee, Idumaea, Peraea), but mostly excluding the Yahwistic population of Samaria. Although Palestine was part of the Roman East, the daily life of Jews — and especially the Jews of Palestine — was distinguished by an observance of biblical (pentateuchal) law and especially purity laws relating to the Jerusalem temple that has left material traces. This book seeks to identify and correlate evidence of these Jewish "footprints" in the archaeological record and literary sources. These footprints relate to a broad spectrum of quotidian activities, from dining practices to toilet habits to Sabbath observance to burial customs.

This introductory chapter sets the stage for the discussion of various categories of activities by considering the characteristics that distinguished the Jews of Palestine from other peoples in the Roman world. Many of the features that set Jews apart stemmed from their worship of the God of Israel and the observance of his laws. Debates about the proper observance of these laws created sectarian divisions among the Jewish population. These divisions not only resulted from differences in opinion with regard to religious practice but also reflected socio-economic realities in late Second Temple–period Palestine.

Sectarianism in Late Second Temple–Period Palestine

Jewish Palestine of the first century swarmed with different sects. Every sect probably had its divisions and subdivisions. Even the Pharisees themselves were reported to have been divided into seven categories. It is therefore precarious to ascribe our documents definitely to any of the known three major Jewish sects.[1]

The [Dead Sea] Scrolls confirm that in the [late] Second Temple period there existed in Israel three main movements: the Pharisees, Sadducees, and Essenes.[2]

By the late Second Temple period various movements and sects had developed among the Jewish population of Palestine, the best-attested of which are the Pharisees, Sadducees, Essenes, and Jesus' movement.[3] These groups were differentiated by their approaches to the interpretation and practice of biblical law, with many of the disagreements among them centering on the Jerusalem temple and especially purity observance relating to the sacrificial cult.

Much of our information about these groups comes from literary sources, the most important of which are Flavius Josephus, rabbinic (especially tannaitic) literature, the New Testament (especially the Synoptic Gospels), and Qumran literature (the Dead Sea Scrolls).[4] To these sources we may add Philo Judaeus and Pliny the Elder, especially on the Essenes.[5] The problems inherent in using the information provided by these sources, which sometimes appears to be contradictory not only between different sources but even internally, are well known.[6] They include the authors' biases and agendas, the question of their sources of information (and the reliability of these sources), chronological issues (especially in cases where the composition postdates 70, sometimes by a century or more), the relationship between the authors and the groups mentioned or described, and the intended audience(s) and purpose(s) of the work.[7] This does not mean that the information provided by these sources should be disregarded altogether, but rather that these works must be evaluated and used critically and responsibly. As Ya'akov Sussman remarked (referring to rabbinic literature and the Dead Sea Scrolls), these sources "complement [or complete] and illuminate each other."[8]

As a Jew who lived in Palestine before 70 and claimed to have personal familiarity with these groups, Josephus provides valuable information, despite his well-known biases and misrepresentations.[9] Much of our information on the Pharisees, Sadducees, and Essenes comes from *War* 2.119-65; *Ant.* 13.171-73, 293-98; and 18.12-20. Some of Josephus's observations seem to be echoed in the New Testament, for example, concerning resurrection: "The Sadducees say that there is no resurrection, or angel, or spirit; but the Pharisees acknowledge all three" (Acts 23:8). A saying attributed to Rabbi Akiba is usually understood in light of Josephus's description of the Pharisees' approach to free will: "Everything is foreseen, and free choice is given" (*m. 'Abot* 3:15).[10]

For the purposes of this study, I make certain assumptions, some of which are of necessity simplifications. The Sadducees were members of the Jerusalem elite or governing class, including some high priests, although not all of the high priests and aristocracy were Sadducees.[11] The Pharisees are related (but not identical) to the rabbis of the period after 70 C.E., with whom they share some similar approaches to the interpretation and practice of Jewish law.[12] Anthony Saldarini described the Pharisees as a "retainer class" that was both a religious group and political force and often interacted with the governing class.[13] Saldarini noted that this retainer class is not analogous to a modern middle class as its members lacked independent power and were dependent on the governing class.[14] Emil Schürer defined as follows the relationship between Sadducees and Pharisees: "the contrast between Sadducees and Pharisees is not one of a priestly party versus a party of the religiously observant, but of a clerical and lay aristocracy vis-à-vis an essentially lay group which derived its authority from learning."[15]

I identify the group that settled at Qumran and the wider movement of which it was a part with Josephus's Essenes. Priests — and especially dispossessed Zadokite priests — played prominent roles in the establishment and leadership of this sect, although not all members were descended from the house of Zadok or other priestly families.[16] Other members of the wider movement lived in Jerusalem and elsewhere around Palestine but have not left identifiable remains in the archaeological record.[17] For the purposes of this study I usually refer to the group at Qumran as the Qumran community, Qumran sect, or sectarians and reserve the term Essene when dealing with the testimony of ancient authors or with the wider movement. In my opinion it is accurate to describe the Qumran community and the larger movement of which it was a part as a sect, but I do not consider the other groups and movements to be sects as they are not characterized by the same extreme exclusivity and withdrawal or separation from the larger society.[18]

I focus on Jesus as he is portrayed especially in the Synoptic Gospels but generally do not consider the practices of the Jerusalem community led by James and Peter after Jesus' death, as the literary and archaeological information is too meager.[19] In my opinion our earliest sources about Jesus and his socio-economic setting indicate that he was a lower-class Galilean Jew.[20]

Purity and Holiness

They shall consecrate my temple and fear my temple, for I dwell among them. (11QT 46:11-12)

Purity therefore, first, serves as an important mode of differentiation and definition for the sects known to us in the first century B.C. and A.D.[21]

Ancient Jews worshipped the God of Israel as their national deity and lived according to his laws.[22] These laws require Jews ("Israel") to be in a state of ritual purity when they enter God's presence:[23] "they must not defile their camp, where I dwell among them" (Num 5:3).[24] The Hebrew Bible contains legislation listing items, people, or processes that convey impurity and mandates methods of purification.[25] Many types of impurity are due to natural processes that are a result of the human condition, such as death, skin diseases, and sexual discharges. It is not a sin to contract these impurities, which temporarily contaminate people and certain objects in close proximity.[26] Although the means of purification vary depending on the cause or nature of the impurity (for example, corpse impurity versus having a genital discharge) and the status of the person who has contracted it (priest versus layperson), for most types of impurity the Hebrew Bible requires bathing or washing in water and the passage of a certain amount of time.[27] The Hebrew Bible also considers certain moral offenses — mainly sexual transgressions (such as adultery, homosexual relations, and bestiality), idolatry, and murder (bloodshed) — as defiling. These acts not only make the transgressor impure but they pollute the land and people of Israel:[28] "Thus the land became defiled; and I punished it for its iniquity, and the land vomited out its inhabitants . . ." (Lev 18:25).[29]

God's presence dwelled in the tabernacle among the Israelites (the "camp") during their desert wanderings: "And have them make me a sanctuary, so that I may dwell among them" (Exod 25:8). Later the two successive temples on Jerusalem's Temple Mount provided the main point of contact between God and his people. Ancient Jews do not seem to have debated the need to purify themselves before entering the Jerusalem temple.[30] However, during the late Second Temple period disagreements developed about whether (and to what degree) purity laws should be observed *beyond the boundaries* of the temple cult.[31] These disagreements reflect a lack of consensus about where God's presence dwelled or was supposed to dwell: was God's presence confined to the Jerusalem temple or did it dwell among all Israel — or was Israel expected to strive to attain the purity necessary so that God's presence could again dwell in their midst?[32]

A related point of disagreement concerned whether Jews were expected to live in imitation of God's holiness *(imitatio Dei)*, as expressed for example in Lev 11:45: "you shall be holy, for I am holy."[33] Disagreements arose because the various sources of the Hebrew Bible present different notions of holiness.[34] According to the Priestly Code, the temple (or sanctuary) and priests are holy but the Israelites and their camp are not. Nevertheless, all who dwell in the camp must observe the laws of purity because of God's presence. The Holiness Code extends divine holiness as well as priestly sanctity to the entire Land of Israel and its inhabitants (not just the sanctuary and priests). According to the Deuteronomist (and E and J), the people of Israel are holy because they were chosen by God.[35] Hannah Harrington notes that the Qumran sect was distinguished from other groups, not by their definition of holiness, but in the level of holiness they required of ordinary Jews.[36]

The lifestyle of the Qumran sect reflects their belief that God's presence was not restricted to one place (the Jerusalem temple), just as the desert camp with the tent of meeting in its midst moved with the Israelites during their wanderings.[37] The *Damascus Document* explicitly describes sectarian communities as "camps":[38] "And this (is) the rule for the settlers of [the] [camps] who walk in accordance with these (rules) . . ." (CD 12:22-23).[39] Therefore, unlike other Jews the sectarians followed laws that applied to the desert camp of the Israelites, such as defecating in a pit dug outside the camp, which was required because "the Lord your God travels along with your camp, to save you and to hand over your enemies to you, therefore your camp must be holy, so that he may not see anything indecent among you and turn away from you" (Deut 23:12-14).[40] Because the sect was conceived of as a substitute temple or sanctuary in the midst of which angels dwelled, members were expected to maintain the level of purity required for priests on a daily basis:[41]

> "{no madman, or lunatic shall enter, no simpleton, or fool, no blind man, or maimed, or lame, or deaf man, and no minor, none of these shall enter into the Community, for the Angels of Holiness are [in their midst]}." (4Q266 8 I, 6-9)[42]

Unlike the Qumran sect, the Pharisees did not withdraw from the sacrificial cult even if they may have criticized the temple priesthood.[43] Vered Noam has identified two approaches to purity among the Pharisees and rabbis: the first approach limits purity concerns strictly to the temple on the basis of scripture, and the second expands purity observance to everyday life outside the temple cult based not on scripture but on custom.[44] These apparent contradictions suggest a mixed view concerning the divine presence and notion of holiness, which at the same time are confined to the temple but encompass all of Israel.[45]

A major point of disagreement between the Pharisees and the Qumran sect was whether the biblical purity laws required for the desert camp of the Israelites applied to the entire city of Jerusalem or only to the temple.[46] The Qumran sect held a maximalist position, equating Jerusalem with the desert camp: "And we think that the temple [is the place of the tent of meeting, and Je]rusale[m] is the camp; and out[side] the camp [is outside of Jerusalem;] it is the camp of their cities" (4Q394=4QMMT 3-7 II 16-18). This is why the sectarians sought to ban from Jerusalem all types of impurity (even human excrement) as well as all who carry or spread impurity, including dogs and chickens.[47] In contrast, the Pharisees seem to have limited the observance of the purity laws required for the desert camp to the temple, with a lesser degree of purity required for the rest of the city and even the Temple Mount, as suggested by rabbinic literature:

> And just as in the wilderness there were three camps, the camp of the Indwelling Presence of God, the camp of the Levites, and the camp of the Israelites, so there were in Jerusalem [three camps]: From the gate of Jerusalem to the gate of the Temple Mount is the camp of Israel. From the gate of the Temple Mount up to Nicanor's Gate is the camp of the Levites. From the Nicanor's Gate and inward is the camp of the

7

Indwelling Presence of God. And that [corresponded to the place within] the curtains in the wilderness. In the time of journeying, no aspect of sanctity applied to them, and people were not liable concerning them on account of uncleanness. (*t. Kelim B. Qam.* 1:12)[48]

Like other Jews, Jesus presumably observed the laws of purity that regulated participation in the temple cult. It is anachronistic to suppose that Jesus disregarded purity laws altogether.[49] Paul too seems to have purified himself before entering the Jerusalem temple, as the episode leading up to his arrest suggests:

Then Paul took the men, and the next day, having purified himself, he entered the temple with them, making public the completion of the days of purification when the sacrifice would be made for each of them. (Acts 21:26)[50]

The Gospels attribute to Jesus a strict position on certain points of law.[51] For example, Jesus reportedly prohibited divorce and remarriage after divorce (Matt 5:31-32; 19:1-10), a position similar to that of the Qumran sect and the house of Shammai but different from the house of Hillel and probably the Sadducees (as illustrated by the episode involving Herod Antipas).[52] Jesus seems to have emphasized the avoidance of impurity caused by certain immoral or unethical acts (such as remarriage after divorce, which he equated with adultery) over impurity caused by natural processes, requiring of his followers moral and ethical behavior to achieve the holiness *(imitatio Dei)* necessary for entering the kingdom of God.[53] This was based on the biblical tradition that some moral violations could cause the divine presence to abandon the temple and Land of Israel altogether.[54] Jesus reportedly associated wealth with immoral and unethical behavior, which is why the wealthy would find it difficult to enter the kingdom of God (Mark 10:24-25). That Jesus linked immoral and unethical behavior with the lifestyle of the wealthy is suggested by early sayings attributed to him and his renunciation of personal possessions, as for example:

No one can serve two masters; for a slave will either hate the one and love the other, or be devoted to the one and despise the other. You cannot serve God and *mammon* [Hebrew: wealth]. (Matt 6:24; see also Luke 16:13)[55]

8

The Socio-Economics of Sectarianism

If "sect" is interpreted as implying doctrinal deviation from a norm, such a term is to be avoided, since we cannot be sure that in late Second Temple Judaism there was a "norm."[56]

The Ruling Class and Urban Elite

Differences between the Jewish groups and movements of the late Second Temple period should be understood in light of socio-economic factors as well as cultic or religious considerations. As Donald Ariel has observed, "The divergence in approach to ritual purity also characterized different social strata."[57] For example, the Sadducees were drawn from the Jerusalem elite, including some of the high priests. They cooperated with the Romans and sought to preserve the status quo.[58] Our sources suggest that the Sadducees rejected innovations in Judaism, such as the belief in the resurrection of the dead, and considered written law (Torah) but not oral law as authoritative.[59]

Jewish royalty — consisting of Herod and his family and successors and the Hasmoneans — occupied the pinnacle of society. Remains of Hasmonean palaces have been discovered at Jericho and Judean desert sites such as Alexandrium-Sartaba and Hyrcania. Herod's palaces have been uncovered around Palestine, including at Jericho, Masada, Herodium, Cypros, Machaerus, and Caesarea Maritima (see Figs. 1-6).[60] The Hasmonean and Herodian palaces were designed and decorated in Hellenistic and Roman fashion, including lavish interior decoration, expensive furniture, and spacious triclinia for receptions and formal dinners and banquets.[61]

Occupying the top of the social pyramid just below the royalty was the Jerusalem elite. Vivid evidence of their lifestyle comes from the mansions in the Jewish Quarter in Jerusalem's upper city (or western hill), which Nahman Avigad, the excavator, described as follows:

> Construction in the Upper City was dense, with the houses built quite close together; but the individual dwelling units were extensive, and inner courtyards lent them the character of luxury villas. These homes were richly ornamented with frescoes, stucco work, and mosaic floors, and were equipped with complex bathing facilities, as well as contain-

ing the luxury goods and artistic objects which signify a high standard of living. This, then, was an upper class quarter, where the noble families of Jerusalem lived, with the High Priest at their head. Here they built their homes in accordance with the dominant fashion of the Hellenistic-Roman period. It is generally assumed that that Jerusalemite nobility was of the Sadducee faction, whose members included the Hellenizers; the lower classes tended more to the Pharisee faction, which opposed foreign influences. Thus, it can be assumed that this quarter was occupied chiefly by Sadducees.[62]

The Jewish Quarter mansions consisted of numerous rooms surrounding a central courtyard. They were two to three stories high and had basement rooms that contained storage facilities and workshops. The mansions were richly decorated in Roman fashion, with Pompeian style paintings and stucco on the walls, mosaic floors, bathing installations with bathtubs, and elegant furniture such as carved stone tables (see Figs. 12, 16, 18).[63] The finds include imported glass, fine red-slipped dining ware, and imported amphoras (see Figs. 9-11).[64] Avigad noted that the presence of numerous miqva'ot and stone vessels in these mansions indicates that the inhabitants observed purity laws (see Figs. 7, 14-15).[65] A stone weight inscribed "(of) [belonging to] Bar Kathros" found in the basement of a mansion called the Burnt House suggests that the residence belonged to this priestly family.[66]

Remains of similar mansions were discovered on Mount Zion.[67] As in the Jewish Quarter, these mansions were equipped with miqva'ot and were decorated with high quality wall paintings and stucco. But whereas no figured images (representations of living creatures) were discovered in the Jewish Quarter mansions, the motifs in the wall paintings from Mount Zion include birds.[68] As the excavator Magen Broshi concluded, "The location of our site on the summit of the Upper City and the elegant, sophisticated murals leave no doubt that this quarter was occupied by the more affluent residents of Jerusalem."[69] Interestingly, Christian tradition identifies this site as the location of the house of the high priest Caiaphas.[70] The only other figured images found to date in a residential Jewish context of the late Second Temple period in Jerusalem were discovered in a residential quarter to the south and west of the Temple Mount. Benjamin Mazar's excavations in this area brought to light fragments of a stuccoed animal frieze including a lion, lioness, antelope, rabbit, and pig (!)[71]

Opposition to the Jerusalem elite's ostentatious display of wealth is expressed in the New Testament and other sources.[72] For example, the author of the *Assumption of Moses,* a pseudepigraphic work that was probably composed in the Herodian era, condemns the wealthy for their luxurious lifestyle and hypocrisy in the observance of purity:

> And these shall stir up the poison of their minds, being treacherous men, self-pleasers, dissemblers in all their own affairs and lovers of banquets at every hour of the day, gluttons, gourmands. . . . Devourers of the goods of the (poor) saying that they do so on the ground of their justice, but in reality to destroy them, complainers, deceitful, concealing themselves lest they should be recognized, impious, filled with lawlessness and iniquity from sunrise to sunset: saying: "We shall have feastings and luxury, eating and drinking, and we shall esteem ourselves as princes." And though their hands and their minds touch unclean things, yet their mouth shall speak great things, and they shall say furthermore: "Do not touch me lest you should pollute me in the place (where I stand"). (*As. Mos.* 7:3-10)[73]

Rural Elites

In Palestine as elsewhere, the Romans established their rule through the local aristocracy, that is, wealthy private landowners.[74] However, as Martin Goodman observes, "The relationship between patron and client which was fundamental in, for instance, Roman culture was not found among Jews."[75] Social categories among Jews were religiously based (for example, priests versus Israelites or being a member of a sect or movement), not economically defined.[76] And whereas among the Greeks and Romans priests held an honorary position, in Judaism the priesthood was a hereditary caste.[77]

These differences in social structure are reflected in the archaeological landscape, as the large plantations or estates centered on rural villas that dot the Italian countryside in the first century B.C.E. and first century C.E. are unattested in Galilee and Judea.[78] Only a few rural villas have been found in Palestine, near the coast and in Samaria and Idumaea, and they are modest in comparison to contemporary "classic villas" in Italy.[79] Of the sites that Yizhar Hirschfeld identified as "manor houses," only Ḥorvat 'Eleq near Caesarea and Khirbet el-Muraq (Ḥilkiah's palace) in Idumaea approach Italian "classic villas" in terms of size, architectural features (such as peristyle courtyards and Roman-style bath houses), and decorative elements (see Fig. 20).[80] Furthermore, the inhabitants of the fortified villa at Ḥorvat ʿEleq apparently were not Jewish, as indicated by the discovery of a small altar associated with agricultural installations, domesticated pig bones, a Roman-style bath house with hypocaust system, inscriptions only in Greek, and a ceramic corpus with imported *orlo bifida* and Pompeian Red Ware cooking vessels, imported amphoras, Roman discus lamps decorated with figured images, and Eastern and Western Terra Sigillata.[81] The presence of these finds combined with the absence of miqvaʾot and stone (chalk or limestone) vessels means there is no support for Hirschfeld's identification of the owners of the villa at Ḥorvat ʿEleq as members of the Judean ruling class.[82] The other "manor houses" that Hirschfeld mentions are better described as farm houses or fortified road stations (except for the sectarian settlement at Qumran).[83] They include Ḥorvat Mazad, the only site on Hirschfeld's list that is located in Judea proper (as opposed to Idumaea), which the excavators and others have identified as a road station.[84] A large farm house with wine and oil presses dating to the first century B.C.E. and first century C.E. is located at Qalandiya, eight kilometers northwest of Jerusalem. The presence of miqvaʾot and the large number of stone vessels indicate that the occupants were Jewish.[85] The farm house lacks a bath house and interior decoration. Two complete amphoras and several amphora fragments were found but no other imported wares.[86]

The Sectarian Settlement at Qumran

Sectarian literature from Qumran describes wealth as one of the nets of Belial (CD 4.15-16) and criticizes the Wicked Priest and other priests in Jerusalem for accumulating riches through violence and plundering:

> "Surely wealth will corrupt the boaster. . . . They shall say: Ah, one who amasses the wealth of others! How long will he load himself with debts?" [Hab. 2:5-6]. Its interpretation concerns the Wicked Priest, who . . . deserted God and betrayed the laws for the sake of riches. And he robbed and hoarded wealth from the violent men who had rebelled against God. And he seized public money. . . . (1QpHab 8.3-12)

> Its interpretation concerns the last priests of Jerusalem, who will accumulate riches and loot from plundering the nations. (1QpHab 9.4-5)

The Qumran sect considered the Jerusalem temple to be polluted by wealth and enjoined members "to abstain from wicked wealth which defiles, either by promise or by vow, and from the wealth of the temple" (CD 6:15-16). Not surprisingly, the sectarian settlement at Qumran presents a stark contrast to the elite mansions of Jerusalem's Jewish Quarter. This settlement, which the excavator Roland de Vaux aptly described as a "community center," contains rooms used for communal purposes (such as dining rooms) and workshops (see Figs. 22, 24). Most or perhaps all of the members seem to have lived (slept) not inside the settlement but outside it, in tents, huts, and some of the nearby caves.[87] The settlement appears to have been conceived along the lines of a biblical camp in desert exile.[88]

The lavish interior decoration and furnishings of the Jewish Quarter mansions (as well as the palaces associated with the priestly and royal elite at nearby Jericho) are unattested at Qumran. The settlement at Qumran reflects the sectarians' opposition to the ostentatious lifestyle of the Jerusalem elite, which stemmed from their belief that the temple priesthood was polluted by wealth and the incorrect observance of God's laws. The construction of the buildings at Qumran — which have floors of dirt or rough paving stones, walls of field stones and roughly hewn stones framing doorways and reinforcing corners, and flat mud and reed roofs — parallels that of contemporary villages around Palestine.[89] As at Qumran, most village houses lack interior decoration and therefore show little evidence of social differentiation.[90]

A Rural, Agrarian Society

Saldarini noted that unlike modern industrial societies, ancient agrarian societies such as Judea consisted of two main groups, a large lower class and a small, elite governing class. The lower class population produced the food and goods that supported the elite lifestyle.[91] As Saldarini put it, the goal of a lower-class family's work year was "wantlessness" — that is, survival.[92] The governing class made up about 1-2 percent of the population, and the retainer class comprised another 5 percent.[93] The non-elite population included farmers as well as artisans such as Jesus' family: "Since 90% of the people in antiquity were farmers, most village residents were farmers. The larger towns and perhaps some villages also had specialists, like skilled artisans, whose poverty and low social standing were similar to that of peasants."[94] At the margins of society were the indigent, itinerant, and landless — that is, the destitute.[95]

John Meier paints a similar picture of Jesus' social setting.[96] Like Saldarini, he places Jesus not among the poorest members of Palestinian society (who included day laborers, the dispossessed, and slaves), but rather among the large lower-class population that lived just above subsistence level but not in grinding poverty by ancient standards.[97] I agree with Meier that "He [Jesus] was indeed in one sense poor, and a comfortable, middle-class urban American would find living conditions in ancient Nazareth appalling. But Jesus was probably no poorer or less respectable than almost anyone else in Nazareth, or for that matter in most of Galilee."[98]

Saldarini reminds us that the agrarian, non-elite population was largely absent from ancient cities (many of which could more accurately be described as towns or large villages), which existed to serve the needs of the governing class.[99] Since Jesus seems to have worked mainly among the lower-class residents of rural Galilee, it is not surprising that the Gospel accounts include no references to him visiting Sepphoris and Tiberias, the two main urban centers in the region.[100] An accurate understanding of Jesus' socio-economic background and his audience is necessary to ascertain his attitude towards the observance of biblical law.

Saldarini relied heavily on the work of Gerhard Lenski in presenting a highly dichotomized picture of ancient Palestinian society consisting of a small upper class and large lower class.[101] Recent studies of Roman society have painted a more nuanced picture, suggesting that a substantial part of the population (perhaps around 20 percent) was situated economically between the elite at the pinnacle of the pyramid and a large poorer class at the bottom.[102] Even according to this model a small proportion (3-5 percent) of the population controlled a large share of the economic assets.[103] Furthermore, even if we assume that this model is valid for Palestine — which was arguably less urbanized than Italy and Egypt, for example — the majority of the population still occupied the bottom of the social and economic pyramid.[104] They had little disposable income and lived close to the subsistence level, struggling to maintain a state of "wantlessness."[105]

These lower-class Jews populate the Gospel accounts. They are villagers who own houses and have a few possessions but are not destitute like the leper who begs Jesus to heal him in Mark 1:40 (see Fig. 21). The agrarian nature of rural Galilee is reflected in Jesus' parables and teachings, which mention picking and sowing grain, netting fish, herding sheep, and so on. References to patched clothing (Mark 2:21), hired laborers in vineyards

(Matt 20:1-16), and debtors sold into slavery (Matt 18:23-35) must have reso-nated with Jesus' audience.[106] When people of substantial means are men-tioned they are singled out, as, for example, the man who is instructed by Jesus to give his "many possessions" to the poor (Mark 10:17-22) and the ob-servation that only royalty can afford soft robes (Matt 11:8).[107]

Conclusion

The Jewish population of late Second Temple–period Palestine was distin-guished from their Gentile neighbors by an observance of biblical law that impacted their daily lives. In the following chapters we examine evidence of quotidian activities: ritual purification, diet, household vessels, dining customs, Sabbath observance, fasting, coins, clothing, oil, spit, toilet hab-its, and tombs and burial customs. The aim is not to provide a comprehen-sive overview, but rather to discuss selected aspects of Jewish daily life based on archaeological and literary information. The final chapter con-cludes with a brief consideration of the aftermath of the destruction of the Jerusalem temple in 70 C.E.

CHAPTER 2

Purifying the Body and Hands

Ritual Baths (Miqva'ot)

Ritual immersion baths *(miqva'ot)* became common in Palestine in the late first century B.C.E., and approximately 700 ancient miqva'ot — most of them dating to the first century C.E. (before 70) — have been found so far.[1] The widespread distribution of miqva'ot attests to the observance of purity laws among various sectors of the population in the late Second Temple period.[2]

For purification from most types of impurity, the Hebrew Bible requires the affected person to wash or bathe in water and wait for a certain amount of time to pass (usually until sundown). Sometimes this was done in combination with other rites such as washing one's clothing or (in the case of corpse impurity) being sprinkled with water mixed with the ashes of an unblemished red heifer.[3] Because there are few perennial sources of water in Palestine, artificial pools were developed for year-round use. Rabbinic halakhah requires the pool to have a minimum volume of 40 seahs (500-1000 liters) of water, whereas Qumran law seems to have mandated only that the water completely cover the bather.[4] Miqva'ot are equipped with steps that enabled the bather to immerse and sometimes additional features such as partitions or double doorways (see Fig. 23). A small number of miqva'ot have a small storage pool *('otsar)* to hold pure (undrawn) water which could be added to the immersion pool if the level fell below the minimum amount required.[5]

The biggest concentrations of miqva'ot — and the largest miqva'ot — are associated with the Jerusalem temple and priestly groups. They include clusters of miqva'ot around the Temple Mount and along the main pilgrimage routes to Jerusalem, miqva'ot in the priestly residences in Jerusalem's Jewish Quarter and at Jericho, and a large number of sizeable miqva'ot at Qumran.[6] Recent excavations have revealed that in the late Second Temple period the Pool of Siloam in Jerusalem — which is mentioned in John 9:7 as the site where Jesus cured a blind man — was an enormous immersion pool that could have accommodated masses of pilgrims.[7] A concentration of miqva'ot in the houses on the Sepphoris acropolis might be connected with the presence of priestly families.[8]

According to Boaz Zissu and David Amit, late Second Temple–period Jewish villages have between one to seven miqva'ot each.[9] Miqva'ot often are found in association with agricultural installations and especially grape and olive presses, as the production of wine and olive oil involved liquids, which are more susceptible than solids to contracting and transmitting impurity.[10] The large size of some miqva'ot found in villages and their location outside of residences suggests communal use, although miqva'ot are also attested in private residences.[11]

Examples of miqva'ot in Judean villages include four miqva'ot (three inside buildings and one in an open area) in the village at Qiryat Sefer (north of Modi'in).[12] The farmhouse at Qalandiya (northwest of Jerusalem) was equipped with two miqva'ot.[13] Three miqva'ot were found in association with poorly-preserved remains of a Jewish village at Pisgat Ze'ev, just north of Jerusalem.[14] The village of Ḥurvat Burnat in the Shefelah had seven miqva'ot, one of which may have been designated for communal use.[15] Examples of miqva'ot from Galilean villages include two small stepped pools found in buildings on the southeast slope of Yodefat, one in association with an olive press.[16] Andrea Berlin notes that at Gamla there are only two miqva'ot for over fourteen houses in Area B (a first-century B.C.E. neighborhood) and three miqva'ot for more than one hundred habitation caves at Arbel. None of the houses in Area R at Gamla has a miqveh, and there is only one small miqveh in this area (inside an oil press complex).[17] No miqva'ot have been discovered in the village at Capernaum, although the Sea of Galilee could have been used for immersion.[18]

Hand Washing before Meals

According to the Gospels, the Pharisees and scribes criticized Jesus and his disciples for not washing their hands before eating:

Now when the Pharisees and some of the scribes who had come from Jerusalem gathered around him, they noticed that some of his disciples were eating with defiled hands, that is, without washing them. (For the Pharisees, and all the Jews, do not eat unless they thoroughly wash their hands, thus observing the tradition of the elders; and they do not eat anything from the market unless they [immerse themselves], and there are also many other traditions that they observe, the washing of cups, pots, and bronze kettles.) So the Pharisees and the scribes asked him, "Why do your disciples not live according to the tradition of the elders but eat with defiled hands?" (Mark 7:1-5; see also Matt 15:1-2)[19]

Jesus called his critics hypocrites who honor God with their lips but not their hearts, and responded that "it is not what goes into the mouth that defiles a person, but it is what comes out of the mouth that defiles" (Matt 15:11; also Mark 7:15).[20]

The need for hand washing before meals arose because the Pharisees and perhaps other groups demanded that ordinary food be eaten in a state of purity that otherwise was required only for sacrificial food, as described in the Mishnah:

They wash the hands for eating unconsecrated food *(hullin)*, tithe *(ma'aser)*, and heave offering *(terumah)*; and for eating food in the status of Holy Things *(qodesh)* they immerse [the hands in a miqveh]. *(m. Ḥag. 2:5)*[21]

The practice of hand washing before meals might be based on Exod 30:17-21, according to which priests must wash their hands and feet before entering the tent of meeting or approaching the altar:

The Lord spoke to Moses: You shall make a bronze basin with a bronze stand for washing. You shall put it between the tent of meeting and the altar, and you shall put water in it; with the water Aaron and his sons shall wash their hands and their feet. When they go into the tent of meeting, or when they come near the altar to minister, to make an offering by fire to the Lord, they shall wash with water, so that they may not die. They shall wash their hands and their feet, so that they may not die: it shall be a perpetual ordinance for them, for him and for his descendants throughout their generations.

Jubilees 21:16 expands on Exodus by requiring priests to wash their hands and feet before and after sacrificing, in order to remove all signs of blood.[22] Nevertheless, it is unclear why some Jews came to expect everyone to wash their hands before all meals, as the biblical legislation refers only to priests coming into contact with sacrifices.[23]

It has been suggested that plastered basins found at some archaeological sites were used for the immersion of hands. For example, Asher Grossberg identifies thirty water basins at Masada as miqva'ot for immersing hands.[24] He notes that ostraca mentioning priestly tithes and "hallowed [holy] things" were found at Masada, including one inscribed "priest's tithe" *(m'śr khn)*. Several storage jars are inscribed with the Hebrew letters *tav* (ת) and *tet* (ט), which Yigael Yadin identified as abbreviations for *terumah* ("heave offering") and *tebel* ("produce from which tithes and *terumah* have not been separated"), respectively:[25]

> One who finds a vessel upon which is inscribed [the letter] *qof* [the produce it contains is in the status of] an offering, *mem* [the produce it contains is in the status of first] tithe, *dalet* [the produce it contains is] doubtfully tithed, *tet* [the produce it contains is] certainly untithed, *tav* [the produce it contains is in the status of] heave offering, for in the time of danger they wrote [only the letter] *tav* instead of [writing out the full word] *terumah* (heave offering). (*m. Ma'aś. Š.* 4:11)

Four ostraca from Masada (all inscribed in the same hand) bear the inscription "fit for the purity of hallowed things *(kšr[yn] lṭhrt hqdš)*," with "fit" apparently referring to the storage jars or to the storerooms in which the jars were found.[26] There are also inscriptions that read "clean for hallowed things *(ṭhwr lqdš)*" or "for hallowed things *(lqwdš')*."[27] Some storage jars bear inscriptions indicating that their contents (wine or oil) were either suited or not suited "for the purity of hallowed things." These jars had been smashed after being emptied, apparently to prevent reuse.[28] Inscriptions indicate that other jars had been disqualified *(pswl')*, presumably as containers of hallowed things.[29] Finally, an ostracon found in a casemate room (L1237) is inscribed "A[nani]as the High Priest, 'Aqavia his son."[30] Yadin identified this high priest as Ananias son of Nedebaus, who is mentioned by Josephus and whose son Eleazar was the "captain of the temple" and a leader of the revolutionary party at the time the First Jewish Revolt broke out. Yadin and Joseph Naveh suggest that Ananias had another (otherwise unknown) son named ʿAqavia, who was present at Masada and certified the jar's contents as clean.[31]

Yadin and Naveh considered the ostraca as evidence that the rebels at Masada continued to collect and set aside priestly tithes and consecrated food.[32] Other scholars have suggested that these ostraca indicate that among the rebels at Masada were individuals who ate ordinary food *(hullin)* in accordance with the purity laws governing the consumption of hallowed (holy) things *(qodesh),* with the *tet* inscribed on some jars being an abbreviation for *tahor* ("pure"):[33]

> For his whole life Yohanan b. Gudegedah ate his food in accord with the requirements of cleanness applying to Holy Things . . . (*m. Ḥag.* 2:7)[34]

According to Grossberg the numerous water basins at Masada were used by these individuals for immersing their hands before eating *hullin.*[35] Similarly, Yoel Elitzur identifies a large number of water basins in Jerusalem as miqvaʾot for hand immersion, arguing that they were needed for purification before the consumption of sacrificial meat.[36]

The connection between hand washing and the consumption of food and drink is reflected in a debate between the houses of Hillel and Shammai.[37] As usual, the house of Shammai takes a stricter position, requiring that hands be pure before coming into contact with liquids (which can act as an agent transmitting impurity to food and other items):[38]

> The House of Shammai say: "They wash the hands and then mix the cup [of wine]." But the House of Hillel say: "They mix the cup and then wash the hands." (*m. Ber.* 8:2)[39]

A baraita in the Tosefta indicates that sometimes wine was used for washing hands:

> Undiluted wine — they recite over it the benediction, "Creator of the fruit of the tree," and they may wash their hands with it. And once they have diluted it with water, they recite over it the benediction, "Creator of the fruit of the vine," and they may not wash their hands with it, the words of R. Eliezer. And sages say, "In either case they recite over it the benediction, 'Creator of the fruit of the vine,' and they may not wash their hands with it." (*t. Ber.* 4:3)[40]

From a passage in Petronius's *Satyricon* we learn that this custom was widespread enough among the Jews to be familiar to the Romans:

> Then two long-haired Ethiopians came in holding little wineskins —
> like those used to dampen the sand at the amphitheater — and they
> poured wine over our hands. (34:4)[41]

Hand Washing and Internal versus External Purity

The Synoptic Gospels reflect an awareness of purity observances that were debated by Jewish groups. In the passages cited above, Jesus reportedly not only calls into question the need to wash hands before eating nonsacral foods, but associates immoral or unethical behavior with impurity.[42] This view is also expressed in one of the seven prophetic "woes" attributed to Jesus:

> Woe to you, scribes and Pharisees, hypocrites! For you clean the out-
> side of the cup and of the plate, but inside they are full of greed and
> self-indulgence. You blind Pharisee! First clean the inside of the cup, so
> that the outside also may become clean. (Matt 23:25; see also Luke
> 11:39-40)[43]

Echoes of these debates are preserved in rabbinic literature, which contains extensive discussions about whether impurity affects the insides and/or outsides of vessels.[44] These discussions include the definition of what constitutes a vessel and which parts belong to the inside or outside:[45]

> All vessels have outsides and an inside. "For example, the mattresses,
> and the pillows, and the sacks, and the packing bags," the words of
> R. Judah. And R. Meir says, "Whatever has hems has outer parts and
> an inner part. Whatever does not have hems does not have outer parts
> and an inner part." "The table and the side table have outer parts and
> an inner part," the words of R. Judah. R. Meir says, "They have no
> outer parts." (*m. Kelim* 25:1)

Jesus seems to have taken a position opposite to that of the rabbis, and presumably the Pharisees, who are frequently portrayed as his opponents in the Synoptic Gospels. Whereas Jesus reportedly argued that impurity is not the result of external processes but comes from within (because it is caused by immoral or unethical behavior),[46] the rabbis ruled that impurity can affect the outside of a vessel without contaminating the inside:[47]

> . . . a utensil whose outer parts are made unclean — its inner part is not made unclean. (*m. Kelim* 25:4)

> A utensil, the outer parts of which have been made unclean with liquids — the outer parts are unclean. Its inside, its rims, hangers, and handles are clean. [If] its inside is made unclean, the whole is unclean. (*m. Kelim* 25:6)

Luke connects washing and internal versus external purity:[48]

> While he was speaking, a Pharisee invited him to dine with him; so he went in and took his place at the table. The Pharisee was amazed to see that he did not first wash *(ebaptisthē)* before dinner. Then the Lord [Jesus] said to him, "Now you Pharisees clean the outside of the cup and of the dish, but inside you are full of greed and wickedness. Did not the one who made the outside make the inside also?" (Luke 11:37-40)[49]

The rabbis associated hand washing with internal versus external purity:

> All utensils have outer parts and an inner part, and they [further] have a part by which they are held. R. Tarfon says, "[This distinction in the outer parts applies only] to a large wooden trough." R. Aqiba says, "To cups." R. Meir says, "To the unclean and the clean hands." Said R. Yose, "They have spoken only concerning clean hands alone." "How so?" "[If] one's hands were clean, and the outer parts of the cup were unclean, [and] one took [the cup] with its holding part, he need not worry lest his hands be made unclean on the outer parts of the cup." [If] one was drinking from a cup, the outer parts of which are unclean, one does not worry lest the liquid which is in his mouth be made unclean on the outer parts of the cup and go and render the [whole] cup unclean. (*m. Kelim* 25:7)

In the Gospel accounts, Jesus not only inverts the Pharisaic/rabbinic view (impurity comes from within instead of from outside), but he relates the discussion to the human body instead of inanimate objects.[50] Jesus' disagreement with the Pharisees about hand washing reflects a different understanding of scriptural tradition and a rejection of legal innovations and expansions that do not have a scriptural basis.[51] In the Sermon on the Mount as reported by Matthew, Jesus says "Blessed are the pure in heart, for they will see God" (Matt 5:8). Scholars have noted the parallel with Psalm 24:3-4: "Who shall ascend the hill of the Lord? And who shall stand in his holy place? Those who have clean hands and pure hearts."[52] Whereas the Pharisees emphasized the need to have clean hands in order to enter God's presence, Jesus stressed the purity of the heart. The importance of moral and ethical behavior for entering God's presence can be seen in Psalm 15: "O Lord, who may abide in your tent? Who may dwell on your holy hill? Those who walk blamelessly, and do what is right, and speak the truth from their heart" (Ps 15:1-2). The Qumran sect seems to have viewed ritual and moral purity as one, as expressed in 4Q Beatitudes, which praises wisdom: "Blessed are those who search for her [the wisdom given by God] with pure hands and do not pursue her with a treacherous [heart]" (4Q525 2-3 II.1).[53]

Jesus' association of immoral or unethical behavior with impurity (something that comes from within a person) is illustrated by the Gospel's use of Isa 40:3 ("Make straight the way of the Lord"), which calls the faithful to repent and undergo baptism in preparation for the coming kingdom of heaven (Matt 3:1-3; John 1:23). In contrast, at Qumran this verse was understood as referring to "the study of the Law wh[i]ch he commanded through the hand of Moses, in order to act in compliance with all that is revealed from age to age . . ." (1QS 8:14-15).[54]

A reference to "morning bathers" in the Tosefta suggests that other groups rejected the Pharisaic/rabbinic distinction between internal and external purity:[55]

> Those who immerse at dawn say, "We complain against you, Pharisees. For you mention the divine name at dawn without first immersing." Say Pharisees, "We complain against you, those who immerse at dawn. For you make mention of the divine name in a body which contains uncleanness." (*t. Yad.* 2:20)

Jesus and Food Laws

According to the Gospel of Mark, Jesus not only opposed the Pharisaic innovation requiring hand washing before (nonsacral) meals, but he rejected biblical laws prohibiting the consumption of unclean food:

> Then he [Jesus] called the crowd again and said to them, "Listen to me, all of you, and understand: there is nothing outside a person that by going in can defile, but the things that come out are what defile." When he had left the crowd and entered the house, his disciples asked him about the parable. He said to them, "Then do you also fail to understand? Do you not see that whatever goes into a person from outside cannot defile, since it enters, not the heart but the stomach, and goes out into the sewer?" (Thus he declared all foods clean). And he said, "It is what comes out of a person that defiles. For it is from within, from the human heart, that evil intentions come: fornication, theft, murder, adultery, avarice, wickedness, deceit, licentiousness, envy, slander, pride, folly. All these evil things come from within, and they defile a person." (Mark 7:14-23; see also Matt 15:10-20)[56]

Nevertheless, it is difficult to believe that Jesus did not observe the food laws, as he seems to have followed other biblical injunctions such as wearing *tzitzit* (see below).[57] Furthermore, had Jesus permitted the consumption of foods that are prohibited by biblical law (such as unclean species of animals, fowl, and insects), we might expect this to be reflected in his opponents' attacks. Instead they criticize Jesus' disciples for not washing their hands before meals, which Jesus rejects as a human innovation that is not biblical law.[58]

In my opinion, Jesus was responding to the Pharisaic requirement that ordinary food be eaten in a state of purity that otherwise was required only for sacrificial food.[59] Consequently, "A vessel whose outer side alone is unclean does not render ordinary food unclean. But if the food is connected with the cult, then it is a Holy Thing, and if so, it is made unclean by touching the outer side of the vessel."[60] Pharisaic observance meant that even ordinary food becomes impure through contact with the outside of an impure vessel. That this is what Jesus had in mind is suggested by the connection between washing hands, internal and external purity, and clean versus unclean food in Mark 7:1-23. Although Jesus apparently opposed the Pharisaic requirement that ordinary food be eaten in a state of purity, I see no evidence that he rejected biblical food laws prohibiting the consumption of unclean animals and requiring temple offerings to be eaten in a state of purity.[61] However, after Jesus' death his sayings were understood as meaning that Jesus abolished the need to observe biblical food laws altogether.[62]

Scrolls and Hand Impurity

In rabbinic Judaism Torah scrolls are associated with impurity, defiling the hands of those who touch them.[63] A number of passages in rabbinic literature attest to debates concerning which scrolls are holy or sacred and therefore defile the hands:[64]

> The blank spaces in a scroll, whether above or below or at the beginning or at the end impart uncleanness to hands. R. Judah says: "That which is at the end does not impart uncleanness unless one will affix the roller to it." A scroll which was erased and in which remain eighty-five letters — such as the paragraph, *And it came to pass when the ark set forward* [Num. 10:35-36], imparts uncleanness to hands. A scroll in which eighty-five letters are written, such as the paragraph, *And it came to pass when the ark set forward,* imparts uncleanness to hands. All sacred scriptures impart uncleanness to hands. The Song of Songs and Qohelet impart uncleanness to hands. R. Judah says, "The Song of Songs imparts uncleanness to hands, but as to Qohelet there is a dispute." R. Yose says, "Qohelet does not impart uncleanness to hands, but as to the Song of Songs there is a dispute." (*m. Yad.* 3:4-5)

> Rab Judah said in the name of Samuel: [The scroll] of Esther does not make the hands unclean. Are we to infer from this that Samuel was of the opinion that Esther was not composed under the inspiration of the holy spirit? How can this be, seeing that Samuel has said that Esther was composed under the inspiration of the holy spirit? — It was composed to be recited [by heart], but not to be written." (*b. Meg.* 7a)

> All scrolls render the hands unclean, except for the scroll of the courtyard (ʿ*ezra* = Temple court). (*m. Kelim* 15:6)

Martin Goodman observed that this last ruling enabled priests serving in the temple to touch Torah scrolls without defiling their hands, although scrolls taken outside cause defilement, as do those brought in from outside:[65]

> The Scroll of Ezra which went forth outside [the court] renders the hands unclean. And not only of the Scroll of Ezra alone did they speak, but even the Prophets and the Pentateuch. And another scroll which entered there renders the hands clean. (*t. Kelim B. Meṣiʿa* 5:8)

The rabbis seem also to have debated which Jewish writings have the status of sacred scripture:

> The Aramaic [passages] which are in Ezra and Daniel impart uncleanness to hands. The Aramaic [passages contained in Scriptures] written in Hebrew, or a Hebrew [version] written in Aramaic or [passages written in archaic] Hebrew script do not impart uncleanness to hands. [Holy Scriptures] impart uncleanness to hands only if written in Assyrian characters (*ašwryt* = square Jewish script), on parchment, and with ink." (*m. Yad.* 4:5)[66]

Rabbinic literature contains hints that these debates began before 70 C.E.[67] The Mishnah records a difference of opinion between the houses of Hillel and Shammai:

> R. Simon [Ishmael] says, "Three opinions of the House of Shammai's more lenient, and the House of Hillel's more stringent, rulings": "[The Book of Qohelet] does not render the hands unclean," according to the House of Shammai. And the House of Hillel say, "It renders the hands unclean." (*m. ʿEd.* 5:3)

> R. Simeon says: "Qohelet is among the lenient rulings of the House of Shammai and strict rulings of the House of Hillel." (*m. Yad.* 3:5)

Although many scholars attribute these debates to questions surrounding the canonical status of certain books, Sid Leiman concluded that the real issue concerned which works were considered divinely inspired.[68] Michael Broyde suggests that the controversies surrounding Esther, Ecclesiastes (Qohelet), and the Song of Songs are due to the absence of the tetragrammaton from these three works alone among the books of the Hebrew Bible.[69] If this is correct, it might explain why the house of Shammai did not consider Qohelet defiling and would mean that this ruling has nothing to do with leniency.

A passage from the Mishnah attests to debates about which scrolls or writings defile the hands:

> Say Sadducees: We complain against you, Pharisees. For you say, "Holy Scriptures impart uncleanness to hands, but the books of *Hamiras* [Homer?] do not impart uncleanness to the hands." Said Rabbi Yohanan b. Zakkai, "And do we have against the Pharisees in this matter alone?" Lo, they say, "The bones of an ass are clean, but the bones of Yohanan, high priest, are unclean." They said to him, "According to their preciousness is their uncleanness. So that a man should not make the bones of his father and mother into spoons." He said to them, "So too Holy Scriptures: According to their preciousness is their uncleanness. But the books of *Hamiras* [Homer?], which are not precious, do not impart uncleanness to hands." (*m. Yad.* 4:6)

The nature of the criticism leveled by the Sadducees named in this passage against the Pharisees is obscure. Perhaps, unlike the Pharisees, in their view touching both Torah scrolls and profane works defiled the hands. Or, they might have considered profane works but not Torah scrolls as defiling, or perhaps did not consider any scrolls as defiling.[70]

Did the Qumran community consider touching Torah scrolls as defiling the hands? Elsewhere I have suggested that ovoid and cylindrical jars were used for a variety of storage purposes and are common at Qumran because they were adopted as distinctively shaped containers for the pure goods of the sect (see Fig. 27).[71] My suggestion assumes that scrolls were stored in jars because they had a high degree of purity, like the sect's food and drink.[72] Although we have no direct evidence indicating whether the Qumran sect considered touching Torah scrolls as defiling the hands, indirect evidence suggests they might not have shared the rabbinic view. First, there is an absence of evidence. In contrast to the rabbis, sectarian legislation displays no concern that touching Torah scrolls conveys impurity. This silence is loud in light of the fact that more than nine hundred scrolls had been deposited in the caves around Qumran. Second, several factors suggest that the Mishnaic passage cited above in which the Sadducees disagree with Pharisees about scroll impurity reflects an early debate, including the attribution of a ruling to Rabbi Yohanan b. Zakkai. The subsequent passage (*m. Yad.* 4:7) contains the well-known disagreement between Sadducees and Pharisees about whether an unbroken liquid stream *(niṣoq)* conveys impurity.[73] The fact that this is paralleled in 4QMMT might indicate that the debate concerning scroll impurity in the preceding Mishnaic passage is also early and perhaps reflects a sectarian view.

It is also possible that the sectarians (and perhaps other groups such as priests/Sadducees) considered touching holy scrolls as defiling the entire body, not just the hands.[74] After all, we might expect the Qumran sect to have a more stringent view than the rabbis with regard to purity issues.[75] In my opinion, the fact that biblical purity laws do not refer to hands causing impurity independently of the rest of the body makes it unlikely that the Qumran sect accepted the principle of hand defilement. *Jubilees* 21:16 requires priests to wash their hands and feet before and after sacrificing but makes it clear that the purpose was to remove all traces of blood, while full body immersion was still necessary before approaching the altar. A passage in the Mishnah suggests that the notion that hands alone can become impure was not universally accepted even among the rabbis: "But whom did they excommunicate? It was Eliezer b. Hanokh, who cast doubt on [the sages' ruling about] the cleanness of hands" (*m. 'Ed.* 5:6).[76] Furthermore, the rabbis ruled that although touching a Torah scroll defiles the hands, the affected person must undergo purification through total immersion in a miqveh, not just hand washing or hand immersion.[77] Thus, the sectarians might have stored the scrolls in caves because of (im)purity concerns. Perhaps the impurity caused by scrolls is not covered by Qumran legislation because it was taken for granted.

In any event, it seems that the pure goods of the sect stored in the cylindrical jars at Qumran could have included scrolls as well as food and drink. I believe that the distinctive shape of the jars signaled the purity of their contents, thereby controlling and restricting access to these goods:[78]

> He should not go into the waters to share in the pure food of the men of holiness, for one is not cleansed unless one turns away from one's wickedness, for he is unclean among all the transgressors of his word. (1QS 5:13-14)

A passage in the Mishnah suggests that *terumah* is rendered impure through contact with Torah scrolls ("the book") and the hands:

> These render heave offering unfit: he who eats food unclean in the first remove; and he who eats food unclean in the second remove; and he

who drinks unclean liquid; he whose head and the greater part of whose body enters drawn water; and one who was clean on whose head and the greater part of whose body three logs of drawn water fall; and the book *(whspr)*, and the hands *(whydyym)*, and the *tebul-yom;* and food and utensils which have been made unclean by [unclean] liquids. (*m. Zabim* 5:12)

The Babylonian Talmud refers to storing *terumah* with Torah scrolls:[79]

And why did the rabbis impose uncleanness upon a book? Said R. Mesharshiya: Because originally food of terumah was stored near the Scroll of the Law, with the argument, "This is holy and that is holy." But when it was seen that they [the Sacred Books] came to harm, the rabbis decreed uncleanness upon them. "And the hands?" Because hands are fidgety. It was taught: Also hands which came into contact with a Book disqualify terumah, on account of R. Parnok['s dictum]. For R. Parnok said in R. Johanan's name: One who holds a scroll of the Law naked [without its wrapping] will be buried naked. (*b. Šabb.* 14a)

The juxtaposition of food of *terumah* and sacred scrolls in this passage is interesting, as at Qumran the term *taharah* ("purity") seems to correspond with *terumah*.[80] If the sectarians stored pure food and drink (analogous to *terumah*) and scrolls in the caves around Qumran, this may be analogous to storing *terumah* and Torah scrolls in proximity, a practice to which the rabbis objected.[81]

Linen scroll wrappers decorated with blue lines representing a blueprint of the temple as described in the *Temple Scroll* were found in Cave 1 at Qumran.[82] Yadin suggested that the design of the wrappers was intended to symbolize hiding the scrolls away in the temple, as was the practice in Jerusalem.[83] A baraita in the Babylonian Talmud refers to storing Torah scrolls:

Then said Eleazar b. Poʿirah to King Jannai: "O King Jannai! That is the law even for the most humble man in Israel, and thou, a King and a High Priest, shall that be thy law [too]!" "Then what shall I do?" "If thou wilt take my advice, trample them down." "But what shall happen with the Torah?" "Behold, it is rolled up and lying in the corner *(hry krwkh wmwnht bqrn zwyt):* whoever wishes to study, let him go and study!" (*b. Qidd.* 66a)

The Soncino Edition of the Babylonian Talmud translates *krekh* as referring to a rolled-up Torah scroll. However, Joseph Baumgarten translated this word as "wrapped up": "Behold, it is wrapped up and deposited in a corner; whoever wishes to study it let him come and study it."[84] According to Baumgarten this baraita and the scholion to *Megillat Ta'anit* attest to the practice of wrapping and depositing written books of the law (attributed in these sources to the Sadducees):

> *On the 4th day of Tammuz the Book of Decrees was abrogated.* The Sadducees had a Book of Decrees written and deposited *(ktwb wmwnḥ)* specifying, These are stoned, these are burned, etc. . . . and when they would sit in deliberation and someone would question their source, they would show him in the Book . . . but they were unable to produce any proof from the Torah.[85]

However, the scholion refers to writing and depositing (or publicizing) books, not wrapping them. Clearer evidence for the practice of wrapping Torah scrolls is attested in the Tosefta and the Babylonian Talmud, where *gll* describes rolling (a scroll) and *mtpḥt* denotes the cloth wrapper:

> He who makes an ark and coverings *(mtpḥwt)* for a [holy] scroll, before one has made use of them for the Most High, an ordinary person is permitted to make use of them. Once one has made use of them for the Most High, an ordinary person is no longer permitted to make use of them. But one may lend a cloth for a scroll and go and take it back from him [to whom it was lent for such a purpose and then make use of it for a lesser purpose]. Clothes for covering a given set of scrolls they may use for different scrolls, but they may not make use of them for other purposes. (*t. Meg.* 2:13)

> R. Parnak said in the name of R. Johanan: Whoever takes hold of a scroll of the Torah without a covering (naked) is buried without a covering. Without a covering, think you? — Say rather, without the covering protection of religious performances. Without religious performances, think you? — No, said Abaye; he is buried without the covering protection of that religious performance. R. Jannai the son of the old R. Jannai said in the name of the great R. Jannai: Is it better that the covering [of the scroll] should be rolled up [with the scroll]

and not that the scroll of the Torah should be rolled up [inside the covering] *(mwṭb tygll ḥmṭpḥt w'l ygll spr twrh)*. (*b. Meg.* 32a)

Although scroll wrappers were found at Qumran, sectarian legislation provides no indication that they considered scroll containers, straps, and wrappers as defiling, in contrast to the rabbis:

> The thongs and straps which one sewed onto a book, even though it is not permitted to keep them, impart defilement to hands. A container of books, and a box of books, and the wrappings of a book, when they are clean, impart defilement to hands.

> *(hmšyḥwt wḥrṣw'wt štprn bspr ""p š'ynw rš'y lqyymn mṭm'wt. tyq hsprym wmṭpḥwt wtybh šl spr bzmn šhn ṭhwrwt mṭm'wt 't hydym)*
> (*t. Yad.* 2:12)

And whereas according to the rabbis phylacteries also defile the hands, there is no evidence that the Qumran sect shared this view:[86]

> The straps of tefillin [while they are still attached] to the tefillin impart uncleanness to hands. R. Simeon says, "The straps of tefillin [under any circumstances] do not impart uncleanness to hands." (*m. Yad.* 3:3)

The basic question — why, according to the rabbis, scrolls defile the hands — is still unanswered. Perhaps the concept is related to the Persian and Roman custom of making an offering with the hand(s) covered or veiled, a practice that was a feature of the cult of Isis and continued in the Byzantine world.[87] The notion that hands must be covered when touching offerings or sacred objects might be reflected in the Jewish practice of wrapping Torah scrolls and perhaps explains why some Jews considered touching Torah scrolls as defiling the hands.

CHAPTER 3

Creeping and Swarming Creatures, Locusts, Fish, Dogs, Chickens, and Pigs

Do not give what is holy to dogs. . . ."

Matt 7:6

Creeping and Swarming Creatures

Matthew 23:13-36 attributes to Jesus a series of seven prophetic "woes" against the scribes and Pharisees. Jesus' criticism includes a halakhic point: "You blind guides! You strain out a gnat but swallow a camel!" (Matt 23:24).[1]

Biblical law prohibits the consumption of camels and gnats:

> But among those that chew the cud or have divided hoofs, you shall not eat the following: the camel, for even though it chews the cud, it does not have divided hoofs; it is unclean *(tame')* for you. (Lev 11:4)

> All winged insects that walk upon all fours are detestable *(sheqetz)* to you. But among the winged insects that walk on all fours you may eat those that have jointed legs above their feet, with which to leap on the ground. Of them you may eat: the locust according to its kind, the bald locust according to its kind, the cricket according to its kind, and the grasshopper according to its kind. But all other winged insects that have four feet are detestable to you." (Lev 11:20-23)

These are unclean *(ṭame')* for you among the creatures that swarm *(sheretz)* upon the earth: the weasel, the mouse, the great lizard according to its kind, the gecko, the land crocodile, the lizard, the sand lizard, and the chameleon. These are unclean for you among all that swarm; whoever touches one of them when they are dead shall be unclean until the evening. (Lev 11:29-31)

These passages in Leviticus 11 distinguish between living creatures that are forbidden as food but do not cause impurity (described as *sheqetz*), and swarming land creatures *(sheretz)* that are forbidden as food and whose carcasses convey impurity (which are described as unclean [*ṭame'*]).[2] The latter consist of the eight species listed in Lev 11:29-30: the weasel, mouse, great lizard, gecko, land crocodile, lizard, sand lizard, and chameleon. According to Lev 11:39, the carcass of a clean (permitted) animal also conveys impurity: "If an animal of which you may eat dies, anyone who touches its carcass shall be unclean until the evening."

Leviticus 11:41-44 complicates the picture, as it not only prohibits the consumption of all swarming things but associates them with impurity *(ṭum'ah)*:[3]

All creatures that swarm *(sheretz)* upon the earth are detestable *(sheqetz)*; they shall not be eaten. Whatever moves on its belly, and whatever moves on all fours, or whatever has many feet, all the creatures that swarm upon the earth, you shall not eat; for they are detestable. You shall not make yourself detestable with any creature that swarms; you shall not defile yourselves (*ṭame'* niphal) with them, and so become unclean *(ṭame')*. For I am the Lord your God; sanctify yourselves therefore, and be holy, for I am holy. You shall not defile yourselves with any swarming creature *(sheretz)* that moves [or creeps] *(haromes)* on the earth."

Deuteronomy 14:19 further complicates matters by repeating the prohibition of Lev 11:20 but describes winged insects as unclean *(ṭame')* rather than detestable *(sheqetz)*:

And all winged insects *(sheretz ha'of)* are unclean *(ṭame')* for you; they shall not be eaten. You may eat any clean winged creature. (Deut 14:19-20)[4]

Jacob Milgrom points out that because the Deuteronomist uses *sheqetz* to denote idolatry only, forbidden animals are described as *tame'* ("impure").[5]

In light of the confusion created by Leviticus and Deuteronomy, it is not surprising that Jewish groups in the late Second Temple period and later disagreed about which swarming creatures are not only forbidden but impure. The rabbis understood Leviticus as meaning that only the eight species listed in Lev 11:29-30 are unclean and therefore did not consider insects to be a source of impurity.[6]

The *Damascus Document* indicates that the Qumran sect understood Leviticus and Deuteronomy as meaning that all swarming creatures — and not just the eight species — are a source of impurity:

> Let no man pollute his soul with any living and swarming [or creeping] creatures *(remes)* by eating of them, whether it be the larvae of bees or any living thing which swarms [or creeps] *(tirmos)* in the water. . . . (So much for) the rule of the settlement of the towns in Israel in accordance with these precepts, to separate between the impure *(tame')* and the pure *(tahor)* and to make known (the distinction) between the holy and the profane. (CD 12:12-13, 19-20)[7]

This legislation makes it clear that the Qumran sect viewed the consumption of all forbidden foods as defiling and appears to be a polemic against those who (like the later rabbis) understood from Leviticus 11 that only the eight species are unclean.[8] The polemic is sharpened by the sectarians' use of the term *remes* to denote all swarming creatures as unclean, in contrast to the rabbinic distinction between the eight unclean species *(sheretz)* and other forbidden but not unclean creeping and swarming creatures *(sheqetz)*. The use of the term *remes* shows that the legislation in the *Damascus Document* is based on Lev 11:44, in which God commands his people to be holy and not defile themselves by eating any swarming or creeping creatures:

> For I am the Lord your God; sanctify yourselves therefore, and be holy, for I am holy. You shall not defile yourselves *(tame'* niphal) with any swarming creature *(sheretz)* that moves [or creeps] *(haromes)* on the earth.

Furthermore, Lev 22:5 prohibits priests from even touching "any swarming thing by which he may be made unclean *(tame')*."[9]

Whereas Lev 11:41-44 prohibits the consumption of creatures that swarm **on the earth** ("You shall not defile yourselves with any swarming creature *[sheretz]* that moves [or creeps] *[haromes]* on the earth"), the *Damascus Document* refers to swarming creatures **in water** (. . . "whether it be the larvae of bees or any living thing which swarms [or creeps] *(tirmos)* in the water"; CD 12:12-13). This seems to be a harmonization of the prohibitions in Lev 11:41-44 (involving swarming land creatures) and Lev 11:9-12 (involving swarming water creatures): "These you may eat, of all that are in the waters. Everything in the waters that has fins and scales, whether in the seas or in the streams — you may eat. But anything in the seas or the streams that does not have fins and scales, of the swarming creatures in the waters and among all the other living creatures in the waters — they are detestable to you and detestable they shall remain. Of their flesh you shall not eat, and their carcasses you shall regard as detestable. Everything in the waters that does not have fins and scales is detestable to you."

Apparently some Jewish groups of the late Second Temple period, including the Qumran sect, understood the legislation in Leviticus as prohibiting the consumption of all swarming creatures in water — not just fish without fins and scales but land-based swarming creatures such as insects and larvae as well. Matthew 23:24 indicates that some Jews strained liquids to prevent the ingestion of these creatures. Rabbinic literature shows that after 70 C.E. debates continued concerning whether biblical law prohibits the consumption of swarming land-based creatures found in water. The rabbis permitted the consumption of these creatures (see, e.g., *b. Ḥul.* 66b-67a), and they even ruled that a person is not liable for ingesting insects and larvae that generated inside fruits and vegetables because they had never crawled on the ground: "[If he ate] a mite which is [found] in lentils, or gnats that are [found] in pods, or worms that are [found] in dates and dried figs, he is exempt" (*t. Ter.* 7:11; see also *b. Ḥul.* 67b).[10] That this was a common problem is illustrated by the remains of ancient wheat, barley, dates, figs, and walnuts found in the excavations at Masada, which were infested with insects and their larvae.[11]

Not only did the rabbis permit the ingestion of swarming land-based creatures found in water, but they condemned as heterodoxy the straining of wine and vinegar to remove these creatures, suggesting that some Jews continued this practice after 70:

[And as to] gnats which are [found] in wine and vinegar, lo, these are permitted. [If] he strained them [out of the wine or vinegar], lo, these are forbidden. R. Judah says, "One who strains wine and vinegar, and one who recites a blessing for the sun [t. Ber. 6:6] — lo, this is heresy (drk 'ḥrt)." (t. Ter. 7:11)[12]

R. Hisda said to R. Huna, There is [a Baraita] taught that supports your contention: [The verse,] "And every creeping thing that creepeth upon the earth [is a detestable thing; it shall not be eaten — Lev 11:41]," includes insects found in liquids that have been passed through a strainer. The reason [then that they are forbidden] is because they had passed through a strainer, but had they not passed through a strainer they would be permitted. (b. Ḥul. 67a)

Thus, Matt 23:24 alludes to a halakhic controversy which divided Jews before and after 70. Jesus' criticism seems to be aimed at groups (designated as "scribes" and "Pharisees") who strained gnats out of liquids. I believe that Jesus refers here not to the Qumran sect (Essenes) but to members of the Jerusalem elite who strictly observed biblical food laws yet consumed imported delicacies and exotic types of cuisine, as we have seen. The Aramaic wordplay on gnat and camel (qalma and gamla) suggests a relatively early date for Matt 23:24.[13]

There is no archaeological evidence that the Qumran community strained liquids, as the only published example of a strainer jug dates to Period III (post-68 occupation).[14] Jugs with strainer necks — and sometimes with a drinking spout — are found at other Judean sites in the first century C.E., including Masada, Jericho, and Jerusalem.[15] Strainer jugs made of Nabataean cream ware were likely the source of inspiration for the strainer jugs found at Judean sites.[16] There is no indication that strainer jugs were used in connection with the sort of purity concerns discussed above, which were not a factor for the Nabataeans. Instead, the distribution of strainer jugs — primarily at sites around the Dead Sea — reflects regional influence in pottery types. Presumably the strainers kept out the swarms of flies and other insects that plague the Jordan Valley and Dead Sea region in the summer.[17] If some Jewish groups did strain liquids, they must have used other materials such as mesh or cloth. In fact, the holes in the strainer jugs usually are too big to strain out tiny insects like gnats, and therefore would have been unsuitable for this purpose.

Locusts, Fish, and Bread

The Qumran sect followed biblical law in permitting the consumption of certain types of winged insects such as locusts but required that they be cooked alive before being eaten:[18]

> [These among] the winged [insects] you may eat: the locust according to its kind, the ba[ld] locust according to its kind, the cri{c}ket according to its kind, and the grasshopper according to its kind. These among the winged insects you may eat: those that go on all fours which have legs above their feet, with which to leap from the earth and fly with their wings. You shall not eat the carcass of any winged thing or animal . . . (11QT 48:3-6)[19]

> And all species of locusts shall be put into fire or water while still alive, for this is the precept of their creation. (CD 12:14-15)

Whereas sectarian law prohibited the consumption of live locusts and locusts that were already dead (had died naturally), the rabbis ruled that live and dead locusts could be eaten:

> [A man] may eat fish and locusts whether they are alive or dead and need not scruple. (*t. Ter.* 9:6)[20]

Interestingly, the reference in this passage to fish followed by locusts recalls the *Damascus Document*, reversing the order in Leviticus 11:

> And they should not eat fish unless they were torn alive and their blood sh[e]d. And all species of locusts shall be put into fire or water while still alive . . . (CD 12:13-15)

This means that sectarian law permitted only the consumption of fish that were caught live and then slaughtered to drain the blood.[21] The Hebrew Bible forbids the ingestion of the blood of birds and animals, which must be drained during the ritual of slaughtering:

> You must not eat any blood whatever, either of bird or of animal, in any of your settlements. Any one of you who eats any blood shall be cut off from your kin. (Lev 7:26-27)

Only be sure that you do not eat the blood; for the blood is the life, and you shall not eat the life with the meat. Do not eat it; you shall pour it on the ground like water. (Deuteronomy 12:23-24)

Whereas the Hebrew Bible mentions only animals and birds in connection with the blood prohibition, the sectarians extended this prohibition to include fish, thereby necessitating their slaughter to drain the blood.[22] In contrast, the rabbis allowed the consumption of live fish and condemned the slaughtering of fish as heterodoxy:[23]

> Jacob of Kefar Nibburaya gave a decision in Tyre that fish require ritual slaughtering. R. Haggai heard it and sent for him to come. He said to him: "Whence did you derive your decision?" The other replied, "From the following: *Let the waters swarm with swarms of living creatures, and let fowl fly* (Gen 1:20). As fowls, I argued, require ritual slaughter, so should fishes require ritual slaughter." Said R. Haggai to them [his assistants]: "Lay him down to be flagellated." The other objected: "Shall a man who has uttered words of Torah be flagellated?" "You have not given a fitting decision," said R. Haggai. "Whence do you say so?" asked the other. He answered him: "From the following: *If flocks and herds be* slain *for them . . . or if all the fish of the sea be* gathered together *for them*. This shows that the former have to be slaughtered and the latter have to be gathered." The other said: "Proceed with your beating, for there is a benefit in taking it." (*Midr. Num. Rab.* 19:3)[24]

Jacob's appeal to Gen 1:20 as the basis for his ruling echoes the *Damascus Document*'s requirement to slaughter fish, which immediately follows a prohibition against eating living and swarming creatures:

> Let no man pollute his soul with any living and swarming creatures by eating of them, whether it be the larvae of bees or any living thing which swarms in the water. And they should not eat fish unless they were torn alive and their blood sh[e]d. (CD 12:11-14)

Sectarian law also prohibited the consumption of any creatures that were already dead: "You shall not eat the carcass of any winged thing or animal . . ." (11QT 48:6).[25]

The sectarian position derives from an injunction that prohibits *priests* from eating "of anything, whether bird or animal, that died of itself or was torn by animals" (Ezek 44:31).[26]

The sectarian prohibition against consuming fish blood means that popular Roman fish sauces would have been forbidden, even if prepared with biblically permitted species (fish with scales).[27] Roman fish sauces — *garum, muria, liquamen,* and *allec* — were used as seasonings and condiments in various dishes. They were made by fermenting fish such as anchovies or mackerel together with additional ingredients including fish intestines, gills, fish blood, and salt.[28] The discovery of amphoras and fish bones indicates that Herod imported high quality *garum* and *allec* from Spain to his palaces at Masada, Jericho, and Herodium.[29] Spanish amphoras for fish sauce have also been found in the area of Herod's palace in Jerusalem.[30] North African amphoras dating to the first century B.C.E. that probably contained salted fish or fish sauce are published from Area E in Jerusalem's Jewish Quarter excavations.[31] Although no examples are published yet, Nahman Avigad's reference to amphora handles bearing Latin stamps leaves open the possibility that amphoras for fish sauce dating to the first century C.E. were found elsewhere in the Jewish Quarter excavations.[32]

Helek or *hilek (hḥylq;* apparently *allec)* and *muries (muria; mwryys)* are listed among the things belonging to Gentiles that the rabbis prohibited (*m. 'Abod. Zar.* 2:4; 2:6).[33] In the Palestinian Talmud (*'Abod. Zar.* 32a) and Babylonian Talmud (*'Abod. Zar.* 39a), this prohibition was attributed to the possibility that Gentile products might contain nonkosher species of fish:[34]

> What is the meaning of HELEK? — R. Nahman b. Abba said in the name of Rab: It is the *sultanith.* Why is it prohibited? Because other species [of fish] of a similar kind [but prohibited] are caught together with it. (*b. 'Abod. Zar.* 39a)

The rabbinic discussions suggest that after 70, fish sauce was popular among Jews, some of whom may have continued indulging in imported Gentile products.

John the Baptist is known for his diet of locusts and wild honey (Mark 1:6 says "he ate locusts"; Matt 3:4 says "his food was locusts").[35] Although admittedly an argument from silence, it seems unlikely that John followed sectarian law and ate only locusts that he caught alive and then cooked, as such an exceptional practice presumably would have been noticed and mentioned in the Gospel accounts.[36] Not only does John's diet reflect his ascetic lifestyle but it suggests a concern with purity, as he reportedly consumed only wild, not processed food.[37] The association between purity and food that is grown or caught in the wild is expressed in 2 Maccabees:

> But Judas Maccabeus, with about nine others, got away to the wilderness, and kept himself and his companions alive in the mountains as wild animals do; they continued to live on what grew wild, so that they might not share in the defilement. (2 Macc 5:27)

The Gospels describe Jesus feeding multitudes with a few loaves and fish (Mark 6:32-44, Matt 14:13-21, Luke 9:10b-17; Mark 8:1-10, Matt 15:32-39; see also John 6:1-15).[38] In my opinion bread and fish are mentioned in these accounts (whether they have any historical basis or not) because these two foods were dietary staples of the rural population around the Sea of Galilee.[39]

Fish and locusts are mentioned together in a debate between the houses of Hillel and Shammai about the biblical prohibition against boiling a kid in its mother's milk (Exod 23:19; 34:26; Deut 14:21).[40] This is a rare case in which the house of Shammai ruled more leniently, allowing fowl and cheese to be served (but not eaten) together:

> Every [kind of] flesh [of cattle, wild beast, and fowl] it is prohibited to cook in milk, except for the flesh of fish and locusts. And it is prohibited to serve it up onto the table with cheese, except for the flesh of fish and locusts. He who vows [to abstain] from flesh is permitted [to make use of] the flesh of fish and locusts. "Fowl goes up onto the table with cheese, but it is not eaten," the words of the House of Shammai. And the House of Hillel say, "It does not go up, and it is not eaten." Said R. Yose, "This is one of the lenient rulings of the House of Shammai and the strict rulings of the House of Hillel." Concerning what sort of table did they speak? Concerning a table on which one lays out cooking, one puts this beside that and does not scruple. (*m. Ḥul.* 8:1)[41]

There is no mention of this prohibition in sectarian literature from Qumran, although E. P. Sanders probably is correct in concluding that "many people would not cook meat or cheese together" even before 70.[42] However, the ruling of the house of Shammai indicates that some Jews served meat and poultry together with cheese. In my opinion, these were likely members of the elite who could afford the luxury of serving different types of food including meat at a single meal. On the other hand, the house of Shammai was more stringent in ruling that fish become susceptible to impurity when they are caught, whereas according to the house of Hillel fish become susceptible only when they die (*m. ʿUq.* 3:8).

Mark 8:14-21 relates what happened when Jesus' disciples found themselves in a boat with only one loaf of bread:

> Now the disciples had forgotten to bring any bread; and they had only one loaf with them in the boat. And he cautioned them, saying, "Watch out — beware of the yeast of the Pharisees and the yeast of the Herodians [or Herod]." They said to one another, "It is because we have no bread." And becoming aware of it, Jesus said to them, "Why are you talking about having no bread? Do you still not perceive or understand? Are your hearts hardened? Do you have eyes, and fail to see? Do you have ears, and fail to hear? And do you not remember? When I broke the five loaves for the five thousand, how many baskets full of broken pieces did you collect?" They said to him, "Twelve." "And the seven for the four thousand, how many baskets full of broken pieces did you collect?" And they said to him, "Seven." Then he said to them, "Do you not yet understand?"

The significance of the numbers mentioned in this passage has been the subject of much speculation. Joel Marcus notes a connection with the miraculous feeding story of the loaves and fishes that precedes this episode (Mark 8:1-9). He suggests that the numbers twelve and seven (and their multiples) likely connoted "eschatological fullness" by invoking images of the seven days of creation and the future restoration of the twelve tribes of Israel.[43] Yigael Yadin suggested that the numbers of baskets mentioned in this passage — twelve and seven — symbolized the bread of the Pharisees and the bread of the Herodians, respectively. The twelve baskets alluded to the twelve loaves of the Presence eaten every week by the priests in the Jerusalem temple. Yadin proposed that the "Herodians" mentioned in this passage practiced a different rite involving seven loaves instead of twelve and identified them with the Essenes because the *Temple Scroll* mandates the offering of seven baskets of bread, one on each day, at the annual festival of the ordination of priests.[44] Interestingly, the parallel passage in Matthew (16:5-12) substitutes Sadducees for Herodians.[45]

Dogs, Chickens, and Pigs

The Animal Bone Deposits at Qumran

One of the most puzzling discoveries at Qumran are deposits of animal bones that were placed between large potsherds or inside jars, either flush with or on top of the ancient ground level and covered with little or no earth (see Fig. 26). The bones belonged to adult sheep and goats, lambs or kids, calves, and cows or oxen.[46] Roland de Vaux noted that the bones must be the remains of meals, since all were clean but some were charred, indicating that the meat was boiled or roasted on a spit.[47] The suggestion made by some scholars that the community wanted to keep scavengers away from the bones is contradicted by the fact that it would have been easier to dump the bones into Wadi Qumran and by the absence of analogous deposits at other sites; are we to assume that scavengers were a problem only at Qumran?[48] Furthermore, this suggestion is based on the mistaken assumption that the bones were buried, whereas de Vaux describes them as being placed flush with or on top of the ground. Therefore, the bones would have attracted predators, scavengers, and insects, not deterred them! Therefore de Vaux's association of the animal bone deposits with religious or ritual meals that were eaten by the community still seems most likely.[49]

It is interesting to consider the animal bone deposits at Qumran in light of sectarian purity concerns. Lawrence Schiffman notes that the author of 4QMMT was opposed to dogs scavenging the bones of sacrificed animals in Jerusalem because, according to sectarian law, bones are a source of impurity:[50]

> And one should not let] dogs [enter the h]oly [camp] [because they might eat some of the b]ones from the te[mple with] the flesh o[n them. Because Jerusalem is the] holy camp, i[t is] [the place which He has chosen] from among all [the tribes of] Israel, since Je[rusalem] is [the head of the camps of Israel]. . . . And concerning] [the uncleanness of a corpse] of a man we s[a]y that every [bone, whether stripped of flesh or complete is subject to the l]aw concerning a dead or murde[red person.] (4Q397 frags. 6-13)[51]

Yadin remarked on the polemical nature of a passage in the *Temple Scroll*, which requires that "whoever carries any part of their bones, or of their carcass, skin and flesh and nail, shall wash his clothes and bathe in water . . ." (11QT 51:4-5), thereby expanding on Lev 11:25 (which refers only to the carcass) to include the bones, skin, and nails.[52]

In contrast, the rabbis ruled that animal bones, skin, and nails do not cause the degree of impurity associated with a carcass:[53]

> The hide, and grease, and sediment, and flayed-off meat, and bones, and sinews, and horns and hooves join together [with the meat to which they are attached to form the requisite volume] to impart food uncleanness, but [they do] not [join together to impart] uncleanness of carrion. (*m. Ḥul.* 9:1)

> "and everything upon which any part of their carcass falls"; any part of their carcass, not any part of their bones, nor of their teeth nor of their nails nor of their hair shall be unclean. (*Sifra, Sherazim* x:2 [55b])[54]

This debate is echoed in a Mishnaic passage in which the Sadducees criticize the Pharisees for considering human bones but not animal bones as impure:

> Say Sadducees: We complain against you, Pharisees. For you say, "Holy Scriptures impart uncleanness to hands, but the books of *Hamiras* [Homer?] do not impart uncleanness to the hands." Said Rabbi Yohanan b. Zakkai, "And do we have against the Pharisees in this matter alone?" Lo, they say, "The bones of an ass are clean, but the bones of Yohanan, high priest, are unclean." They said to him, "According to their preciousness is their uncleanness. So that a man should not make the bones of his father and mother into spoons." He said to them, "So too Holy Scriptures: According to their preciousness is their uncleanness. But the books of *Hamiras* [Homer?], which are not precious, do not impart uncleanness to hands." (*m. Yad.* 4:6)[55]

The animal bone deposits at Qumran likely represent the remains of communal meals at which meat was consumed. I have suggested that because the sectarians considered these meals to be a substitute for participation in the temple sacrifices, they disposed of the remains of animals that they consumed in a manner analogous to those sacrificed in the temple.[56] As Edwin Firmage observes, "Indeed, it was not uncommon [in antiquity] for a single animal to provide both the sacrifice and the meal. Every use of meat thus became a sacral meal, and every act of animal slaughter a sacrifice. The [Hebrew] Bible makes this connection explicit. In Israelite priestly literature, sacrifice and slaughter were nearly synonymous."[57] Many of the pottery vessels found with the animal bones at Qumran appear to have been broken before they were deposited, a phenomenon that brings to mind the biblical injunction regarding the *ḥaṭṭ'at* (individual sin offering): "An earthen vessel in which it was boiled shall be broken" (Lev 6:28).[58]

The distribution of the animal bone deposits at Qumran — on the fringes of the settlement and outside the main buildings — seems to reflect a sectarian hierarchy of sacred space, with the main parts of the settlement symbolizing the "temple" or "sanctuary" and the surrounding or adjacent areas corresponding to the "sacred camp."[59] Forty years ago David Flusser noted that the sectarians conceptualized their community as structured along the lines of the eschatological city of Jerusalem, as expressed in 4QIsaiah Pesher (4Q164, following Isa 54:11-12).[60]

Chickens and Dogs in Jerusalem and the Desert Camp

Our understanding of the animal bone deposits at Qumran can be refined in light of David Henschke's observations about sectarian regulations governing the slaughter of nonsacrificial animals in Jerusalem.[61] Leviticus prohibits the slaughter of nonsacrificial animals and permits the consumption of meat only after the animal has been sacrificed as "Holy Things" *(qdšym)* on the altar:[62]

> If anyone of the house of Israel slaughters an ox or a lamb or a goat in the camp, or slaughters it outside the camp, and does not bring it to the entrance of the tent of meeting, to present it as an offering to the Lord before the tabernacle of the Lord, he shall be held guilty of bloodshed; he has shed blood, and he shall be cut off from the people. (Lev 17:3-4)

The rabbis allowed the slaughter and consumption of nonsacrificial animals everywhere (including in Jerusalem but not in the temple), as prescribed in Deuteronomy:[63]

> When the Lord your God enlarges your territory, as he has promised you, and you say, "I am going to eat some meat," because you wish to eat meat, you may eat meat whenever you have the desire. If the place

44

where the Lord your God will choose to put his name is too far from you, and you slaughter as I have commanded you any of your herd or flock that the Lord has given you, then you may eat within your towns whenever you desire. (Deut 12:20-21)

The Qumran sect did not reject Deuteronomy but instead understood its legislation together with Leviticus's as allowing the slaughter and consumption of nonsacrificial animals only outside Jerusalem:[64]

And you shall not slaughter a clean ox or sheep or goat in all your towns, near to my temple (within) a distance of a three-days' journey; nay, but inside my temple you shall slaughter it, making it a burnt offering or a peace offering, and you shall eat and rejoice before me at the place on which I shall choo[se] to put my name. And every clean animal which has a blemish, you shall eat it within your towns, far from my temple, thirty stadia *(rs)* around it; you shall not slaughter near my temple, for it is foul flesh. (11QT 52:13-18)

Because the sectarians considered Jerusalem to be the sacred camp in the midst of which God dwells, they extended temple prohibitions to the entire city but excluded other camps or settlements.[65] The author of 4QMMT reiterates the prohibition against eating nonsacrificial animals slaughtered in Jerusalem and seems to condemn those who violate this injunction:[66]

[And concer]ning what is written: [. . .] [. . .] outside the camp a bull, or a sheep or a goat, for [. . . in the north of the camp.] And we think that the temple [is the place of the tent of meeting, and Je]rusale[m] is the camp; and out[side] the camp [is outside of Jerusalem;] it is the camp of their cities. (4Q394 14-18)

[. . .] they do [no]t slaughter in the temple. (4Q396 1)

The term "outside the camp" appears to denote an area to the north of Jerusalem that was set aside for the disposal of ashes and sacrificial remains:[67]

Outside the ca[mp . . .] . . . [. . .] removing the ashes from [the altar] and bur[ning there the sin-offering, for Jerusalem] is the place which . . . (4Q394 18-19)

The Tosefta also refers to this area in Jerusalem:[68]

> Where do they burn them? In the great house of ashes, outside of Jerusalem, north of Jerusalem, beyond the three camps. Rows of priests were set up around the fire, because of the crush of the crowd, so that they should not push to see and fall into the fire. (*t. Kippurim* 3:17)

Having demonstrated that the sectarians identified Jerusalem as the sacred camp and prohibited the slaughter and consumption of nonsacrificial animals throughout the city, Henschke reconsiders 4QMMT's ban against dogs:

> And one should not let] dogs [enter the h]oly [camp] [because they might eat some of the b]ones from the te[mple with] the flesh o[n them. Because Jerusalem is the] holy camp . . . (4Q397 58-59)

He concludes that since the sectarians required all meat consumed in Jerusalem to be sacrificial, only sacrificial remains would be available for dogs to eat. This is why the author of 4QMMT sought to ban dogs from Jerusalem. In contrast, because the rabbis permitted the slaughter and consumption of nonsacrificial animals in Jerusalem (the scraps of which could be fed to dogs), they did not consider dogs to be a problem, as the lack of rabbinic legislation on this matter indicates.[69]

The possibility that the sectarians conceived of the settlement at Qumran along the lines of the sacred camp is supported by the composition of the animal bone deposits (but see below). The biblical legislation discussed above mentions the same species that are represented in the deposits at Qumran, specifically sheep and goats, lambs or kids, calves, and cows or oxen: "If anyone of the house of Israel slaughters an ox or a lamb or a goat in the camp . . ." (Lev 17:3; see also 11QT 52:13). The analogy with the sacred camp is further supported by the absence of poultry from the animal bone deposits, which makes no sense if we assume that the communal meals were considered a substitute for participation in the temple sacrifices, as the Hebrew Bible permits the consumption of pigeons and turtledoves as sacrificial offerings. The absence of fowl among the animal bone deposits cannot be the result of environmental factors (that is, an argument that chickens cannot survive at Qumran), as large numbers of poultry bones were found in the excavations at 'Ein Gedi and 'Ein Boqeq.[70]

Two passages in the *Temple Scroll* might shed light on the absence of poultry from the animal bone deposits at Qumran. Although sectarian law does not forbid the consumption of permitted species of fowl,[71] the *Temple Scroll* bans all birds from the temple precincts. The first passage refers to unclean species:

> (let) no]t fly [any] / unclean bird over [my] temp[le and you shall make spikes on the wall of the court and over] the roofs of the gates [of] / the outer court. And an [unclean bird shall not] be within my temple for [ev]er / and ever, all the days that [I dwe]ll among them. (11QT 46:1-4)

Yadin noted that this passage recalls Josephus's description of the "scarecrow" on the roof of Herod's temple: "From its summit protruded sharp golden spikes to prevent birds from settling upon it and polluting the roof" (*War* 5.224).[72] The concern seems to be that unclean birds flying or perching overhead would pollute the temple with their secretions and perhaps with their carcasses.[73]

A second passage in the *Temple Scroll* might explain why even permitted species of fowl such as chickens are unrepresented among the animal bone deposits at Qumran:

> [. . .] . . . [. . .] to enter my city [. . .] a cock (or chicken; *trngwl*) you shall not rai[se . . .] *(tgdlw)* in the entire temple [. . .] the temp[le . . .] (11Q21/11QTc)[74]

Elisha Qimron notes that although the words *trngwl* and "to raise" [animals] do not occur in the Hebrew Bible, they appear together in rabbinic literature:[75]

> They do not rear chickens in Jerusalem, on account of the Holy Things, nor do priests [rear chickens] anywhere in the Land of Israel, because of the [necessity to preserve] the cleanness [of heave offering and certain other foods which are handed over to the priests]. (*m. B. Qam. 7:7*)

Although chickens are a clean (permitted) species, some groups apparently sought to ban them as well as dogs from Jerusalem due to purity concerns.[76] The polemics of 4QMMT (and the lack of rabbinic concern) suggest that dogs wandered freely around Jerusalem and perhaps scavenged sacrificial remains. The Mishnah's reference to a ban against raising chickens in Jerusalem might reflect similar concerns about scavenging.[77] If such a prohibition existed, however, it does not seem to have been enforced, judging from the discovery of poultry bones in contexts dating to the late Second Temple period in Jerusalem.[78] A bizarre incident recorded in the Mishnah also attests to the presence of chickens in Jerusalem before 70:

> R. Judah b. Baba gave testimony concerning five matters: . . . that a chicken was stoned in Jerusalem because it had killed a human being. (*m. 'Ed.* 6:1)[79]

Recent excavations by Randall Price on the marl terrace to the south of the Qumran settlement have brought to light additional animal bone deposits.[80] These deposits, which are concentrated along (and even under) the boundary wall marking the eastern edge of the settlement, differ in some respects from those described by de Vaux.[81] First, the animal bone deposits discovered by Price had been buried (inside pottery vessels or with potsherds), not laid on top of or flush with the ancient ground level. Second, whereas de Vaux described some of the animal bones as charred, Price reports significant quantities of ash together with charred bones in the deposits. Third, out of approximately two thousand specimens that Price recovered, a small percentage consists of gazelle bones. Although the Hebrew Bible permits the consumption of gazelle and deer, nondomesticated species could not be offered for sacrifice.

The presence of gazelle (albeit in very small quantities) among the animal bone deposits discovered by Price might invalidate my suggestion that the Qumran community conceived of the settlement along the lines of the sacred desert camp, as gazelle meat could not be sacrificial. However, there is another possibility. Price assigns the animal bone deposits that he found to the pre-31 B.C.E. phase of Period Ib. This could account for the differences between Price's deposits, which are located at the southern end of the marl terrace, and those discovered by de Vaux, which surround the settlement's buildings and mostly appear to postdate the earthquake of 31.[82] If this is the case, it may be that before 31 B.C.E. the Qumran community did not consider the settlement analogous to Jerusalem or the sacred desert camp, and therefore the animals that they consumed included nondomesticated species. Perhaps this accounts for the presence of two to three poultry bones among the approximately two thousand specimens that Price reports.[83] If the settlement was reorganized along the lines of the sacred desert camp after 31, nonsacrificial species would no longer have been consumed. The possibility that the Qumran settlement was reorganized along the lines of the ideal city of Jerusalem and the sacred desert camp is further suggested by the apparent failure to replace the destroyed toilet in L51 after the earthquake.[84]

As observed above, the rabbis rejected the notion that all meat consumed in Jerusalem must be sacrificial and allowed nonsacrificial meat to be eaten in the city.[85] The discovery of small numbers of gazelle and deer bones in contexts dating to the late Second Temple period in Jerusalem indicates that nonsacrificial meat was consumed by some of the city's inhabitants.[86] This evidence supports Schiffman's observation that "the Pharisees and those who followed them, including the Hasmoneans in this period, did perform nonsacral slaughter in this area, and it was against this practice that the authors of both the 'Halakhic Letter' [4QMMT] and the *Temple Scroll* polemicized."[87]

The *Temple Scroll* not only prohibits the consumption of nonsacrificial meat in Jerusalem but bans the importation of skins of clean animals that have not been slaughtered in Jerusalem (and therefore are nonsacrificial) and their use as containers for temple offerings:

> All skin of clean animals that will be slaughtered within their cities, they shall not bring into it [the temple city]. . . . And they shall not defile my temple with the skins of their abominable offerings which they will sacrifice in their land . . . (11QT 47: 7-8, 13-14)

Yadin noted the polemical tone of the ban on animal skins, which has no direct scriptural basis and contradicts (later) rabbinic law.[88] A decree attributed to Antiochus III suggests that a ban on the consumption of nonsacrificial meat and the importation of unclean animal skins was observed in Jerusalem around 200 B.C.E.:

> Nor shall anyone bring into the city the flesh of horses or of mules or of wild or tame asses, or of leopards, foxes or hares, or, in general, of any animals forbidden to the Jews. Nor is it lawful to bring in their skins or even to breed any of these animals in the city. But only the sacrificial animals known to their ancestors and necessary for the propitiation of God shall they be permitted to use. Any person who violates any of these statutes shall pay to the priests a fine of three thousand drachmas of silver. (Josephus, *Ant.* 12.145-46)[89]

The *Temple Scroll* thus seems to extend a pre-Hasmonean ban against importing into Jerusalem the skins of unclean animals to all animals not sacrificed in the Jerusalem temple.[90] This extrabiblical ban originated in priestly circles.[91]

The Hebrew Bible allows the consumption of permitted nondomesticated species of animals and birds only after the blood has been poured out:[92]

> But whenever you desire, you may slaughter and eat meat in any of your settlements, according to the blessing that the Lord your God has granted you. The unclean and the clean alike may partake of it, as of the gazelle and the deer. But you must not partake of the blood; you shall pour it on the ground like water. (Deut 12:15-16)

> If the place where the Lord has chosen to establish His name is too far from you, you may slaughter any of the cattle or sheep that the Lord gives you, as I have instructed you; and you may eat to your heart's content in your settlements. Eat it, however, as the gazelle and the deer are eaten: the unclean may eat it together with the clean. But make sure that you do not partake of the blood; for the blood is the life, and you must not consume the life with the flesh. You must not partake of it; you must pour it out on the ground like water . . . (Deut 12:21-24)

Leviticus 17:13 mandates that the blood drained from wild animals and birds must be covered: "And if any Israelite or any stranger who resides among them hunts down an animal or a bird that may be eaten, he shall pour out its blood and cover it with earth."

The author of the *Temple Scroll* harmonized Deuteronomy's legislation with Lev 17:13, with the result that the blood of all animals that have not been sacrificed must be drained and covered:

> Within your towns you shall eat it; the unclean and the clean among you alike may eat it, as though it were a gazelle or a hart. Only you shall not eat its blood; you shall pour it upon the earth like water, and cover it with dust. (11QT 52:10-12; also 11QT 53:4-6)[93]

Perhaps the animal bone deposits discovered by Price should be understood in light of the *Temple Scroll's* legislation mandating the burial of the blood of all nonsacrificial animals, assuming that blood was disposed of together with bones and other inedible parts of the animals. If there is indeed a chronological distinction between the animal bone deposits discovered by Price (pre-31) and de Vaux (post-31), it could be that the earlier deposits were buried because the meat consumed was considered nonsacrificial. The exclusion of nondomesticated species from the (apparently) later deposits and their placement on top of the ground suggest an analogy with sacrificial offerings, and the absence of poultry hints at conceptual parallels with Jerusalem and the sacred desert camp.

The evidence reviewed here suggests that after 31 B.C.E. the Qumran community reorganized the settlement along the lines of the sacred desert camp. They followed the relevant biblical laws according to their understanding, which meant that all meat consumed was considered sacrificial (or as a substitute for sacrifices) and included sheep, ox, and goats. No poultry seems to have been raised or consumed at Qumran, and presumably there were no dogs in the settlement either.[94] We do not know how and where the animals consumed at Qumran were slaughtered.

Dogs and Pigs

m. Baba Qamma 7:7 says that chickens are not raised in Jerusalem on account of "the Holy Things" *(hqdšym)*. This is followed by a reference to pigs and dogs, supporting Qimron's association of chickens and dogs with impurity: "They do not rear pigs anywhere. A person should not rear a dog, unless it is kept tied up by a chain."[95] This concern seems to be echoed in a saying that Matthew attributes to Jesus in the Sermon on the Mount: "Do not give what is holy *(to hagion)* to dogs; and do not throw your pearls before swine, or they will trample them under foot and turn and maul you" (Matt 7:6). The *Gospel of Thomas* (93) has a slightly different version: "Jesus said, 'Do not give what is holy to dogs, lest they throw them on the dungheap *(kopria)*. Do not throw the pearls to swine, lest they [. . .] it [. . .].'"[96] The *Didache* contains a similar verse:

> Let no one eat or drink of your eucharist save those who have been baptized in the name of the Lord, since the Lord has said, "Do not give what is holy to the dogs." (9:5)[97]

These passages seem to reflect a concern similar to that voiced by the author of 4QMMT, that dogs will eat sacred food or sacrificial offerings.[98]

Huub van de Sandt suggests that the phrase "what is holy" refers to sacrificial food, based on rabbinic rulings to the effect that "Holy things (dedicated sacrifices) are not to be redeemed to feed them to dogs."[99] Ugaritic and Hittite texts express a similar view that dogs should not have access to sacrificial offerings.[100] Furthermore, in the Hittite texts dogs and pigs are considered unclean, defiling temple and sacrificial offerings through their presence: "Maintain great respect for the sacrificial loaves (and) libation vessel(s) of the gods. . . . If a pig or dog does somehow force its way to the utensils of wood or clay that you have, and the kitchen worker does not throw it out, but gives it to the gods to eat from an unclean (vessel), to that one will the gods give excrement and urine to eat and drink."[101]

Jesus' statement about not giving what is holy to dogs is echoed in Exodus, where God enjoins the Israelites to be holy by avoiding unclean meat (specifically *ṭrph*, "meat torn by animals"), which should be thrown to the dogs:

> You shall be a people holy to me; therefore you shall not eat any meat that is mangled by beasts in the field; you shall throw it to the dogs. (Exod 22:31)

Here the Israelites are commanded to throw unclean meat to dogs, whereas Jesus says that holy things should not be given to dogs. Another biblical passage brings to mind Jesus' saying about dogs:

> None of the daughters of Israel shall be a temple prostitute; none of the sons of Israel shall be a temple prostitute. You shall not bring the fee of a prostitute or the pay of a dog *(ûmĕḥîr kēleb)* into the house of the Lord your God in payment for any vow, for both of these are abhorrent [an abomination] to the Lord your God. (Deut 23:18; MT 23:19)

Scholars disagree about whether the "pay of a dog" should be understood literally or refers to male cultic prostitution.[102] Either way, here too Jesus inverts the biblical injunction; instead of forbidding one from donating the pay of a dog to God, he prohibits giving what is holy to dogs.

A connection between dogs and impurity (or profanity/lack of holiness) is suggested by the parallel reference to swine in Matt 7:6.[103] Elsewhere in early Christian literature dogs and pigs represent filth and (moral) impurity. For example, Oxyrhynchus papyrus fragment 840 mentions dogs and pigs wallowing in a miqveh in Jerusalem called the "pool of David":

> You have washed yourself in these running waters where dogs and pigs have wallowed day and night . . . (2.7)[104]

The references to pigs in association with dogs and chickens in rabbinic and early Christian literature suggest that these creatures were considered sources of impurity and filth, despite the fact that poultry is permitted by biblical law and was raised and consumed by Jews.[105]

CHAPTER 4

Household Vessels: Pottery, Oil Lamps, Glass, Stone, and Dung

Antigonus of Soko had two disciples who used to study his words. . . . So they arose and withdrew from the Torah and split into two sects, the Sadducees and the Boethusians: Sadducees named after Zadok, Boethusians after Boethus. And they used silver vessels and gold vessels all their lives — not because they were ostentatious; but the Sadducees said, "It is a tradition amongst the Pharisees to afflict themselves in this world; yet in the world to come they will have nothing."

'Abot R. Nat. 5[1]

Now, for the Pharisees, they live meanly, and despise delicacies in diet.

Josephus, *Ant.* 18.12; Whiston's translation

Pottery

Imported Wares

In the late Hellenistic and early Roman periods, fine ceramic tablewares (dining and serving dishes) in the eastern Mediterranean typically were covered with a glossy red coating called a slip. The most common type of red-slipped ware found at sites in Palestine is Eastern Terra Sigillata A (ESA), which was produced in Syria-Phoenicia.[2] This ware is characterized by the light yellow color of the clay and an uneven or blotchy, flakey orange-red slip (see Fig. 10). ESA and other imported fine wares are rare or absent from Jerusalem, Jericho, and elite contexts elsewhere in Judea before the middle of Herod's reign. Rachel Bar-Nathan attributes this phenomenon to the widespread observance of purity laws by the Judean elite during the Hasmonean period, which she relates to "unwritten Sadducean laws and customs" in Jericho and Jerusalem.[3] But if Bar-Nathan is correct, why did these elite Jews change their purity observance during Herod's reign and begin to acquire and use imported wares?

The discovery of amphoras (jars for transporting products such as wine) in elite Judean contexts of the Hasmonean period contradicts Bar-Nathan's suggestion.[4] For example, amphoras dating from the mid–second century to first century B.C.E. are represented on Jerusalem's western hill, albeit in small numbers (see Fig. 9).[5] Bar-Nathan also refers to "five or six Rhodian and Knidian sherds" from the Hasmonean palaces at Jericho.[6] These amphoras indicate that in the Hasmonean period some affluent Jews indulged in wines imported from Rhodes, Kos, Italy, and North Africa.[7] Nevertheless, the Jewish population of Hasmonean-period Jerusalem consumed significantly less Rhodian wine than the inhabitants of other cities around the eastern Mediterranean including Alexandria.[8] The non-Jewish (probably Hellenized Phoenician) residents of the Late Hellenistic villa at Tel Anafa in Israel's Upper Galilee also consumed much larger quantities of imported wine than their contemporaries in Jerusalem but did not enjoy the same variety, as indicated by the fact that all but one of the 137 stamped amphora handles found in the excavations come from Rhodes (the single exception is from Knidos).[9] Hellenistic influence on the Judean elite is also evident in the architectural features and decoration of the Hasmonean palaces at Jericho, including walls decorated with frescoes and stucco, mosaic floors, bath houses, swimming pools, garden triclinia, and Greek architectural elements such as Doric columns and a triglyph and metope frieze.[10]

To account for the absence of imported fine wares such as ESA in Hasmonean-period contexts in Judea, I have emphasized economic and regional factors, that is, the high cost of overland transport from coastal ports and Phoenicia inland to Judea and the Dead Sea region.[11] As we shall see, fine red-slipped wares are found in Hasmonean-period contexts at sites in Galilee, where the cost of transport was less of a factor. Not surprisingly, red-slipped wares and other imports are also common at coastal sites around the eastern Mediterranean and on Cyprus.[12]

The appearance of a variety of imported wares at Jericho and Jerusalem (and other inland Judean sites) in the middle of Herod's reign should be understood in the context of the close ties between Herod and his family, on the one hand, and Augustus and members of the imperial family such as Marcus Agrippa, on the other hand.[13] The fashions and customs introduced by Herod were adopted and imitated (on a more limited scale) by the Judean elite. Roman influence is evident in the introduction of new types of interior decoration (such as Pompeian-style wall paintings) and the remodeling of some mansions on Jerusalem's western hill to include formal dining rooms (see Figs. 12, 16).[14] The mansions were equipped with Hellenistic-style dining rooms that provided a setting for lavish gatherings in which diners reclined on couches at individual tables and consumed delicacies served on fine dishes.[15] The finds include luxury glass, expensive red-slipped ceramic tableware, and imported amphoras (see Figs. 9-11, 18).[16] On the other hand, Nahman Avigad noted that the presence of numerous miqva'ot and stone vessels in these mansions indicate that the inhabitants observed Jewish purity laws (see Figs. 7, 14-15).[17]

As Renate Rosenthal-Heginbottom remarked in her discussion of ceramic imports from the Jewish Quarter excavations: "the imported pottery from Area A is clear evidence for the substantial changes in lifestyle, culinary tastes, trade connections, and marketing strategies which took place during the reign of Herod; yet it was relevant to a minority only [the elite]."[18] For example, ESA begins to appear in quantities in Herod's palaces at Jericho and Jerusalem and in the homes of Jerusalem's wealthiest Jews around 20-10 B.C.E.[19] At the same time, a high-quality, thin-walled tableware painted with delicate floral designs (usually referred to as Jerusalem[ite] painted pottery and consisting mostly of bowls) began to be produced in Jerusalem (see Fig. 30 [from Masada]).[20] Other ceramic imports that appeared in Jerusalem during Herod's reign (albeit in small quantities) include Italian thin-walled ware, Cypriot Eastern Sigillata D, Western Terra Sigillata, and Pompeian Red Ware (see Fig. 31 [from Masada]).[21]

Rosenthal-Heginbottom observed that "The appearance of Italian pans in the houses of the upper class Jewish inhabitants in Jerusalem means that . . . Jews were open to Roman culinary influences and prepared to try and taste new food. Herod the Great could have become acquainted with the dish during his stay in Rome, had it introduced to his household, whence it was copied by others."[22] Italian pans are characterized by a broad, shallow body and flat base (see Fig. 31). Their form is ideally suited to the preparation of *patinae* and *patellae,* popular Roman dishes similar to a quiche or frittata in which an egg mixture was poured over chopped meat, fish, vegetables, and/or fruit and then baked or cooked over a fire.[23] There is no need to assume that the preparation of these dishes violated biblical dietary laws, as *patinae* and *patellae* could be made without forbidden ingredients such as pork. As Andrea Berlin concludes, "in the wealthy homes of the Upper City of Jerusalem, however, there occur imported Italian pans and close, locally produced versions, making it probable that pans were used for Roman cuisine and understood as a vehicle for Roman culture."[24]

Amphoras found in the Jewish Quarter mansions and elsewhere on the western hill indicate that during the Herodian period the Jerusalem elite also consumed imported wine, a phenomenon that puzzled Avigad:[25] "These [amphoras] are evidence that the inhabitants of the house enjoyed wine imported from Italy. But how was 'gentile' wine used here in a period when the Jews generally adhered to the precepts forbidding consumption of such foreign products? It would seem that there have always been more and less observant Jews."[26] Donald Ariel notes that we still do not know when laws prohibiting the eating of Gentile food originated and became common.[27] The finds from the Jewish Quarter suggest that even if prohibitions against the consumption of Gentile food originated before 70 c.e., they were not universally accepted or observed.[28]

Some of these fashions trickled down and were adopted on a more modest scale by local Jewish or Judaized elites outside Jerusalem during the first century c.e. For example, the rural villa at Khirbet el-Muraq (Ḥilkiah's Palace) in Idumaea is equipped with a Roman-style bathhouse complete with hypocaust, a stuccoed formal dining room, and a peristyle courtyard (see Fig. 20).[29] Roman-style wall paintings have been found in an early Roman house on Sepphoris's acropolis, in one house at Yodefat (Jotapata), and in two houses at Gamla.[30] Fragments of fourteen imported Pompeian Red Ware pans and seven lids were also found at Gamla.[31] A few Jewish potters in Galilee and Jerusalem produced local versions of pans in the first century c.e., but these are limited in quantity and distribution.[32] Interestingly, there are no comparable finds from Judean villages, as Berlin observes: "Only in Jerusalem, however, is there a full array of remains reflecting foreign dining habits, including decorated table vessels for serving and personal use and even Italian-style cooking pans for Roman recipes."[33] Even affluent dwellings of the first century c.e. at Sepphoris have yielded few fine wares and no imported amphoras.[34]

The finds from Jerusalem's Jewish Quarter mansions indicate that their elite residents acquired and used imported dishes, prepared Roman-style cuisine, and consumed imported foodstuffs. The mansions, richly decorated with Pompeian-style wall paintings, stucco, mosaic floors, and stone furniture provided a setting for a highly Romanized lifestyle — a display of conspicuous consumption. The Jerusalem elite provide an interesting example of hybridity and adaptation to biblical law. For example, the fine, lathe-turned stone dishes found in large quantities in the Jewish Quarter mansions are modeled after imported fine wares in other materials (Figs. 14-15; see below).[35] These expensive stone dishes provided an elegant table setting for consuming temple offerings and priestly foods in conformity with Jewish purity laws.[36] The Romanization of the lifestyle of the Jerusalem elite in the middle of Herod's reign coincides with the introduction of stone vessels and ossuaries, on the one hand, and the disappearance of ESA among the Jewish population of Galilee, on the other hand.[37]

Local Pottery

Large numbers of locally-produced, undecorated dining dishes (plates, cups, and bowls) were discovered in miqva'ot in the Hasmonean palaces at Jericho and in some of the Jewish Quarter mansions (see Figs. 7-8).[38] Bar-Nathan suggests that this phenomenon attests to an otherwise unknown "Sadducean halakhah," according to which ceramic vessels could be purified through immersion in a miqveh.[39] She speculates that the Sadducees understood the relevant Biblical passage as including all materials that can withstand fire, instead of limiting it only to the specified metals: ". . . gold, silver, bronze, iron, tin, and lead — everything that can withstand fire, shall be passed through fire, and it shall be clean. Nevertheless it shall also be purified with the water for purification; and whatever cannot withstand fire, shall be passed through the water" (Num 31:22-23). Alternatively, it may be that the Sadducees and/or other groups understood this passage as meaning that any materials not mentioned are insusceptible to impurity (such as pottery, glass, and stone).[40]

Rabbinic halakhah follows Leviticus in mandating that ceramic vessels can acquire impurity and once impure must be broken, as they cannot be purified: "And if any of them falls into any earthen vessel, all that is in it shall be unclean, and you shall break the vessel" (Lev 11:33; see *m. Kelim* 2:1) Hundreds of dining dishes were discovered at Qumran, stored in annexes to the communal dining rooms (L86 and L114) but not deposited in miqva'ot as in Jerusalem and Jericho (see Fig. 25).[41] This suggests that the Qumran community interpreted the injunction in Num 31:22-23 in a more restricted manner, as did the rabbis. Apparently the sectarians also followed Lev 11:33, for the requirement to break impure pottery vessels is reiterated in the *Temple Scroll:*

> And all earthen vessels shall be broken, for they are unclean and cannot become clean again forever. (11QT 50:17-19; see also 11QT 49:8)

If Bar-Nathan's suggestion is correct, it means that the Sadducees and/or other groups ignored Lev 11:33, which at first glance seems difficult to accept.[42] However, the polemical tone of the *Temple Scroll's* injunction — which emphasizes that *all* ceramic vessels must be broken and adds that they cannot become clean *forever* — suggests that some contemporary Jews thought (and did) otherwise.[43]

Even if the dishes found in the miqva'ot in Jerusalem and Jericho are evidence of an unknown "Sadducean halakhah" that allowed pottery to be purified through immersion, this practice apparently was abandoned after the Hasmonean period, as deposits of intact vessels in miqva'ot cease to be attested. Instead, large numbers of cooking pots that were neatly pierced by holes after firing have been discovered in first-century c.e. deposits around Jerusalem, including in debris inside Herod's Gate in the Old City,[44] in cisterns and pits associated with houses to the south and west of the Temple Mount,[45] and in a cistern in the largest mansion in the Jewish Quarter, which yielded thirty-five pierced but intact cooking pots (see Fig. 13).[46] If these cooking pots were pierced in order to render them unusable due to purity concerns (as proposed by Avigad, Meir Ben-Dov, and others), the specimens from the Jewish Quarter mansion would indicate that by the first century c.e. the Jerusalem elite, like other Jews, agreed that pottery vessels cannot be purified and must be discarded.[47]

Village Dining and Pottery

Palestinian villages of the first century b.c.e. and first century c.e. typically consisted of dwelling units clustered around shared courtyards or open spaces, sometimes separated by alleys (see Fig. 21). Agricultural and industrial installations such as wine and oil presses are found inside some of the buildings and in the surrounding areas.[48] Jewish families in villages and towns generally gathered for common meals in household contexts,[49] in a setting that recalls Jesus' dinner at Levi's house:

> As he sat at dinner in Levi's house, many tax collectors and sinners were also sitting with Jesus and his disciples — for there were many who followed him. When the scribes of the Pharisees saw that he was eating with sinners and tax collectors, they said to his disciples, "Why does he eat with tax collectors and sinners?" (Mark 2:15-16; see also Matt 9:10-11; Luke 5:29-30)[50]

Archaeological evidence indicates that when Jewish villagers at Gamla gathered for a meal at home in the first century B.C.E., they shared food out of one or two large serving vessels and used a small bowl or saucer for individual servings.[51] Typical fare consisted of soups, beans, lentils, and stews (with meat or chicken):[52]

> A woman should not fill a pot with peas and pulse and put it into the oven on the eve of the Sabbath at dusk. (t. Šabb. 3:1)

During the first century C.E. the number of cooking vessels per household at Gamla increased whereas serving vessels and tableware declined dramatically in number, suggesting that diners began to eat directly out of cooking pots instead of serving vessels and perhaps used bread to hold the food.[53] Berlin describes the dining habits of the Gamla villagers as "basic, perhaps even ascetic."[54] Similarly, the pottery from the Jewish villages at 'Ein Gedi, Pisgat Ze'ev (just north of Jerusalem), and Qiryat Sefer (north of Modi'in) consists almost entirely of local, undecorated wares, with few fine wares or imports.[55] This picture brings to mind Josephus's remark that the Pharisees live meanly and despise delicacies in diet (Ant. 18.12; although I am not suggesting that the inhabitants of these villages necessarily were Pharisees), in contrast to the Jerusalem elite, who used Roman-style dishes for the preparation and consumption of exotic cuisine.

Whereas in Jerusalem and Judea fine red-slipped wares and other imports are rare before the reign of Herod, Galilee displays the opposite pattern: there ESA is found at Jewish sites during the first century B.C.E. but disappears during the first century C.E., an interesting phenomenon considering that ESA was easily obtainable in the northern part of the country and remained common at non-Jewish sites in Galilee and Samaria.[56] Berlin does not believe that this phenomenon is connected with new purity practices among the Jewish population of Galilee, "since at the same time ESA became a regular part of household assemblages in Jerusalem, especially in the wealthy homes of priests living in sight of the Temple in the Upper City."[57] Instead, she attributes the disappearance of ESA to the Jewish population's desire to make "a political statement of solidarity and affiliation with a traditional, simple, unadorned, Jewish lifestyle, as well as demonstrating a unified opposition to the newly looming Roman presence."[58]

However, the apparent absence of ESA in first-century B.C.E. contexts at Yodefat and the discovery of a small number of imported Pompeian Red Ware pans and lids in first-century C.E. contexts at Gamla indicate that the picture might not be uniform throughout Galilee.[59] In fact, Berlin acknowledges that the appearance of stone vessels in Jewish villages and towns at about the same time that ESA disappears points to a connection with purity observance: "Across Galilee and Gaulanitis, the disappearance of ESA coincides with the appearance of chalk vessels, a pattern that might suggest that Jews now considered ESA impure."[60] The adoption by the Jerusalem elite of a wide range of imported wares (including but not limited to ESA) in the middle of Herod's reign, together with the presence of miqva'ot and stone vessels, suggests that these wealthy Jews either did not consider Gentile products impure or that they might have limited purity observance to the realm of the temple cult.

The establishment of new potters' workshops and the appearance of new ceramic types in the mid-to-late first century B.C.E. also might attest to the spread of purity observance among broad sectors of the Jewish population.[61] According to rabbinic law, pottery vessels become susceptible to impurity once they have been finished or fired:

Earthenware vessels — from what point [in their manufacture] do they receive uncleanness? "From [the point at which] their manufacture is completed," the words of R. Meir. R. Judah says, "When they have been fired in the furnace." (*t. Kelim B. Qam.* 3:12)

Dina Avshalom-Gorni and Nimrod Getzov have noted that, whereas Phoenician storage jars are represented in Hellenistic contexts at Yodefat in Galilee, by the first century C.E. they were replaced by a locally-produced type of jar with bag-shaped or barrel-shaped body (see Fig. 33 [from Masada]). In contrast, the inhabitants of the Phoenician settlement of Bet

Zeneta continued to use typical Phoenician jars, which have a conical body. Avshalom-Gorni and Getzov propose that the Jewish population of Yodefat preferred the bag-shaped jars due to purity concerns: "Buyers were advised to witness the firing of the vessels in the kiln in order to be certain that no Gentile handled the vessel during its manufacture, thus rendering it impure."[62] Berlin has suggested that bag-shaped storage jars were developed in the late first century B.C.E. as distinctively shaped containers for (ritually) pure olive oil.[63] She also links the establishment of new potters' workshops in the mid-to-late first century B.C.E. at Binyanei Ha'uma in Jerusalem and Kfar Hananya in Galilee to the spread of purity observance.[64] It is not clear whether some Jews now began to regard Gentiles and their products as inherently impure (as proposed by Gedaliah Alon), or whether they had other concerns related to the difficulty of ensuring the purity of any pottery imported from a distance, or the fact that Gentiles did not observe Jewish purity laws, or the possibility that Gentile products were associated with idolatrous practices (as suggested by Christine Hayes).[65]

Pottery at Qumran

The presence of a potters' workshop at Qumran should be understood in light of the sect's purity concerns and dining habits, which required multiple sets of dishes (see below).[66] A wide variety of ceramic vessels from Qumran and the nearby caves (including cylindrical jars) have been subjected to Neutron Activation Analysis (NAA) to determine the origin of the clay. One set of tests identified two different chemical groups among the Qumran pottery: one of Jerusalem clay and the other of non-Jerusalem clay.[67] Petrographic analysis of a large number of vessels including cylindrical jars and other vessels from the caves and settlement indicates that most of the pieces are made of Motza Formation clay from the Jerusalem area.[68] The authors of this study concluded that "The Qumran jars under investigation were made of a raw material which is not present in the vicinity of the Qumran site."[69]

A second set of NAA tests (by a different team) identified five chemical groups among the Qumran pottery.[70] The majority of vessels are made of clay from one of two sources, one identified as coming from Jerusalem and the other a non-Jerusalem source. A small number of pieces (Chemical Groups III and V) match pottery from Jericho. This means that either some of the Qumran vessels were manufactured at Jericho (or vice versa) or that the potters at Jericho and Qumran were using some of the same clay sources. It is worth noting that although Jan Gunneweg and Marta Balla describe Chemical Group I (the largest group) as "local to Qumran," no evidence of a local clay source has yet been identified.[71] In other words, although it makes sense to assume there was a clay source in the vicinity of Qumran, one has not been located yet.

Because no ovoid or cylindrical jars have been found in Jerusalem and because of the high cost of overland transport and the risk of cracking or breakage of pottery, I have suggested that some of the Qumran vessels were manufactured of clay brought from Jerusalem, instead of understanding the NAA results as meaning that finished vessels were transported to Qumran from Jerusalem.[72] The cost of transporting finished vessels overland from Jerusalem to Qumran (bundled on pack animals) would have been prohibitively expensive due to the risk of breakage along the way. Furthermore, pottery vessels transported in this way were in danger of incurring impurity through contact with impure objects, creatures, or people. Perhaps a similar concern underlies the rabbinic view that the purity of vessels brought from beyond certain distances cannot be trusted:

> From Modi'im inwards [the potters] are trusted in respect of earthenware vessels; from Modi'im outwards they are not trusted. For instance, if the potter who sells the pots enters inwards of Modi'im, then the same potter in respect of the same pots and of the same buyers is trustworthy, but if he went outwards [of Modi'im] he is not trusted. (*m. Ḥag.* 3:5)

The rarity or absence of imports (ESA and other imported wares) at Qumran should be understood in light of purity concerns as well as economic considerations. Presumably, even if the Qumran community could have afforded to purchase imported wares, they would have chosen not to do so because of purity concerns, in contrast to the Jerusalem and Jericho elite. Not only did the sectarians consider Gentiles impure, but they regarded only themselves as the true Israel and treated even other Jews as Gentiles.[73] The sectarian view seems to be based on Lev 19:16-18:

> You shall not go around as a slanderer (or talebearer) among your people, and you shall not profit by the blood of your neighbor: I am the Lord. You shall not hate in your heart anyone of your kin; you shall reprove your neighbor, or you will incur guilt yourself. You shall not take

vengeance or bear a grudge against any of your people, but you shall love your neighbor as yourself; I am the Lord.

Aharon Shemesh has demonstrated that the sectarians understood "your people" and "your kin" in this verse as referring only to other members of the sect, and therefore they were obligated to hate all others (including Jews) based on Nah 1:2: "the Lord takes vengeance on his adversaries and rages against his enemies."[74] On the other hand, the rabbis interpreted "your people" and "your kin" in Lev 19:16-18 as all of Israel, even sinners, and identified the adversaries of Nah 1:2 as Gentiles.[75] According to Mark 12:31, Jesus regarded the injunction to love your neighbor as yourself as the second most important commandment.[76] Matthew reports that Jesus included even one's enemies among those who should be loved:

> "You have heard that it was said, 'You shall love your neighbor and hate your enemy.' But I say to you, Love your enemies and pray for those who persecute you, so that you may be children of your Father in heaven; for he makes his sun rise on the evil and on the good, and sends rain on the righteous and on the unrighteous. For if you love those who love you, what reward do you have? Do not even the tax collectors do the same? And if you greet only your brothers and sisters, what more are you doing than others? Do not even the Gentiles do the same? Be perfect, therefore, as your heavenly Father is perfect." (Matt 5:43-48)

This passage shows that Lev 19:16-18 generally was understood as meaning that one should love one's neighbors and hate one's enemies (however they are defined), despite the fact that this verse says nothing about hating others.[77] Jesus' statement should be understood in the context of a wider debate over the meaning of this verse. Because in Jesus' view holiness is required to enter the kingdom of God (according to the Gospel accounts), one must love all others in order to imitate God's perfection (*imitatio Dei*).

Oil Lamps

In the late first century B.C.E. — at about the same time that stone vessels appeared and miqva'ot became increasingly common — a new type of oil lamp appeared in Palestine.[78] The lamps are wheel-made, have a round body with a large filling hole, and a short, flaring nozzle that was knife-pared (see Fig. 34). In form, wheel-made lamps are a composite of earlier Judean mold-made lamps with radiating lines around a large filling hole and Roman mold-made lamps with a closed, decorated discus and short, flaring nozzle. Berlin observes that wheel-made lamps were not necessarily less expensive to manufacture than mold-made lamps (and therefore were not less expensive, as scholars sometimes assume).[79]

Although Berlin attributes the popularity of wheel-made lamps among the Jewish and Judaized populations of Palestine to a preference for an austere lifestyle, I believe that the motivating factor was a desire to avoid the figured images that typically decorate Roman mold-made lamps (see Fig. 35). This is suggested by the apparent absence of Roman discus lamps from the Jewish Quarter mansions, whose wealthy Romanized residents avoided figured images in other media including pottery, interior decoration, and furniture.[80] On the other hand, imported lamps that are not decorated with figured images have been found in the Jewish Quarter excavations, together with large numbers of wheel-made lamps.[81] All of the lamps from the Hasmonean palaces at Jericho are local types without figured decoration.[82] Four small fragments of imported Roman discus lamps (none preserving figured decoration) were found in Herodian-period levels at Jericho, together with wheel-made lamps.[83] A number of Roman lamps with figured decoration on the discus were discovered at Masada, many of them associated with the Roman garrisons that occupied the site between Herod's death in 4 B.C.E. and the outbreak of the First Jewish Revolt and following the fall of the mountain in 73/74 C.E.[84] Although wheel-made lamps are most common at Jewish sites in Palestine, they are also attested at non-Jewish sites, including in Samaria, on the coast, in Transjordan, and in the Negev.[85] However, not all Jews seem to have avoided acquiring and using Roman lamps with figured decoration on the discus, as indicated by the discovery of a few examples at Ḥorvat ʿAqav.[86]

In light of Exod 35:3, which prohibits kindling a fire on the Sabbath, the rabbis discussed what measures may be taken to keep an oil lamp burning through the night (*t. Šabb.* 2:4-6). They prohibited reading the Torah on Sabbath (Friday) night by the light of an oil lamp because a forgetful person might tip it to obtain better light (thereby violating the Sabbath):

> But they do not read on Sabbath nights by the light of a lamp, even if it
> is above him, even if it is in another room, even if it is inside the tenth

of ten rooms, one inside another. But he may make use of a light which is located inside a cup or inside a dish, and he need not scruple about the matter. Rabban Simeon b. Gamaliel says, "Children prepare their chapters on Sabbath nights with the light of a lamp." Said R. Ishmael, "One time I read by the light of a lamp, and [forgetfully], I wanted to tilt it [to get more oil on the wick.]. I said, 'How great are the words of sages, who rule. "They do not read on Sabbath nights by the light of a lamp."'" R. Nathan says, "He [Ishmael] most certainly did tilt it. And written on his notebook is the following: 'Ishmael b. Elisha tilted a lamp on the Sabbath. When the sanctuary will be rebuilt, he will bring a sin-offering.'" (*t. Šabb.* 1:11-13)

Oil lamps must have been used for similar purposes by the Qumran sectarians, who according to the *Community Rule* spent one-third of each night studying Torah:

And the Many shall be on watch together for a third of each night of the year in order to read the book *(lqrw' bspr)*, explain the regulation *(wldrwš mšpṭ)*, and bless together *(wlbrk byḥd)*. (1QS 6:7-8)

Glass

Although glass is not listed among the materials from which vessels that acquire impurity are made (Num 31:22-23) — presumably because it was not yet in use when this legislation was written — the rabbis ruled that glass vessels are susceptible to impurity:[87]

Glass utensils [are susceptible to uncleanness because of a decree] of the words of scribes. . . . This [rule] is more strict concerning glass utensils than leather or wooden utensils. (*t. Kelim B. Bat.* 7:7)[88]

And concerning the laws about territory of the Gentiles: Did not R. Zeira bar Abina in the name of R. Jeremiah say, "Yose b. Yoezer of Seridah and Yose b. Yohanan of Jerusalem decreed that the territory of the Gentiles should be unclean, and likewise that is the case for glass utensils?" (*y. Šabb.* 1:4 [3d])

Now Shimon b. Shetah made three decrees: . . . that glassware is susceptible to becoming unclean. Did not R. Zeira, R. Abuna in the name of R. Jeremiah say, "Yosé b. Yoezer of Seridah, and Yosé b. Yohanan of Jerusalem decreed that the land of the peoples should be unclean, and likewise that is the case for glass utensils"? (*y. Ketub.* 8:11 [32c])

Ziona Grossmark notes that the earliest rabbinic legislation declaring glass impure is associated with a pair of sages who are thought to have lived in the mid-second century B.C.E., precisely the period when glass vessels (which previously had been a rare luxury commodity) began to flood the Palestinian markets. Glass vessels became even more common after the invention of glassblowing in the mid-first century B.C.E. and the adoption of this technology by Jewish craftsmen, leading to changes and modifications in rabbinic legislation regarding the impurity of glass and the manufacturing process.[89]

It is not clear whether any groups before 70 (including the Pharisees) considered glass susceptible to impurity. Sectarian legislation from Qumran does not mention glass in connection with purity. Small quantities of glass — mostly fragments belonging to relatively inexpensive types of vessels — are represented at archaeological sites around the country, including at Qumran. In my opinion, it is likely that the sectarians considered glass susceptible to impurity. However, it is possible that some groups such as the Sadducees took the omission of glass from the list in Numbers to mean that it is insusceptible to impurity. In this connection it is interesting to consider the finds from the Jewish Quarter mansions, which include locally-produced and imported luxury glass vessels such as an exquisite vase signed by the Sidonian craftsman Ennion (see Fig. 11).[90] Yael Gorin-Rosen remarks, "Apparently the residents . . . in the Jewish Quarter area in the second part of the 1st century BCE could afford luxurious glass vessels of local manufacture as well as imported objects."[91] Of course, the discovery of glass in an elite context is not surprising and does not necessarily relate to purity observance.

Glass refuse was discovered in the fill of a miqveh in the Jewish Quarter that was sealed by a stone pavement during the reign of Herod the Great.[92] The refuse, which represents waste from a glass factory, consists of glass fragments, wasters, pieces of raw glass, and slag (see Fig. 17). The glass objects represented among the fragments include cast bowls, small blown-glass perfume bottles, applicators or stirring rods ("kohl sticks"), spindle whorls, gaming pieces, and inlays.[93] These finds provide the earliest evidence of blown glass discovered until now.[94] Avigad was surprised to find evidence of glass manufacturing in a major urban center and not closer to a source of silica sand.[95] Berlin proposes that the establishment of a pot-ters' workshop at Binyanei Ha'uma (modern Jerusalem's convention cen-ter) at the same time as the glass workshop and the local stone vessel in-dustry attests to an increased interest in "household purity" among Jerusalem's Jewish population.[96] If this is true, it would suggest that by the second half of the first century B.C.E. the notion that glass was susceptible to impurity was widely accepted.

A relatively large quantity of glass was found in recent excavations at Shu'afat, just north of Jerusalem.[97] This village provides important evi-dence of Jewish settlement in Jerusalem's immediate environs during the period between the two revolts (70-132 C.E.).[98] The poor quality and sim-plicity of the glass from Shu'afat might indicate that it was produced in a local workshop that catered to the needs of the Jewish population.[99]

Robert Donceel and Pauline Donceel-Voûte have claimed that a large quantity of glassware was found in de Vaux's excavations at Qum-ran, including high-quality imports from Italy, indicating that the site was a villa rustica rather than a sectarian settlement. They catalogued about 150 fragments belonging to approximately 89 vessels.[100] The Donceels' findings are widely cited by advocates of the alternative interpretations of Qumran, such as Yizhar Hirschfeld, who identified the site as a manor house:

> Among the most striking discoveries at Qumran are the rich assem-blages of glass vessels and jewelry. Some of the vessels were imported from the Phoenician coast, whereas others resemble glassware that was produced in Italy. Moreover, there are traces of a local glass industry at Qumran, where raw materials of a light green glass have been found. The presence of a large collection of glassware at the site (never men-tioned by the excavators) is an indication of industrial and commer-cial, rather than religious, activity.[101]

In fact, the glass from Qumran is modest in quantity and quality. In comparison, the Jewish village at Shu'afat yielded over one thousand glass fragments, although it was occupied for a much shorter period than Qum-ran.[102] Furthermore, some of the glass from Qumran comes from post-68 C.E. (nonsectarian) contexts or from mixed (and therefore undatable) contexts such as dumps. According to Dennis Mizzi, who has studied the glass from de Vaux's excavations at Qumran, the assemblage consists mostly of inexpensive, free-blown, naturally-colored vessels such as cups, bowls, goblets, and bottles.[103] The finer wares include fragments of a mold-blown beaker, a fluted bowl, and two goblets, only one of which definitely comes from a pre-68 C.E. context (the other three are from post-68 or mixed contexts).[104] Only four pieces of sagged-glass vessels (a more expensive type) were found in de Vaux's excavations, two from post-68 C.E. contexts and two from mixed contexts.[105] There are no examples of fine-cast colored and colorless tablewares, polychrome glass/mosaic, or core-formed vessels, although one fragment (or perhaps two) of a mold-blown beaker was found in de Vaux's excavations ("Sidonian glass").[106]

Mizzi notes that the glass from Qumran is consistent in quantity and type with glass from other sites in the Dead Sea region and does not support claims that Qumran was a villa or manor house or an industrial or commercial center: "It cannot be emphasised enough that most probably not all glass vessels were considered as luxurious wares and that not all glass vessels were expensive. Thus, the evidence is really at odds with the idea that the glass from Qumran betrays the existence of a very wealthy community who lived a life of luxury and not with the presence of a sectarian community."[107] At the same time Mizzi cautions against "over-interpreting" the lack of fine wares, which are rare or unattested at many other sites as well. The picture presented by the glass from Qumran parallels the lack of imported fine wares among the pottery and is consistent with other sites in the Dead Sea region.[108]

According to rabbinic halakhah, vessels made of glass, wood, leather, and bone that have become impure can be purified by being broken:

> Vessels of wood, and vessels of leather, and vessels of bone, and vessels of glass: when they are flat, they are clean, and when they form receptacles, they are [susceptible of becoming] unclean. [If] they are broken, they are clean. [As to] vessels of clay and vessels of alum crystal, their [capacity to receive] uncleanness is alike. They [both] become unclean and convey uncleanness by [their] contained airspace, and they impart uncleanness from their outer sides. But they do not contract uncleanness from their outer parts. And breaking them is purifying them. (*m. Kelim* 2:1)

Underlying this legislation is the rabbinic notion of intention; that is, a vessel is susceptible to impurity as long as it can fulfill the function for which it was intended but becomes pure after it is broken and can no longer be used. Similarly, vessels made of glass, pottery, wood, leather, and bone become susceptible to impurity only after the manufacturing process is completed and they can fulfill their intended function:

> A spoiled jar which is found in the furnace, [if found] before its manufacture is completed, is clean; [if found] after its manufacture is completed, is unclean. (*m. Kelim* 2:6)

In contrast, intention does not seem to have played a role in sectarian legislation, for the *Temple Scroll* does not distinguish between finished and unfinished or broken vessels but instead declares everything unclean in a house where someone has died:

> And when a man dies in your cities, every house in which a dead (man) died shall become unclean, seven days; everything which is in the house and every one who comes into the house shall become unclean, seven days. (11QT 49:5-6)[109]

Similarly, according to the *Damascus Document* (CD 12:5-6), even dust and stones can acquire corpse impurity.

Stone Vessels

Most scholars attribute the popularity of soft chalk or limestone vessels (here referred to simply as stone vessels) to the observance of purity laws among broad sectors of the Jewish population in the late Second Temple period, as suggested by (later) rabbinic legislation.[110] The ubiquity of stone vessels at settlements in Judea and Galilee, combined with their absence from sites inhabited by the Yahwistic population of Samaria, reinforces the impression that they were connected with the observance of purity laws relating to the Jerusalem temple cult.[111] Stone vessels are found in different socio-economic contexts, including the mansions in Jerusalem's Jewish Quarter, the settlement at Qumran, and villages and towns around Judea and Galilee.[112] As Shimon Gibson remarks, "The widespread distribution of these vessels, however, in so many different contexts, both urban and rural, supports the notion that they were not actually used by any one particular socio-economic or religious group within Judaism."[113] Even so, the largest numbers of stone vessels seem to come from sites in Jerusalem, and most of the workshops found so far are located in Jerusalem's environs.[114]

Berlin divides stone vessels into four functional groups: (1) large, wide-mouthed, lathe-turned jars; (2) handled mugs (sometimes called "measuring cups") with chiseled or knife-pared exteriors; (3) lathe-turned or finely carved large vessels for serving food and drink; (4) lathe-turned small dishes for individual use (see Figs. 14-15).[115] Mugs predominate over the other groups.[116]

How were stone vessels used? According to Berlin, the purpose of the large lathe-turned serving vessels and smaller fine dining dishes was display, a proposal that is supported by the large numbers of these types discovered in the Jewish Quarter mansions and by their shapes, which imitate vessels in other materials (such as metal and red-slipped pottery).[117] A number of scholars have suggested that the large, lathe-turned jars contained water for purification, as illustrated by the episode of the wedding at Cana in John 2:6: "Now standing there were six stone water jars for the Jewish rites of purification, each holding twenty or thirty gallons."[118] Stone mugs likely were used to pour water for hand washing, not as measuring cups.[119] A passage in the Mishnah might refer to these mugs:

[In Jerusalem] . . . they brought oxen with doors laid upon their backs, and on these the children sat bearing in their hands cups of stone. When they reached [the spring or pool of] Siloam they alighted and filled the cups with water and got up again and sat upon the boards. Rabbi Jose says: "The child used to let down his cup and fill it without alighting." (*m. Parah* 3:2)[120]

Another passage refers to the use of stone, dung, and unfired clay vessels for hand washing: "With all sorts of utensils do they pour [water] for hands, even with utensils made of dung, utensils made of stone, utensils made of [unbaked] clay" (*m. Yad.* 1:2). The possibility that stone mugs were used in purification rituals is supported by Berlin's observation that their shape seems to be new, without similar forms in other media.[121]

In the first century C.E., half of the vessels in every household in Area R at Gamla were of stone, specifically mugs and saucers. But Berlin notes that this picture is skewed, as there were only seven to ten stone vessels per household over the course of two generations: "It is clear that so small an amount could not have served all residents every day as receptacles for food and drink. Instead, the types and number found suggest occasional and/or specific uses: the mugs for pouring water for hand-washing before meals, perhaps, and the small saucers for holding spices in the weekly ceremony that ends the Sabbath."[122] A total of 258 diagnostic fragments of stone vessels are recorded from the Gamla excavations, most of which come from areas that were occupied only in the first century C.E. (Areas R and S).[123] About 120 fragments of stone vessels, 80 of which are diagnostic pieces, are mentioned as having been found at Yodefat, suggesting a picture similar to Gamla.[124] In contrast, only 60 fragments of stone vessels were recovered in the village at Qiryat Sefer (north of Modi'in), and the excavations at 'Ein Gedi yielded only 35 fragments of stone vessels.[125]

Stone vessels appear to have become popular because many Jews considered stone insusceptible to impurity, whereas according to rabbinic halakhah vessels made of processed or fired materials such as pottery, metal, and glass are susceptible to impurity:

> Every utensil of metal which has a name of its own is unclean, except for the door, and for the bolt, and for the lock, and the hinge socket, and the hinge, and the clapper, and the threshold groove, which are made [to be joined] to the ground. (*m. Kelim* 11:2)

> Utensils of wood, utensils of leather, utensils of bone, utensils of glass: when they are flat, they are clean. And when they form receptacles, they are unclean. [If] they have been broken, they are clean. (*m. Kelim* 15:1)

> These utensils afford protection with a tightly stopped-up cover: vessels [made] of dung, vessels of stone . . . (*m. Kelim* 10:1)

> [If] they were utensils of dung, utensils of stone, utensils of clod [which were set on the hatchway] — the whole is clean. (*m. 'Ohal.* 5:5)

> With all utensils do they mix, even with utensils of dung, and with utensils of stone, and with utensils of clod. (*m. Parah* 5:5)[126]

> And they concur that they effect surface contact between water [which is unclean], contained in a stone vessel [which is insusceptible to uncleanness, and the water of an immersion pool] in order to render [the unclean water] clean. (*m. Beṣah* 2:3; see also *t. Šabb.* 16:11)

The rabbis ruled that the contents of tightly sealed vessels are insusceptible to defilement: "These vessels afford protection [from impurity] with a tightly stopped-up cover: Vessels made of dung, vessels of stone, vessels of unfired earth, vessels of [fired] clay, and vessels of alum crystal" (*m. Kelim* 10:1). In contrast, according to the *Temple Scroll* even the contents of sealed pottery vessels are rendered impure in a house where someone has died, at least for those scrupulous in their observance of purity laws: "And earthen vessels shall be unclean, and all that is in them shall be unclean for every clean man, and the open (vessels) shall be unclean for every man of Israel" (11QT 49:8-9).[127] The author's expansion is evident when compared with Num 19:14-15, which is the basis for this legislation: "This is the law when someone dies in a tent: everyone who comes into the tent, and everyone who is in the tent, shall be unclean seven days. And every open vessel with no cover fastened on it is unclean."

Despite the fact that according to sectarian law stone could contract impurity through contact with oil, stone vessels are attested at Qumran.[128] If stone mugs were used for hand washing, as Berlin suggests, does their presence at Qumran indicate that the sectarians washed their hands before meals (or on other occasions)? There is no clear answer to this question, as sectarian literature contains no legislation about hand washing and outside sources such as Josephus do not refer to the Essenes washing their hands.[129] This (lack of) evidence might indicate that the sectarians did not wash their hands but instead immersed themselves before all meals.[130] Perhaps the sectarians did not distinguish between internal and external impurity or between parts of the body but considered the whole person defiled.[131] This would explain why immersion without repentance does not purify:[132]

> He should not go into the waters to share in the pure food of the men of holiness, for one is not cleansed unless one turns away from one's wickedness, for he is unclean among all the transgressors of his word. (1QS 5:13-14; see also 3:4-9)[133]

Several texts from Qumran suggest that full immersion was required before all meals, even for the consumption of nonsacral food (*ḥullin*).[134] For example, according to sectarian legislation an impure person must immerse before eating and drinking (see 4Q512 col. 2 frags. 7-9; 4Q514 frag. 1; 4Q274 frags. 1-2). The *Community Rule* (1QS 5:13) indicates that members had to immerse before partaking of the pure food and drink of the sect ("He should not go into the waters to share in the pure food of the men of holiness . . ."append).[135] Furthermore, Josephus tells us that the Essenes purified themselves through immersion before participating in communal meals (*War* 2.129).

Josephus's description of the communal meals of the Essenes — and his comparison of the dining room to a temple or holy precinct — raises the possibility that the sectarians considered the food consumed at those meals to have the status of *qodesh* or *terumah* (the latter if, unlike the rabbis, they required full immersion or just hand immersion for eating food in the status of *terumah*). Perhaps they differentiated, as the rabbis did, between the purification methods required before consuming foods of different status:

> They wash the hands for eating unconsecrated food *(hullin)*, tithe *(ma'aser)*, and heave offering *(terumah)*; and for eating food in the status of Holy Things *(qodeshim)* they immerse [the hands in a miqveh]; and as to [the preparation of] purification water [through the burning of the red cow], if one's hands are made unclean, his entire body is deemed to be unclean as well" (*m. Hag.* 2:5; see also *m. Hal.* 1:9 and *m. Bik.* 2:1)[136]

In this case, in addition to the immersion required before all meals, the sectarians might have washed their hands before (and after?) consuming food at the status of *qodesh* or *terumah*. This possibility is suggested by *Jub.* 21:16 (based on Exod 30:17-21), which requires priests to wash hands and feet before and after coming into contact with sacrifices, in addition to full immersion prior to approaching the altar. If the sectarians did not practice hand washing, they must have used the stone mugs from Qumran for other purposes.

The popularity of stone vessels at sites around the country surely reflects the observance of purity laws among broad sectors of the Jewish population. However, the presence of stone vessels alone does not necessarily indicate a concern with purity, as they were widely available and could have been used without any connection to purity observance. This is especially true of mugs, which presumably cost less than the finer, lathe-turned vessels.[137] Although stone vessels may have been more expensive than locally-produced pottery, the investment paid off in the long term because of their durability. For example, it is not clear whether a few stone vessels found at 'Ein Boqeq attest to Jewish purity observance or even Jewish presence, as this site is located on the border with Nabataea and many of the finds are typically Nabataean.[138]

Dung Vessels

According to the Mishnah, vessels made of unfired clay or animal dung —
like vessels made of stone — are insusceptible to impurity (*m. Kelim* 4:5;
m. 'Ohal. 5:5):

> Clay vessels — from what time do they receive uncleanness? When
> they are fired in the furnace. And that is the completion of their manu-
> facture. (*m. Kelim* 4:5)

> These vessels afford protection [from impurity] with a tightly
> stopped-up cover: Vessels made of dung, vessels of stone, vessels of un-
> fired earth, vessels of [fired] clay, and vessels of alum crystal. (*m. Kelim*
> 10:1)

> A dung basket which was damaged [so as to be unable to] hold pome-
> granates — R. Meir declares unclean. And sages declare clean, because
> [if] the primary purpose is annulled, the secondary purpose is an-
> nulled. (*m. Kelim* 19:10)

Large bowls and basins made of unfired animal dung and clay have
been published from Masada, where they were found in contexts associated with rebel occupation at the time of the First Revolt (see Fig. 32).[139]
However, the presence of these vessels does not necessarily provide evidence for purity practices among the Jewish rebels at Masada. Instead, the
Mishnah's legislation should be understood as referring to a type of vessel
that was in widespread use among the Jewish population (and perhaps
non-Jewish populations as well).[140] The examples from Masada were preserved due to the arid conditions and the circumstances surrounding the
site's destruction. Because these crude, handmade vessels were manufactured from materials that were readily available to all sectors of the population, it is not surprising to find them in a siege context where they easily
could have been made on the spot.

Although the Mishnah indicates that some Jewish groups considered
dung vessels insusceptible to impurity, it is not clear whether this legislation originated in the period before 70 and, if so, how widely it was accepted or observed. Qumran literature indicates that according to sectarian law, unfired earth and clay vessels become susceptible to impurity
through contact with oil, like stone vessels.[141] For this reason stone and

unfired earth or clay vessels are excluded from the items listed in the *Temple Scroll* that can be purified:

> ... they shall purify the house and all its vessels, (including) mills and mortars, and all vessels made of wood, iron, and bronze, and all vessels that may be purified. (11QT 49:14-15)[142]

Dung was also used to repair pots, although the rabbis considered these pots impure because they still functioned as vessels, not because of the dung: "A jar which cracked and which [one] plastered over with dung, even though one might remove the dung and the sherds fall apart, is unclean, because the name of 'vessel' has not ceased [to apply to] it" (*m. Kelim* 3:4).

It is likely that some Jews used dung vessels because they were cheap and easy to manufacture in the household context, without any connection to purity concerns. Therefore, although the discovery of dung vessels is interesting because of the references in the Mishnah, their presence at Masada might — but does not necessarily — provide evidence of purity observance among the Jewish rebels. As E. P. Sanders cautions, "One of the difficulties in reading rabbinic literature is deciding when people did something because 'the rabbis had decreed it' and when common and widely accepted practices happen to be recorded in the Mishnah."[143]

CHAPTER 5

Dining Customs and Communal Meals

How we eat and what we eat is one of the fundamental ways we define ourselves as social beings and members of a given group.

Bray, "The Commensal Politics of Early States"

For the House of Shammai say, "A Zab who is a Pharisee should not eat with a Zab who is of common folk." And the House of Hillel permit it.

t. Šabb. 1:14

Dining among the Poor

Dining practices are a means of self-definition, often signifying membership in or exclusion from a community.[1] This is reflected, for example, in the spacious triclinia of the Hasmonean and Herodian palaces, which were used for receptions and formal dinners and banquets. The presence of these triclinia suggests that the Jewish ruling class structured itself according to Roman social norms, since seating arrangements at a Roman banquet were governed by rules that reflected each diner's rank and status in society.[2] Focusing on the other end of the social spectrum, John Dominic Crossan has proposed that for Jesus, "Commensality was, rather, a strategy for building or rebuilding peasant community on radically different prin-

77

ciples from those of honor and shame, patronage and clientage. It was based on an egalitarian sharing of spiritual and material power at the most grass-roots level."[3]

The poorest members of Jewish society — the destitute — begged and scavenged for food or were provided for out of a communal fund or soup kitchen:

> Now during those days, when the disciples were increasing in number, the Hellenists complained against the Hebrews because their widows were being neglected in the daily distribution of food. (Acts 6:1)

> They give to a poor man traveling from place to place no less than a loaf [of bread] worth a *dupondion*, [made from wheat which costs at least] one *sela* for four *seahs*. [If such a poor person] stayed overnight, they give him enough [to pay] for a night's lodging. [If such a poor person] spent the Sabbath, they give him food for three meals. Whoever has sufficient food for two meals may not take [food] from a soup kitchen. (*m. Pe'ah* 8:7)[4]

Because Jesus asked his disciples to live an itinerant lifestyle (Mark 6:8-9; Matt 10:9-10),[5] he allowed them to harvest grain on the Sabbath over the protests of the Pharisees, on the grounds that they needed to eat (Mark 2:23-28; a slightly different version in Matt 12:1-8).[6] Biblical law requires that unharvested parts of fields and crops be left to the poor to glean, and the rabbis devoted an entire tractate (Pe'ah) of the Mishnah, Tosefta, and Jerusalem Talmud to this subject.[7] The book of Ruth tells the story of an impoverished woman who gleaned to survive: "She said, 'Please, let me glean and gather among the sheaves behind the reapers.'" (2:7) Ruth ate the bread, vinegar, and parched grain that Boaz gave her while sitting on the ground among the other harvesters:

> At mealtime Boaz said to her, "Come here, and eat some of this bread, and dip your morsel in the sour wine [vinegar]." So she sat beside the reapers, and he heaped up for her some parched grain. (Ruth 2:14)

Rabbinic literature indicates that bread dipped in sour wine or vinegar remained a staple of the Palestinian diet through the Roman period: "He who is concerned about his teeth may not suck vinegar through them. But he dunks [his bread] in the normal way . . ." (*m. Šabb.* 14:4)

The rabbis discussed the status of a field in which two different kinds of wheat are grown:

He who sows his field with two types of wheat — [if] he harvests [the wheat] in one lot, [he] designates one [portion of produce as] *pe'ah* [gleanings]. [But if he harvests the wheat in] two lots, [he] designates two [portions of produce as] *pe'ah*. It happened that R. Simon of Mispah sowed [his field with two types of wheat]. (*m. Pe'ah* 2:5-6)

Plant samples recovered from archaeological excavations confirm that different species of wheat were cultivated in ancient Palestine.[8]

Communal Meals at Qumran

Since it [the Qumran community] thought of itself as a human sanctuary, its ingestion would have been the closest thing to the offering of sacrifice, which also involved the consumption of food and drink.[9]

Our most complete literary and archaeological information for the communal meals and dining practices of a Jewish group of the late Second Temple period comes from Qumran. Albert Baumgarten has observed that the process of admission to the Essenes was organized around food regulations.[10]

Much of our information about the communal meals of the Essenes comes from Josephus:

They reassemble in the same place and, girded with linen loin cloths, bathe themselves thus in cold water. After this purification they assemble in a special building to which no one is admitted who is not of the same faith; they themselves only enter the refectory if they are pure, as though into a holy precinct. When they are quietly seated *(kathisantōn)*, the baker serves out the loaves of bread in order, and the cook serves only one bowlful of one dish to each man; but a priest says grace before meat; and it is unlawful for any one to taste of the food before grace be said. . . . No shouting or disturbance ever defiles the house; they allow each other to speak in turn. To those outside, this silence of the men inside seems a great mystery; but the cause of it is their invariable sobriety and the fact that their food and drink are so measured out that they are satisfied and no more. (*War* 2.129-33)

This passage corresponds on many points with information from the Dead Sea Scrolls and the archaeological remains at Qumran. For example, according to Josephus only full members are allowed to participate in the communal meals. Josephus repeats this point elsewhere: "And before he is allowed to touch their common food, he is obliged to take tremendous oaths" (*War* 2.139; Whiston's translation). Various sectarian scrolls indicate that only full members were allowed access to the pure food and drink of the sect:[11]

> And when he draws near to the council of the community he shall not come in contact with the pure food of the community . . . until he completes one full year. . . . Let him not come into contact with the liq-uid food of the community until he completes a second year. (1QS 6:16-21)[12]

> And furthermore concerning the lepers, we s[ay that they shall not c]ome (into contact) with the sacred pure food. (4QMMT B64-65)

> And he shall not eat (pure food) while in his initial impurity who has not begun to become pure from his source. (4QOrdc 1:7)[13]

The *Rule of the Community* describes as follows the messianic banquet, which may have been modeled after the sect's communal meals:[14]

> And when they gather [at the tab]le of community *(yḥd)* [or to drink the n]ew wine, and the table of the community is prepared [and the] new wine [is mixed] for drinking, [no one should stretch out] his hand to the first-fruit of the bread and of [the new wine] before the priest, for [he is the one who bl]esses the first-fruit of bread and of the new win[e and stretches out] his hands towards the bread. (1Q28a 2:17-19)

According to Josephus, members purified themselves by immersing in a pool before entering the dining room. Like the other sectarian practices described here, this was done in imitation of the priests in the Jerusalem temple, who purified themselves through immersion before offering sacri-fices.[15] In fact, Josephus explicitly compares the communal dining room to a temple.[16] Josephus's description is supported by the placement of some of the largest miqva'ot at Qumran by the entrances to the communal dining rooms: L56-58 by L77, and the pair of miqva'ot in L117 and L118 by the dining room above L111, L120, L121, L122, and L123 (see Fig. 24).[17]

According to Josephus, members wore a linen loin cloth even during ritual immersion (*War* 2.129). Elsewhere he states that female Essenes bathe wearing a dress (*War* 2.161).[18] A sectarian document refers to a *zab* immersing himself while clothed:

> [And when] he [has complet]ed the seven days of [his purifi]cation [ ], [then] he shall launder his garments in wa[ter and bathe his flesh in water] and cover (himself with) his garments and bless wh[ere he stands saying, "Blessed are you] God of Isra[el]." (4Q512)

Dining While Seated or Reclining

Josephus's use of the term *kathisantōn* and the absence of couches in the communal dining rooms at Qumran indicate that the sectarians sat when they ate instead of reclining in the Greco-Roman manner.[19] Lawrence Schiffman has observed that sectarian scrolls describe participants in the messianic banquet dining while seated instead of reclining.[20] Interestingly, the *Temple Scroll* describes seats *(mwšbwt)* rather than couches for dining in the temple court: "And [in]side the cou[rt] you shall m[a]ke s[i]tting pl[a]ces for the priests, and tables in front of the sitting places" (11QT 37:8-9). The Qumran sectarians appear to differ from the Therapeutae, who Philo says conducted their communal meals while reclining on rough couches (*On the Contemplative Life* 69).

Jewish villagers in Galilee generally dined while sitting on the ground instead of reclining on couches.[21] Rabbinic literature refers both to dining seats and couches:

> But the couches *(mškbwt)* and seats *(mšbwt)* and clay utensils which are sealed with a tight seal are clean. (*m. Tehar.* 7:5)

When the rabbis legislate for communal meals or banquets they generally refer to the custom of reclining, as for example:

> A householder who was reclining at table and eating . . . (*t. Ber.* 4:20)

What is the order for reclining [when several eat together]? When there are two couches *(mṭwt), the greatest [in importance] among them reclines at the head of the first, the second [in importance] to him reclines below him. (t. Ber.* 5:6)

The Gospel accounts describe Jesus as welcoming everyone to dine with him:

And as he sat at dinner in Levi's house, many tax collectors and sinners were also sitting *(katakeisthai)* with Jesus and his disciples — for there were many who followed him. When the scribes of the Pharisees saw that he was eating with sinners and tax collectors, they said to his disciples, "Why does he eat with tax collectors and sinners?" When Jesus heard this, he said to them, "Those who are well have no need of a physician, but those who are sick; I have come to call not the righteous but sinners." (Mark 2:15-17; see also Matt 9:9-13; Luke 5:27-32)[22]

The use of the verb *katakeimai* (Liddell and Scott: "to recline at meals")[23] in all three Synoptic accounts suggests that unlike the Qumran community, Jesus did not reject the Greco-Roman custom of reclining while dining. Luke 13:29 refers to reclining at a banquet in the kingdom of God:

Then people will come from east and west, from north and south, and will recline at table *(anaklithēsotai)* in the kingdom of God.

On the other hand, of the canonical Gospels only John describes someone reclining while dining at Jesus' last supper: "One of his disciples — the one whom Jesus loved — was reclining *(anakeimenos)* next to him" (John 13:23).

The Meal

Josephus describes the Essenes dining in silence due to their sobriety, in contrast to symposia where the large quantities of wine consumed led to boisterous noise and talking. Like high priests serving in the Jerusalem temple, the sectarians drank new wine *(tyrwš)* in measured amounts that were not intoxicating.[24] The *Rule of the Community* refers to new wine at the messianic banquet:

> And when they gather [at the tab]le of community *(yḥd)* [or to drink the n]ew wine, and the table of the community is prepared [and the] new wine [is mixed] for drinking, [no one should stretch out] his hand to the firstfruit of the bread and of [the new wine] before the priest." (1Q 28a 2:17-19)[25]

As in Josephus's description of the Essenes, the *Community Rule* mentions a priest reciting a blessing over the bread or new wine before the communal meals (1QS 6:5-6):

> And when [the table has been prepared for eating or the n]ew wine [for drinking, the] priest shall [be first to stretch out his hand to bless the firstfruit of the bread] and of the wine. (1QS 6:4-6)[26]

According to Josephus, each member was served an individual dish with his portion of food. As Todd Beall observed, "Josephus stresses the order, frugality, (*one* plate of *one* kind of food given to each) and equality of treatment (each receiving the same portion) in the Essene community with respect to the meal."[27] At communal meals in the Roman world, diners typically shared food out of common dishes, as for example in Mark's description of Jesus' last supper: "He [Jesus] said to them, 'It is one of the twelve [who will betray me], one who is dipping bread into the bowl with me" (Mark 14:20). Although they expected diners to purify themselves first, the rabbis (and presumably Pharisees) also seem to have shared food out of common dishes:

> Two wait for another [to begin eating] with regard to [partaking of food from] a single plate. Three do not wait. (*t. Ber.* 5:7)

The sectarian custom of dining from individual dishes accounts for the discovery of hundreds of small plates, cups, and bowls in pantries attached to the two communal dining rooms at Qumran (L86 and L114) (see Fig. 25).[28] Although Josephus presents this practice as an ascetic ideal, it presumably stemmed from the sectarians' concern that impurity could be spread by sharing food and drink.[29] For this reason access to the pure food and drink of the sect was restricted to members who had passed through the required stages of initiation.[30]

Josephus singles out for description the sectarian custom of eating out of individual dishes ("the cook serves only one bowlful of one dish to each man"). This custom appears to have been widespread in the first century B.C.E., judging from the large numbers of plates, saucers, and bowls found at sites around the country. Berlin describes as follows the evidence from Gamla: "Each person had a small plain buff fabric bowl for his own portion."[31] These are the same types of dishes found by the hundreds in miqva'ot in Jericho and Jerusalem and in the pantries at Qumran (L86 and L114).[32] However, whereas this practice seems to have been abandoned by the rest of the Jewish population by the first century C.E., members of the Qumran community continued to dine on individual dishes, apparently prompting Josephus's observation.[33]

Josephus remarks that not only does each member receive his own individual dish, but everyone is served the same portion. His observation is borne out by the large numbers of nearly identical small plates, cups, and bowls in the pantries at Qumran. Could it be that equal portions were served not only for reasons of frugality and equality of treatment but because the pure food of the sect was considered analogous to *terumah* (heave offering or priestly tithe)? Jacob Milgrom notes that at Qumran the term *taharah* ("purity") seems to correspond with *terumah:* "instead of terumot Qumran employed the term tahara by which they meant that their food should be maintained in a state of purity."[34] Sectarian literature from Qumran specifies standard measures for separating *terumah* of wheat, barley, and oil, following Ezek 45:11, 13, whereas rabbinic halakhah does not fix the amount to be set aside and even forbids measuring it.[35] In fact, Josephus notes that the Essenes are served measured amounts of food and drink: "To those outside, this silence of the men inside seems a great mystery; but the cause of it is their invariable sobriety and the fact that **their food and drink are so measured out** that they are satisfied and no more" (*War* 2.132-33). Therefore, the equal portions of food served at Qumran might indicate that the sectarians considered their pure food analogous to *terumah*.[36]

CHAPTER 6

Sabbath Observance and Fasting

Sabbath Observance

Josephus informs us that the Essenes observed the Sabbath so strictly that they prepared all food in advance and did not move any vessels: "Moreover, they are stricter than any other of the Jews in resting from their labors on the seventh day; for they not only get their food ready the day before, that they may not be obliged to kindle a fire on that day, but they will not remove any vessel out of its place" (*War* 2.147; Whiston's translation).

Josephus's observations correspond on several points with information from the Dead Sea Scrolls. Sectarian law prohibited consuming any food on the Sabbath that had not been prepared in advance: "No one is to eat on the Sabbath day except what has been prepared" (CD 10:22).[1] In contrast, the rabbis ruled that in some cases the process of cooking may continue after the beginning of the Sabbath:

> They do not roast meat, onions, and eggs, unless there is time for them to be roasted while it is still day. They do not put bread into an oven at dusk, nor cakes on the coals *(hghlym)*, unless there is time for them to form a crust [even] on the top surface while it is still day. R. Eliezer says, "Sufficient time for its bottom surface [only] to form a crust." They lower the Passover offering into an oven at dusk [when the fourteenth of Nisan falls on a Friday]. And they light the fire in the fireplace of the House of the Hearth. But in the provinces, [they do so only if] there is sufficient time for the flame to catch over the larger part of [the wood]. R. Judah says, "In the case of charcoal *(phmym)*

[one may light the fire if there is time for the fire to catch] any quantity [of charcoal] whatsoever." (*m. Šabb.* 1:10-11)

Josephus's observation that the Essenes do not kindle a fire on the Sabbath is puzzling, as this biblical injunction (Exod 35:3) was widely observed by Jews. For this reason Lawrence Schiffman interpreted Josephus's statement as meaning that the Essenes prohibited cooking and baking food on the Sabbath but not other kinds of preparation, "Otherwise why would Josephus cite fear of making a fire on the Sabbath as the reason for preparing food before the holy day?"[2] However, in my opinion, Josephus here highlights a disagreement between the Essenes and other Jewish groups concerning the use of fire on the Sabbath. This is the subject of a scroll fragment from Qumran (4Q421 frag. 13 = 4Q264a 2), which forbids the discussion of profane matters on the Sabbath, followed by a prohibition relating to the burning of fire:

...] *'l yʿr 'iš ghl[y] 'š lpn[y* . . .[3]
". . .] not shall a man kindle (or pour) coal[s of] fire befo[re . . .]"

Vered Noam and Elisha Qimron demonstrate that this fragment relates to the biblical prohibition against kindling a fire on the Sabbath, and specifically to a debate about whether biblical law permits leaving an already kindled fire burning on the Sabbath.[4] On the basis of this fragment, Noam and Qimron suggest that sectarian law prohibited leaving a fire burning (even if already kindled) on the Sabbath.[5] The Mishnah preserves a related series of disputes between the houses of Hillel and Shammai concerning whether activities begun before the Sabbath must be completed before the Sabbath begins, with both agreeing that an already kindled fire may continue to burn on the Sabbath (see *m. Šabb.* 1:5-8).[6]

Josephus's observation about the Essenes complements information from the Dead Sea Scrolls and rabbinic literature. The sectarians required all food preparation to be completed in advance of the Sabbath, and they prohibited leaving any fires burning on the Sabbath. Perhaps Josephus linked these two points ("for they not only get their food ready the day before, that they may not be obliged to kindle a fire on that day") because food could not continue to cook without a fire burning.

Josephus also remarks that the Essenes will "not remove any vessel out of its place" on the Sabbath. The prohibition against carrying on the Sabbath is stated in Jeremiah: "And do not carry a burden out of your houses [or 'domain'; *ršwt*] on the Sabbath or do any work" (17:22).[7] In the late Second Temple and rabbinic periods, Jews debated what constituted a burden and how a domain was defined.[8] For example, the sectarians did not recognize the rabbinic innovation of an *'eruv*, an artificial device that enlarged the public and private domain by extending the distance that one is allowed to walk and making it possible to carry objects beyond the confines of a house on the Sabbath (see *m. 'Erub.; t. Šabb.* 1:5).[9] The Sadducees seem to have rejected this innovation as well:[10]

> Said Rabban Gamaliel, "A Sadducean lived with us in the same alley-way in Jerusalem." And his father said to us, "Make haste and bring all sorts of utensils into the alleyway before he brings out his and prohibits you [from carrying about in it]." R. Judah says it in another version, "Make haste and do all your needs in the alleyway before he brings out his utensils and prohibits you [from using it]." The men of a courtyard, one of whom forgot and did not participate in the *erub* with the others — his house is prohibited, both for him and for them, from bringing things in and from taking things out. And theirs are permitted both for him and for them. (*m. 'Erub.* 6:2-3)

The rabbis also distinguished between the acts of lifting an object (*'qyrh*) and placing it elsewhere (*hnḥh*), prohibiting only the combination of the two on the Sabbath.[11] In contrast, sectarian legislation strictly prohibited moving vessels on the Sabbath:

> No one should remove anything from the house to outside, or from outside to the house. Even if he is in a hut (*swkh*) he should remove nothing from it nor bring anything into it. (CD 11:7-9)[12]

The book of *Jubilees* contains the same prohibition and threatens violators with death:[13]

> . . . and that they should not prepare thereon anything to be eaten or drunk, and (that it is not lawful) to draw water, or bring in or take out thereon through their gates any burden, which they had not prepared for themselves on the sixth day in their dwellings. And they shall not bring in nor take out from house to house on that day. (*Jub.* 2:29-30)

> And whoever takes up any burden to carry it out of his tent or out of his house shall die. (50:8; see also 2:29-30)[14]

Josephus's statement that the Essenes "will not remove any vessel out of its place *(metakinēsai)*" on the Sabbath seems to correspond with the sectarian prohibition against moving a vessel even without carrying it outside.[15] Perhaps embedding cylindrical jars in the floors of the settlement at Qumran was a means of ensuring the observance of this regulation, as the jars could not have been moved out of their places.[16]

Fasting

Ancient sources suggest that fasting was common among some ancient Jews, not only at mandated times such as Yom Kippur but also on a voluntary individual basis.[17] Rabbinic literature contains a great deal of discussion of fasting, including an entire tractate *(Ta'anit)* of the Mishnah, Tosefta, and both Talmudim devoted to the subject. The possibility that some Jews fasted on certain days of the week on a regular basis is suggested by the Gospel accounts:[18]

> Now John's disciples and the Pharisees were fasting; and people came and said to him, "Why do John's disciples and the disciples of the Pharisees fast, but your disciples do not fast?" Jesus said to them, "The wedding guests cannot fast while the bridegroom is with them, can they? As long as they have the bridegroom with them, they cannot fast. The days will come when the bridegroom is taken away from them, and then they will fast on that day." (Mark 2:18-20)

> He [Jesus] also told this parable to some who trusted in themselves that they were righteous and regarded others with contempt: "Two men went up to the temple to pray, one a Pharisee and the other a tax collector. The Pharisee, standing by himself, was praying thus, 'God, I thank you that I am not like other people: thieves, rogues, adulterers, or even like this tax collector. I fast twice a week; I give a tenth of all my income.'" (Luke 18:9-12)[19]

Evidence for individual fasting by Jews on a regular basis also comes from an early Christian work called the *Didache* (Teachings of the Twelve Apostles), which probably dates to the latter part of the first century C.E.:

> Let your fasts not [take place] with [those of] the hypocrites. They fast

on Monday and Thursday; you, though, should fast on Wednesday and Friday. (8.1)[20]

Most scholars identify the hypocrites as pious Jews, perhaps even Pharisees.[21] No matter their identity, this polemic suggests that some first-century Jews regularly fasted on Mondays and Thursdays.[22]

The Mishnah and Tosefta provide additional evidence that Mondays and Thursdays were set aside for individual and public fasting, usually if no rain had fallen by certain dates:

> [If] the seventeenth day of Marheshvan came and rain did not fall, individuals began to fast a sequence of three fasts [Monday, Thursday, Monday]. (*m. Ta'an.* 1:4)

> [Once] the new moon of Kislev has come and rain has not fallen, the court decrees a sequence of three fasts for the whole community. (*m. Ta'an.* 1:5)

> Once these [fasts] have gone by and they have not been answered, the court decrees a sequence of three more fasts for the community. (*m. Ta'an.* 1:6)

> But the first three fasts are on Monday, Thursday, and Monday. And the second set of three fast days are on Thursday, Monday, and Thursday. (*m. Ta'an.* 2:9)

> Monday and Thursday are set aside for public fasts. (*t. Ta'an.* 2:4)

Recently Joseph Zias, James Tabor, and Stephanie Harter-Lailheugue have argued that the Qumran sectarians were able to refrain from defecating on the Sabbath (see below) because they fasted on Friday, claiming that "Some scholars have suggested that the Qumran members likely abstained from eating on Friday so as to avoid having to go to the toilet until after sundown Saturday evening."[23] However, the only authority they cite — Samuel Kottek — says no such thing in his 1983 article and 1994 book on medicine and the Essenes.[24]

In fact, there is no evidence that the Qumran sect fasted on Fridays or other weekdays. Noah Hacham has shown that Yom Kippur was the only communal fast day observed at Qumran.[25] Furthermore, none of our ancient sources on the Essenes refers to fasting, a silence that is loud considering Josephus's and Philo's concern to highlight the ascetic and virtuous lifestyle of the community.[26] For example, Philo describes in great detail fasting by the Therapeutae:

> . . . and no one of them may take any meat or drink before the setting of the sun, since they judge that the work of philosophising is one which is worthy of the light, but that the care for the necessities of the body is suitable only to darkness, on which account they appropriate the day to the one occupation, and a brief portion of the night to the other; and some men, in whom there is implanted a more fervent desire of knowledge, can endure to cherish a recollection of their food for three days without even tasting it, and some men are so delighted, and enjoy themselves so exceedingly when regaled by wisdom which supplies them with her doctrines in all possible wealth and abundance, that they can even hold out twice as great a length of time, and will scarcely at the end of six days taste even necessary food, being accustomed, as they say that grasshoppers are, to feed on air, their song, as I imagine, making their scarcity tolerable to them. (*Contempl.* 34-35)

Is it possible that the Qumran sect fasted on the Sabbath? It is difficult for us to conceive of Jewish fasting on the Sabbath because the day is now celebrated with prayer in synagogues and by gathering with family and friends for large meals, following rabbinic norms. The rabbis prohibited fasting on the Sabbath and required the consumption of three or four meals, whereas on other days usually only two meals were eaten:[27]

> R. Aha, R. Abbahu in the name of R. Yose b. Haninah: "It is forbidden to a person to fast on the Sabbath beyond six hours [noon]." . . . [If it rained] after noon, they should complete the day in fasting [*m. Ta'an.* 3:10]. For the greater part of the day already had passed in a status of sanctification. [It follows that once they have fasted until noon the day is deemed to have been a day observed in fasting. Hence one may not fast up to the midpoint of the day on the Sabbath.]." (*y. Ta'an.* 3:9 [76a]; *y. Ned.* 8:1 [40d]).

> Our rabbis taught: How many meals must one eat on the Sabbath? Three. R. Hidka said: Four. R. Johanan observed, Both expound the same verse: "And Moses said, Eat that today; for today is a Sabbath unto the Lord; today you shall not find it in the field." (*b. Šabb.* 117b)

Some rabbis even recommended abstaining from eating on Friday afternoon in order to increase the appetite on the Sabbath:

> "A man should not eat on the eve of the Sabbath from afternoon onwards, so that he should be hungry at the start of the Sabbath," the words of R. Judah. R. Yosé says, "He may continue to eat until it grows dark." Rabban Simeon b. Gamaliel and R. Judah and R. Yosé were reclining [and eating] in Acre and the Sabbath began. Said Rabban Simeon b. Gamaliel to R. Yosé, "Rabbi, if it is your wish, we shall stop [eating] on account of the [beginning of the] Sabbath." He said to him, "Every day you prefer my opinion to Judah's, and now you prefer Judah's opinion to mine!?" . . . He said to him, "If so, then let us not stop, lest the law be established permanently [in accord with our actions]." (*t. Ber.* 5:1-2)

The rabbinic injunction to eat more on the Sabbath than on other days is based on the biblical precedent of God providing the Israelites with twice as much manna on Friday, so they would not have to gather food the following day (Exod 16:22).[28] Nevertheless, there is evidence that some ancient Jews fasted on the Sabbath. Yitzhak Gilat assembled the rabbinic testimony regarding fasting on the Sabbath, citing passages that attest to debates among rabbis.[29] For example, in the Babylonian Talmud R. Eliezer is quoted as saying that since on a festival *(ywm ṭwb)* one can either eat and drink or sit and study, the time is better spent studying Torah (*b. Pesaḥ.* 68b = *Beṣah* 15b).[30] The same *sugiya* refers to another rabbi who fasted all year round including on Sabbaths:

> Mar son of Rabina would fast the whole year, except on the Feast of Weeks, Purim, and the eve of the Day of Atonement. (*b. Pesaḥ.* 68b)

Some rabbis permitted fasting on the Sabbath if it was done because of a bad dream:[31]

> [Mine] is a fast for a [bad] dream, and Rabbah b. Mehasiah said in the name of R. Hama b. Guriah, in the name of Rab: Fasting is as efficacious for the bad dream as fire is for tow, and upon this R. Hisda commented: And [the fast must be] on the same day; and R. Joseph added: Even if [the day] is the Sabbath. What amends shall he make [for having fasted on the Sabbath]? — He should observe an additional fast. (*b. Taʻan.* 12b; see also *b. Šabb.* 11a)

The strident tone eventually adopted by the rabbis against fasting on the Sabbath and their insistence on eating multiple meals suggest a response to a widespread custom:[32]

> The fact, however, is as R. Hiyya b. Abba said: "For both the withholding of rain and the exile we may fast at one and the same time, but we may not fast on Friday or the Sabbath because of the honor of the Sabbath." (*Midr. Rab. Lam.* i.16, 51)[33]

The rabbis even forbade fasting on the ninth of Ab if it falls on a Sabbath, albeit with dissenting opinions:

> As to the Sabbaths and festivals — it is permitted to fast on the day before them and on the day after them. . . . Abba Yosé b. Dosa'i says in the name of R. Yosé the Galilean, "[If] one has taken an oath to fast on the eve of the Sabbath, lo, such an oath is taken in vain." (*t. Ta'an.* 2:6)

> On the ninth of Ab which coincided with the eve of the Sabbath [Friday] a person eats food in the volume of an egg and drinks liquid in the volume of an egg, "so that this person should not enter [the Sabbath] when he is subject to pain," the words of R. Judah. R. Yosé says, "Lo, this person should fast and complete the fast day." (*t. Ta'an.* 2:7)

> On the ninth of Ab which coincides with the Sabbath, a person eats whatever he requires and drinks whatever he requires. (*t. Ta'an.* 3:13)

The Hebrew Bible does not explicitly forbid fasting on the Sabbath. The scriptural basis for the rabbinic injunction seems to be Isa 58:13, "if you call the Sabbath a delight," which was interpreted by the rabbis as a prohibition against fasting.[34] However, some Jews and even some rabbis understood 'ng ("delight") as meaning that one should devote the Sabbath to Torah study instead of eating.[35]

According to the Gospel accounts, Jesus allowed his disciples to pick grain on the Sabbath instead of going hungry, over the protests of the Pharisees:

> One Sabbath he was going through the grainfields; and as they made their way his disciples began to pluck heads of grain. The Pharisees said to him, "Look, why are they doing what is not lawful on the Sab-

bath?" And he said to them, "Have you never read what David did when he and his companions were hungry and in need of food? He entered the house of God, when Abiathar was high priest, and ate the bread of the Presence, which it is not lawful for any but the priests to eat, and he gave some to his companions." Then he said to them, "The Sabbath was made for humankind, and not humankind for the Sabbath." (Mark 2:23-27; see also Matt 12:1-8; Luke 6:1-5)

Perhaps this episode, which usually is understood as a halakhic debate over which activities are permitted on the Sabbath, also represents Jesus' response to the practice of fasting on the Sabbath among some Jewish groups.

A number of Latin authors refer to Jewish fasting on the Sabbath.[36] In his biography of Augustus, Suetonius cites a letter written by the emperor to his stepson Tiberius:

Not even a Jew, my dear Tiberius, fasts so scrupulously on his sabbaths as I have today, for it was not until after the first hour of the night that I ate two mouthfuls of bread in the bath before I began to be anointed [oiled — J.M.]. (*Divus Augustus* 76.2)

Pompeius Trogus, a historian of the early first century C.E., describes the Jewish Sabbath as a fast day:

. . . he [Moyses], for all time, consecrated the seventh day, which used to be called the Sabbath by the custom of nation, for a fast-day *(ieiunio)*, because that day had ended at once their hunger and their wanderings. (apud Justin, *Historiae Philippicae* 36.2.14)

Petronius, writing in the time of Nero, also refers to the Jewish Sabbath as a fast day:

The Jew may worship his pig-god and clamor in the ears of high heaven, but unless he also cuts back his foreskin with the knife, he shall go forth from the people and emigrate to Greek cities, and shall not tremble at the fasts of Sabbath imposed by the law *(et non ieiuna sabbata lege tremet)*. (Fragment 37 = Stern[37] no. 195)

In an epigram dated to the year 88 C.E., the poet Martial refers to the stinking breath of Jewish women fasting on the Sabbath:

The stench of the bed of a drained marsh; of the raw vapors of sulphur springs; the putrid reek of a sea-water fishpond; of a stale he-goat in the midst of his amours; of the military boot of a fagged out veteran; of a fleece twice dyed with purple; of the breath of fasting Sabbatarian women . . . (*Epigrammata* 4.4)

Although some scholars have dismissed these references to Jewish fasting on the Sabbath on the grounds that the Latin authors were confused or ignorant of Jewish customs, I agree with those who believe that this reflects actual practice among some Jews.[38] However, whereas Margaret Williams argues that Sabbath fasting was limited to the Jews of Rome,[39] rabbinic evidence suggests that this practice was more widespread.[40]

Having determined that some ancient Jews fasted on the Sabbath, the question remains whether the Qumran sect followed this custom. At first glance this idea is attractive not only because it might explain how the sectarians managed to refrain from defecating on the Sabbath (see below) but also because of the importance they placed on Torah study. After all, the *Community Rule* (or *Manual of Discipline*) describes members spending one-third of each night in studying the Torah:

And the Many shall be on watch together for a third of each night of the year in order to read the book *(lqrw' bspr)*, explain the regulation *(wldrwš mšpṭ)*, and bless together *(wlbrk byḥd)*. (1QS 6:7-8)

Another scroll indicates that the Qumran sect read and studied the Torah on the Sabbath:

[Let no man check the scrol]l of a book by reading its writing on the [Sabbath] day, [but] they may read [and] learn from them. (4Q421 frag 1: 4-5)[41]

Did the sectarians devote the Sabbath to Torah study instead of eating? Various sources indicate that the Qumran sect did not fast on the Sabbath. First, positive evidence that the sectarians ate on the Sabbath comes from the *Damascus Document*, which contains legislation governing cooking and eating:

No one shall eat (anything) on the Sabbath day except that which has been prepared *(mwkn)* (in advance) or from that which is decaying in the field. (CD 10:22-23)

Another piece of legislation forbids eating outside the camp on the Sabbath:

> Let him not drink or eat except if he (or: that which) is in the camp. (CD 10:23)

The book of *Jubilees* (2:21, 32; 50:9) positively enjoins eating and drinking on the Sabbath, but prohibits consuming food that has not been prepared in advance (2:29; 50:8). The discovery of fragments belonging to at least fourteen to fifteen different copies of *Jubilees* among the Dead Sea Scrolls indicates the importance of this work to the Qumran community.[42] Similarly, Josephus says that the Essenes prepare food for the Sabbath in advance:

> Moreover, they are stricter than any other of the Jews in resting from their labors on the seventh day; *for they not only get their food ready the day before,* that they may not be obliged to kindle a fire on that day, but they will not remove any vessel out of its place, nor go to stool thereon. (*War* 2.147; Whiston's translation)

The *Damascus Document,* Josephus, and the book of *Jubilees* therefore provide evidence that the sectarians ate on the Sabbath, albeit with strict regulations. The book of *Jubilees* even prescribes death for those who fast on the Sabbath:[43]

> And (as for) any man who does work on it, or who goes on a journey . . . or who fasts or makes war on the day of the Sabbath, let the man who does any of these on the day of the Sabbath die. (*Jub* 50:12-13)

A document from Cave 4 (4Q264a = 4QHalakhah B) prohibits talking about profane matters on the Sabbath but permits speaking for the purposes of prayer and to eat and drink:

> Let no-one plan [aloud] [. . .] about all matters of work or about wealth or [about gain . . .] [. . .] on the day of the sa[bba]th. And one should not sp[eak a wor]d except to [speak] [holy words. According to the precept one shall spe]ak to praise God. Indeed one may speak [a word] regarding eating or dr[inking . . .].[44]

This exception attests to the importance placed by the sectarians on eating and drinking on the Sabbath.

According to the sectarian calendar, Yom Kippur could not fall on the Sabbath, thereby preventing the Sabbath from being a fast day.[45] Adele Berlin has noted that other fast days (such as the Ninth of Av) that fell on Fridays and Saturdays according to the sectarian calendar do not appear to have been observed at Qumran.[46] Therefore, although in antiquity some Jews apparently fasted on the Sabbath, sectarian legislation regulating the preparation and consumption of food (and Josephus's testimony) combined with prohibitions against fasting indicate that the Qumran sect did not fast on weekdays or on the Sabbath.[47]

Fig. 1 *(left):* Aerial view of Masada looking north

Fig. 2 *(below):* Fresco in the lower terrace of the northern palace complex at Masada

Fig. 3: Mosaic floor in the western palace at Masada

Fig. 4: View of the Hasmonean and Herodian palaces at Jericho
on the north bank of Wadi Qelt

Fig. 5: The western peristyle courtyard of the north wing of Herod's third palace at Jericho, showing *opus reticulatum* walls (mud bricks laid in a net pattern characteristic of Roman architecture)

Fig. 6: View of Herodium with Lower Herodium in the foreground

Fig. 7 *(right):*
Deposit of
bowls in a
miqveh in the
Jewish Quarter

Fig. 8 *(below):*
Bowls from a
deposit in a
miqveh in the
Jewish Quarter

Fig. 9: Imported amphoras from the Jewish Quarter

Fig. 10: Eastern Terra Sigillata from the Jewish Quarter

Fig. 11: Glass vase made
by Ennion from the
Jewish Quarter

Fig. 12: Pompeian
style wall painting
in a mansion in the
Jewish Quarter

Fig. 13: Cooking pots pierced by holes from a cistern in the Jewish Quarter

Fig. 14: Stone vessels from the Jewish Quarter

Fig. 15 *(above):*
Stone vessels
from the
Jewish Quarter

Fig. 16 *(right):*
Mosaic floor
from the
Jewish Quarter

Fig. 17: Refuse from a glass factory in the Jewish Quarter

Fig. 18: Stone table with Eastern Terra Sigillata vessels from the Jewish Quarter

Fig. 19: Pottery assemblage of the late first century B.C.E. from the Jewish Quarter, including fusiform and piriform unguentaria

Fig. 20: View of Khirbet el-Muraq (Hilkiah's Palace)

Fig. 21: Village house with a window wall
(internal partition wall with windows) at Qazrin

Fig. 22: View of the settlement at Qumran

Fig. 23 *(above):*
Miqveh with
earthquake
crack at
Qumran
(L48-49)

Fig. 24 *(right):*
Plan of
Qumran

Fig. 25: Pottery in the pantry (L86/89) at Qumran

Fig. 26: Animal bone deposit at Qumran

Fig. 27: Cylindrical jars and bowl-shaped lids from Qumran

Fig. 28: Unexcavated grave in the cemetery at Qumran

Fig. 29 *(above):*
Excavated grave
in the cemetery
at Qumran

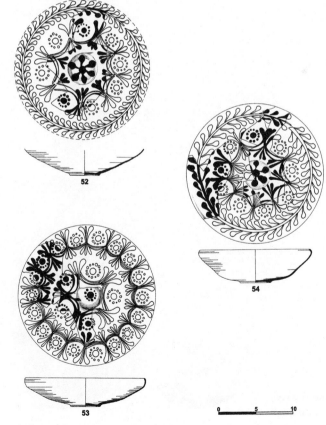

Fig. 30 *(left):*
Jerusalem
painted bowls
from Masada

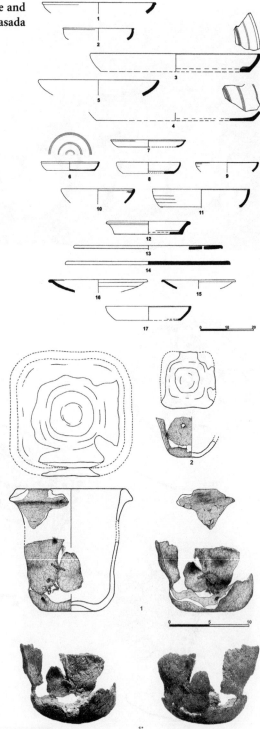

Fig. 31: Pompeian Red Ware and Orlo Bifida pans from Masada

Fig. 32: Dung vessels from Masada

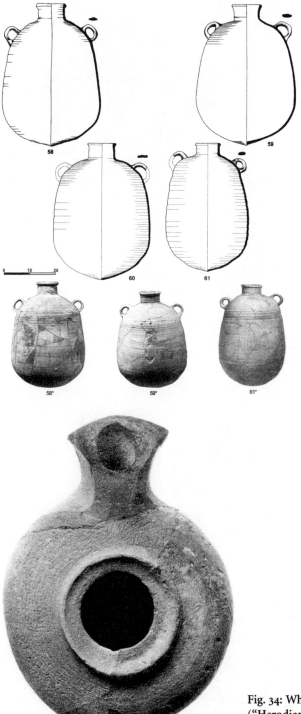

Fig. 33: Bag-shaped
storage jars from
Masada

Fig. 34: Wheel-made
("Herodian") oil lamp
from Masada

Fig. 35: Roman discus
oil lamp from Jerusalem

Fig. 36: Coins of Alexander Jannaeus found by the Dead Sea

Fig. 37: Tyrian sheqel from Masada

Fig. 38: Wool tunic from the Cave of Letters

Fig. 39: Roman luxury latrine in the Scholastica Baths at Ephesus

Fig. 40: Street at Pompeii with stepping stones, and a fountain at upper left

Fig. 41: Late Iron Age toilet in Jerusalem's City of David

Fig. 42: Late Iron Age rock-cut tomb at Ketef Hinnom

Fig. 43 *(right):*
Jason's Tomb
in Jerusalem

Fig. 44 *(below):*
Loculi in the
Akeldama tombs

Fig. 45 *(left):*
Ossuaries in a
loculus in the
Akeldama tombs

Fig. 46 *(below):*
Ossuary from
the Akeldama
tombs carved
with rosettes and
an amphora

Fig. 47: Rock-cut tomb in the Ben-Hinnom Valley

Fig. 48: Cinerary urn from Antalya, Turkey

CHAPTER 7

Coins

Jewish groups of the late Second Temple period had different attitudes towards the accumulation of wealth and sharing of possessions. Coins shed light on some of these issues, including the opposition of some Jewish groups to the annual payment of a temple tax, the pooling of possessions at Qumran, and the nullification of the second tithe.

Coins and the Qumran Caves

Roland de Vaux observed that whereas coins were plentiful in the settlement at Qumran, not a single coin was found in the caves in which pottery was abundant. He tentatively connected this phenomenon with the pooling of possessions described by ancient authors as characteristic of the Essenes.[1] Philo says:

> For all the wages which they earn in the day's work they do not keep as their private property, but throw them into the common stock and allow the benefit thus accruing to be shared by those who wish to use it. (*Good Person* 12.86)[2]

Josephus has a similar description:

> They despise riches, and their sharing of goods is admirable; there is not found among them any one who has greater wealth than another. For it is a law that those entering the sect transfer their property to the

97

order *(ousia)*; consequently, among them all there appears neither abject poverty nor superabundance of wealth, but the possessions of each are mingled together *(ktēmatōn anamemigmenōn)*, and there is, as among brothers, one property communal to all. (*War* 2.122)

Pliny simply states that the Essenes live "without money" (*Nat. Hist.* 5.73).

Sectarian legislation presents a similar picture.[3] The *Damascus Document* forbids members from buying and selling to each other, commanding them instead to exchange goods and services: "And let no man of all who enter the covenant of God buy from or sell to the Sons of Dawn, but rather (give) hand to hand" (CD 13:14-15).[4] The *Community Rule* enjoins members to constitute a community apart "in law *(twrh)* and possessions *(hwn)*" (1QS 5:2). Individuals were required to transfer their personal property to the sect upon admission:

All those who submit freely to his truth will convey all their knowledge, their energies, and their riches *(hwnm)* to the Community of God. (1QS 1:11-12)

According to the admission procedures described in 1QS 6:17-22, during the first year initiates were denied access to the pure food and could not share (mingle) their property with the sect's. During the second year initiates were allowed access to the pure food but not the pure drink, and handed over their property *(hwn)* and earnings *(ml'kh)* to the inspector *(mbqr)* for safekeeping in a separate account. If admitted after the completion of the second year, initiates could partake of the pure food and drink and their property was mingled with the sect's *(wl'rb 't hwnw)*. Both Josephus and the *Community Rule* refer to the mingling of possessions upon admission to the common entity *(ousia)*, a term that may be equivalent to *yaḥad*.[5] Members who knowingly lied about their possessions were penalized (1QS 6:25).

A Hebrew-language ostracon found while cleaning the outside of Qumran's eastern perimeter wall in 1996 records the transfer of property in Jericho belonging to a man named Ḥoni to another man named Eleazar.[6] Despite the contested reading of a word in line 8 as *yḥd*, many scholars agree that the transaction involved the transfer to the sectarian community of private property belonging to a new initiate.[7]

Sectarian literature describes wealth as one of the nets of Belial (CD 4:15-16) and criticizes the Wicked Priest and other priests in Jerusalem for heaping up riches through violence and plundering:[8]

"Surely wealth *(hwn)* will corrupt the boaster. . . . They shall say: Ah, one who amasses the wealth of others! How long will he load himself with debts?" [Hab 2:5-6]. Its interpretation concerns the Wicked Priest, who . . . deserted God and betrayed the laws for the sake of riches *(hwn)*. And he robbed and hoarded wealth *(hwn)* from the violent men who had rebelled against God. And he seized public money. (1QpHab 8.3-12)

Its interpretation concerns the last priests of Jerusalem, who will accumulate riches and loot from plundering the nations. (1QpHab 9.4-5)

Members were enjoined "to abstain from wicked wealth which defiles, either by promise or by vow, and from the wealth of the temple." (CD 6:15-16)[9]

Archaeological remains of the Hasmonean palaces at Jericho and rock-cut burial caves such as Jason's Tomb and the Tomb of Bene Hezir in Jerusalem indicate that by the first century B.C.E. the Jerusalem elite had adopted a lifestyle based on the conspicuous consumption and display of wealth. The Herodian mansions in the Jewish Quarter, whose owners and occupants included priestly families, were richly decorated with expensive furniture and Roman-style wall paintings, stucco, and mosaics. The author of the *Pesher Habakkuk* opposed such an ostentatious accumulation and display of wealth: "Woe to anyone putting ill-gotten gains in his house [Hab 2:9]" (1QpHab 9.12).

On the basis of de Vaux's observation that coins are abundant in the settlement at Qumran but absent from the caves, Todd Beall concluded that "the testimony of Josephus concerning common ownership of property seems to be consistent with the situation at Qumran, at least during one phase of the community's existence."[10] However, Catherine Murphy concluded that coins are not numerous even in the settlement at Qumran. About half of the 1,234 coins that de Vaux discovered at Qumran belong to the hoard from L120, which may be a collection related to the Temple tax. Murphy observes:

the [remaining] total of 499 coins is not an especially large amount for a site that was occupied for over 190 years; a rough distribution would yield only 2.6 coins per year. . . . Apart from the coin hoard, which appears to have represented a special kind of collection, the coins from Qumran represent a rather meager haul. Bronze and a few scattered silver coins that may date to the sectarian period number just under five hundred; this contrasts, for example, to the 2,275 coins from the second, third and fourth years of the First Jewish Revolt found at Masada (that is, 758.3 coins per year against 2.6 per year at Qumran). Even if the hoard is included in the Qumran total, the number of coins per year is only 5.6.[11]

If the occupation of the Qumran settlement is estimated at 150 years rather than 190 years, the number of coins per year (minus the hoard) is 3.3. In comparison, the Jewish village at Shu'afat, just north of Jerusalem, which was occupied between the two revolts (ca. 70-132), yielded almost 900 coins, although over half of the identifiable specimens come from four hoards discovered in the excavations.[12]

Donald Ariel argues (*pace* Murphy) that coins are relatively plentiful at Qumran: "More coins were found at Qumran than all of the sites in the Judean Desert, with the exception of Jericho and Masada."[13] If the hoard from L120 is excluded from consideration, the number of coins from Qumran is comparable to that found in the contemporary farmhouse at Qalandiya north of Jerusalem (464). Although some of the tiny bronze coins come from hoards or deposits, the relatively large number of coins overall has led Ariel to question whether Qalandiya is a "regular farmstead."[14]

In light of Ariel's observation about the relatively large number of coins from Qumran, their absence from the surrounding caves is even more remarkable. De Vaux observed that "We did not find a single coin in the thirty or more caves which were used as living quarters, storage-places, or hiding-places by the members of the group."[15] No coins were found in the residential caves in the marl terrace at Qumran that Hanan Eshel and Magen Broshi excavated.[16] In contrast, coins are ubiquitous in caves used for habitation and refuge during the late Second Temple period and the Bar Kokhba Revolt elsewhere along the Dead Sea and around Judea, including the Cave of Horror and Cave of Letters in Naḥal Ḥever, the Cave of the Pool in Naḥal David at 'Ein Gedi, the el-Jai Cave in Naḥal Michmash, the caves in Wadi Murabba'at, the Caves of Yahel, Makukh, and Sela near Jericho, and in the en-Na'saneh Cave in Wadi Daliyeh.[17] Coins have been found in underground tunnels and dwelling places around Judea that were occupied at the time of the Bar Kokhba Revolt.[18] The rock huts above 'Ein Gedi that Yizhar Hirschfeld excavated and identified as an Essene settlement yielded one coin of the Bar Kokhba Revolt.[19] Coins were also discovered in burial caves at Jericho and 'Ein Gedi.[20]

In contrast to other settlements in Judea where caves were used also for burials, the Qumran community reserved the nearby caves for habitation and for storing the pure goods of the sect (including scrolls). That some of these caves were used for habitation is indicated by the presence of domestic types of pottery (such as cooking pots and oil lamps) and the discovery of mats (in Cave 10 and a marl-terrace cave) and a mezuzah (in Cave 8).[21] The absence of coins from the Qumran caves, which are ubiquitous in contemporary habitation and refuge caves elsewhere along the Dead Sea, is best understood in light of the practice of pooling possessions upon admission to the sect.

Coins and the Jerusalem Temple

Then they came to Jerusalem. And he entered the temple and began to drive out those who were selling and those who were buying in the temple, and he overturned the tables of the money changers and the seats of those who sold doves; and he would not allow anyone to carry anything through the temple. He was teaching and saying, "Is it not written, 'My house shall be called a house of prayer for all the nations'? But you have made it a den of robbers." (Mark 11:15-17; see also Matt 21:12-15; Luke 19:45-46; John 2:13-16)

Tyrian Silver Coins and the Temple Tax

Jonathan Klawans has suggested that a concern for the poor motivated Jesus' "cleansing of the temple," in which he overturned the tables of the money changers and dove-sellers.[22] I believe that Klawans is correct in linking the money changers and dove-sellers, which he connects with financial obligations to the temple that were a hardship for the poor.[23] As the cheapest form of animal sacrifice, pigeons and doves were offered by the impoverished who could not afford more expensive animals such as sheep and goats. Citing rabbinic sources, Klawans suggests that money changers were connected with economic hardship because of a small surcharge on the exchange that was assessed at the temple.[24] This may be true, but I believe it is more likely that the hardship was due to the fact that an annual payment of the temple tax, which previously was a one-time payment upon reaching adulthood, had only recently been instituted (see *m. Šeqal.* 3:3).[25] The financial burden created by this innovation was increased by the requirement that the tax must be paid in Tyrian sheqels (tetradrachmas), a silver currency purchased by pilgrims at the temple (see Fig. 37). This currency probably was favored because of the high quality of the silver, which was 92 percent silver or better.[26] Scraping together the cash needed to exchange and purchase the Tyrian silver coins annually must have been a great hardship on the poor.

Klawans concludes that "the temple incident is a further reflection of Jesus' consistent concern with giving to the poor, which was balanced by a firm renunciation of wealth."[27] Jesus was not opposed to the observance of purity laws, but as Klawans says, "Jesus believed that the poor should not have to pay what they could not easily afford."[28]

Jesus' movement was not alone in opposing the institution of an annual temple tax.[29] The Qumran sect also refused to recognize this innovation, interpreting pentateuchal law literally to mean that the tax should be paid only once in a lifetime, upon reaching the age of twenty:[30]

> [Concer]ning [the ransom:] the money of valuation which one gives as ransom *(kpr)* for his own person will be half [a shekel,] only on[ce] will he give it in all his days. The shekel comprises twenty geras in the she[kel of the temple.] (4Q159 = 4QOrdinances[a] frag. 1 II + 9: 7)

The *Temple Scroll* also seems to enjoin a one-time payment:

> . . . that he shall fulfill the law [   ] for himself(?) to the Lord, half a shekel, a statute for ever, a memorial in their settlements(?); the shekel is twenty(?) gerahs. (11QT 39:8-9)

A hoard of 561 coins from Qumran that consists almost exclusively of Tyrian tetradrachmas might represent a collection of the tax.[31] This possibility is strengthened by a comparison with coin assemblages from contemporary sites around the Dead Sea. For example, only one Tyrian shekel and one half-shekel were found at Masada (in a hoard dating to the time of the First Jewish Revolt), and both had been deliberately defaced.[32] As Yaakov Meshorer remarked, "The three shekel hoards found at Masada are peculiar from the point of view that they contain no Tyrian shekels."[33] Hanan Eshel and Magen Broshi note that the ratio between silver coins minted at Tyre and silver coins of the First Jewish Revolt found at Masada is 4:73 and at Qumran is 513:0.[34] Tyrian silver coins are rare at other sites around the Dead Sea. None was found among the 1,247 coins recovered during seven seasons of excavations at 'Ein Gedi, and no specimens are attested among the 837 coins dating to before 70 C.E. from Herodian Jericho.[35] There are also no Tyrian silver coins from 'Ein Feshkha, 'Ein el-Ghuweir, 'Ein Boqeq, or 'Ein ez-Zara.[36]

Eyal Regev proposes that male members of the Qumran community made a one-time half-shekel payment to the sect upon reaching the age of twenty (the age of adulthood and full admission), with no direct connection to the funding of the sacrificial cult in the Jerusalem temple. Instead, as 4QOrdinances[a] suggests, this payment was considered a ransom for the people of Israel. According to Regev, the Qumran sect did not accept the principle that the temple sacrifices should be paid for out of public funds (in the form of an annual tax).[37] Whether or not this is the case, the Tyrian tetradrachmas from Qumran are best understood as a one-time payment made by male members upon reaching the age of twenty, as ransom and/ or as a collection of the tax to be paid to the temple at a future date.

Bronze Coin Deposits by the Dead Sea

A discovery involving coins to the south of Qumran, near a site called Khirbet Mazin or Qasr el-Yehud (ancient Madin), also might relate to the Jerusalem temple. This site is located about 5 km. south of Qumran and ca. 2 km. south of 'Ein Feshkha. Excavations by Pesach Bar-Adon at Khirbet Mazin revealed a massive Hasmonean-period structure that apparently functioned as a dock, slipway, and pier for boats on the Dead Sea.[38] The pottery published from Bar-Adon's excavations at Khirbet Mazin appears to represent a homogeneous assemblage of the Hasmonean period. Specifically, most of the ceramic types can be dated from ca. 80 B.C.E. to the middle of Herod the Great's reign.[39] Bar-Adon also mentions finding "body sherds, handles, and bases belonging to many amphoras."[40] Only three amphoras are illustrated: two toes and an angular stamped Rhodian handle (illegible), described by Bar-Adon as "Herodian" but probably dating to the first century B.C.E.[41] Although the chronology of the pottery does not rule out the possibility that Khirbet Mazin functioned as a dock only during the reign of Alexander Jannaeus, it seems more likely that occupation continued afterwards, perhaps until the time of Herod.

A recent reinvestigation of the site by Yizhar Hirschfeld brought to light 1,735 coins, deposited along a 50-meter-long strip of shore in a small nearby inlet.[42] Another 189 coins were discovered by Moshe Dothan on the shore of Khirbet Mazin in 1990.[43] The coin finds are a result of the dropping level and receding shoreline of the Dead Sea.[44] All of the 1,735 coins found by Hirschfeld are small bronze denominations, and all but one represent a type minted by Alexander Jannaeus that bears a Greek inscription ("of King Alexander") surrounding an inverted-arm anchor on the obverse and on the reverse a star with eight rays within a diadem and the name "Jonathan the King" in Palaeo-Hebrew letters (Group K).[45] Most of the coins show little wear but are poorly minted. The only coin in the group that does not belong to this type is a specimen from late in the reign of Alexander Jannaeus (Group L; ca. 80/79 B.C.E. or later).[46]

Another eight hundred coins found next to the Khirbet Mazin shore in 2004 by Yuval Peleg represent the same Jannaeus type (Group K), with only one exception (a Hasmonean coin with illegible ruler).[47] Hirschfeld and Ariel associate the coins with Khirbet Mazin's occupation and believe that the homogeneous composition of the deposits indicates that the dock was used for nautical purposes only during the reign of Alexander Jannaeus. Because the coins originally were submerged underwater, Hirschfeld and Ariel suggest that they come from a sunken boat and might have been part of a payment for mercenaries.[48]

The coins found at Khirbet Mazin are apparently part of a much larger deposit, which so far may have yielded three hundred thousand coins according to reports from antiquities dealers (see Fig. 36).[49] The coins seem to be spread along the Dead Sea shoreline between Khirbet Mazin and 'Ein Feshkha.[50] Hanan Eshel and Boaz Zissu find the suggestion that the coins come from a sunken boat "unpersuasive" and instead relate the deposits to a practice described in rabbinic literature.[51] According to this practice, money consecrated for vows, offerings, and tithes that could not be brought to the Jerusalem temple should be cast into the Dead Sea:[52]

> A woman who took a vow to be a Nazir. . . . [Now if] she had coins which she had not designated for any specific purpose, they fall to a freewill offering. [If the] coins [were] designated [for a specific purpose] — those designated for a sin offering are to go off to the Salt Sea. (*m. Naz.* 4:4)

> He who sets aside coins for his Nazirite offering[s] . . . they are not available for benefit. . . . [If] they were designated [for their particular,

respective purposes], the money set aside for the sin offering is to go to the Salt Sea. (*m. Me'il.* 3:2)

He who sets aside coins for a sin offering, which were lost, and [who] offered up a sin offering in their stead, and afterward the coins turned up — let them go to the Salt Sea. (*m. Tem.* 4:2)

And coins do not go to the Salt Sea except in the case of those [sin offerings] which are found after the owner has effected atonement. (*m. Tem.* 4:3)

And if one has declared something holy, pledged a valuation, declared something *herem,* or raised up [produce as a tithe or offering], a garment [in question] is to be burned, a beast [in question] is to be destroyed. What does one do? He locks the gate before it, and it dies on its own. And coins [so designated] are to be thrown into the Dead Sea. (*y. Šeqal.* 8:4 [51b])

The rabbinic rulings are based on Deut 14:24-26, according to which people who live at a distance from Jerusalem may sell the agricultural produce and animals that they are supposed to tithe and then spend the money on food and drink in Jerusalem:

But if, when the Lord your God has blessed you, the distance is so great that you are unable to transport it, because the place where the Lord your God will choose to set his name is too far away from you, then you may turn it into money. With the money secure in hand, go to the place that the Lord your God will choose; spend the money for whatever you wish — oxen, sheep, wine, strong drink, or whatever you desire. And you shall eat there in the presence of the Lord your God, you and your household rejoicing together.

Eshel and Zissu note that the Mishnah describes this practice as "nullification," referring to the use of small bronze coins for the nullification of the second tithe (see *m. Ma'aś. Š.* 4:5; 4:8).[53] Although the rabbinic rulings relate to the period after the temple's destruction, Eshel and Zissu suggest that they have their roots in a common practice among dissident Jewish groups such as the Essenes before 70. Because these groups refused to participate in the sacrificial cult in the Jerusalem temple, they might have disposed of coins that were consecrated for vows, offerings, and tithes by casting them into the Dead Sea.[54] Hirschfeld and Ariel reject this suggestion for three reasons. First, they note that these deposits have been reported only along the northwest shore of the Dead Sea.[55] But this is an argument from silence, as there could be undiscovered deposits elsewhere. It is also possible that it was customary to dispose of the coins in one area. Second, Hirschfeld and Ariel object that "this nullification was based upon the assumption that the metal would be damaged by the salt water, while in fact the lack of oxygen in the Dead Sea helped to preserve these coins."[56] However, ancient Jews presumably did not know that the anaerobic conditions in the Dead Sea would preserve the coins instead of corroding them. Hirschfeld and Ariel's third objection raises the major question: why do all of the coins date within a range of forty years, with the overwhelming majority representing a single type that dates to the eighties of the first century B.C.E.?[57] Although I can offer no answer to this question, I still find Eshel and Zissu's suggestion persuasive. Perhaps the choice of this particular coin type was due to their low value and quality, easy availability and large circulating numbers, and/or local custom.

CHAPTER 8

Clothing and Tzitzit

Clothing

Male nudity was an accepted part of life in Palestine as in other parts of the Roman world.[1] A passage from the Tosefta suggests that it was not unusual to see naked men at work in the field or elsewhere:

> One who was standing naked while in the field or while doing his work [when the time came to recite the Shemaʿ] — behold, this one covers himself with straw or stubble or with anything, and recites [the Shemaʿ]. (*t. Ber.* 2:13)[2]

Nudity was the norm in some public places such as bath houses:[3]

> One who enters a bathhouse . . . if it is a place where people stand naked, he may not greet [his fellows] there, and obviously he may not recite the Shemaʿ or the Prayer there. . . . [If it is] a place where people stand both naked and dressed, he may greet [his fellows] there, but he may not recite the Shemaʿ or the Prayer there. (*t. Ber.* 2:20)

> Hillel the Elder says, "Do not appear naked [where others go clothed], and do not appear clothed [where others go naked] . . ." (*t. Ber.* 2:21)

In these passages the rabbis do not object to male nudity in public but only to someone reciting the Shemaʿ and other prayers while naked.[4] Furthermore, male criminals routinely were stripped before being flogged and executed. For example, Cicero describes as follows Verres's mistreatment of a Roman citizen named Gavius of Consa:

... he [Verres] suddenly ordered the man to be flung down, stripped naked and tied up in the open market-place, and rods to be got ready. . . . He then ordered the man to be flogged severely all over his body. (*Against Verres* 2.5.160-61)

Even the Mishnah prescribes stripping convicted male felons prior to execution (in this case by stoning):[5]

[When] he was four cubits from the place of stoning, they remove his clothes. "In the case of a man, they cover him up in front, and in the case of a woman, they cover her up in front and behind," the words of R. Judah. And sages say, "A man is stoned naked, but a woman is not stoned naked." (*m. Sanh.* 6:3)

That Jesus was crucified in the nude was taken for granted by Melito of Sardis, writing in the second century:

The Master has been treated in unseemly fashion, his body naked, and not even deemed worthy of a covering that [his nakedness] might not be seen. Therefore the lights [of heaven] turned away, and the day darkened, that it might hide him who was stripped upon the cross. (*Peri Pascha* 96-97)[6]

Therefore, even in Roman Palestine male nudity was accepted and expected in certain situations. Although stripping a criminal prior to flogging and execution was part of the process of humiliation and dehumanization, male nudity was not always associated with punishment or shameful circumstances. In some situations it was simply taken for granted as a necessity, as for example in bathhouses or when attending to one's bodily needs. In contrast, the Qumran community differed from everyone else — including other Jews — in an extreme concern with modesty that affected even their toilet habits (see Chapter 10). According to Josephus, Essene men wore a linen loincloth during ritual immersion and female Essenes immersed clothed in a dress (*War* 2.161), in contrast to rabbinic halakhah which requires full nudity.[7] Male sectarians wore a linen loincloth under their tunics to ensure that the genitals were not exposed, in imitation of the temple priesthood, whereas most people wore nothing under tunics. A similar concern with modesty is expressed in the book of *Jubilees,* which is well-represented at Qumran: "And to Adam alone did He give (the wherewithal) to cover his shame, of all the beasts and cattle. On this account, it is prescribed on the heavenly tablets as touching all those who know the judgment of the law, that they should cover their shame, and should not uncover themselves as the Gentiles uncover themselves" (*Jub* 3:30-31)[8]

According to Josephus, the Essenes replaced clothing and shoes only after they were threadbare or ragged: "Their dress and outward behavior are like those of children whose teacher rears them in fear; they do not change their garments or shoes until they are completely torn or worn out" (*War* 2.126). Legislation in the *Community Rule* prohibits indecent exposure that results from wearing torn or tattered clothing: "And whoever takes out his *yad* ("penis") from under his clothes, or if these are rags which allow his nakedness to be seen, he will be punished thirty days" (1QS 7:13-14). The fact that this problem was addressed specifically in the sect's penal code suggests that the exposure of genitalia due to the wearing of ragged clothing was a common or likely occurrence.[9] It also raises the possibility that male sectarians wore a linen loincloth only on certain occasions such as during communal meals and ritual immersion; otherwise the casual exposure of the genitalia due to ragged clothing (specifically tunics) should not have been a common problem. This possibility may be supported by Josephus's apparent reference to the Essenes girding themselves with a linen loincloth before immersing and entering the dining room and laying aside their "sacred garments" after the meal (*War* 2.129, 131), analogous to priests officiating in the Jerusalem temple (see below).[10]

Ragged clothing was not an unusual sight to the rabbis either:

> He who is wearing ragged clothing recites the Shema‛ and translates, but he does not read in the Torah, pass before the ark, or raise his hands. (*m. Meg.* 4:6)[11]

Ragged clothing was familiar to Jesus' audience as well, as indicated by a parable referring to an old patched cloak (Mark 2:21).

Josephus says that the Essenes wear white clothing, including a linen loincloth (*perizōma*):[12]

> They make a point . . . of being always clothed in white garments. (*War* 2.123)

. . . and girded with linen loincloths, bathe themselves in cold water. (*War* 2.129)

. . . and he is given a hatchet, the loincloth which I have mentioned, and a white garment. (*War* 2.137)

. . . The women bathe wearing a dress (*endymata* [pl.]), whereas the men wear a loincloth. (*War* 2.161)

Both the Slavonic version of *War* and Hippolytus describe the loincloth as linen, and Hippolytus describes the garments worn during the communal meals as linen (and also the dress worn by Essene women when they bathe).[13] The priests serving in the Jerusalem temple wore a linen loincloth, as God commanded: "You shall make for them [the priests] linen undergarments *(miknĕsê-bād)* to cover their naked flesh; they shall reach from the hips to the thighs" (Exod 28:42; see also Exod 20:26; Lev 16:4; Ezek 44:18). Failure to follow this injunction would result in death:

> Aaron and his sons shall wear them [the linen undergarments] when they go into the tent of meeting, or when they come near the altar to minister in the holy place; or they will bring guilt on themselves and die. (Exod 28:43)

A sectarian scroll called 4Q512 (4Q Ritual of Purification B) refers to wearing a garment — identified by Joseph Baumgarten as a loincloth — during ritual immersion:

> And he will cover himself with his clothes *(wksh 't bgdyw)* and bless o[n (the place) where he stands . . .].[14]

In my opinion, archaeological evidence combined with the testimony of Josephus and Hippolytus indicates that sectarian men wore loinclothes, tunics, and mantles made of linen. In contrast, archaeological evidence suggests that most Jews wore wool clothing, much of it colored (see Fig. 38).[15] Eibert Tigchelaar disagrees, arguing that the literary references to the white clothing of the Essenes do not necessarily denote linen since "There were also white woolen clothes and dyed linen clothes . . . though tunics could be linen, this is much less to be expected of mantles."[16] However, linen *is* more difficult to dye than wool.[17] With one exception, all of the linen textiles from Masada are undyed, and none of the linen textiles from the Cave of Letters has colored, decorated patterns.[18] Furthermore, even the undyed woolen tunics and mantles found at Masada and in the Cave of Letters have colored bands or stripes.[19] On the other hand, linen garments with self-stripes created by using a different weave instead of a different color have been found in the Cave of Letters, Wadi Murabbat, and the Cave of Avior near Jericho.[20] Yigael Yadin suggested that self-stripes represent an attempt to create *clavi* while complying with the rule of *shaatnez* (the biblical prohibition against mixing different materials in a single garment; see below), which resulted from the difficulty of dying linen and the prohibition against adding colored woolen bands.[21] Finally, the discovery of an almost complete linen mantle in Cave 7 at Qumran supports the possibility that this was a standard article of sectarian clothing.[22] Therefore, I find it unlikely that the Essenes usually wore white woolen garments and reserved linen only for ritual occasions such as communal meals, as Tigchelaar suggests.[23] The sectarians extended the requirements of the temple priesthood (based on their understanding of biblical law) to all full members. This affected every aspect of their daily lives, even their toilet habits. Therefore, the sectarians modeled their clothing after priestly garments, which according to the Hebrew Bible, the *Temple Scroll,* and Josephus were made of linen.[24]

Aharon Oppenheimer observed that "the importance attached to the purity and impurity of garments is evident from the fact that it was one of the criteria which defined the difference, in the realm of purity, between various strata of people."[25] Perhaps purity concerns were one reason new members were given clothing when they joined the Essenes, as Philo and Josephus describe (*Good Person* 86; *Hypothetica* 11.12; *War* 2.137).[26]

Tzitzit

The Lord said to Moses: "Speak to the Israelites, and tell them to make fringes on the corners of their garments throughout their generations and to put a blue cord on the fringe at each corner." (Num 15:37-38)

You shall make tassels on the four corners of the cloak with which you cover yourself. (Deut 22:12)

*You shall bind them as a sign on your hand, and fix them as an
emblem on your forehead. (Deut 11:18; see also Deut 6:8-9; Exod
13:9, 16)*

Tzitzit and the Qumran Sect

It is difficult to determine how widespread the binding of *tefillin* (phylacteries) and wearing of *tzitzit* (fringes attached to the edges of a mantle)
were in late Second Temple–period Palestine because these items are made
of perishable materials.[27] Some evidence comes from the Dead Sea region,
where the arid climate preserved not only scrolls but other organic materials. Phylactery fragments and cases were discovered in Caves 1, 4, 5, and 8 at
Qumran.[28]

Yadin suggested that a bundle of dyed, unspun wool from the Cave
of Letters in Naḥal Ḥever belonged to unfinished *tzitzit*, although well-
preserved wool mantles found in the cave did not have fringes.[29] Yadin attributed the lack of *tzitzit* on the mantles to their discovery in burial
niches, citing a passage from the Babylonian Talmud that refers to the removal of fringes before using a mantle as a burial wrapper or shroud.
However, this passage (*b. Ber.* 18a) does not deal with the removal of *tzitzit*
from a mantle but instead considers whether someone watching a corpse is
required to put on *tefillin* and recite the Shemaʿ.[30] Perhaps Yadin had in
mind tractate *Sem.* 12:11: "Abba Saul b. Bothnith used to say to his sons,
'Bury me at the feet of my father and remove the thread of blue from [the
tzitzit of] my cloak'" (Soncino translation). But this passage refers only to
the removal of the blue thread rather than the entire fringe from the mantle. Elsewhere, Abba Saul b. Bothnith ruled that *tzitzit* should be removed
from mantles used as shrouds, whereas other sages held the opposite opinion, on the grounds that *tzitzit* are not inherently sacred.[31]

The Babylonian Talmud's tractate *Menaḥot*, which contains an extended discussion of *tzitzit* (38a-44b), presents conflicting opinions on the
requirement to remove them from mantles used as shrouds:

> R. Tobi b. Kisna said in the name of Samuel, The garments put away in
> a chest are subject to *zitzith*. Samuel, however, admits that where an
> old man made it for his shroud it is exempt, for the Divine Law says,
> *Wherewith thou coverest thyself* (Deut 22:12), and this is not intended
> for ordinary covering. Nevertheless, when the time comes for its use

we should insert fringes in it, on account of the injunction, *Whoso mocketh the poor blasphemeth his Maker* (Prov 17:5)." (*b. Menaḥ.* 41a)

These passages suggest that there was no uniformity of practice or consensus with regard to the removal of *tzitzit* from mantles used as shrouds. This means we cannot assume, as Yadin did, that the mantles from the Cave of Letters had *tzitzit* that were removed prior to their use in burials. Furthermore, mantles belonging to Jewish rebels who occupied Masada at the time of the First Jewish Revolt also lack *tzitzit*, and none of them comes from burial contexts.[32] The absence of archaeological evidence for the wearing of *tzitzit* by the refugees at Masada and in the Cave of Letters is important because these Jews represented a broad swath of the local population who came from various places of origin and different socioeconomic backgrounds.

We do not know whether members of the Qumran community had fringes attached to their garments, as the caves surrounding the site have yielded few remains of clothing associated with the sectarian settlement. Although there are no definite references to the wearing of *tzitzit* in sectarian literature, the *Temple Scroll* might contain a section reiterating the Deuteronomic requirement to attach tassels *(gdylm)* to the corners of the mantle (11QT 65).[33] As we have seen, the Essenes wore all-white clothing, apparently undyed linen.[34] Because the blue thread of the *tzitzit* is wool, attaching *tzitzit* to a linen garment would violate the biblical prohibition against combining these materials in a single garment *(sha'atnez)*: "You shall not wear clothes made of wool and linen woven together" (Deut 22:11). A passage from 4QMMT indicates that the Qumran sect observed the law of *sha'atnez*: "and concerning clot[hing, that no] materials are to be mixed" (4Q396 77-78).[35]

Although it is possible that the sectarians did not wear *tzitzit* attached to their garments, this seems unlikely in view of their observance of other biblical laws, including the binding of phylacteries. Debates preserved in rabbinic literature indicate that some Jews wore *tzitzit* attached to linen garments:

A linen garment, as to fringes — The House of Shammai declare exempt. And the House of Hillel declare liable. (*m. 'Ed.* 4:10)

Our Rabbis taught: A linen garment is, according to Beth Shammai, exempt from *zitzith;* but Beth Hillel declares it liable. The *halachah* is in accordance with Beth Hillel. R. Eliezer son of R. Zadok said, Is it not a fact that any one in Jerusalem who attaches blue threads [to his linen garment] causes amazement? Rabbi said, If that is so, why did they forbid it? Because people are not versed in the law. (*b. Menaḥ.* 40a)

These debates concern whether the positive commandment of wearing *tzitzit* (which includes blue wool thread) overrides the prohibition against *sha'atnez*.[36] The dyed, unspun wool from the Cave of Letters included undyed linen threads for tying the tassels, suggesting that linen and wool were sometimes combined in *tzitzit*.[37] A passage from *b. Menaḥot* (39b) shows that some rabbis accepted the practice of attaching *tzitzit* with blue wool thread to linen mantles:

> Samuel said in the name of Levi, Woolen threads fulfill [the precept of *tzitzit*] in linen garments. The question was raised: Linen threads — why do they fulfill [the precept of *tzitzit*] in a woolen garment? Do we hold that only woolen threads fulfill [the precept] in a linen garment, for since blue [woolen threads] fulfill [the precept in any garment] while [woolen threads] also fulfill the precept, but linen threads cannot fulfill the precept in a woolen garment; or, we can argue, since it is written, "Thou shalt not wear mingled stuff, wool and linen together; thou shalt make thee twisted cords," accordingly it matters not whether woolen threads are put in a linen garment or linen threads in a woolen garment? — Come and hear. Rehabah said in the name of Rab Judah, "Woolen threads fulfill the precept in a linen garment and linen threads in a woolen garment. . . ."[38]

In support of this ruling, the rabbis pointed out that even the high priests violated the prohibition of *sha'atnez* in order to wear *tzitzit*:

> The Master said, "All must observe the law of *tzitzith*, priest and Levites and Israelites." Is not this obvious? For if priests and Levites and Israelites were exempt, then who would observe it? — It was stated particularly on account of priests. For I might have argued, since it is written, *Thou shalt not wear mingled stuff, wool and linen together,* and [it is followed by,] *Thou shalt make thee twisted cords* (Deut 22:11, 12), that only those who are forbidden to wear mingled stuff must observe the law of *tzitzith* and as priests are permitted to wear mingled stuff they need not observe [the law of *tzitzith*]; we are therefore taught [that they, too, are bound], for although while performing the service

[in the temple] they may wear [mingled stuff] they certainly may not wear it when not performing the service." (*b. Menaḥ.* 43a; see also *t. Kil.* 5:27)[39]

If the Qumran community agreed that the requirement to wear *tzitzit* overrides the prohibition against *sha'atnez*, they might have worn *tzitzit* with blue wool threads attached to linen mantles. Perhaps they rationalized this practice as the rabbis did, by citing priestly precedent. However, the sectarians often differed from the rabbis on specific points of law, and even the rabbis did not agree among themselves. As we have seen, for example, the house of Shammai reportedly forbade attaching *tzitzit* with a purple thread of wool to a linen mantle (*b. Menaḥ.* 40a), as does an anonymous ruling in the Mishnah: "A fringe of wool [fastened] onto [a garment of flax {linen} is prohibited, because [the threads of the fringe] interlace the web [of the garment]" (*m. Kil.* 9:9). If the Qumran sect shared this view, which seems likely given their strict observance of the prohibition against *sha'atnez*, perhaps their solution was to attach all-linen *tzitzit*.[40] This possibility is supported by rabbinic and sectarian literature. Rava bar Rav Chana ruled that "Since it is possible to fulfill the mitzvah in linen garments with white threads of their own kind, i.e. linen, in which case the *tzitzit* will not constitute *sha'atnez*, we may not use threads of wool, which do constitute *sha'atnez*" (*b. Menaḥ.* 40a; Schottenstein edition)

Whereas the biblical law of *sha'atnez* refers only to mixing linen and wool in a single garment (which the rabbis followed), sectarian legislation extended the prohibition against mixing *to all materials*:

You shall not wear clothes made of wool and linen woven together. (Deut 22:11)

Nothing is prohibited on account of [the laws of] diverse kinds except [wool and flax {linen} which are] spun or woven [together], as it is written, You shall not wear *sha'atnez* (Deut 22:11) — something which is hackled, spun, or woven. (*m. Kil.* 9:8)

and concerning clot[hing, that no] materials are to be mixed. (4Q396 77-78)[41]

The possibility that the sectarians did not mix materials for *tzitzit* but instead wore linen *tzitzit* attached to a linen mantle is supported by the fact that the biblical passage prohibiting *sha'atnez* is followed immediately by the injunction to wear fringes: "You shall make tassels on the four corners of the cloak with which you cover yourself" (Deut 22:12). Since 4QMMT indicates that the sectarians did not mix any materials in their clothing, I believe it is likely that they fulfilled this commandment by wearing all-linen *tzitzit*.

Many Jews including the rabbis apparently assumed that the *ptil tekelet* ("blue thread") of Num 15:38 is wool, which may have come about because wool is easier to dye than linen. The rabbis do not even discuss the possibility of a linen *ptil tekelet*. However, linen scroll wrappers with a pattern woven in individual blue linen threads (apparently depicting a blueprint of the Jerusalem temple) were discovered in Cave 1 at Qumran.[42] This raises the possibility that the sectarians used blue linen threads instead of wool as the *ptil tekelet* in *tzitzit*. In fact, sectarian literature seems to contain polemics in this matter. As we have seen, not only did the rabbis take for granted that the *ptil tekelet* is always of wool, but they cited priestly precedent to support the mixing of wool and linen: "And these priests, since *sha'atnez* is permitted for them in the priestly vestments . . ." (*b. Menah.* 43a; Schottenstein edition). The Schottenstein edition of the Babylonian Talmud notes that Rashi understood this passage as referring to the sash or belt *('bnt)* worn by the priests, which according to the rabbis contained wool and linen: ". . . and the sash *('bnt)* of fine twisted linen, and of blue *(tklt)*, purple, and crimson yarns, embroidered with needlework" (Exod 39:29)[43]

However, according to the Qumran sectarians priestly clothing must be made entirely of linen, as the *War Scroll* makes clear:

> . . . clad in garments of white byssus [linen]; a linen tunic and linen trousers, and girt with a linen girdle of twined byssus, blue, purple and scarlet, and a brocaded pattern, cunningly wrought, and turbaned headdresses on their heads. (7:9-10)

As Yadin noted, "the author's emphasis on 'byssus', 'white', 'linen' suggests that he wished to rule out any doubt on this matter."[44] This work and the passage from 4QMMT (77-78) cited above suggest that the sectarians opposed the mixing of wool and linen in *tzitzit* and wore all-linen *tzitzit* with a blue *ptil tekelet* attached to their linen mantles.

The possibility that binding *tefillin* and wearing *tzitzit* gradually became more common (although not universal) only in the centuries following the destruction of the temple is suggested by a lack of legislation in the

Mishnah.[45] Instead, injunctions about *tefillin* and *tzitzit* are recorded in the Talmudim and minor tractates.[46] Despite the lack of archaeological evidence, literary sources indicate that *tefillin* and *tzitzit* were a familiar sight in Palestine in the late Second Temple period and must have been worn regularly by some Jews.[47] Matthew describes Jesus criticizing the scribes and Pharisees for making "their phylacteries broad and their fringes long" (Matt 23:5).[48] Justin Martyr's testimony suggests that *tefillin* and *tzitzit* were recognizable even to some Gentiles in the early second century:

> For He enjoined you to place around you [a fringe] of purple dye, in order that you might not forget God; and he commanded you to wear a phylactery, certain characters, which indeed we consider holy, being engraved on very thin parchment; and by this means stirring you up to retain a constant remembrance of God. (*Dial.* 46)[49]

Jesus and Tzitzit

The Synoptic Gospels describe Jesus wearing a fringed mantle while performing healings. One episode involves a woman suffering from prolonged vaginal bleeding:[50]

> Then suddenly a woman who had been suffering from hemorrhages for twelve years came up behind him and touched the fringe of his cloak, for she said to herself, "If I only touch his cloak, I will be made well." (Matt 9:20-21)

In Luke's version the woman sneaks up behind Jesus:

> She came up behind him and touched the fringe of his clothes. (Luke 8:44; Mark's version of this episode [5:27] omits the reference to a fringe and mentions only Jesus' cloak [*himation*])[51]

In another episode throngs of people seek to be healed by touching the fringe of Jesus' mantle:

> After the people of that place recognized him, they sent word throughout the region and brought all who were sick to him, and begged him that they might touch even the fringe of his cloak; and all who touched it were healed. (Matt 14:35-36)

Mark's version is similar:

> And wherever he went, into villages or cities or farms, they laid the sick in the marketplaces, and begged him that they might touch even the fringe of his cloak; and all who touched it were healed. (Mark 6:56)

All of the Gospels refer to fringe as *kraspedon,* a Greek word that can also mean "edge" or "hem." But the episode in Matt 23:5, according to which Jesus condemns the scribes and Pharisees for wearing long fringes, suggests that *kraspedon* should be understood in the other passages as referring to the fringe of a mantle rather than the hem. The LXX also uses the term *kraspedon* for *tzitzit* (Num 15:37).[52] The Synoptic Gospels suggest that Jesus belonged to a minority of Jews who wore a fringed mantle, for it is hard to imagine why the Gospel writers would have fabricated a detail of clothing that was unfamiliar to most non-Jewish readers and reflected a strict observance of Jewish law by Jesus.[53] Furthermore, the Gospel accounts accurately describe the fringe being attached to a mantle *(himation)* rather than another garment such as a tunic.[54] Notice too that Matt 23:5 reports that Jesus criticized the scribes and Pharisees for wearing *long tzitzit* but not for wearing *tzitzit* in general (and for wearing *broad* phylacteries but not for wearing phylacteries).[55]

Although Jesus' healings would have brought him into contact with impure people, it is unclear whether all Jews believed that impurity was transmitted by touching clothing or *tzitzit.* Biblical law mandates that "leprous" clothing and clothing worn by people with certain skin afflictions (usually rendered in English as "leprosy" but not limited to Hansen's Disease) must be washed or destroyed (Lev 13-14; see also *m. Neg.* 11-12). Several texts from Qumran refer to the washing of clothing in connection with purification rites (see, e.g., 4Q512; 4Q514; 4Q274). According to rabbinic law, clothing acquires secondary impurity (*magʿa* impurity) through contact with any source of primary impurity. Clothing, bedding, furniture, and other items acquire primary impurity if they have been under pressure (e.g., through sitting, lying, leaning, or walking) of a *zab* or *zabah* or a menstruating woman or a woman after childbirth (*midras* impurity).[56] Anyone who touches an object with *midras* impurity contracts secondary impurity.[57] This is based on Leviticus 15:

> Every bed on which the one with the discharge lies shall be unclean; and everything on which he sits shall be unclean. Anyone who touches

his bed shall wash his clothes, and bathe in water, and be unclean until the evening. All who sit on anything on which the one with the discharge has sat shall wash their clothes, and bathe in water, and be unclean until the evening. All who touch the body of the one with the discharge shall wash their clothes, and bathe in water, and be unclean until the evening. . . . All who touch anything that was under him shall be unclean until the evening, and all who carry such a thing shall wash their clothes, and bathe in water, and be unclean until the evening. (Lev 15:4-10)[58]

The rabbis seem to have considered pressure as well as intention factors in conveying impurity to clothing:[59]

"An unclean person who hits the clean person, and the clean person who hits the unclean — the clothes of the clean person are unclean," the words of R. Meir. And sages say, "[If] a clean person hits the unclean, the clothes of the clean person are clean. [If] an unclean person hits the clean, since if the clean person draws back, lo, the unclean person falls down, the clothes of the clean person are unclean." R. Simeon says, "[If] he hits him with knuckles, he is unclean. [If] he hits him with the back of his hand, he is clean." (*t. Zabim* 4:1)[60]

Leviticus 11:24-25 and 11:39-40 mandate that whereas touching animal carcasses makes a person impure until sundown, only someone who carries or eats a carcass (the latter in the case of a clean animal) must wash their clothes. The author of the *Temple Scroll* expanded upon Leviticus' legislation by requiring a person to wash clothing after touching a carcass (11QT 51:1-5).[61] In contrast, the rabbis ruled that a person who has come into contact with the carcass of a clean animal does not defile clothing by touching it:

But it is not the case that the one who touches defiles clothing. Therefore, the text is (only) "The one who touches . . . is impure until evening" (Lev 11:39) and not, "the one who touches . . . defiles clothing." (Sifra on Lev 11:39-40)[62]

Touching does not convey uncleanness to clothes. But would it not follow that since carrying, which is slighter (in conveying uncleanness), does convey uncleanness to clothes, touching, which is more severe (in conveying uncleanness), should definitely convey uncleanness to clothes?! Therefore Scriptures say: "whoever touches shall be unclean until the evening" — to teach us that "he who touches does not make his clothes unclean." (Sifra, Sheraẓim iv:7 [51b])[63]

Thomas Kazen argues that "there are reasons to think that even a discharger [*zab* or *zabah*] touching the clothes of a clean person would be seen as transmitting something like a first-degree impurity during the Second Temple period."[64] A passage from the Mishnah indicates that some Jews (in this case the *haverim*) avoided contact with the clothing of those who were not scrupulous about purity observance: "He who undertakes to be a *haver* . . . does not receive him [the *am ha'aretz*] as his guest while he [the *am ha'aretz*] is wearing his [the *am ha'aretz's*] own clothes" (*m. Demai* 2:3).[65] However, the fact that Jesus' opponents are not presented as attacking him for coming into contact with impure people implies that either Jesus was not considered as defiled when unclean people touched his *tzitzit* or that it was assumed he would undergo the necessary purification before entering the temple.[66] As E. P. Sanders concluded, "Common people, one gathers from rabbinic discussions, did not worry about *midras* impurity, except when they entered the temple, and possibly then they did not worry about *midras* impurity on their clothes."[67] This evidence suggests that most Jews would not have been concerned by the potential impurity conveyed by unclean people touching Jesus' *tzitzit*.[68] Perhaps those who sought healing touched Jesus' *tzitzit* rather than a part of his body out of sensitivity to purity concerns.[69]

CHAPTER 9

Oil and Spit

Oil and Bathing

According to Josephus, the Essenes consider oil to be defiling and do not allow themselves to be anointed without their consent:

> They think that oil is a defilement (*kēlis,* "stain"); and if any one of them be anointed without his own approbation, it is wiped off his body; for they think to be unwashed is a good thing. (*War* 2.123; Whiston's translation)

In contrast to rabbinic halakhah, the sectarians believed that stone and unfired clay vessels (like wood) can become impure if they come into contact with oil and that oil stains on these materials can transmit impurity:[1]

> And all the [vessels of] wood and the stones and the dust which are defiled by man's impurity, while with stains of oil in them, in accordance with their uncleanness will make whoever touches them impure. (CD 12:15-17)

> And on the day on which they will take the dead body out of it, they shall sweep the house of any defiling smirch of oil, and wine, and moisture of water. (11QT 49:11)[2]

Josephus's observation that the Essenes consider oil defiling therefore seems to be accurate.[3] Josephus adds that the Essenes forbid others to anoint them without their approval but does not say that they avoid oil altogether.[4] Yigael Yadin noted that although the Essenes refrained from oiling their bodies on an everyday basis, anointing with new oil was part of the ritual of the Feast of the Firstfruits of Oil.[5] The Essenes' attitude must be due to purity concerns, despite the fact that Josephus attributes it to a preference for being unwashed.[6] I believe that Josephus did this in order to present the sectarians' lifestyle as an ascetic ideal to his Roman audience.[7] Similarly, Hegesippus reports that James the Just (brother of Jesus) abstained from using oil, linking it with James' refusal to bathe: "he did not anoint himself with oil, and he did not use the bath" (apud Eusebius, *Hist. eccl.* 2:23).[8] This could indicate that James had purity concerns similar to those of the Essenes or might reflect his ascetic lifestyle (or both).[9] Whatever his motives, Josephus's characterization of the Essenes as unwashed is supported by other evidence.

In the ancient Mediterranean world oil was used for washing, as illustrated for example by a passage in the deuterocanonical appendix to the book of Daniel on Susanna:

> She said to her maids, "Bring me olive oil and ointments, and shut the garden doors so that I can bathe." (Sus 1:17)

That this was an ancient custom is illustrated by the book of Ruth, where Naomi instructs Ruth, "Now wash and anoint yourself, and put on your best clothes" (3:3).

The Oxyrhynchus papyrus fragment 840, which presents a debate between a "Pharisee" priest named Levi and Jesus, also connects "anointing" with bathing:

> ... and you have cleansed and wiped the outside skin which the prostitutes and flute-girls anoint, which they wash, and wipe, and make beautiful for human desire. (2:8)[10]

The Babylonian Talmud describes the use of oil in connection with bathing, specifically in hot water:

> If one bathes in hot water and does not have a cold shower bath, he is like iron put into fire but not into cold water. If one bathes without anointing, he is like water [poured] over a barrel. (*b. Šabb.* 41a)

The Gospels mention the use of perfumed oil in connection with the washing of feet:

And a woman in the city, who was a sinner, having learned that he [Jesus] was eating in the Pharisee's house, brought an alabaster jar of ointment *(myrou)*. She stood behind him at his feet, weeping, and began to bathe his feet with her tears and to dry them with her hair. Then she continued kissing his feet and anointing them with the ointment. (Luke 7:37-38)[11]

Mary took a pound of costly perfume made of pure nard *(myrou nardou)*, anointed Jesus' feet, and wiped them with her hair. The house was filled with the fragrance of the perfume. (John 12:3)

These sources describe two different practices: the use of oil in bathing and the washing and anointing of feet with oil. Whereas oil was used throughout the Roman world for bathing, some scholars have suggested that washing and anointing the feet with perfumed oil was an Eastern and perhaps specifically Jewish custom associated with the offering of hospitality and respect.[12] Petronius's *Satyricon* might allude to this oriental practice:

I'm ashamed to say what happened next. Following some unheard of custom, several long-haired boys presented us with ointment *(unguentum)* in a silver basin and rubbed it on our feet as we lay there, after tying little garlands around our ankles and calves! Then some of the ointment was poured into the wine bowl and the lamp! (70:8)[13]

Rabbinic literature describes a peculiar ritual involving oil:[14]

The House of Shammai say, "[At the end of the meal] one holds the cup of wine [for the benedictions after meals] in his right hand and the perfumed oil [for cleaning one's hands] in his left. He recites the benediction over the wine and afterward recites the blessing over the oil." And the House of Hillel say, "One holds the perfumed oil in his right hand and the cup of wine in his left. He recites the benediction over the oil and smears it on the head of the servant. If the servant is a disciple of the sages, [then instead] one smears [the oil] on the wall, for it is not befitting a disciple of the sages to go about perfumed." (*t. Ber.* 5:29)

That this custom was practiced even among Jews outside Palestine is indicated by a passage in Petronius's *Satyricon*, in which Trimalchio dries his hands on the head of a slave:[15]

> After emptying his bladder, he called for water for his hands, sprinkled it lightly on his fingers and then wiped them dry on the head of a young slave. (27:6)[16]

These sources suggest that anointing the head as well as the feet with oil was a widespread Jewish custom. In Luke 7:46, Jesus reportedly criticizes Simon the Pharisee for not offering a guest the usual hospitality: "You did not anoint *(aleiphō)* my head with oil *(elaion)*, but she has anointed my feet with ointment *(myron)*."

The sectarians apparently differed from other Jews in refusing the anointing with oil that was a common gesture of hospitality and respect, due to purity concerns. This explains Josephus's observation that the Essenes forbid others to anoint them without their consent. Furthermore, archaeological evidence from Qumran suggests that the sectarians did not bathe in the Roman manner, supporting Josephus's statement that the Essenes prefer to remain unwashed. There are no above-ground bathtubs or bathhouses at Qumran and no heated pools or bathing facilities. In contrast, the Hasmonean and Herodian palaces at Jericho and around the Dead Sea were equipped with bathing facilities, as were the mansions in Jerusalem's Jewish Quarter.[17] In describing immersion before the communal meal (*War* 2.129), Josephus mentions that the Essenes "bathe (wash) their bodies in cold water *(psychrois hydasin).*" In addition, the hundreds of pottery vessels from Qumran published by Roland de Vaux include only three (piriform) unguentaria from the settlement and none from the caves.[18] Unguentaria are small bottles for perfumed oil; fusiform unguentaria were the dominant type until Herod's reign, when they were replaced by piriform unguentaria (see Fig. 19).[19]

The fact that only three unguentaria from Qumran are published is admittedly an argument from silence, as there is still no final report on the pottery or glass. Nonetheless, a comparison with other Judean sites is instructive. Three ceramic unguentaria from 'Ein Feshkha are published, and five from 'Ein el-Ghuweir (all piriform), but both sites have smaller ceramic assemblages than Qumran and were occupied for shorter periods.[20] Dozens of ceramic unguentaria were found at Masada, many of them in contexts dating to the First Revolt, including a local variant that is unattested at

Qumran ("the Judean kohl bottle").[21] Rachel Bar-Nathan published more than twenty examples of fusiform and piriform unguentaria from the Hasmonean and Herodian palaces at Jericho, some from miqva'ot in the palace and others from the industrial complex.[22] Judean kohl bottles and ceramic alabastra are also attested at Herodian Jericho.[23] Fusiform and piriform unguentaria are well-represented in Jerusalem's Jewish Quarter, and there are a few examples of Judean kohl bottles and ceramic alabastra.[24] No ceramic unguentaria from the Second Temple period village at 'Ein Gedi have been published (which is interesting considering its importance as a center for the cultivation of opobalsam), although there are a few examples of glass unguentaria ("candlestick bottles").[25] However, fusiform and piriform unguentaria are well-represented in the Hasmonean and Herodian period burial caves at 'Ein Gedi, and there is also a specimen made of alabaster.[26]

The rarity of unguentaria at Qumran suggests a limited use of oil for washing or anointing, whereas the absence of bathing facilities indicates that the community did not bathe in the Roman manner. This evidence supports Josephus's observation about the Essenes with regard to washing and the use of oil. Andrea Berlin notes that in the first century C.E. at Gamla, perfume and oil containers comprised 8.5 percent of every household's pottery (compared with only 0.1 percent in the first century B.C.E.). She attributes this phenomenon to Roman influence on the Jewish villagers.[27] Berlin's observation about changes in Jewish customs or practices in the first century B.C.E. and first century C.E. is important. Writing in the first century C.E., Josephus must have been struck by the Essenes' avoidance of oil, as by this time other Jews apparently had adopted the Roman custom. Similarly, whereas by the first century C.E. other Jews shared food from common dishes, the Essenes continued the common first century B.C.E. practice of being served their portions individually. In both cases the Essenes seem to have retained earlier customs or practices, presumably because of purity concerns.

Spit and Spitting

Josephus informs us that the Essenes refrained from spitting in assemblies as well as to the right:

> They also avoid spitting **in the midst of them** *(eis mesous),* or on the right side. (*War* 2.147; Whiston's translation)

Similarly, the *Community Rule* penalizes members who spit during an assembly:

And the person who spits **in the midst** *('l twk)* of a meeting of the Many shall be punished thirty days. (1QS 7:13)[28]

Presumably the basis for this prohibition is Lev 15:8, which states that a *zab's* spit conveys impurity:

If the one with the discharge spits on persons who are clean, then they shall wash their clothes, and bathe in water, and be unclean until the evening.

The rabbis forbade spitting on the Temple Mount:

And one should not use [the Temple Mount] for a shortcut. And spitting [there likewise is forbidden, as is proven by an argument] *a minori ad majus* [if you may not use it for a shortcut, you obviously may not spit there]. (*m. Ber.* 9:5; see also *b. Ber.* 62b-63a, where the rabbis prohibit spitting on the Temple Mount but are divided over whether it is permitted in a synagogue)[29]

The rabbinic prohibition was motivated by a desire to show respect for the temple rather than being due to purity concerns, as a passage in the Tosefta indicates:[30]

And spitting [is forbidden on the Temple Mount] by a fortiori reasoning [*m. Ber* 9:5] [as follows]: Now if [with respect to wearing] a shoe, which is not contemptuous, the Torah said, "Do not enter [the Temple Mount] wearing a shoe," how much more so is spitting, which is contemptuous, [to be forbidden on the Temple Mount]. (*t. Ber.* 6:19)

This does not preclude the possibility that a ban on spitting in the Jerusalem temple originated out of purity concerns. Alternatively, it could be that whereas the rabbis understood this prohibition as a show of respect, the sectarians attributed it to purity concerns. The possibility that spitting was indeed prohibited in the Jerusalem temple (and is not a rabbinic fiction) is supported by evidence of a similar ban in Roman temples:

What, do you even enter our temples in such a state, where it is not lawful to spit or blow one's nose, when you yourself are nothing more than spit and rheum? (Epictetus, *Discourses* 4.11:32)[31]

In some cases the rabbis considered spit a source of impurity, especially if it came from a Gentile:

Our Rabbis taught: The scholars were once in need of something from a noblewoman where all the great men of Rome were to be found. "Who will go?" "I will go," replied R. Joshua. So R. Joshua and his disciples went. . . . After he came out he descended, had a ritual bath, and learnt with his disciples. Said he to them . . . "When I descended and had a ritual bath, of what did you suspect me?" "We thought, perhaps some spittle spurted from her mouth upon the Rabbi's garments." "By the [Temple] Service!" exclaimed he to them, "it was even so." (*b. Šabb.* 127b)[32]

"All drops of spit which are found in Jerusalem are assumed to be clean, except for those [found in] the Upper Market Place," the words of R. Meir. (*m. Šeqal.* 8:1)[33]

[If there is] one [female] idiot in the village or [one] Gentile woman or one Samaritan woman all drops of spit which are in the village are unclean. (*m. Ṭehar.* 5:8)

There is also a discussion about spitting in the Palestinian Talmud:

R. Halafta B. Saul taught: "One who breaks wind while wearing his tefillin — this is a bad sign for him." [But the same does not apply to one who sneezes.] This accords with that which has been said, "[Breaking wind] below [is a bad sign]. But [sneezing] above is not." This accords with that which R. Haninah said, "I saw Rabbi yawn, and sneeze and cover his mouth with his hand [to yawn during his recitation of the Prayer]. But I did not see him spit." R. Yohanan said, "Even spitting [is permitted] if it serves to clear one's throat." Spitting in front of oneself is forbidden. Behind is permitted. To his right is forbidden. To his left is permitted. This follows what is written, "A thousand may fall at your side; [ten thousand at your right hand]" [Ps 91:7] [i.e., the right side is more important]. Everyone agrees that one who needs to spit into his jacket [or a handkerchief is permitted to do so, but he] is forbidden [to spit anywhere during his recitation of Prayer]. R. Joshua b. Levi said, "Spitting in the synagogue is like spitting in [God's] eye." R. Jonah used to spit and then smooth it over [with his foot]. R. Jeremiah, R. Samuel bar Halafta in the name of R. Ada b. Ahavah, "One who prays should not spit until he moves four cubits [from the place in which he prays]." Said R. Yose b. R. Abun, "Likewise one who spits should not pray until he moves four cubits [from the place he spit]." (y. Ber. 3:5)

Here again the rabbis are concerned with showing respect to holy places or while praying. R. Yohanan's statement forbidding spitting to the front or right recalls sectarian practice. However, whereas the rabbis banned spitting while praying, the sectarians refrained from spitting to the front and right in their assemblies. This seems to be an example of the sectarians universalizing a practice that otherwise was observed in a restricted or limited manner, prompting Josephus's remark. Perhaps the sect associated the left side not only with a superstitious sense of evil but with impurity, as reflected in the Community Rule's prohibition against gesticulating with the left hand (1QS 7:15), which was used to clean oneself after defecation.[34]

Whereas spitting on the Temple Mount may have been forbidden or at least frowned upon, there seems to have been no general prohibition against spitting in public, including spitting on others in certain situations. According to Mark (14:65), those present at Jesus' trial spat on him: "Some began to spit on him." In fact, biblical law (Deut 25:5-10) requires a childless widow to spit in her brother-in-law's face if he refuses to marry her (the halitzah ceremony).[35]

The Romans used saliva for protection against the evil eye, as Pliny describes:

I have however pointed out that the best of all safeguards against serpents is the saliva of a fasting human being, but our daily experience may teach us yet other values of its use. We spit on epileptics in a fit, that is, we throw back infection. In a similar way we ward off witchcraft and the bad luck that follows meeting a person lame in the right leg. We also ask for forgiveness of the gods for a too presumptuous hope by spitting on the ground three times by way of ritual, thus increasing its efficacy, and marking early incipient boils three times with fasting saliva. (Nat. Hist. 38.7.36)

Similarly, Jesus reportedly used saliva in his miraculous healings:

> He took him aside in private, away from the crowd, and put his fingers into his ears, and he spat and touched his tongue. (Mark 7:33)

> He took the blind man by the hand and led him out of the village; and when he had put saliva on his eyes and laid his hands on him, he asked him, "Can you see anything?" (Mark 8:23; see also the healing of a blind man in John 9:1-12, in which Jesus mixes saliva and dirt to make mud, which he puts on the man's eyes).

To conclude, the spit of certain people such as the *zab* and Gentile was considered impure and apparently was avoided by Jews who were scrupulous in the observance of purity. The sectarians extended the prohibition against spitting in the Jerusalem temple to their assemblies, presumably because they conceived of their community as a substitute temple.

CHAPTER 10

Toilets and Toilet Habits

Cacator sic valeas, ut tu hoc locum transeas.
(Shit with comfort and good cheer, so long as you do not do it here.)

(*CIL* IV.6641; graffito on a wall at Pompeii[1])

Modern Westerners tend to view the ancient world through a highly sanitized lens. In fact, despite sophisticated aqueduct systems and other technologies, the Roman world was a filthy, malodorous, and unhealthy place, certainly by contemporary standards. If we could be transported back in time, it is unlikely that most of us would survive exposure to the widespread dirt and diseases, to which we lack immunity. Human waste fouled the streets and sidewalks of even the most advanced Roman cities. Because toilet facilities serve one of the most basic human needs and toilet habits are deeply embedded within cultural and social norms, few of us realize that our modern, Western obsession with toilet privacy and hygiene was not shared by ancient peoples. This chapter examines the toilets and toilet practices characteristic of the Roman world in general and the Jews of Palestine in particular.[2] Within this world, the Qumran sectarians were distinguished by their concern with toilet privacy, and unlike other Jews, they considered excrement impure and defecation to be a ritually polluting activity.

Ancient Toilet Facilities and Sanitary Arrangements

Perhaps the best-known examples of ancient toilets are Roman luxury latrines, which were often part of a public bathhouse. They were equipped with stone or wooden seats pierced with holes along one or more sides of a room (see Fig. 39). The seats were mounted above a constantly running stream of water from the bathhouse, which carried off the sewage.[3] Since these latrines relied on a constant supply of fresh water piped in by aqueduct, they are rarely found outside Roman civic bathhouses or other public establishments. Roman luxury latrines seem to be unattested in Palestine before 70 C.E., and are relatively rare even in the following centuries.[4]

The arrangement of side-by-side seats indicates that there was no expectation of privacy in Roman luxury latrines.[5] To the contrary, there seems to have been a great deal of socializing, judging from remarks made by Roman authors such as Martial:

> You read to me as I stand, you read to me as I sit,
> You read to me as I run, you read to me as I shit. (Martial III.44)[6]

Sanitary arrangements otherwise varied greatly in the ancient Mediterranean world, even during the time of the Roman Empire. Because many private homes lacked toilet installations, residents availed themselves of chamber pots. Chamber pots could be vessels designed for that purpose or consisted of recycled (broken) jars, as Varro describes:[7]

> He/she retrieves the Chian amphora of the wealthy for use as a common chamber pot. (*Menippean Satires* 192.104)[8]

Rabbinic literature also contains references to chamber pots:[9]

> Pots into which Israelites and Gentiles urinate — if the greater part is from the unclean [Gentile source], it [the urine in the pot] is unclean. (*m. Makš.* 2:3)

> [As regards] the chamber pot of a *zab* or a *zabah* — the [water of the] first and second [washings of the pot] conveys uncleanness. But the [water of the] third [rinsing] is clean. Under what circumstances? When one put water in it [to rinse it]. But when one did not put water

into it [but rinsed it with clean urine] — even up to the tenth [rinsing] — it conveys uncleanness. (*t. Ter.* 10:13)

The contents of chamber pots were emptied into the streets or into cesspits along the streets, which is why better-designed Roman cities such as Pompeii had high curbs with stepping-stones (see Fig. 40). According to Juvenal, it was not uncommon for pedestrians to be soaked by the contents of chamber pots tossed from houses above:

> And now regard the different and diverse perils of the night. See what a height it is to that towering roof from which a potsherd comes crack upon my head every time that some broken or leaky vessel is pitched out of the window! See with what a smash it strikes and dents the pavement! There's death in every open window as you pass along at night. You may be deemed a fool, improvident of sudden accident if you go out to dinner without having made your will. You can but hope, and put up a piteous prayer in your hearth that they may be content to pour down on you only the contents of their slop-basins. (Juvenal, *Satires* III.268-77)[10]

In more advanced Roman cities, the waste in the streets was washed away by the overflow from public fountains, which ran through gutters into underground sewers.[11] In towns and cities that lacked central drainage and sewer systems, waste flooded the streets after heavy rains.[12]

When individuals had no access to built toilet facilities, they relieved themselves anywhere they could, including in streets and alleys, staircases of dwellings, bathhouses and other public buildings, and tombs.[13] Public urination and even defecation do not appear to have been unusual sights, as indicated by signs and graffiti found in cities around the Roman world requesting that individuals relieve themselves elsewhere:

> Twelve gods and goddesses and Jupiter, the biggest and the best, will be angry with whoever urinates or defecates here. (*CIL* VI.29848; from the Baths of Titus in Rome)[14]

> If you shit against the walls and we catch you, you will be punished. (*CIL* IV.7038; from Regio V at Pompeii)[15]

> Whoever refrains from littering or pissing or shitting on this street may the goddesses in general favor. If he does not do so let him watch out. (*CIL* III.1966; from Salona in Croatia)[16]

Rabbinic literature indicates that the situation was no better in Palestine:

> One should not enter filthy alleyways [*mbw'wt mṭwnpwt,* "soiled with excrement"] and recite the Shemaʿ." (*t. Ber.* 2:17)

When built toilet facilities are found in private dwellings in the Roman world, they usually consist of a stone or wooden seat set over a cesspit.[17] Other household waste such as garbage was also thrown into the cesspit, which is why toilets in Roman houses were often located in or next to the kitchen.[18] Manure merchants who were paid to clean cesspits sold the contents as fertilizer.[19] A passage in the Mishnah seems to describe a toilet seat made of leather stretched over a metal frame, presumably set over a cesspit:

> A toilet *('slh)* is susceptible to midras uncleanness and to corpse uncleanness. [If] it was separated, the leather is susceptible to midras uncleanness, and the iron to corpse uncleanness. (*m. Kelim* 22:9)

A late Iron Age residence called the House of Ahiel in Jerusalem's City of David contained a toilet installation consisting of a square stone seat pierced by a hole still in its original position over a cesspit (see Fig. 41).[20] Roland de Vaux found a toilet of this type in L51 at Qumran, a room on the eastern side of the settlement (see Fig. 24). The toilet consisted of a mud-lined pit filled with thin layers of dirty soil *("terre sale"),* into which was set a terracotta pipe surrounded by stones.[21] Since no toilet seat was found in L51 at Qumran, it might have been made of wood or other perishable materials. However, a pierced stone block that de Vaux described finding in L44, which is adjacent to and east of L51, could be the toilet seat. De Vaux tentatively identified this object as part of a conduit or chimney flue.[22]

Literary Information on the Toilets and Toilet Habits of the Qumran Sect

The *Temple Scroll, War Scroll,* and Josephus indicate that the Qumran sect had different toilet habits from other ancient Jews and Romans. In these scrolls, toilets are referred to by the biblical term "the hand" or "the place for a hand *(maqom yad)*."[23] In Qumranic Hebrew the term "hand" *(yad)* means "penis."[24] The *War Scroll* mandates the placement of toilets at a distance of 2000 cubits from the camps:

> There shall be a space between all their camps and the place of the "hand," about two thousand cubits, and no unseemly evil thing shall be seen in the vicinity of their encampments. (1QM 7:6-7)

The relevant passage in the *Temple Scroll* reads:

> And you shall make them a place for a hand outside the city, to which they shall go out, to the northwest of the city — roofed houses with pits within them into which the excrement will descend, so that it will not be visible at any distance from the city, three thousand cubits. (11QT 46:13-16)

Because the sectarians observed in their everyday lives the laws of the desert camp, they relieved themselves in private and buried their excrement in a pit as prescribed in Deut 23:9-14(MT 10-15):[25]

> When you are encamped against your enemies you shall guard against any impropriety. If one of you becomes unclean (impure) because of a nocturnal emission, then he shall go outside the camp; he must not come within the camp. When evening comes, he shall wash himself with water, and when the sun has set, he may come back into the camp. You shall have a designated area outside the camp to which you shall go. With your utensils you shall have a trowel *(ytd)*; when you relieve yourself outside, you shall dig a hole with it and then cover up your excrement. Because the Lord your God travels along with your camp, to save you and to hand over your enemies to you, therefore your camp must be holy, so that he may not see anything indecent among you and turn away from you.

The peculiar sectarian concern that defecation be done in private and excrement buried is reflected in the *Temple Scroll*'s legislation, which requires that built toilet facilities (in permanent settlements such as Jerusalem and Qumran) be enclosed, roofed structures containing a pit. Josephus's description of the toilet practices of the Essenes shows that the sectarians took care to defecate in private and buried the excrement in a pit when they did not have access to built toilet facilities:

(On the Sabbath they do not) even go to stool. On other days they dig a trench a foot deep with a mattock *(skalidi)* — such is the nature of the hatchet which they present to neophytes — and wrapping their mantle about them, that they may not offend the rays of the deity, sit above it. They then replace the excavated soil in the trench. For this purpose they select the more retired spots. And though this discharge of the excrements is a natural function, they make it a rule to wash themselves after it, as if defiled. (*War* 2.147-49)[26]

The literary evidence and the presence of a toilet at Qumran indicate that the sectarians attended to their bodily functions in various ways. When they did not have access to built toilet facilities in permanent settlements, they relieved themselves in the manner described by Josephus. The fact that the toilet practices described in these sources are complementary rather than contradictory is indicated by the relevant passage in Deuteronomy (23:13). This passage mandates digging a pit for one-time use when an individual is outside the camp and therefore does not have access to permanent toilet facilities.[27]

The location of the toilet in L51 on the eastern side of the main building suggests that the distance regulations mandated for toilets in the *War Scroll* and *Temple Scroll* did not apply to the settlement at Qumran. These sources make a point of requiring minimum distances from the war camp for the placement of toilets at the end of days and the ideal city of Jerusalem. However, the fact that the toilet in L51 does not seem to have been replaced after the earthquake of 31 B.C.E. suggests that the sectarians reorganized the settlement at Qumran along the lines of their ideal Jerusalem.[28] Even before 31 the toilet in L51 could not have served the needs of the entire community. Therefore most of the members (before 31) must have relieved themselves outside the settlement (and after 31 all members did), in built facilities and in the manner described by Josephus.[29]

The silence of ancient Roman sources concerning the placement and construction of domestic latrines reflects a lack of regulation or concern, in contrast to the Qumran community.[30] Josephus was struck by the fact that the Essenes secluded themselves when defecating outdoors, as opposed to the contemporary practice of openly relieving oneself. This corresponds with the *Temple Scroll*'s requirement that toilets be located within an enclosed, roofed structure, thereby ensuring privacy.[31] Similarly, Herodotus thought it odd that the Persians would not defecate in view of others; "To vomit or obey natural calls in the presence of another is forbidden among them" (*Hist.* 1.133).

The sectarian concern for toilet privacy reflected in the *Temple Scroll* and by Josephus's testimony was exceptional in the Roman world.[32] The *Temple Scroll* describes the type of toilet found at Qumran and undoubtedly in other permanent settlements, but it and the *War Scroll* added a distance regulation because of the state of purity required in the ideal holy city of Jerusalem or during the holy war at the end of days and to ensure that nothing indecent would be visible.[33]

Yigael Yadin noted that the distances mandated by the *Temple Scroll* and *War Scroll* placed the toilets beyond the Sabbath limits.[34] The prohibition against traveling beyond a set limit on the Sabbath is based on Exod 16:29:[35] "See! The Lord has given you the sabbath, therefore on the sixth day he gives you food for two days; each of you stay where you are; do not leave your place on the seventh day." Similarly, Josephus observed that the Essenes did not defecate on the Sabbath.[36] If this regulation was observed at Qumran, the inhabitants would have refrained from using the toilet in L51 on the Sabbath. Sectarian legislation does not specify penalties for defecating on the Sabbath, which, of course, cannot always be avoided. Presumably, in their view defecating on the Sabbath simply rendered the affected person impure, analogous to other types of bodily discharges.[37] On the other hand, the legislation in the *War Scroll* and *Temple Scroll* — which places the toilets beyond the Sabbath limits — is prescriptive and idealizing.

The sectarians differed from other Jews in regarding defecation as a polluting activity and therefore required immersion afterwards as Josephus describes.[38] I do not believe it is a coincidence that the only doorway in the room with the toilet at Qumran opens onto a miqveh (L48-49) (see Fig. 23). Another miqveh located by the entrance at the northwest side of the settlement (L138) might have been used by members who exited in that direction to relieve themselves, if we assume that toilets were located to the northwest of Qumran as mandated for Jerusalem in the *Temple Scroll* (see Fig. 24).[39]

Defecation and Excrement in Rabbinic Judaism

In contrast to the sectarian view, rabbinic Judaism does not associate excrement and defecation with impurity:[40]

These do not become unclean and do not impart susceptibility to uncleanness: (1) sweat, (2) stinking pus, (3) excrement, (4) blood which exudes with them, and (5) liquid [which is excreted with a stillborn child] at the eighth month. (*m. Makš.* 6:7)

According to the Mishnah (*Kelim* 10:2), excrement can be used to seal a clay vessel. In the Palestinian Talmud Rabbi Yosé ruled that defecation is associated with purity instead of impurity because its evacuation leaves the body clean:[41]

And is excrement [a matter of ritual] impurity; is it not merely [rather a matter of] cleanliness [being considered filth]? (*y. Pesaḥ.* 7:12)

A similar view is expressed in the Babylonian Talmud:

R. Papa said: "If there be excrement in its place [*bmqwmh*, "in the anus"], he must not read the Shemaʿ." How shall we imagine this case? If to say that it is invisible, that is self-evident: if to say that it is unseen — surely "The Torah was not given to the ministering angels!" — This has but reference to a situation in which it is obvious when he sits and invisible when he stands. But what is the difference between this and one who has filth (*ṣw'h*, "excrement") on his body, for it has been stated: Where one who has filth on his body, or whose hands are in a privy. R. Huna permits the reading of the Shemaʿ and R. Hisda forbids it. — In its place filth is most execrable *(npyš zwhm')*, away from it, it is less so *(l' npyš zwhm')*. (*b. Yoma* 30a)

In other words, if excrement is visible in the anus when a person sits or squats, he is not allowed to recite the Shemaʿ. Here the rabbis note that the need to defecate distinguishes humans from angels. Elsewhere in the Babylonian Talmud Moses is said to have emptied his bowels in order to undergo an angelic transformation so that he could receive the Torah:

Moses went up in the cloud, and was covered by the cloud and was sanctified by the cloud in order that he might receive the Torah for Israel in sanctity. . . . R. Nathan says: the purpose of scripture was that he [= Moses] might be purged of all food and drink in his bowels so as to make him like the ministering angels. (*b. Yoma* 4a-b)

Although the rabbis did not associate excrement with impurity, like the Qumran sectarians they seem to have understood the passage from Deuteronomy as meaning that excrement is indecent and should be hidden from God's view.[42] A rabbinic ruling that cites Deut 23:15 makes explicit their rationale:

> "Since the Lord your God moves about in your camp [to protect you and to deliver your enemies to you, let your camp be holy; let Him not find anything unseemly among you and turn away from you] (Deut 23:15)." From there they deduced that a person [A] should not recite the Shema' adjacent to a soaking pool [e.g., of flax] and [B] should not enter a bathhouse or tannery with scrolls [of the Bible] or phylacteries in hand. (Sifre Deut 258)[43]

For this reason the rabbis prohibited reciting the Shema' in the vicinity of human and animal excrement, urine, and other sources of foul odors.[44] Effectively this means that the Shema' cannot be recited while one is defecating or in a toilet:

> They remove themselves only from human [excrement] and from canine [excrement], if they use it [the latter] for tanning hides. [If one had with him in his house a vessel for excrement or for urine [chamber pot], behold, he removes himself four 'amot from it and recites [the Shema']. (t. Ber. 2:16)

> One should not stand to pray [i.e., recite the Prayer] if he needs to relieve himself, as Scripture states, Prepare to meet your God, O Israel. (t. Ber. 2:17)

> One should not urinate where he prays until he has removed himself four 'amot [before urinating]. (t. Ber. 2:18)[45]

The Babylonian Talmud indicates that some rabbis took care to defecate in private, recalling sectarian practice and presumably in accordance with their understanding of Deuteronomy:[46]

> Our Rabbis taught: Who is a modest man? One who eases himself by night in the place where he eased himself by day [i.e., a long way off]. Is that so? Has not Rab Judah said in the name of Rab: A man should

always accustom himself [to consult nature] in the early morning and in the evening so that he may have no need to go a long distance? And again, in the daytime Raba used to go as far as a mile, but at night he said to his attendant, Clear me a spot in the street of the town, and so too R. Zera said to his attendant, See if there is anyone behind the Seminary as I wish to ease myself. — Do not read "in the place," but read, "in the same way as he eases himself by day." R. Ashi said, You may even retain the reading "place," the reference being to a private corner.

The [above] text [states:] "Rab Judah said in the name of Rab: A man should always accustom himself to consult nature morning and evening so that he may have no need to go a long distance." It has been taught similarly, Ben 'Azzai said: Go forth before dawn and after dark, so that you should not have to go far. (*b. Ber.* 62a)

One rabbinic injunction comes close to sectarian practice by mandating defecation in a pit in the event of a war, citing the same passage in Deuteronomy:

He who goes forth to fight in an optional war goes back and squats down [to defecate], digs a hole, and covers up [his excrement], since it says, *You shall dig a hole with it and turn back and cover up your excrement* (Deut 23:13). (*t. Meg.* 3:25)[47]

Excrement and Impurity

Although the rabbis understood Deuteronomy as meaning that excrement should be kept away from God's presence or view, they did not associate it with impurity.[48] On the other hand, the Mishnah's description of the toilet in the Jerusalem temple indicates that, like the Qumran sect, the priests considered excrement impure and therefore required immersion in a miqveh after defecation: "This governing principle applied in the temple: Whoever covers his feet [and defecates] requires immersion" (*m. Yoma* 3:2). Because the sect extended the priestly purity laws to its members, they viewed defecation as a polluting activity and required immersion afterwards.

A passage in Ezekiel suggests that the association of human excrement with impurity originated in priestly circles:

You shall eat it as a barley-cake, baking it in their sight on human dung (*běgellê ṣē'at hā'ādām*, lit., "dung that comes out of a man"). The Lord said, "Thus shall the people of Israel eat their bread, unclean, among the nations to which I will drive them." Then I said, "Ah Lord God! I have never defiled myself; from my youth up until now I have never eaten what died of itself or was torn by animals, nor has carrion flesh come into my mouth." Then he said to me, "*See, I will let you have cow's dung instead of human dung, on which you may prepare your bread.*" (Ezek 4:12-15)[49]

The rabbis did not consider human excrement to be defiling because there is no pentateuchal basis for such a view.[50] However, unlike the rabbis, the sectarians considered the Prophets as authoritative scripture for legal purposes.[51] Therefore they apparently understood Ezekiel 4 as a scriptural basis for the impurity of human excrement. There may also be a connection between Ezekiel and the sectarians' abstention from defecation on the Sabbath. Lutz Doering has noted that Ezekiel associates profanation of the Sabbath with pollution: "When the sanctification of the Sabbath consists, among others, of avoiding pollution, the Sabbath regulations become open for purity rules."[52] The influence of this view is evident in the book of *Jubilees* (50:8), which prohibits sexual intercourse on the Sabbath, apparently because of purity concerns.[53] Therefore, the Qumran sect probably refrained from defecating on the Sabbath because they considered it a polluting activity, which might also be the reason that sectarian law banned sexual relations on the Sabbath. The connections with legislation in Ezekiel and *Jubilees* suggest that these prohibitions may have originated in priestly circles.[54]

The sectarian association of excrement with impurity is expressed in other ways. For example, the *Damascus Document* prohibits ritual immersion in *mym ṣw'ym*, which is usually translated "dirty water" but likely refers to water containing excrement:

Concerning purification with water. No one should bathe in water which is dirty or which is less than the amount which covers a man. No one should purify a vessel in it. (CD 10:10-12)[55]

A few lines below this the *Damascus Document* forbids wearing clothes soiled with excrement on the Sabbath:

No one is to wear dirty clothes *(bgdym ṣw'ym)* . . . (CD 11:3)[56]

In contrast, rabbinic discussions about ritual immersion focus on the color and odor of the water but do not refer to *mym ṣw'ym*.[57] For example:

> Three *logs* of [drawn] water — and into them fell a *qartob* of wine — and lo, their color is the color of wine — and they fell into the immersion pool — they have not rendered it unfit. Three *logs* of water, lacking a *qartob* — and a *qartob* of milk fell into them, and lo, their color is the color of the water — and they fell into the immersion pool — they have not rendered it unfit. R. Yohanan b. Nuri says, "All follows the color *(hkwl hwlk 'ḥr hnr'h)*." (*m. Miqw.* 7:5)

> But he [a *zab*] should not cover himself with foul water *(bmym hr'ym)* or in water used for soaking [flax] *(bmy hmšrh)*, unless he has poured into it [some fresh] water. And how far should one distance himself from them [from foul water] and from excrement [before he may recite]? Four cubits. (*m. Ber.* 3:5)

This last piece of legislation is necessary because a *zab* recites the Shemaʿ while immersing.

Apparently it was not uncommon to drink water dirtied with manure *(my zblyn)*, although some rabbis originally prohibited it on festivals:

> They drink manure-water, palm-water, and a cup of root-water on the festival. For at first they would rule, They do not drink manure-water, palm-water, and a cup of root-water on a festival, until R. ʿAqiba came and taught that they drink manure-water, palm-water, and a cup of root-water on the festival. (*t. Moʿed* 2:10)

Traditions in relatively late rabbinic sources indicate that some rabbis condoned wearing clothing soiled with excrement as part of an ascetic lifestyle, a view that Joshua Schwartz suggests might reflect the influence of Christian monastic habits:

> If one wastes away over the words of the Torah, eats dried-out dates and wears soiled clothing and sits faithfully at the door of the Sages, every passerby says, "Probably that's a fool!" But in the end thou wilt find the whole Torah at his command. (*'Abot R. Nat.* A, 11)[58]

An episode described in the Gospels might provide evidence for Jesus' position on the impurity of excrement, and perhaps suggests that this was a matter of debate among different Jewish groups and sects. Mark 7:1-23 records a dispute between Jesus and the scribes and Pharisees over the need to wash the hands before eating, to which Jesus responds: "There is nothing outside a person that by going in can defile, but the things that come out are what defile" (Mark 7:15).[59] The parallel passage in Matthew (15:11) reads: "It is not what goes into the mouth that defiles a person, but it is what comes out of the mouth that defiles." Notice that Matthew has clarified the Markan statement by adding that it is what goes in and out *of the mouth* that does or does not defile.

In the following passage in Mark, Jesus reiterates his position:

> When he had left the crowd and entered the house, his disciples asked him about the parable. He said to them, "Then do you also fail to understand? Do you not see that whatever goes into a person from outside cannot defile, since it enters, not the heart, but the stomach, and goes out into the sewer?" (Thus he declared all foods clean.) And he said, "It is what comes out from a person that defiles. For it is from within, from the human heart, that evil intentions come; fornication, theft, murder, adultery, avarice, wickedness, deceit, licentiousness, envy, slander, pride, folly. All these evil things come from within, and they defile a person." (Mark 7:17-23)

These passages might suggest that, unlike the Qumran sectarians, Jesus did not consider excrement (that is, what passes through the stomach and into the sewer) to be impure.[60]

The Temple Toilet

A passage in the Mishnah sheds light on why the *Temple Scroll* mandates the placement of the toilets to the northwest of Jerusalem. The miqveh associated with the toilet used by the priests in the temple was located in the Chamber of Immersion. The toilet and immersion facilities were located in underground rooms beneath the northwest side of the temple courtyard: "Through that [room in the Beit Hamoked, the Chamber of the Hearth] on the northwestern side do they go down to the room for immersion" (*m. Mid.* 1:6). The *Temple Scroll* mandates the placement of toilets in the ideal city of Jerusalem to the northwest of the city because in the second temple the toilet facilities were located on the northwest side.[61]

The Mishnah's description of the temple facilities highlights the toilet's privacy:

> [If] one of them should have a nocturnal emission of semen, he goes out, proceeding along the passage that leads below the building — and lamps flicker on this side and on that — and he reaches the immersion room, and there was a fire there, and a privy *(byt kys' šl kbwd)* in good taste. And this was its good taste: [if] he found it locked, he knows that someone is there; [if he found it] open, he knows that no one is there. He went down and immersed and came up and dried off, and warmed himself by the fire. (*m. Tamid* 1:1)

In other words, the room containing the toilet used by the priests serving in the Jerusalem temple had a door that could be closed or locked to ensure privacy. Similarly, a concern for toilet privacy explains the placement of the toilet at Qumran in a room at the eastern edge of the settlement and at the extreme western end of the room. Not only was this toilet located in a roofed house like the toilets mandated by the *Temple Scroll*, but it would not have been visible to passersby. In fact, the only way to view the toilet from outside L51 would be from the eastern wall of L52, a spot that no one was likely to pass by casually (see Fig. 24).[62] Furthermore, de Vaux's discovery of a wooden beam and many nails by the threshold indicates that the doorway in L51 was originally closed by a door.[63]

Magen Broshi has suggested that the Mishnah's detailed description of the toilet in the Jerusalem temple (*m. Mid.* 1:1) is a polemical response to an attempted ban of toilets from Jerusalem (as represented in the *Temple Scroll's* legislation).[64] In addition, whereas the sectarians used the Deuteronomic term "hand" or "place of the hand" to denote a toilet, in rabbinic literature toilets are described by the term "house of the seat," following *m. Middot's* description of the temple's toilet *(byt kys' šl kbwd)*.[65]

The placement of the doorway on the south side of L51 at Qumran might reflect a custom that was also observed outside sectarian circles, as suggested by a passage in the Babylonian Talmud:

> Our Rabbis taught: One who defecates *(hnpnh)* in Judea should not do so east and west but north and south. In Galilee he should do so only east and west." (*b. Ber.* 61b; modified from the Soncino translation, which reads "One who consults nature . . .")[66]

To conclude, the Qumran sect differed from other Jews in considering excrement impure and defecation to be a ritually polluting activity. Because of these unique purity concerns — and because they lived according to the biblical laws governing the desert camp — the sectarians were distinguished in their toilet practices from the rest of the population. Nevertheless, the Deuteronomic injunction to hide excrement from God's view also influenced the legal rulings and toilet habits of some rabbis.

CHAPTER 11

Tombs and Burial Customs

Ancient Jewish tombs and burial customs have been much in the news, thanks to recent reports of two sensational archaeological discoveries. In November 2002 the media broke a story about a small stone box called an ossuary (the "James ossuary") inscribed in Aramaic with the name "James son of Joseph brother of Jesus."[1] In March 2007, a Discovery Channel program and related book claimed that the tomb of Jesus and his family had been discovered in southern Jerusalem's Talpiyot (or Talpiot) neighborhood.[2] To understand the burials of Jesus and James, it is necessary first to consider the evidence for ancient Jewish tombs and burial customs in Jerusalem.

Scholarly and public attention has focused almost exclusively on the rock-cut tombs that surrounded the ancient city of Jerusalem in the late First Temple period (eighth century to 586 B.C.E.) and the late Second Temple period (first century B.C.E. to 70 C.E.). The following features characterize these tombs:

1. The rock-cut tombs are artificially hewn, underground caves cut into the bedrock slopes around Jerusalem.
2. With few exceptions, the tombs were located outside the walls of the city.
3. Each tomb was used by a family over the course of several generations, as described by the biblical expression "he slept and was gathered to his fathers" (e.g., Judg 2:10; 2 Chr 34:28).
4. When a member of the family died, the body was wrapped in a shroud and sometimes placed in a coffin and was then laid in the

tomb as an individual inhumation, even if the bones were later collected and placed elsewhere.

5. Because of the expense associated with hewing a burial cave into bedrock, only the wealthier members of Jerusalem's population — the upper classes — could afford rock-cut tombs. The lower classes apparently disposed of their dead in a manner that has left fewer traces in the archaeological record, for example, in individual trench graves or cist graves dug into the ground.

6. From the earliest periods, the layout and decoration of Jerusalem's rock-cut tombs exhibited foreign cultural influences and fashions. Evidence for such influence — and indeed, for the use of rock-cut tombs — is attested only in times when Jerusalem's Jewish elite enjoyed an autonomous or semi-autonomous status, that is, in the late First Temple period and the late Second Temple period. During these periods the Jerusalem elite adopted foreign fashions that were introduced by the rulers or governing authorities.[3]

Rock-Cut Tombs in Jerusalem: The Late First Temple Period

Rock-cut tombs of the late First Temple period have been discovered to the west, north, and east of the Old City. They include the tombs at Ketef Hinnom, the caves at St. Étienne (the École Biblique), and the caves in the Silwan (Siloam) village.[4] These tombs typically consist of one or more burial chambers that were entered through a small, unadorned opening cut into the bedrock. Each burial chamber is lined with rock-cut benches around three sides, on which the bodies of the deceased were laid (see Fig. 42). Frequently a pit hewn under one of the benches was used as a repository for the bones of earlier burials. In this way, space was made for new interments when the benches were occupied. An undisturbed repository in the Ketef Hinnom cemetery contained large numbers of skeletons as well as accompanying burial gifts, including ceramic vases and oil lamps, jewelry, seals, a rare early coin, and two silver amulets.[5] Many of the decorative elements in these burial caves, such as the benches with carved headrests and parapets and the cornices carved around the top of the burial chambers (as, e.g., at St. Étienne) reflect Phoenician influence (or Egyptian styles transmitted directly from Egypt or through Phoenician intermediaries).[6] Phoenician influence on the tombs of Jerusalem's elite in the First Temple period is hardly surprising in light of the biblical accounts of Phoenician involve-

ment in the construction of Solomon's temple, as well as later contacts between the Israelites and their neighbors to the north.[7]

Rock-Cut Tombs in Jerusalem: The Late Second Temple Period

After the destruction of Jerusalem and Solomon's temple in 586 B.C.E.,
rock-cut tombs reappeared only in the Hasmonean period, when Jerusalem again came under Jewish rule. Although the Maccabees were re-
nowned for their opposition to the introduction of Hellenistic culture to
Judea, the Hasmonean rulers show signs of Hellenization soon after the establishment of their kingdom. This is perhaps best illustrated by the monumental family tomb and victory memorial built by Simon in their hometown of Modiin, in which he interred the remains of his parents and
brothers. Although no remains of this tomb survive, our literary sources
leave little doubt that it was inspired by the tomb of Mausolus of Caria —
the so-called Mausoleum at Halicarnassus — which was one of the seven
wonders of the ancient world:[8]

> And Simon built a monument over the tomb of his father and his
> brothers; he made it high so that it might be seen, with polished stone
> at the front and back. He also erected seven pyramids, opposite one
> another, for his father and mother and four brothers. For the pyramids
> he devised an elaborate setting, erecting about them great columns,
> and on the columns he put suits of armor for a permanent memorial,
> and beside the suits of armor he carved ships, so that they could be
> seen by all who sail the sea. This is the tomb that he built in Modein; it
> remains to this day. (1 Macc 13:27-30)

> However, Simon sent some to the city Basca to bring away his brother's
> bones, and buried them in their own city Modin; and all the people
> made great lamentation over him. Simon also erected a very large
> monument for his father and his brethren, of white and polished
> stone, and raised it to a great height, and so as to be seen a long way off,
> and made cloisters about it, and set up pillars, which were of one stone
> apiece; a work it was wonderful to see. Moreover, he built seven pyra-
> mids also for his parents and his brethren, one for each of them, which
> were made very surprising, both for their largeness and beauty, and
> which have been preserved to this day. (Josephus, *Ant.* 13.210-11)[9]

Like the Mausoleum, the tomb of the Maccabees consisted of a tall podium with a templelike building surrounded by columns and capped by a pyramidal roof (actually seven pyramids, one for each family member). As Andrea Berlin notes, none of these features is found in earlier Jewish or Phoenician tombs in Palestine.[10] Pyramidal, conical, or columnar tomb markers became popular among Jerusalem's elite in the first century B.C.E. and first century C.E. (as well as among neighboring peoples such as the Nabateans). Jews referred to this type of tomb marker as a *nefesh* ("soul").[11]

It is not surprising that the Hasmoneans adopted elements of Hellenistic culture to display their status.[12] By the first half of the second century B.C.E., Jerusalem's elite, including the high priests, were predisposed to embrace Hellenistic culture. These elite families (most prominently, the Tobiads, Simonites, and Oniads) had allied themselves alternately with the Ptolemies, the Seleucids, and/or the Romans.[13] In 175 B.C.E., while the high priest Onias III was in Antioch, his brother Jason seized the high priesthood for himself. Jason requested (and received) Antiochus IV's permission to refound Jerusalem as a Greek polis and established a gymnasium for the education of the city's Jewish youth:

> When Seleucus died and Antiochus, who was called Epiphanes, succeeded to the kingdom, Jason the brother of Onias obtained the high priesthood by corruption, promising the king at an interview three hundred sixty talents of silver, and from another source of revenue eighty talents. In addition to this he promised to pay one hundred fifty more if permission were given to establish by his authority a gymnasium and a body of youth for it, and to enroll the people of Jerusalem as citizens of Antioch. When the king assented and Jason came to office, he at once shifted his compatriots over to the Greek way of life. (2 Macc 4:7-10)

Commenting on this episode, Martin Hengel noted, "The initiative here clearly came from the Hellenists in Jerusalem, who presumably had the majority of the priests and lay nobility, who in practice held all power in their hands, on their side."[14] 2 Maccabees describes how the high priests hurried to finish their sacrifices so they could watch the games:

> He [Jason] took delight in establishing a gymnasium right under the citadel, and he introduced the noblest of the young men to wear the Greek hat. There was such an extreme of Hellenization and increase in

the adoption of foreign ways because of the surpassing wickedness of Jason, who was ungodly and no high true priest, that the priests were no longer intent upon their service at the altar. (2 Macc. 4:12-14)

Berlin attributes the adoption of Hellenistic material culture by Simon to the fact that Jonathan, his brother and predecessor, established himself as a dynast who was involved in international politics. Upon Jonathan's death, Simon transformed the "unpretentious family tomb into a dynastic monument fit for a king," modeled after the monuments of the Hellenistic East.[15] Beginning with John Hyrcanus I, Simon's successors adopted Greek names.[16]

Jason's Tomb demonstrates that the Jerusalem elite soon imitated the new tomb style introduced by Simon, which itself was inspired by the Mausoleum at Halicarnassus. Berlin describes Jason's Tomb as "the earliest surviving 'display tomb' in Jerusalem."[17] This Hasmonean-period tomb is located in the western Jerusalem neighborhood of Rehavia (see Fig. 43).[18] The modern name derives from a graffito incised on one of the walls which asks the visitor to lament the death of Jason.[19] Jason's Tomb continues the earlier tradition of rock-cut burial caves in Jerusalem but with several innovations.[20] A large stone pyramid was constructed above the tomb. The tomb was approached through a series of long, open courtyards (like a dromos) which gave access to a porch. The porch's entablature was supported by a single Doric column in-antis (that is, a Doric column set between the thickened, projecting ends of the porch walls).[21] The porch gave access to two rooms: a burial chamber (A) and a charnel room (B). Instead of having rock-cut benches as in First Temple–period tombs, loculi *(kwkym, kokhim)* were cut into the walls of the burial chamber in Jason's Tomb (see Fig. 44; Akeldama tombs). Each loculus was designed to hold an individual inhumation. Like the pyramidal marker and the porch with a column, loculi reflect Hellenistic influence. Loculi are common in tombs in Hellenistic Alexandria and make their first recorded appearance in Palestine at Marisa in Idumaea.[22] Instead of depositing the remains of earlier burials in a pit or repository, as in First Temple–period tombs, the bones cleared out of the loculi in Jason's Tomb were placed in the charnel room.[23]

Elements of continuity and change in the tradition of Jerusalem's rock-cut tombs can be discerned in Jason's Tomb. On the one hand, the Jerusalem elite revived the ancient tradition of interring their dead in rock-cut family tombs consisting of one or more burial chambers that were used over the course of several generations. Furthermore, the custom of making space for new burials by depositing the earlier remains elsewhere in the tomb continued. On the other hand, new elements reflecting foreign influence and fashions were introduced. These elements included using loculi instead of benches to accommodate the bodies inside the burial chamber(s) and decorating the tomb's exterior, sometimes with a Greek-style porch and a pyramid or other monument marking the site of the tomb.

The features that appeared in Jason's Tomb remained characteristic of Jewish rock-cut tombs in Jerusalem until the end of the Second Temple period. The differences between individual rock-cut tombs of the late Second Temple period in Jerusalem mostly concern their size and degree of elaboration; that is, the number of burial chambers, the presence or absence of a porch (with or without columns), the addition of decoration (typically around the main entrance to the burial chambers and/or on the porch façade), and the presence or absence of one or more monumental tomb markers. Herod's tomb and memorial to himself — the mountain of Herodium — displays the same features but on a much larger scale: a tomb structure containing a burial chamber and a monumental conical marker.[24]

Rock-cut tombs surround Jerusalem on the north, east, and south (see Fig. 47). Well-known examples include the tomb of Bene Ḥezir in the Kidron Valley, the tomb of Queen Helena of Adiabene (the so-called Tomb of the Kings) near the American Colony Hotel, the Sanhedria tombs, and Nicanor's tomb on Mount Scopus.[25] Pausanias singles out the tomb of Queen Helena together with the Mausoleum at Halicarnassus for special mention:

> I know of many wonderful graves, and will mention two of them, the one at Halicarnassus and one in the land of the Hebrews. The one at Halicarnassus was made for Mausolus, king of the city, and it is of such vast size, and so notable for all its ornament, that the Romans in their great admiration of it call remarkable tombs in their country "Mausolea." The Hebrews have a grave *(taphos)*, that of Helen, a native woman, in the city of Jerusalem, which the Roman Emperor razed to the ground. (*Descr.* 8.16:4-5)

However, most of Jerusalem's rock-cut tombs are not display tombs but are relatively modest, with an undecorated entrance and a single burial chamber with loculi.[26]

Why Ossuaries?

In the middle of Herod's reign, around 20-15 B.C.E., ossuaries first appeared in Jerusalem's rock-cut tombs.[27] There is no doubt that ossuaries were used as containers for bones removed from loculi. The question is why ossuaries were introduced at this time and why they disappear from Jerusalem after 70 C.E. (with evidence of their use on a smaller and more modest scale in southern Judea and Galilee until the third century).[28] Most of these small rectangular containers are made of stone quarried in the Jerusalem area, usually soft chalk and less frequently harder limestone (see Figs. 45-46).[29] They have flat, rounded, or gabled lids. The ossuaries can be plain or decorated (usually with incised or chip-carved designs, rarely in relief, and sometimes with painting).[30] Sometimes the name(s) of the deceased (and infrequently other information such as their title or occupation) were incised on the front, back, side, or lid of the ossuary.[31] Most of the inscriptions are in Aramaic, Hebrew, or Greek (less frequently, in more than one language), and usually they are crudely executed, having been added inside the tomb by family members involved in collecting the remains.[32]

There is no correlation between the relative wealth and status of the deceased and the ornamentation of the ossuary, since plain and uninscribed ossuaries have been found in tombs belonging to some of ancient Jerusalem's most prominent families.[33] The same is true of the tombs themselves, as indicated by the modest size and appearance of the tomb of the Caiaphas family.[34] Interestingly, some of the largest and most lavishly-decorated tombs belonged to émigré families living in Jerusalem: the tomb of Queen Helena of Adiabene (which according to Josephus was crowned by three pyramidal markers [*Ant.* 10.95]),[35] Nicanor's tomb (which contains more burial chambers than any other Jerusalem tomb),[36] and Caves 2 and 3 of the Akeldama tombs (which are unique in the quality and quantity of decoration inside the burial chambers).[37] Perhaps these families constructed especially large and lavish tombs to establish their standing among the local elite.

Levy Yitzhak Rahmani connected the appearance of ossuaries with the Pharisaic belief in the individual, physical resurrection of the dead.[38] Prior to the introduction of ossuaries, the remains of earlier burials in rock-cut tombs were collected in pits, repositories, or charnel rooms. The skeletons were therefore mingled and susceptible to separation, breakage, and even loss. This means that in the event of a physical resurrection, an individual would be restored to life missing vital body parts. In addition,

Rahmani argues that the collection of bones in an ossuary corresponds with the Pharisaic notion that the decay of the flesh is connected with the expiation of sin.[39] In other words, each individual's remains were preserved intact in an ossuary, in a sinless state, awaiting future resurrection.

Many scholars have pointed to difficulties with Rahmani's explanation.[40] For example, ossuaries frequently contain the bones of more than one individual, and sometimes parts of the skeleton are missing.[41] In fact, the rabbis ruled that it was not necessary to collect all of the bones:

> Is there a lower limit to the number of bones? Nichomachi taught before R. Zeira, "There is no lower limit [to the number of bones that must be collected in a case of] the gathering of bones [for secondary burial, so that even if only a few bones have been collected, the rites of mourning are invoked]." (*y. Mo'ed Qaṭ.* 1:5)

Furthermore, even in tombs with ossuaries some skeletons were still deposited in pits or repositories.[42] In my opinion, the greatest difficulty with Rahmani's explanation is that our sources associate the belief in individual, physical resurrection of the dead with the Pharisees (see, e.g., Josephus, *Ant.* 18.12). These same sources tell us that the Sadducees rejected this concept (*Ant.* 18.16; Matt 22:23). But there is no doubt that monumental rock-cut tombs with ossuaries belonged to Jerusalem's elite, many of whom were Sadducees.[43] In fact, some of these tombs and ossuaries belonged to high priestly families, such as the tomb of Bene Ḥezir and the tomb and ossuaries of the Caiaphas family.[44] In other words, ossuaries were used by the same members of Jerusalem society who reportedly rejected the concept of individual, physical resurrection of the dead.[45] Of course, not all of these tombs and ossuaries were used by Sadducees, but undoubtedly many were.[46] It is not a coincidence that outside of Jerusalem, the largest cemetery with rock-cut loculus tombs containing ossuaries is at Jericho, which was the site of the Hasmonean and Herodian winter palaces and the center of a priestly community.[47] Rahmani argues that the Pharisaic belief in individual, physical resurrection was adopted by the Sadducees by the first century C.E.[48] But our sources — Josephus and the New Testament — date to this period, and in fact were composed in the late first century. Why assume that they are anachronistic in this regard?

Instead, I prefer a suggestion made by Lee Levine and Gideon Foerster, who have each attributed the appearance of ossuaries to Roman influence on the Jerusalem elite.[49] In the late first century B.C.E. and first century C.E. cremation was the prevailing burial rite among the Romans.[50] The ashes of the deceased were placed in small stone containers called *cineraria* (cinerary urns), which are usually casket-shaped and have gabled lids (see Fig. 48). Sometimes they have carved decoration and/or inscriptions.[51] Although they are not uncommon, Roman cinerary urns are not well-studied. They are rarely displayed or illustrated; only a handful can be seen in larger museums such as the Metropolitan Museum of Art or the Boston Museum of Fine Arts, and these examples tend to be exceptional in terms of their decoration.[52]

Cinerary urns were in widespread use around the Roman world, including Rhodes, Asia Minor, and North Africa. Stone cinerary urns still containing cremated remains are displayed in the Archaeological Museum in Afyon in western-central Anatolia.[53] Aside from the fact that they contain cremations, the Afyon urns are virtually identical to the plain Jerusalem ossuaries: the same size, shape, and with the same kind of lids. Small stone containers or chests *(ostothecai)* used for the secondary collection of bones are also found in Asia Minor.[54] Like their Judean counterparts, these stone boxes can have carved decoration and sometimes contain the remains of more than one individual.[55] Closer to Judea, the Nabatean cemetery at Mampsis in the Negev yielded an ossuary containing bones wrapped in linen.[56] This evidence suggests that the appearance of ossuaries in Judea is related to funerary customs and fashions that were prevalent in the Roman world instead of to Jewish expectations of resurrection. Finally, the frequent use of the Hebrew or Aramaic term *gluskoma* (from the Greek *glōssokomon*, meaning "casket") to refer to Judean ossuaries and the occurrence on one ossuary of the word *kayka* (written in Palmyrene script and meaning "amphora" in the sense of a funerary urn) provide another indication that Roman cinerary urns were the source of inspiration.[57]

Rahmani has objected to Levine's and Foerster's proposal on the grounds that Jerusalem's elite could not have imitated a practice with which they were unacquainted.[58] However, we have seen that other Hellenized features in tombs and burial customs were adopted by Jerusalem's elite without personal contact or familiarity (as were other aspects of Hellenistic and Roman culture). Monumental tombs marked by a pyramid became a raging fashion after Simon constructed the family tomb at Modiin.[59] The ultimate source of inspiration for these tombs was the Mausoleum at Halicarnassus, which presumably none of Jerusalem's elite in the Hasmonean period — not even Simon — ever saw. Loculi, which also originated in the Hellenistic world, quickly became universal in Jerusalem's rock-cut tombs.[60] The spread of these features has little or nothing to do with religious beliefs in the afterlife and everything to do with social status. Jerusalem's elite were prohibited by Jewish law from cremating their dead. Instead, they could and did adopt the external trappings of cremation by depositing the bones of the deceased in ossuaries (urns).[61] Like loculi, once ossuaries appeared, they quickly became universal in rock-cut tombs.

The practice of recording name(s) on ossuaries should be understood as reflecting a concern for recording and preserving the memory of the deceased.[62] The preservation of the names of ancestors was of great importance to the upper classes and priestly families, and above all the high priestly families, who based their social standing and claims of legitimacy on their lineage.[63] An ossuary bearing the Hebrew inscription "house of David" illustrates this concern nicely.[64]

The disappearance of ossuaries supports the suggestion that they were inspired by Roman cinerary urns. If the use of ossuaries was connected with the concept of the individual, physical resurrection of the dead, they should have become even more popular after 70 C.E., when this belief became normative in Judaism. In fact, the opposite is true.[65] After 70, ossuaries disappeared from Jerusalem because the Jewish elite who used the rock-cut tombs were now dead or dispersed. The appearance of crude ossuaries in Galilee and southern Judea probably is connected with the emigration or displacement of members of Jerusalem's elite to these regions after the First Revolt.[66] By the mid-to-late third century the custom of ossilegium died out.[67] At the largest and most prestigious cemetery of this period — Beth She'arim in Lower Galilee — the prevailing burial rite consists of individual inhumations in large stone sarcophagi or hewn troughs in rock-cut tombs.[68] Most of the sarcophagi are crude local products made of limestone, with a few Roman imports of marble.[69] Many of the burial caves at Beth She'arim belonged to individual families, but there are also catacombs containing burials of different elite families.[70] The burial customs at Beth She'arim parallel contemporary developments in Rome and the provinces during the second and third centuries, when inhumation in large stone sarcophagi in catacombs supplanted cremation as the preferred burial rite.[71]

The production of ossuaries (and other stone vessels) was one component of Jerusalem's economy during the late Second Temple period.[72] It is not a coincidence that ossuaries first appeared during Herod's reign.

This period is characterized by a heavy dose of Hellenistic-Roman influence on other aspects of the lifestyle of Jerusalem's elite, with a wide range of imported and locally-produced consumer goods appearing around 20-10 B.C.E. Their mansions were decorated with Roman-style wall paintings, stucco, and mosaics and were furnished with locally-produced stone tables modeled after Roman prototypes.[73] As in the case of the tombs, these fashions were introduced to Judea by the ruler (in this case, Herod) and were imitated or adopted by the Jerusalem elite.

The heavy dose of Roman cultural influence evident in Jerusalem around 20-10 B.C.E. should be understood within the context of contemporary events. It was during these years that Herod undertook the reconstruction of the Jerusalem temple.[74] He established a theater and an amphitheater (or hippodrome) in Jerusalem in which athletic competitions, chariot races, and musical and dramatic contests were held.[75] Herod also maintained close contacts with Augustus. Peter Richardson notes that "Herod developed his friendship with Augustus through his children's education."[76] In 22 B.C.E., Herod sent his sons Alexander and Aristobulus (by his Hasmonean wife Mariamme) to Rome to be educated. Alexander and Aristobulus remained in Rome for five years, staying first with Pollio and then with Augustus.[77] A couple of years later (20 B.C.E.), Augustus traveled to Syria, where he was hosted by Herod.[78] In 17 B.C.E., Herod traveled to Rome to visit Augustus, returning to Judea with his sons who were now young men about nineteen and eighteen years of age.[79] Two years later, Herod entertained Augustus's son-in-law and heir apparent Marcus Agrippa, taking him on a tour of his kingdom.[80] The appearance of ossuaries and other Romanized elements in Jerusalem is a result of the close contacts and interactions between Augustus and his family, on the one hand, and Herod and his family, on the other. It is not surprising that beginning around 20 B.C.E., the lifestyle — and deathstyle — of Jerusalem's elite was heavily influenced by Roman culture.

Tombs and Burial Customs of the Lower Classes and the Qumran Community

Most archaeologists take it for granted that a large proportion of the dead of many ancient societies will have received "invisible" disposal . . . the serious effects of archaeologically invisible disposal are now widely recognized.[81]

In the late Second Temple period the upper classes of Jerusalem and Jericho buried their dead in rock-cut family tombs that were used over the course of several generations. When a family member died the body was wrapped in a shroud and placed in a loculus. When the loculi became filled, space was made for new burials by clearing out the earlier remains and placing them in a pit or on the floor of the tomb. In the middle of Herod's reign small bone boxes called ossuaries were introduced into rock-cut tombs as containers for the remains cleared out of loculi. Because even modest rock-cut tombs were costly, only the more affluent members of Jewish society could afford them.[82]

The association of rock-cut tombs with the upper classes is indicated by several factors. First, rock-cut tombs are concentrated in areas of elite presence, primarily around Jerusalem and Jericho, with scattered examples elsewhere.[83] Second, rock-cut tombs are attested in Jerusalem only in the late First Temple period and late Second Temple period — that is, only when there was an autonomous Jewish elite in the city.[84] The flourishing of the necropolis at Beth She'arim is connected with the displacement and relocation of the Judean elite to Lower Galilee after 70.[85]

The fact that rock-cut tombs accommodated only a small proportion of the population can be demonstrated on the basis of numbers and distribution. Approximately 900 rock-cut tombs of the late first century B.C.E. to the first century C.E. are known from Jerusalem.[86] Eyal Regev has calculated that no more than five to seven people per generation were buried in most of these tombs.[87] If we take the maximum possible estimate (three generations of seven people each buried in all of these tombs), the number of burials (over the course of a century) would total 18,900.[88] During this period Jerusalem's population at any given time was at least 60,000, and perhaps much larger.[89] Even if we double, triple, or quadruple the number of rock-cut tombs, they would still fall far short of accommodating the majority of Jerusalem's population.[90] The concentration of rock-cut tombs around Jerusalem (with smaller numbers in Jericho and scattered examples elsewhere) reflects the concentration of wealth and attests to their connection with the Jerusalem elite. If rock-cut tombs were used also by members of the lower classes (as some scholars claim), they should be widespread throughout Judea and Galilee and not limited mainly to Jerusalem in the late First Temple and late Second Temple periods.[91] The association of rock-cut tombs and ossuaries with the elite is borne out by inscriptions, some of which bear the names of these affluent families and some of which denote the deceased's profession. Jonathan Price has noted that no ossuary inscriptions refer to the deceased having lower-class or lower-middle-class occupations such as bakers or fullers.[92]

The following observation by Ian Morris about ancient Athenian burials is equally relevant to those of late Second Temple–period Palestine, where archaeologists have focused on rock-cut tombs to the exclusion of other burial types because of their visibility in the landscape: "If graves of one period are easier to identify because of surface indications or are more desirable because of their grave goods, they may tend to be over-represented in the archaeological record."[93] The numbers, chronology, and distribution of rock-cut tombs indicate that the majority of the ancient Jewish population must have been disposed of in a manner that left few traces in the archaeological landscape, as is true of other ancient societies in the Mediterranean world.[94] Many Jews apparently buried their dead in individual graves dug into the ground, analogous to the way we bury our dead today. In the Iron Age kingdoms of Israel and Judah, non-elite burials consisted of individual inhumations in simple pit or cist (stone-lined) graves.[95] The practice of burial in pit graves or trench graves continued through the Second Temple period.[96] The body of the deceased, wrapped in a shroud and sometimes placed in a wooden coffin, was laid in a pit or a trench dug into the ground. Sometimes the burial at the base of the trench was sealed off with stone slabs or mud bricks (as at Qumran and Khirbet Qazone), before the trench was filled in with dirt.[97] Often a headstone was erected to mark the site of the grave. The necropolis at Beth She'arim attests to a diversity of burial customs used by the Jewish population, which inside the catacombs included interment in arcosolia, loculi, or in stone, lead, terracotta, or wood sarcophagi, sometimes with secondary collection of bones in pits or ossuaries, and outside the catacombs included burials in trench graves, cist graves, shaft graves, and even a mausoleum.[98]

At Princeton Theological Seminary's Symposium on Afterlife and Burial Practices in Second Temple Judaism, held in Jerusalem on January 16-18, 2008, Amos Kloner claimed that trench graves and other field burials "consumed more area and resources than family tombs; i.e., it was *more expensive* [my emphasis] for families to use this type of burial than the hewn family tombs."[99] However, in a paper presented at the same conference, Shimon Gibson estimated that at least fifty days of work were required to hew a rock-cut tomb, which means that a family would have needed sufficient funds at its disposal to cover the costs. Kloner and Boaz Zissu note that rock-cut tombs were hewn by "experienced professionals" and acknowledge that digging a trench grave required less effort than hewing a loculus.[100] It is difficult to see how a pit grave or trench grave, which presumably could be dug by one or two unskilled individuals in less than a day, could be more expensive than even a small rock-cut tomb. Furthermore, availability of space would not have been a factor outside the city walls.

Because pit graves and trench graves are poor in finds and are much less conspicuous and more susceptible to destruction than rock-cut tombs, relatively few examples are recorded.[101] Remarking on the disposal of the dead in late Iron Age Judah, Alan Millard observes that "Tens of thousands of its citizens died during the almost 350 years of Judah's kingdom. Most of them were buried in shallow graves that have disappeared through erosion and later construction."[102] For ancient Rome (25 B.C.E. to 325 C.E.), John Bodel estimates that the known tombs and burials account for only 1.5 percent of the city's population: "We can only guess by what means and where the other 98.5 percent of the presumed numbers who died there were buried . . . simple surface burials (whether of cremations or inhumations) are perhaps the most likely to have left no trace in the archaeological record."[103] Qumran provides the best evidence for the use of trench graves in late Second Temple–period Judea, where the cemetery is preserved and visible because it is in the desert and was never built over, covered up, or plowed (see Figs. 28-29).[104] Other graves of this type have been found at 'Ein el-Ghuweir and in Jerusalem, where they have been identified as Essene burials.[105] Although it is possible that some or all of those buried in these cemeteries were Essenes, there is no archaeological evidence to support this assumption. Unlike at Qumran, the trench graves in Jerusalem and at 'Ein el-Ghuweir are not associated with identifiable remains of Essene settlements, and they contain proportionate numbers of men, women, and children.[106] In fact, the presence of thousands of trench graves in the first- and second-century C.E. Nabatean cemetery at Khirbet Qazone demonstrates that they are not associated exclusively with Essenes.[107] Some of the headstones at Khirbet Qazone are engraved with symbols of Nabatean deities.[108]

Rabbinic literature refers to burial in pit graves and trench graves without any indication that it was considered shameful or less proper than interment in rock-cut tombs. The Mishnah's tractate 'Ohalot and the Tosefta's tractate 'Ahilot repeatedly describe burials in soil that are pit graves or trench graves:[109]

A man who finds a corpse lying in usual fashion, in the first instance, removes it and the soil around it. [If] one found two, he removes them and their soil. [If] one found three, if there are four cubits between this and that one, and up to eight, about enough space for the bier and its bearers — lo, this is a graveyard. (*m. 'Ohal.* 16:3; see also *m. Naz.* 9:3)

He who ploughs up the grave — lo, he makes [the field into] a grave area. . . . R. Yose says, "[The entire rule of the grave area applies only] where the ground slopes downward, not where it slopes upward." (*m. 'Ohal.* 17:1)

Said R. Judah: One was ploughing and shook the plough and it came out that a [whole] skull of a corpse was cleaving to the plough, and they declared him unclean because he overshadowed the corpse. (*t. 'Ahil.* 15:13)

The following passages appear to distinguish between pit and trench graves and rock-cut tombs:

There are three kinds of grave areas: He who ploughs up the grave — it may be planted with any kind of tree, but it may not be sown with any kind of seed. (*m. 'Ohal.* 18:2)

A field of mourners/tomb niches (*śdh kwkym/bwkym*) — is not planted, and is not sown, but its dust is clean. And they make from it ovens for holy [use]. (*m. 'Ohal.* 18:4)

But that which is buried in its shroud, and in a wooden coffin, on dirt, and does not produce corpse-mould. And he that takes dirt from under it — that is, the dirt of graves — "a ladleful and a bit more." A mixture which is found in the grave and the character of which one does not know, lo, this is the dirt of graves — "a ladleful and a bit more." R. Eleazar b. R. Sadoq explained, "One sifts out the pebbles and the chips which are certain[ly not corpse-matter]. One takes that which is certain [to be corpse-matter] and leaves that which is in doubt. And this is the dirt of graves — 'a ladleful and more.'" (*t. 'Ahil.* 2:3-4)

Other passages refer to graves that are dug (not hewn), in which individuals had been laid in coffins:

[If] they made for him [a Gentile] a coffin and dug a grave for him (*'šw lw 'rwn whprw lw qbr*), an Israelite may be buried therein. But if this was done for an Israelite, he may not ever be buried therein. (*m. Šabb.* 23:4)

He who ploughs on top of the grave, and so he who ploughs on top of the coffin, even covered over with boards and with stones, and even [if he ploughs] on top of them by two heights [of a person], lo, this makes a grave-area. (*t. 'Ahil.* 17:1)

It is curious that although Qumran is literally ringed by caves, the sectarians did not utilize them for the interment of the dead.[110] Instead, they buried their dead in the manner of the lower classes. I believe this reflects the ascetic and communal nature of the sect and their rejection of the Hellenized/Romanized lifestyle (and deathstyle) of the Jerusalem elite.[111] Purity concerns also may have been a factor. Sectarian law expanded on Num 19:14 by mandating that everything inside a house where someone has died contracts corpse impurity, including the nails and pegs in walls and even the contents of sealed vessels (for those strict in purity observance):

This is the law when someone dies in a tent: everyone who comes into the tent, and everyone who is in the tent, shall be unclean seven days. (Num 19:14)

And when a man dies in your cities, every house in which a dead (man) died shall become unclean, seven days; everything which is in the house and every one who comes into the house shall become unclean, seven days. . . . And earthen vessels shall be unclean, and all that is in them shall be unclean for every clean man, and the open (vessels) shall be unclean for every man of Israel. (11QT 49:5)

And any vessel, nail, or peg in a wall which is with a corpse in a house shall become impure with the same impurity as the working implement. (CD 12:18)[112]

In the Masoretic Text, the passage that is the basis for this legislation (Num 19:14) has the word "tent" (*'hl*) instead of "house" (*byt*).[113] The rabbis understood "tent" to mean whatever is under the same roof, and hence their concern with overshadowing.[114] Sectarian legislation replaced the word "tent" with "house," that is, an enclosed space or building (a permanent structure).[115] Therefore, as Yadin observed, "a grave conveys 'the uncleanness of a house' like a dead person."[116] The sectarian understanding of Num 19:14 as referring to corpse impurity in an enclosed space explains why they considered a woman carrying a stillborn child in her womb as impure as a grave:

> And if a woman is pregnant, and her child dies in her womb, all the days on which it is dead inside her, she is unclean like a grave. (11QT 50:10-11)[117]

Furthermore, sectarian law considered even dirt and stones susceptible to impurity:

> And all the wood and the stones and the dust which are defiled by man's impurity, while with stains of oil in them, in accordance with their uncleanness will make whoever touches them impure. (CD 12:15-17)[118]

Therefore, according to sectarian law, anyone entering the closed space of a rock-cut tomb or burial cave would have contracted corpse impurity.[119] Even the rocks and dirt could have conveyed impurity, as oil often was applied to corpses in connection with the burial rites (see, e.g., Mark 14:8, 16:1; Matt 26:12; Luke 23:56, 24:1).[120] This might explain the Qumran community's decision to bury their dead in trench graves, which limited corpse impurity to individuals who came into direct contact with the corpse or the grave (see Num 19:18; 11QT 50:4-6). The fact that the more affluent inhabitants of Jerusalem and Jericho (among them Sadducees and Pharisees) used rock-cut tombs suggests that they may not have considered this type of enclosed space as equivalent to a corpse-impure house or tent.[121]

The sectarians required a corpse-contaminated person to immerse on the first, third, and seventh days after defilement, in contrast to Pharisaic and rabbinic halakhah, which requires immersion only on the seventh day, following Num 19:16-19.[122] Esther Eshel suggests that the sectarians followed a priestly law that might be described in Tob 2:4-5: "Then I sprang up, left the dinner before even tasting it, and removed the body from the square and laid it in one of the rooms until sunset when I might bury it. When I returned, I washed myself and ate my food in sorrow."[123] The discovery of miqva'ot by the entrances to the tomb of Queen Helena of Adiabene in Jerusalem and adjacent to a few other rock-cut tombs in Jerusalem and Jericho might reflect the practice of first-day immersion, as otherwise there is no reason to install a miqveh next to a tomb.[124] Perhaps the observance of this priestly law explains the placement of the largest miqveh at Qumran (L71), next to the gate that provided access to and from the direction of the cemetery.[125] On the other hand, Yonatan Adler suggests that miqva'ot adjacent to rock-cut tombs were used by people who had contracted second-degree corpse impurity by attending the funeral and coming into contact with those with first-degree corpse impurity.[126]

Whereas trench graves at other sites are marked only by a headstone, at Qumran the graves are covered by heaps of stones and have large stones marking both ends, as Roland de Vaux observed: "The tombs [graves] are marked by oval-shaped heaps of stones appearing on the surface, often with a larger stone at either end."[127] In my opinion, the heaps of stones covering the Qumran graves and the large stones set up at both ends were intended to make the graves visible to passersby, so they could be avoided due to purity concerns:[128]

> Whoever in the open field touches one who has been killed by a sword, or who has died naturally, or a human bone, or a grave, shall be unclean seven days. (Num 19:14)[129]

Marking the graves in a conspicuous manner was necessary because, according to sectarian legislation, even dust can transmit impurity:[130]

> And all the wood and the stones and the dust which are defiled by man's impurity, while with stains of oil in them, in accordance with their uncleanness will make whoever touches them impure. (CD 12:15-17)

The piles of stones covering the trench graves at Qumran therefore reflect the sectarians' concern with purity observance. A similar concern is echoed in one of Jesus' prophetic woes against the scribes and Pharisees: "Woe unto you, since you are like unmarked graves, and the people who walk over them do not know it" (Luke 11:44, attributed to Q).[131] This saying obviously refers to pit graves or trench graves, not rock-cut tombs, and it suggests that walking over these graves unawares was a common occurrence.[132] The Lukan version probably is closer to the original than Matthew's:[133] "Woe to you, scribes and Pharisees, hypocrites! For you are like whitewashed tombs, which on the outside look beautiful, but inside they are full of the bones of the dead and of all kinds of filth" (Matt 23:27). Matthew's reference to a beautiful, white-washed exterior denotes a rock-cut tomb. Whereas Luke's version refers to something that is unseen and conveys impurity, Matthew describes something that is beautiful on the outside but dirty and impure on the inside.

The *Temple Scroll* indicates that Jews buried their dead everywhere, even inside houses (a practice to which the author objected):

> And you shall not do as the nations do: everywhere they bury their dead, even within their houses they bury. For you shall set apart places within your land (in) which you shall bury your dead. (11QT 48:11-13)[134]

Bodel's description of the disposal of the dead in Rome mirrors the situation in Palestine:

> The *wealthy and moderately well-to-do* [my emphasis] at Rome had always possessed the means to purchase plots of land beyond city limits where family tombs could be erected. . . . But there had always existed at Rome a section of the population — how broad a section at any one time we cannot say — to whom the opportunity to purchase a grave site or be included in a communal tomb was denied because of impoverishment and a lack of ties to a patron. Not surprisingly, therefore, dead bodies — or parts of them — sometimes turned up in inconvenient places.[135]

In late Republican Rome, large pits called *puticoli* located outside the city walls contained thousands and sometimes tens of thousands of corpses belonging to commoners.[136] Public funerary pyres *(ustrinae)* adjoined the area where public executions took place.[137] The bodies of the poorest members of society, including executed criminals, were thrown into pits in potter's fields or were disposed of randomly.[138] Similarly, according to tradition Judas's blood money was used to pay for a potter's field in Jerusalem (Matt 27:5-8). The Mishnah indicates that even in Palestine the random disposal of bodies was not uncommon:

> A cistern into which they throw abortions or slain people — one gathers bone by bone, and all is clean. (*m. 'Ohal.* 16:5)

He who plows in a pit filled with bones, in a pile of bones, in a field in which a tomb was lost, or in which a tomb was [afterwards] found . . . (*m. 'Ohal.* 17:2)

Dogs gnawed on corpses left lying in the streets of Rome and dug up human remains buried in shallow pits, depositing body parts around the city, as reflected in Suetonius's *Life of Vespasian* (5:4): "Once when he was taking breakfast, a stray dog brought in a human hand from the crossroads and dropped it under the table."[139] The Mishnah indicates that similar conditions prevailed in Palestine:

A dog which ate the flesh of a corpse, and the dog died and was lying on the threshold . . . (*m. 'Ohal.* 11:7; see also *Sem.* 6:8)

These contaminate in the Tent: (1) the corpse, and (2) an olive's bulk [of flesh] from the corpse, and (3) an olive's bulk of corpse dregs, and (4) a ladleful of corpse mold; 5) the backbone, and the skull, and 6) *a limb from the corpse* . . . (*m. 'Ohal.* 2:1)[140]

The author of the polemical Qumran work 4QMMT objected to dogs scavenging sacrificial refuse in the Jerusalem temple:

And one should not let dogs enter the h[o]ly camp, because they might eat some of the [bo]nes from the temp[le with] the flesh on them. (4Q394, frag. 8 col. IV: 8-9)

Perhaps in addition to making the burials visible to passersby, the stones heaped on the trench graves at Qumran were intended to prevent dogs and other scavengers from digging up the remains.

The Burial of Jesus

We have no option to drawing on the evangelists: Their writings represent the best body of evidence we have for reconstructing the historical Jesus.[141]

This review of Jewish tombs and burial customs has provided the background for understanding the manner in which Jesus and his brother

James were buried. According to the Gospel accounts, Jesus expired and was removed from the cross on the eve of the Sabbath (Friday afternoon).[142] The Synoptic Gospels are in broad agreement in their description of this event:[143]

> Although it was now evening, yet since it was the Preparation Day, that is, the day before the Sabbath, Joseph of Arimathea, a highly respected member of the council, who was himself living in expectation of the reign of God, made bold to go to Pilate and ask for Jesus' body. . . . And he [Joseph] bought a linen sheet and took him down from the cross and wrapped him in the sheet, and laid him in a tomb that had been hewn out of the rock, and rolled a stone against the doorway of the tomb. (Mark 15:42-46)

> In the evening a rich man named Joseph of Arimathea, who had himself been a disciple of Jesus, came. He went to Pilate and asked him for Jesus' body. . . . Then Joseph took the body and wrapped it in a piece of clean linen, and laid it in a new tomb that belonged to him, that he had cut in the rock, and he rolled a great stone over the doorway of the tomb, and went away. (Matt 27:57-60)

Joseph of Arimathea seems to have been motivated by a concern for the observance of Jewish law. On the one hand, Deut 21:22-23 mandates burial within twenty-four hours of death, even for those guilty of the worst crimes, whose bodies were hanged after death.[144] On the other hand, Jewish law prohibits burial on the Sabbath and festivals. Because Jesus expired on the cross on the eve of the Sabbath, he had to be buried before sundown on Friday, because waiting until after sundown on Saturday would have exceeded the twenty-four-hour time limit. Since there was no time to prepare a grave, Joseph of Arimathea placed Jesus' body in his family's rock-cut tomb.

Martin Hengel argued that since crucifixion was a sadistic and humiliating form of corporal punishment reserved by the Romans for the lower classes (including slaves), Jesus "died a criminal's death on the tree of shame."[145] Hengel's claim that Jesus was buried in disgrace because he was an executed criminal who died a shameful death is widely accepted and has become entrenched in scholarly literature.[146] In my opinion, this view is based on a misunderstanding of archaeological evidence and Jewish law. Jesus was condemned by the Roman authorities for crimes against

Rome, not by the Sanhedrin for violating Jewish law. The Romans used crucifixion to punish rebellious provincials for incitement to rebellion and acts of treason, whom they considered common "bandits."[147] For this reason, the local (provincial) governor could impose the penalty of crucifixion to maintain peace and order.[148] Although victims of crucifixion could be left on their crosses for days, this was not usually the case.[149]

According to the Mishnah, those found guilty by the Sanhedrin of violating Jewish law were executed by stoning (like James), or were burned, decapitated, or strangled: "Four modes of execution were given in the court: stoning, burning, decapitation, and strangulation" (*m. Sanh.* 7:1).[150] Biblical law requires the body of an executed criminal to be hanged from a tree:

> When someone is convicted of a crime punishable by death and is executed, and you hang him on a tree, his corpse must not remain all night upon the tree; you shall bury him that same day, for anyone hung on a tree is under God's curse. (Deut 21:22-23)[151]

The rabbis (and perhaps Pharisees) understood this passage as referring to the hanging of a corpse after death for the purpose of public display.[152] The Mishnah describes this procedure as involving tying together the hands of the deceased and dangling the body from a pole: "How do they hang him? They drive a post into the ground, and a beam juts out from it, and they tie together his two hands, and thus do they hang him" (*m. Sanh.* 6:4).

In contrast, the Qumran sectarians interpreted Deut 21:22-23 as meaning that the person condemned should be put to death by being hanged alive from a tree.[153] The *Temple Scroll* makes this clear by twice reversing the biblical word order so that hanging precedes dying:

> If a man informs against his people, and delivers his people up to a foreign nation, and does harm to his people, you shall hang him on the tree, and he shall die. On the evidence of two witnesses and on the evidence of three witnesses he shall be put to death, and they shall hang him on the tree. And if a man has committed a crim[e] punishable by death, and has defected into the midst of the nations, and has cursed his people [and] the children of Israel, you shall hang him also on the tree, and he shall die. And their body shall not remain upon the tree all night, but you shall bury them the same day, for those hanged on the tree are accursed by God and men. (11QT 64:6-12)[154]

The author of the *Temple Scroll* elaborated on biblical law by making hanging while alive the punishment for treasonous acts.[155] There is evidence that some Pharisees/rabbis also considered hanging someone alive *(tlyh)* to be a legal form of execution, equating it with strangulation *(ḥnq)*.[156] A reference in the scholion to *Megillat Ta'anit* (iv:1 [75]) seems to indicate that the Sadducean "Book of Decrees" (apparently a penal code) prescribed hanging someone alive *(w'lw šnḥnqyn)* as the penalty for certain crimes.[157]

Some scholars believe that after Judea came under direct Roman rule, crucifixion was imposed only by the Roman authorities.[158] They argue that Jews would not have sanctioned impalement and crucifixion as legal forms of execution because they did not result in immediate death.[159] Other scholars note that some rabbinic sources designate hanging/strangulation [on a tree] by the term *ṣlybh* and argue that crucifixion is meant.[160] Beth Berkowitz cites a midrash from *Sifre Deuteronomy* that seems to equate hanging someone alive with crucifixion:

Is it possible that they hang him alive the way that the kingdom does? The Torah teaches: "[If a man is guilty of a capital offense] and is put to death, and you impale him on a stake . . ." (Deut 21:22)[161]

Whether crucifixion was ever employed as a legal mode of execution by Jews in Palestine before 70 C.E. depends largely on how one understands hanging and strangulation to have been carried out.[162]

Much attention has focused on an episode reported by Josephus in which the Hasmonean king Alexander Jannaeus had eight hundred Pharisee opponents crucified, dining with his concubines as his victims writhed in agony.[163] Jannaeus's actions are described as an atrocity in the *Pesher Nahum* from Qumran (4Q169 frags. 3-4), where crucifixion is described as hanging someone alive *(ḥyym):* "who *hanged living* men [from the tree, committing an atrocity which had not been committed] in Israel since ancient times, for it is [hor]rible for the one *hanged alive* from the tree."[164]

Roman crucifixion involved spreading apart the arms of a live victim, so that he/she could be affixed to the crossbeam by ropes or nails.[165] Josephus knew the difference between the hanging of a dead victim and Roman crucifixion. When referring to the former, he employs the verb *kremannumi* ("to hang"), as for example: "He that blasphemeth God let him be stoned, and let him hang *(kremasthō)* [upon a tree] all that day" (*Ant.* 4.202). In contrast, Josephus uses the verb *anastauroō* ("to crucify") when describing the crucifixion of live victims: "he [Alexander Jannaeus] ordered about eight hundred of them to be crucified *(anastaurōsai)*" (*Ant.* 13.380); "as I came back, I saw many captives crucified *(anestaurōmenous)*" (*Life* 75 [420]).[166]

Josephus indicates that Jews took care to bury victims of Roman crucifixion by sunset in accordance with Deut 21:22-23:

> Nay, they proceeded to that degree of impiety, as to cast away their bodies without burial, although the Jews used to take so much care of the burial of men, that they took down those that were condemned and crucified *(anestaurōmenous)*, and buried them before the going down of the sun. (*War* 4.317)[167]

Although crucifixion victims often were left unburied, the Roman authorities sometimes granted permission to bury them, as Justinian's *Digest* indicates:

> The bodies of those who suffer capital punishment are not to be refused to their relatives; and the deified Augustus writes in the tenth book of his *de Vita Sua* that he observed this [custom]. Today, however, the bodies of those who are executed are buried in the same manner as if this had been sought and granted. But sometimes it is not allowed, particularly [with the bodies] of those condemned for treason. The bodies of those condemned to be burned can also be sought so that the bones and ashes can be collected and handed over for burial. (48.24.1)[168]

> The bodies of executed persons are to be granted to any who seek them for burial. (48.24.3)[169]

Roman legislation is consistent with the Gospel accounts, according to which Joseph of Arimathea requested from Pilate permission to bury Jesus' body: "Joseph of Arimathea, a respected member of the council, who was also himself waiting expectantly for the kingdom of God, went boldly to Pilate and asked for the body of Jesus. . . . When he [Pilate] learned from the centurion that he was dead, he granted the body to Joseph" (Mark 15:43, 45).[170]

The discovery of the remains of a crucified man named Yoḥanan in an ossuary demonstrates that crucifixion victims could be interred in rock-cut family tombs.[171] John Dominic Crossan claims that Yoḥanan's interment in a rock-cut family tomb is exceptional and extraordinary because victims of crucifixion would not have received an honorable burial.[172] However, the Mishnah attaches no stigma to crucifixion by the Roman authorities and does not prohibit victims of crucifixion from being buried with their families.[173] On the other hand, the Sanhedrin excluded those executed for violating Jewish law from burial in family tombs or burial grounds:

> And they did not bury [the felon] in the burial grounds of his ancestors. But there were two graveyards made ready for the use of the court, one for those who were beheaded or strangled, and one for those who were stoned or burned. (*m. Sanh.* 6:5)[174]

Crossan argues that, "with all those thousands of people crucified around Jerusalem in the first century alone, we have so far found only a single crucified skeleton, and that, of course, preserved in an ossuary. Was burial then, the exception rather than the rule, the extraordinary rather than the ordinary case?"[175] In fact, the exact opposite is the case: the discovery of the identifiable remains of even a single victim of crucifixion is exceptional. Crossan's assumption that we should have the physical (archaeological) remains of additional crucified victims is erroneous for several reasons. First, with one exception (the repository in the late Iron Age cemetery at Ketef Hinnom) not a single undisturbed tomb in Jerusalem has ever been discovered and excavated by archaeologists.[176] This means that even in cases where tombs or ossuaries still contain the original physical remains, the skeletons are often disturbed, damaged, or incomplete. Second, the Jerusalem elite who owned rock-cut family tombs with ossuaries favored the preservation of the status quo through accommodation with the Romans. Presumably, relatively few of them were therefore executed by crucifixion. Instead, the majority of victims crucified by the Romans belonged to the lower classes[177] — precisely those who could not afford rock-cut tombs. Third, and most important, the nail in Yohanan's heel was preserved only because of a fluke:

> The most dramatic evidence that this young man was crucified was the nail which penetrated his heel bones. But for this nail, we might never have discovered that the young man had died in this way. *The nail was preserved only because it hit a hard knot when it was pounded into the ol-*

ive wood upright of the cross. The olive wood knot was so hard that, as
the blows on the nail became heavier, the end of the nail bent and
curled. We found a bit of the olive wood (between 1 and 2 cm) on the
tip of the nail. This wood had probably been forced out of the knot
where the curled nail hooked into it. When it came time for the dead
victim to be removed from the cross, the executioners could not pull
out this nail, bent as it was within the cross. The only way to remove
the body was to take an ax or hatchet and amputate the feet.[178]

In other words, the means by which victims were affixed to crosses
usually leave no discernable traces in the physical remains or archaeological record. Some victims were bound with ropes, which were untied when
the body was removed from the cross.[179] When victims were nailed to a
cross, the nails had to be pulled out so that the body could be taken down.
This is exactly how the *Gospel of Peter* (6:21) describes Jesus' crucifixion:
"And then they drew the nails from the hands of the Lord and placed him
on the earth."[180] The nail in Yohanan's ankle was preserved only because it
bent after hitting a knot in the wood and therefore could not be removed
from the body.

Jesus came from a family of modest means that presumably could
not afford a rock-cut tomb.[181] Had Joseph not offered to accommodate Jesus' body in his tomb (according to the Gospel accounts), Jesus likely
would have been disposed of in the manner of the lower classes: in a pit
grave or trench grave dug into the ground. When the Gospels tell us that
Joseph of Arimathea offered Jesus a spot in his tomb, it is because Jesus'
family did not own a rock-cut tomb and there was no time to prepare a
grave — that is, there was no time to *dig* a grave, *not* hew a rock-cut tomb
(!) — before the Sabbath.[182] It is not surprising that Joseph, who is described as a wealthy Jew and perhaps even a member of the Sanhedrin, had
a rock-cut family tomb.[183] The Gospel accounts seem to describe Joseph
placing Jesus' body in one of the loculi in his family's tomb. The "new"
tomb mentioned by Matthew probably refers to a previously unused
loculus. The Gospel accounts include an accurate (although not necessarily historical) description of Jesus' body being wrapped in a linen
shroud.[184] When Joseph departed, he sealed the entrance to the tomb by
blocking the doorway with a rolling stone.[185]

This understanding of the Gospel accounts removes at least some of
the grounds for arguments that Joseph of Arimathea was *not* a follower of
Jesus or that he was a completely fictional character (although, of course, it

does not prove that Joseph existed or that this episode occurred).[186] In addition, the tomb must have belonged to Joseph's family, because rock-cut tombs were family tombs (see below).[187] There is no evidence that the Sanhedrin or Roman authorities paid for and maintained rock-cut tombs for executed criminals from lower-class families.[188] Instead, these unfortunates would have been buried in pit graves or trench graves. This sort of tradition is preserved in the New Testament reference to the Potter's Field (Matt 27:7-8).[189]

There is no need to assume that the Gospel accounts of Joseph of Arimathea offering Jesus a place in his family tomb are legendary or apologetic.[190] The Gospel accounts of Jesus' burial appear to be largely consistent with the archaeological evidence.[191] In other words, although archaeology does not prove there was a follower of Jesus named Joseph of Arimathea or that Pontius Pilate granted his request for Jesus' body, the Gospel accounts describing Jesus' removal from the cross and burial accord well with archaeological evidence and with Jewish law. The source(s) of these accounts were familiar with the manner in which wealthy Jews living in Jerusalem during the time of Jesus disposed of their dead. The circumstances surrounding Jesus' death and burial can be reconstructed as follows.

Jesus expired on the cross shortly before sundown on Friday. Because Jesus came from a lower-class family that did not own a rock-cut tomb, under ordinary circumstances he would have been buried in a pit grave or trench grave. However, there was no time to prepare (dig) a grave before the beginning of the Sabbath. Joseph of Arimathea, a wealthy follower of Jesus, was concerned to ensure that Jesus was buried before sundown in accordance with biblical law. Therefore, Joseph hastened to Pilate and requested permission to take Jesus' body. Joseph laid Jesus' body in a loculus in his own rock-cut tomb, an exceptional measure due to the circumstances as rock-cut tombs were family tombs. When the women entered the tomb of Joseph of Arimathea on Sunday morning, the loculus where Jesus' body had been laid was empty. The theological explanation for this phenomenon is that Jesus was resurrected from the dead. However, once Jesus had been buried in accordance with Jewish law, there was no prohibition against removing the body from the tomb after the end of the Sabbath and reburying it. It is therefore possible that followers or family members removed Jesus' body from Joseph's tomb after the Sabbath ended and buried it in a pit grave or trench grave, as it would have been unusual to leave a nonrelative in a family tomb.[192] No matter which explanation one prefers, the fact that Jesus' body did not remain in Joseph's tomb means that his bones could not have been collected in an ossuary, at least not if we follow the Gospel accounts.

The Talpiyot Tomb

The so-called Talpiyot tomb is a modest, single-chamber loculus tomb that was discovered in 1980 during construction work in Jerusalem's East Talpiyot neighborhood. The tomb was excavated by Joseph Gat, and a final (scientific) report was published in 1996 by Amos Kloner.[193] Of the ten ossuaries found in the tomb, four are plain and six are inscribed (five in Hebrew and one in Greek). The tomb has attracted attention because some of the names on the inscribed ossuaries correspond with figures mentioned in the New Testament in association with Jesus, specifically Yeshua (Jesus), Mariamene (Mary), and Yosé (Joseph). It is mainly on this basis that the claim has been made that this is the [lost] tomb of Jesus and his family.[194] If true, this would mean that the Church of the Holy Sepulcher does not enshrine the site of Jesus' crucifixion and burial, a tradition that goes back at least to the time of Constantine (early fourth century). Furthermore, if true, this claim would mean that Jesus was married and had an otherwise unknown son named Judah (since one ossuary is inscribed "Yehudah son of Yeshua") and that Jesus was not resurrected (since his remains were gathered in an ossuary).

The identification of the Talpiyot tomb as belonging to Jesus' family flies in the face of all available evidence and contradicts the Gospel accounts, which are our earliest sources of information about Jesus' death and burial. This claim is also inconsistent with evidence from these sources indicating that Jesus was a lower-class Jew. Even if we accept the unlikely possibility that Jesus' family had the means to purchase a rock-cut tomb, it would have been located in their hometown of Nazareth, not in Jerusalem. For example, when Simon, the last of the Maccabean brothers and one of the Hasmonean rulers built a large tomb or mausoleum for his family, he constructed it in their hometown of Modiin, not in Jerusalem. In fact, the Gospel accounts indicate that Jesus' family did not own a rock-cut tomb in Jerusalem — for if they had, there would have been no need for Joseph of Arimathea to take Jesus' body and place it in his own family's rock-cut tomb! If Jesus' family did not own a rock-cut tomb, it means they also had no ossuaries.

A number of scholars including Kloner have pointed out that the names on the ossuaries in the Talpiyot tomb are very common among the Jewish population of Jerusalem in the first century.[195] Furthermore, the ossuary inscriptions provide no indication that those interred in this tomb were Galilean (not Judean) in origin, as we would expect in light of Rahmani's observation: "In Jerusalem's tombs, the deceased's place of origin was noted when someone from outside Jerusalem was interred in a local tomb."[196] On ossuaries in rock-cut tombs belonging to Judean families it was customary to indicate the ancestry or lineage of the deceased by naming the father, as, for example, Judah son of John (Yohanan); Shimon son of Alexa; and Martha daughter of Hananya.[197] But in rock-cut tombs owned by non-Judean families (or which contained the remains of family members from outside Judea), it was customary to indicate the deceased's place of origin, as, for example, Simon of Ptolemais; Papias the Bethshanite (of Beth Shean); and Gaios son of Artemon from Berenike.[198] If the Talpiyot tomb indeed belonged to Jesus' family, we would expect at least some of the ossuary inscriptions to reflect their Galilean origin, by reading, for example, Jesus [son of Joseph] of Nazareth (or Jesus the Nazarene), Mary of Magdala, and so on. However, the inscriptions provide no indication that this is the tomb of a Galilean family and instead point to a Judean family.

The claim that the Talpiyot tomb belongs to Jesus' family is based on a string of problematic and unsubstantiated claims, including adding an otherwise unattested Matthew (Matya) to the family of Jesus; identifying an otherwise unknown son of Jesus named Judah (and assuming that Jesus was married); and identifying the Mariamene named on one of the ossuaries in the tomb as Mary Magdalene by interpreting the word *Mara* (which follows the name Mariamene) as the Aramaic term for "master" (arguing that Mariamene was a teacher and leader).[199] To account for the fact that Mary/Mariamene's name is written in Greek, the filmmakers transform the small Jewish town of Migdal/Magdala/Tarichaea on the Sea of Galilee (Mary's hometown) into an important trading center where Greek was spoken.[200] Instead, as in other Jewish towns of this period, generally only the upper classes knew Greek, whereas lower-class Jews spoke Aramaic as their everyday language.[201] Individually each of these points weakens the case for the identification of the Talpiyot tomb as the tomb of Jesus' family, but collectively they are devastating.

To conclude, the identification of the Talpiyot tomb as the tomb of Jesus and his family contradicts the canonical Gospel accounts of the death and burial of Jesus and the earliest Christian traditions about Jesus.

This claim is also inconsistent with all available information — historical and archaeological — about how Jews in the time of Jesus buried their dead, and specifically the evidence we have about lower-class, non-Judean families like that of Jesus.[202] Finally, the fact that not a single source preserves any reference to or tradition about any tomb associated with Jesus aside from Joseph of Arimathea's is a loud silence indeed, especially since Paul's writings and some sources of the Synoptic Gospel accounts antedate 70 c.e. Had Jesus' family owned a rock-cut tomb in Jerusalem, presumably some of his followers would have preserved the memory of its existence (if not its location) and venerated the site.[203] In fact, our earliest sources contradict the identification of the Talpiyot tomb as the tomb of Jesus and his family. For example, Hegesippus reported seeing James' grave in the second century c.e. — but he seems to describe a pit grave or trench grave marked by a headstone (see below) and makes no reference to James having been interred with his brother Jesus in a rock-cut family tomb.

The Burial of James

After Jesus' death his brother James became the leader of Jerusalem's early Christian community.[204] Although marginalized in later Western Christian tradition, James is widely regarded as a righteous and observant Jew. His pious and ascetic lifestyle earned him the nickname "the Just."[205] Even if the Letter of James was not composed by James (which is a matter of debate), its attribution to James suggests that he was known for his opposition to the accumulation of wealth and the lifestyle of the wealthy, as illustrated by the following passages:[206]

> Let the believer who is lowly boast in being raised up, and the rich in being brought low, because the rich will disappear like a flower in the field. For the sun rises with its scorching heat and withers the field; its flower falls, and its beauty perishes. It is the same way with the rich; in the midst of a busy life, they will wither away. (Jas 1:9-11)

> Has not God chosen the poor in the world to be rich in faith and to be heirs of the kingdom that he has promised to those who love him? But you have dishonored the poor. Is it not the rich who oppress you? Is it not they who drag you into court? (2:5-6)

Come now, you rich people, weep and wail for the miseries that are coming to you. Your riches have rotted, and your clothes are moth-eaten. Your gold and silver have rusted, and their rust will be evidence against you, and it will eat your flesh like fire. You have laid up treasure for the last days. Listen! The wages of the laborers who mowed your fields, which you kept back by fraud, cry out, and the cries of the harvesters have reached the ears of the Lord of hosts. You have lived on the earth in luxury and in pleasure . . . (5:1-5)

John Painter notes that "One of the aspects of James that offers some support for the view that the epistle has its context in Judaea and Galilee before the Jewish war is the focus on the exploitation of the poor by the rich."[207] The negative views on wealth expressed in the Letter of James are consistent with the nature of the early Christian community in Jerusalem, which is known for a modest, communal lifestyle, although some members came from wealthy families.[208] In this regard, the early Christian community in Jerusalem resembled the Qumran community.[209]

In 62 or 63 c.e., during a hiatus in the office of procurator, the Jewish high priest Ananus took advantage of the opportunity to condemn James and had him executed by stoning.[210] James's opposition to the wealthy, who of course included the high priests, might explain why Ananus had him put to death.[211] Josephus provides a contemporary account of this episode:

So he [Ananus the high priest] assembled the Sanhedrin of the judges, and brought before them the brother of Jesus, who was called Christ, whose name was James, and some others [or some of his companions;] and when he had formed an accusation against them as breakers of the law, he delivered them to be stoned. (*Ant.* 20.200)[212]

According to the second-century c.e. church historian Hegesippus, James was buried just below the Temple Mount (presumably in the area of the Kidron Valley or Mount of Olives).[213] Hegesippus mentions that in his time the stele marking the grave could still be seen:

So they went up and threw down the Just, and they said to one another, "Let us stone James the Just," and they began to stone him since the fall had not killed him. . . . And a certain man among them, one of the laundrymen, took the club with which he used to beat out the clothes, and hit the Just on the head, and so he suffered martyrdom. And they bur-

ied him on the spot by the temple, and his gravestone *(stele)* still remains by the temple. (apud Eusebius, *Hist. eccl.* 2.23:15-18)[214]

Ben Witherington argues that the "James ossuary" should be understood as the stele described by Hegesippus.[215] However, ossuaries are referred to in ancient inscriptions and literary sources by the Greek words
osteophagos, glōssokomon, and *soros,* and in Hebrew and Aramaic as
gluskoma, 'aron, and *ḥalat.*[216] The Greek word *stele* (Hebrew *maṣṣebah*) denotes a stone such as a cippus or headstone. Stelae were used to mark individual graves dug into the ground, whereas monumental columnar, pyramidal, or conical *nefashot* were erected above rock-cut tombs. Therefore,
Hegesippus's testimony suggests that James was buried in a pit grave or
trench grave marked by a headstone *(stele).*[217]

Jesus was interred in a rock-cut tomb because he was removed from
the cross on the eve of the Sabbath, when there was no time to dig a trench
grave for him, and because a wealthy follower offered a loculus in his own
family tomb. On the other hand, none of our sources indicates that James
was placed in a rock-cut tomb, and in fact all available evidence suggests
the opposite. As we have seen, the family of Jesus and James probably
could not afford a rock-cut tomb.[218] Even if they owned a rock-cut tomb,
the fact that James was executed by stoning for violating Jewish law means
that his remains could not have been placed in it (*m. Sanh.* 6:5).[219] Unlike
Jesus, James did not die on the eve of a Sabbath or holiday, which means
there would have been plenty of time to dig a pit grave or trench grave for
him. And finally, James's opposition to wealth and the wealthy makes it
hard to believe that he would have been buried in the kind of rock-cut
tomb that was a hallmark of the elite lifestyle. James's conflict with the Jerusalem elite might even have led to his execution: "James's conflict with
Ananus was a result of his opposition to the exploitation of the poor by the
rich aristocratic ruling class and in particular the exploitation of the poor
rural priesthood by the aristocratic urban chief priests."[220]

Some scholars have suggested that the early Christian community of
Jerusalem chose to "honor" James by preparing a rock-cut tomb for him or
by offering him a spot in one of their family tombs, analogous to Jesus'
burial.[221] I find it hard to believe that Jerusalem's early Christian community, which lived in communal poverty, would have honored a man who
supposedly believed that "riches are a mark of the ungodly" by burying
him in the manner of the upper classes.[222] Furthermore, the Gospel accounts make it clear that Joseph of Arimathea placed Jesus' body in his

family's tomb because of the unique circumstances surrounding Jesus' death, which included Jesus' expiration on the cross just before the onset of the Sabbath, his abandonment by relatives and followers, and the fact that Jesus' family did not own a rock-cut tomb in Jerusalem into which his body could have been placed (as discussed above). Joseph's concern was to ensure that Jesus was buried in accordance with Jewish law, not "honor" Jesus by interring him in a rock-cut tomb.

The notion that a wealthy patron would "honor" a nonrelative by burying him in a manner that was incompatible with his social class was alien to Jewish Palestine, certainly before 70. The patron-client relationship that was characteristic of other parts of the Roman world was not a feature of Jewish culture at this time.[223] Instead, social categories were religiously based (for example, priests versus Israelites or being a member of a particular sect or movement) but were not economically defined.[224] Charity among Jews was a religious obligation that was unconnected to patronage ties.[225] The Qumran community and early Christian community of Jerusalem supported their members in an egalitarian but impoverished lifestyle through the pooling of possessions, not through patron-client relationships. Even after 70 the rabbis make it clear that the deceased is honored through burial with his/her family:

> Neither a corpse nor the bones of a corpse may be transferred from a wretched place to an honored place, nor, needless to say, from an honored place to a wretched place; but if to the family tomb, even from an honored place to a wretched place, it is permitted, for by this he is honored. (*Sem.* 13:7)[226]

All available evidence indicates that Judean rock-cut tombs were family tombs.[227] By the late Second Temple period, the nuclear family seems to have replaced the extended family as the primary social unit among the Jews. Martin Goodman and Eyal Regev each view the relatively small number of loculi in most rock-cut tombs as reflecting this change in familial social structure.[228] Anthropological analyses of human skeletal remains from several rock-cut tombs of the late Second Temple period have confirmed that the individuals in each tomb were related and that the tombs were family-owned.[229] Inscriptions sometimes indicate family ownership of a tomb or familial relationships among those interred within. For example, an inscription on the architrave informs us that the tomb of Bene Ḥezir belonged to that priestly family: "This is the grave and nefesh of Eleazar Honia Joezer Joudah Simeon Johanan sons of Joseph son of Obed Joseph and Eleazar sons of Honia priests of the sons of Hezir."[230] The name "Caiaphas" is inscribed on two of the ossuaries from that family's tomb.[231] Perhaps the best evidence that these were family tombs comes from the tomb of Goliath in Jericho, which yielded a wealth of skeletal remains and inscribed ossuaries. An analysis of this material indicated that three generations of the Goliath family were interred in the tomb between ca. 10 and 70 C.E.[232] Family members included the parents and their sons and families but not the parents' daughters and their families.[233] Rachel Hachlili and Patricia Smith concluded, "The findings indicated that this was a family tomb."[234] The rabbis took it for granted that the rites of mourning and gathering bones in a tomb (ossilegium) were carried out by relatives (see, e.g., *m. Ber.* 3:1; *y. Pesah.* 8:8; *y. Moʿed Qat.* 1:5).[235]

We have no evidence such as inscriptions or literary testimony that nonfamily members including slaves were interred in Judean rock-cut tombs before 70.[236] Even after 70, when different families purchased space in the catacombs at Beth Sheʿarim, there is no indication that nonfamily members were included among them.[237] As Rabbi Judah reportedly said, "Whomsoever a person may sleep with when he is living, he may be buried with when he is dead" (*Sem.* 13:7).[238] Rabbinic literature indicates that although slaves were members of the household, they were considered material possessions like animals, not as human beings:[239]

> For heathens or slaves, no [mourning] rites whatsoever should be observed, but one may join in the lament, "Alas, O lion! Alas, O mighty one!" . . . One does not receive condolences for slaves.

> And when his [Rabban Gamaliel's] slave Tevi died, he received condolences about him. They said to him: Our teacher, did you not teach us that one does not accept condolences for slaves? He said to them: My slave Tevi was not like other slaves, he was honest. (*Sem.* 1:9-10)
> Hence, about unrelated freed men one accepts condolences? So is the Mishnah: one does not accept condolences for slaves.
> It happened that Rebbi Eliezer's maidservant died and his students came to him for condolences but he did not accept. He entered the courtyard, they followed him there. He entered the house, they followed him there. He told them: I was thinking that you would be burned by lukewarm water but you are not burned even by boiling water. Did they not say that one does not accept condolences for slaves

because slaves are in this like animals? If not does not accept condolences for unrelated free persons, so much more for slaves. If one's slave or animal died, people say to him: The Omnipresent may replace your loss. (*y. Ber.* 2:8; see also *Sem.* 1:10)[240]

On the basis of this evidence, Dov Zlotnick concluded: "Although humane treatment of slaves was enjoined, the master's treatment of his slave was not that of a kinsman but that of a stranger."[241]

There is no indication that the members of Jerusalem's first-century early Christian community abandoned the principle that rock-cut tombs were used by families. In Palestine, the custom of community burial in catacombs is not attested before the second to third centuries (most prominently at Beth She'arim).[242] There is no reason to assume that James was placed in someone else's tomb since we have no testimony that this happened (unlike the case of Jesus). Even if we assume that the early Christians of Jerusalem buried their members as a community instead of as individuals with their families,[243] we should probably envisage a practice analogous to the Qumran burials.[244] In fact, pit graves and trench graves are more suitable than rock-cut tombs for communities in which group membership superseded family ties. Hegesippus's relatively early date (within a century of James's death) and the fact that he was apparently from Palestine (as Eusebius certainly was) suggest that he preserves an accurate tradition about the manner in which James was buried — in a pit grave or trench grave marked by a headstone.[245] The suggestion made by some scholars that all or part of the inscription on the "James ossuary" is an ancient forgery — added by a pious Christian in the fourth to fifth centuries — is anachronistic, since the custom of ossilegium had disappeared from Jerusalem long before then.[246] Contemporary Christians would not have been familiar with the custom of ossilegium. Those who encountered ossuaries in earlier tombs would have had no reason to associate these objects with the first century C.E. or with James.[247]

The evidence that James was buried in a grave dug into the ground and not in a rock-cut tomb renders the controversy over the "James ossuary" moot. Even if the inscription is authentic, it does not refer to James the Just, the brother of Jesus.[248] Ossuaries were introduced into rock-cut tombs to collect the remains removed from loculi.[249] However, ossuaries are not associated with pit graves or trench graves, as there was no reason to exhume the remains and place them in an ossuary in order to make space for new burials.[250] Instead, new graves were dug as the need arose.

In my opinion, the prevailing scholarly views and popular controversies about the burials of Jesus and James are the result of a number of widespread misconceptions:

Ossuaries and ossilegium in Jerusalem tend to be viewed without considering the development of Jewish rock-cut tombs and burial customs over time.

Ossuaries and rock-cut tombs in Jerusalem usually are considered in isolation from their local social and economic context (elite versus non-elite burials).

Ossuaries in Jerusalem generally are discussed in isolation from the larger Mediterranean (Hellenistic and Roman) setting and contemporary trends.

In contrast to other countries and periods for which archaeologists acknowledge the diversity that characterized tombs and burial customs, in late Second Temple–period Judea rock-cut tombs have been the focus of attention to the exclusion of other burial types.

Interpretations of ancient Jewish tombs and burial customs have been influenced by assumptions about beliefs in resurrection and the afterlife.

Ancient literary accounts describing the burials of Jesus and James have been interpreted without a correct understanding of Jewish law and have been influenced by anachronistic assumptions about Jewish society in pre-70 Palestine.

CHAPTER 12

Epilogue — The Aftermath of 70

With the destruction of the temple the primary focal point of Jewish sectarianism disappeared. . . . For most Jews, however, sectarian self-definition ceased to make sense after 70.

Cohen, "The Significance of Yavneh," 45

The standard assumption that these Jewish groups disappeared soon after 70 is therefore no more than an assumption. Furthermore, the presuppositions which have encouraged the assumption are so theologically loaded that historians' suspicions should be instinctive. . . . My hypothesis is that groups and philosophies known from pre-70 Judaism continued for years, perhaps centuries, after the destruction of the Temple.

Goodman, "Sadducees and Essenes
after 70 C.E.," 348, 355

For many Jews the disastrous events of 70 — which culminated with the destruction of the Jerusalem temple — had little or no impact on the most basic aspects of daily life. They consumed the same foods, wore the same types of garments, and attended to their toilet needs in the same manner as before 70. However, some changes can be discerned after 70, most of which reflect the reconfigured social and religious landscape. For now not only

181

was the Jerusalem temple gone, but so were the officiating priests. The remnants of the Jerusalem elite were dispersed, with some families having relocated to Galilee. The sectarian divisions and debates that had focused on the temple cult gradually disappeared, and eventually the rabbis emerged as religious leaders and authorities.

The widely-held view that sectarianism disappeared soon after 70 is based mainly on the silence of rabbinic writings, which provide little indication that Essenes and Pharisees or Sadducees and Pharisees (for example) continued to debate halakhic issues after 70.[1] As David Instone-Brewer remarks, "a good case can be made that all the rival groups simply lost their distinctiveness and impetus with the destruction of the Temple. The Sadducees lost their locus of activity, the Essenes lost the reason for their rebellion, and the Pharisees' attempt to replicate Temple activities in the home, synagogue, and schoolhouse became the only way to express Jewish rites."[2] The groups that were inclusive of all Israel and believed that the divine could be experienced anywhere — that is, the Pharisees and Jesus' movement — survived (in some form) the temple's destruction, whereas the exclusive priestly groups — the Sadducees and Essenes — vanish from view.[3]

The apparent disappearance of these sects after 70 does not mean that Jewish factionalism and debates over purity observance ceased.[4] To the contrary, rabbinic writings present a variety of rulings on purity issues relating to prayer and Torah study as well as the (now defunct) temple cult.[5] However, whereas before 70 debates on halakhic issues divided Jews along sectarian lines, after 70 the rabbis tolerated and preserved different opinions.[6] Most scholars therefore view the rabbinic period as characterized by an inclusive and pluralistic attitude that contrasts with the period before 70.[7] As Instone-Brewer puts it, "This inclusivity is seen in the Mishnah, which was the first Jewish document to express rival views with equal authority, and which appears to 'agree to disagree' except when a clear decision was made by the voting of a majority."[8]

Still, rabbinic tolerance had its limits, with sages who refused to accept the majority opinion being condemned as heretics (often denoted as *minim* [*mynym*] or as Sadducees), as a debate about resurrection in the Babylonian Talmud illustrates:

> A sectarian [*min*] said to R. Ammi: "Ye maintain that the dead will revive; but they turn to dust, and can dust come to life?" — He replied: I will tell thee a parable. This may be compared to a human king who

commanded his servants to build him a great palace in a place where there was no water or earth [for making bricks]. So they went and built it. But after some time it collapsed, so he commanded them to rebuild it in a place where water and earth were to be found; but they replied, "We cannot." Thereupon he became angry with them and said, "If ye could build in a place containing no water or earth, surely ye can where there is!" "Yet," [continued R. Ammi], "If thou dost not believe, go forth into the field and see a mouse, which to-day is but part flesh and part dust, and yet by to-morrow has developed and become all flesh. And shouldst thou say, 'That takes a long time,' go up to the mountains, where thou wilt see but one snail, whilst by to-morrow the rain has descended and it is covered with snails."

A sectarian [*min*] said to Gebiha b. Pesisa, "Woe to you, ye wicked, who maintain that the dead will revive; if even the living die, shall the dead live!" He replied, "Woe to you, ye wicked, who maintain that the dead will not revive: if what was not, [now] lives, — surely what has lived, will live again!" "Thou hast called me wicked," said he, "If I stood up I could kick thee and strip thee of thy hump!" "If thou couldst do that," he retorted, "thou wouldst be called a great doctor, and command large fees." (*b. Sanh.* 91a)[9]

In other words, whereas before 70 there were various groups, movements, or sects with different halakhic practices, after 70 mainstream (rabbinic) Judaism tolerated a plurality of views but only within certain limits.[10] Those who refused to conform were condemned as heretics, as Daniel Boyarin observes:

I find in the fact that the Mishnaic text discussed above [Niddah 4:2] opposed "Sadducees" and "Israel" not evidence for a tolerant, non-sectarian Judaism, but rather for a Catholic Israel, a former "group" that has won the day, or at any rate, that so represents itself and defines all others as simply not in the fold at all. . . . Jewish sectarianism as a form of decentralized pluralism by default had been replaced by the binary opposition of Jewish orthodox and Jewish heretics.[11]

Before 70 even the most extreme or marginal Jewish sects were not prohibited from participating in the sacrificial cult in the Jerusalem temple (including the Essenes and the Jewish followers of Jesus after his death), whereas after 70 Jews who refused to accept the majority opinion were no longer considered Jews at all.[12] It may be that the real schism between the Jews and Samaritans occurred after the Bar Kokhba Revolt, with the Samaritans developing their own Pentateuch during the third and fourth centuries.[13] Boyarin views the creation of heresiological discourse as a rabbinic attempt to define and circumscribe Judaism in relation to Christianity.[14]

What happened to Jewish purity observance after the Jerusalem temple — the place where God's presence dwelled — was destroyed?[15] Some scholars point out that purity issues continued to play a major role in Jewish religious life, as reflected by the centrality of purity laws in rabbinic debates.[16] As John Poirier says, "the relevance of purity was a debated issue for much, if not all, of the period between the destruction of the temple and the late Gaonic period."[17] Other scholars assume that the observance of purity laws declined as time went on and hopes of a rebuilt temple faded.[18] For example, Thomas Kazen observes that the Talmudim contain no Gemara for any Mishnaic tractate belonging to the order of Purities except for Niddah.[19] Both points of view are correct, as rabbinic literature displays a concern with certain types of purity observance but ignores others.[20] Instone-Brewer provides a list summarizing which temple practices continued to be debated by the rabbis after 70, which practices were continued in a limited way for a short period, and which rituals ceased altogether after 70.[21]

A number of passages in the Mishnah reflect the rabbis' struggle to adapt legal observance to the new reality:

> [Laws concerning] sheqel dues and firstfruits apply only in the time of the Temple. But those concerning tithe of grain, tithe of cattle, and of firstlings apply both in the time of the Temple and not in the time of the Temple. He who [nowadays] declares sheqels and firstfruits to be holy — lo, this is deemed holy. R. Simeon says, "He who says, 'Firstfruit is holy,' — they do not enter the status of Holy Things." (*m. Šeqal.* 8:8)

> One who buys [outside Jerusalem with money in the status of second tithe] pieces of fruit: unintentionally [not realizing the coins were consecrated] — let their payment be returned to its [former] place [to the purchaser who bought them by mistake]; on purpose — let [the pieces of fruit] be brought up and eaten in the [holy] place [Jerusalem]. And if the Temple does not exist, let [the pieces of fruit] rot.
> One who buys [outside Jerusalem] a domesticated animal [with

money in the status of second tithe]: intentionally — let its payment return to its [former] place; on purpose — let [the animal] be brought up and eaten in the [holy] place. And if the Temple does not exist, let it be buried with its hide. (*m. Maʿaś. Š.* 1:5-6)[22]

Archaeology sheds valuable light on Judaism in the decades and centuries following the temple's destruction. Objects and installations associated with purity observance, especially miqvaʾot and stone vessels, continue to be attested after 70, although they are not as common and widespread as before.[23] These features are concentrated in regions and sites where remnants of the Jewish elite — among them priestly families — settled after 70, mostly in Lower Galilee (such as at Sepphoris, Tiberias, and Beth Sheʿarim) and southern Judea's periphery.[24] For example, Jewish refugees from ʿEin Gedi who fled to the Cave of Letters in Naḥal Ḥever at the time of the Bar Kokhba Revolt took with them two stone mugs.[25]

Recent excavations at Shuʿafat on Jerusalem's northern outskirts have brought to light a Jewish settlement that dates to the period between the two revolts (70-135), the first ever discovered in the city's vicinity.[26] The settlement consists of large, well-built village-type houses and public buildings laid out along a regular network of streets and alleys. Some of the buildings are equipped with miqvaʾot.[27] The excavators report finding a large number and variety of lathe-turned and hand-carved stone vessels.[28] Among the buildings are Roman-style bathhouses with wall paintings and hypocaust systems, and the finds include pottery manufactured in the kiln works of the Tenth Roman Legion in Jerusalem.[29] Five mold-made ceramic inkwells, apparently products of the legionary kiln works, were discovered on the floor of one room.[30] The evidence of a relatively prosperous, romanized lifestyle combined with Jewish purity observance suggests that this was a settlement of elite families including priests who remained as close as possible to Jerusalem after 70, perhaps awaiting the rebuilding of the temple.[31]

Evidence for the use of objects and installations associated with purity observance — most notably miqvaʾot and stone vessels — declines gradually over time, disappearing over the course of the third to fourth centuries.[32] The kiln works at Kfar Hananya in Galilee, which produced pottery that may have been marketed to a Jewish population concerned with purity (although small quantities are attested at non-Jewish sites), also ceased operating by the end of the fourth century.[33] If the related debates over purity observance continued, it would lend support to Goodman's suggestion that these groups survived in some form long after the temple's destruction.[34] In this case we should consider the possibility that sources such as rabbinic writings and the New Testament contain nuggets of information that reflect contemporary historical reality, however distorted they may be due to the motivations and biases of the authors and editors. For example, some of the practices that the rabbis condemned as heresy (minut) — such as Jacob of Kefar Nibburaya's ritual slaughtering of fish (Midr. Num. Rab. 19:3) — might attest to continued sectarianism in the period after 70.[35] Indeed, Vered Noam and Elisha Qimron have observed that often the rabbis did not identify their opponents in order to avoid creating the impression that their views were equal.[36] Perhaps the numerous and generally hostile references to Pharisees in the canonical Gospels are not entirely anachronistic or inaccurate but instead reflect the continued existence and influence of this group after the temple's destruction.[37]

Whereas the issue of purity observance deeply divided Palestinian Jewish society of the late Second Temple period, with the exception of Paul's claim to be a Pharisee (Acts 23:6, 26:5; Phil 3:5) we have no evidence of sectarianism among Diaspora Jews and no objects or installations associated with purity practices in the Diaspora before 70.[38] As Jacob Neusner concluded, "nearness to the temple cult yields concrete and socially significant interpretations of purity, while distance from the temple (both spatially and temporally) generally results in a metaphorical interpretation of purity laws."[39] He noted that after 70 (and especially after 135) the rabbis came to believe that the temple's purity and holiness could only be replicated in a diminished way.[40] The final blow to Jewish expectations of a rebuilt temple occurred under Julian the Apostate. It is probably not a coincidence that installations and objects associated with purity practices relating to the temple disappeared by the second half of the fourth century.[41] At the same time, however, the first monumental synagogue buildings were erected in Palestine, such as the so-called Synagogue of Severos at Hammath Tiberias.[42] The rich temple imagery and liturgical furniture of these buildings enabled Jews to preserve the memory of the temple and sacrificial cult while awaiting their future reestablishment.

Notes

Notes to Chapter 1

1. Lieberman, "The Discipline in the So-Called Dead Sea Manual of Discipline," 206.

2. Flusser, "Pharisees, Sadducees and Essenes in the Pesher Nahum," 152 (my translation).

3. The corpus of secondary literature on these groups is vast. For the question of who was a Jew/Ioudaios, see Cohen, *The Beginnings of Jewishness*. For the major groups and sects with bibliography, see inter alia: Chalcraft, *Sectarianism in Early Judaism*; Newman, *Proximity to Power*; Neusner and Chilton, *In Quest of the Historical Pharisees*; Kazen, *Jesus and Purity Halakhah*, 44-48, 51-55; Meier, *A Marginal Jew*, 1:289-613; Goodman, *The Ruling Class of Judaea*, 76-108; Saldarini, *Pharisees, Scribes and Sadducees*; Sanders, *Judaism: Practice and Belief*, 317-451; Schürer, *The History of the Jewish People*, 2:384-414 (Pharisees and Sadducees); Baumgarten, *The Flourishing of Jewish Sects* (who focuses on the Hasmonean period). Baumgarten (1-2, 43-44, 50) reminds us that the majority of the Jewish population did not belong to any of these groups and that except for Jesus' movement most members were male. Some scholars have argued that the Pharisees, Sadducees, and Essenes were the only major sects of the late Second Temple period; see Taylor, "Philo of Alexandria on the Essenes," 18; Eshel, "New Information from the Dead Sea Scrolls"; Flusser, "Pharisees, Sadducees and Essenes."

4. See also Epiphanius' *Panarion*. For the relationship of the Pharisees to the later rabbis, see Hezser, *The Social Structure of the Rabbinic Movement*, 69; Cohen, "The Significance of Yavneh," 40-42; Deines, *Jüdische Steingefäße*, 19-23. For introductions to rabbinic literature, see Instone-Brewer, *Prayer and Agriculture*, 6-40; Schürer, *The History of the Jewish People*, 1:68-114. Sussman, "History of the 'Halakha,'" 21, 25-26, remarks on the great similarity between the "halakhic world" of the sages (in language, terminology, and legal details) and the halakhic sectarian literature from Qumran. For Josephus on the Pharisees, see Goodblatt, "The Place of the Pharisees in First Century Judaism." For the identification of the "Herodians" of the Gospels with the Essenes, see Taylor, "Philo of Alexandria on the Essenes," 17. On the other hand, Regev, *The Sadducees and Their Halakhah*, 52-57, identifies

the Herodians with the Boethusians. For the identification of the "scribes" mentioned in the Gospels with priests/Sadducees, see Schwartz, *Studies in the Jewish Background of Christianity*, 89-101 ("'Scribes and Pharisees, Hypocrites': Who are the 'Scribes' in the New Testament?"); Marcus, *Mark 1–8*, 523-24. I try to exercise caution in my use of rabbinic literature for the purposes of this study and rely mostly (but not entirely) on tannaitic sources and traditions.

5. For Josephus and the Essenes, see Beall, *Josephus' Description of the Essenes;* Goodman, "A Note on the Qumran Sectarians"; Baumgarten, "Tannaitic Halakhah and Qumran," 3. Flusser, "Pharisees, Sadducees and Essenes," 133, remarks that "the words of the Essenes themselves show how precise Josephus was" (my translation). For Josephus and the Pharisees, see Mason, *Flavius Josephus on the Pharisees;* and "Josephus' Pharisees: The Narrative." For Josephus and the Sadducees, see Baumbach, "The Sadducees in Josephus." For Philo on the Essenes, see Taylor, "Philo of Alexandria on the Essenes," who compares Philo's account with Josephus's.

6. For discussions see Sanders, *Judaism*, 5-12; Fredriksen, *Jesus of Nazareth*, 18-41 (for the Gospels and Paul).

7. For the methodological difficulties of comparing Qumran law and rabbinic traditions, see Elman, "Some Remarks on 4QMMT"; see also Baumgarten, "Rabbinic Literature as a Source." Instone-Brewer, *Prayer and Agriculture*, 5, notes that one problem with trying to isolate pre-70 traditions in rabbinic literature is that the rabbis were interested in preserving the conclusions of scholarly debate, not their origins.

8. Sussman, "History of the 'Halakha,'" 65 (my translation).

9. Mason, "Pharisaic Dominance before 70 C.E.," 371, notes that some of Josephus's statements about Pharisaic power "have an internal logic that precludes a post-70 association," including his references to the Pharisaic beliefs in fate and the afterlife, the "monastic" lifestyle of the Essenes, and the small aristocratic following of the Sadducees.

10. For a discussion, see Mason, "Josephus' Pharisees: The Philosophy," 56-57.

11. As Sanders, *Judaism*, 318, puts it, "Not all aristocrats were Sadducees, but it may be that all Sadducees were aristocrats." See also Meier, *A Marginal Jew*, 1:393-96; Newman, *Proximity to Power*, 73-82; Schürer, *The History of the Jewish People*, 2:235; Stern, "Aspects of Jewish Society," 609-18 (including the nonpriestly elite); Regev, *The Sadducees and Their Halakhah*, 12-13. For sources on the Sadducees, see Kazen, *Jesus and Purity Halakhah*, 53; Meier, *A Marginal Jew*, 1:389-411; Regev, *The Sadducees and Their Halakhah*, 14-31.

12. For discussions, see Hezser, *The Social Structure of the Rabbinic Movement*, 55-69; Instone-Brewer, *Prayer and Agriculture*, 3-4; Kazen, *Jesus and Purity Halakhah*, 54; Baumgarten, "Rabbinic Literature as a Source," 16 n. 6. But Lightstone, "The Pharisees and Sadducees," 286, after examining Mishnaic passages that claim to present debates between Pharisees and Sadducees, concludes, "we cannot distinguish instances when Mishnaic law may reflect antecedent pharisaic positions from occasions when early rabbinic authors/editors have projected Mishnaic law on the Pharisees so as to represent the latter as their legal predecessors. . . . In the end, we can only say that the authors/editors of the Mishnah and in particular the Tosefta exhibit a strong tendency to represent Mishnaic law as consistent with (allegedly earlier) Pharisaic positions." Nevertheless, Lightstone admits that this evidence shows that the early rabbinic authors/editors saw the Sadducees as the "other" against whom the Pharisees defined themselves. He suggests that the late-second- and third-century rabbis

may have done this in order to construct their own group identity by laying claim to the temple traditions.

13. In contrast, Sanders, *Judaism*, 13, defines the Pharisees as mostly laity, few of whom were socially and financially prominent. He argues (426-27) that the Pharisaic tradition of *prosbul* (which facilitated borrowing and lending near the end of a sabbatical year) was aimed at helping the small landowner or businessman. In my opinion, Sanders and Saldarini are talking about the same economic stratum.

14. See Saldarini, *Pharisees, Scribes and Sadducees*, 39, 42, 46. In the preface to the 2001 reprint of this book, James VanderKam reviews recent scholarship on this subject, including objections to Saldarini's description of the Pharisees as a retainer class (see xviii-xx); see also Baumgarten, *The Flourishing of Jewish Sects*, 51.

15. Schürer, *The History of the Jewish People*, 404.

16. For the identification of Josephus's Essenes with the Qumran community, see Beall, *Josephus' Description of the Essenes;* see also Magness, *The Archaeology of Qumran.* For the centrality of the Zadokite line in the sect's history, see Wacholder, "Historiography of Qumran," 356-63; see also Hultgren, *From the Damascus Covenant to the Covenant of the Community*, 308; Sanders, *Judaism*, 24; Broshi, "Qumran and the Essenes," 464. For the role of priests in the Qumran community, see García Martínez, *Qumranica Minora*, 2:77-93; Jastram, "Hierarchy at Qumran," 363-65; Fraade, "Interpretive Authority in the Studying Community at Qumran," 54, 68; Bergsma, "Qumran Self-Identity," 187. Some scholars now question the authority of priests in general and Zadokites in particular at Qumran; see Kugler, "Making All Experience Religious," 135 n. 17 with bibliog.; Himmelfarb, *A Kingdom of Priests*, 125-28; Baumgarten, "Rabbinic Literature as a Source," 49 n. 124. Nevertheless, Kugler (152) concludes that "In the case of Qumran, the literate elite — the preachers — surely were priests or some other type of temple officials alienated from the Jerusalem cult." For the view that the sectarian inhabitants of Qumran were not Essenes, see Baumgarten, "The Rule of the Martian"; Newman, *Proximity to Power*, 45-50; Goodman, "A Note on the Qumran Sectarians."

17. Eshel, "New Information from the Dead Sea Scrolls," 148, reminds us that the Essenes and Pharisees were subdivided into small groups or parties, typically designated as "houses" (sgl. *byt*). Regev, *Sectarianism in Qumran*, 243-66, considers the Essenes an "outgrowth" (later development) of the Qumran "movement."

18. For a recent discussion, see Regev, *Sectarianism in Qumran*, esp. 15-29, 34-93, who defines the Qumran "sects" (plural) as an example of "introversionist sectarianism." See also Wassen and Jokiranta, "Groups in Tension," who conclude that the communities associated with the *Damascus Document* and the *Community Rule* were sectarian. Newman, *Proximity to Power*, 221, notes that "The Jerusalem Sadducees did not secede even when the court was controlled by Pharisees, and vice versa" (he uses the terms "dissenting groups" and "seceding groups"). According to Shemesh, "The Origins of the Laws of Separatism," 224, the distinguishing characteristic of the Qumran sect was their separatist world view. Sussman, "The History of the 'Halakha' and the Dead Sea Scrolls," 36-37, defines the Qumran community as a sect because of their refusal to accept the majority opinion or view. Himmelfarb, *A Kingdom of Priests*, 81, notes that the Qumran community believed that they alone possessed the truth and would be saved. Chilton, *The Temple of Jesus*, 86, describes the Pharisees as "more a tendency of Judaism than a party or even a movement." Neusner, *The Idea of Purity in Ancient Judaism*, 113, defines the various groups of the late Second Temple period as sectarian.

For a general discussion, see Baumgarten, *The Flourishing of Jewish Sects*, 5-11, who uses the term sect more broadly and notes that the term's meaning depends largely on the examples chosen to determine the paradigm.

19. Of course, I recognize and acknowledge the difficulty of using the Synoptic Gospels as sources of information about the historical Jesus, as they sometimes present different or contradictory accounts and were written a couple of generations after Jesus' death. For this problem, see Meier, *A Marginal Jew*, 1:335; Kazen, *Jesus and Purity Halakhah*, 49, 59-60. Nevertheless, I hope to show that some of the episodes described in the Gospel accounts reflect an awareness of first century C.E. Jewish legal debates and correspond with archaeological evidence from Palestine (which, however, does not mean they actually happened or are associated with the historical Jesus). In this regard my view differs somewhat from Sanders, *Jesus and Judaism*, 264-67. Except for discussing the death of James in the chapter on tombs, I do not deal with Jewish-Christians after Jesus' death. I also shall not consider in a systematic manner the identity of other groups mentioned in our sources such as scribes, Boethusians, *ḥaverim*, and morning bathers. For scribes, see Goodman, "Texts, Scribes, and Power in Roman Judaea"; Himmelfarb, *A Kingdom of Priests*, 11-52.

20. See Flusser, "The Social Message from Qumran," 108-10; Klawans, *Purity, Sacrifice, and the Temple*, 236-41. Instone-Brewer, *Prayer and Agriculture*, 316-17, suggests that Jesus opposed the tithing of herbs (Matt 23:23) because this obligation was a hardship on the lower classes. Fredriksen, *Jesus of Nazareth*, 103, observes that "Jesus is drawn especially to the poor, whose very poverty enriches them spiritually." This is suggested also by Jesus' death by crucifixion, a form of execution that the Romans generally reserved for the lower classes; see Halperin, "Crucifixion," 42.

21. Neusner, *The Idea of Purity in Ancient Judaism*, 108.

22. I exclude from my discussion Jewish communities in the Diaspora, such as those in Mesopotamia, Egypt, and Asia Minor, as we do not have evidence of sectarian divisions analogous to those among their Palestinian counterparts (although Paul describes himself as a Pharisee). Neusner, *The Idea of Purity in Ancient Judaism*, 108-19, suggests that geographical distance from the temple was a factor, causing purity to be viewed allegorically (at least by Philo). For Philo's concern with priestly matters see Himmelfarb, *A Kingdom of Priests*, 143-59.

23. Harrington, *The Purity Texts*, 8-9; Noam, "The Bounds of Non-Priestly Purity," 128, ". . . impurity has no meaning, and, in fact, almost does not exist without the presence of holiness [or the divine]" (my translation). See also Klawans, *Purity, Sacrifice, and the Temple*, 171: "Ritual purity remained for ancient Jews, first and foremost, the prerequisite for encountering the sacred, whether that meant entering the earthly temple, the heavenly one, or — at Qumran — the earthly, temporary, and inadequate substitute for the currently defiled Jerusalem temple." Of course, other ancient religions required purification before entering a deity's presence; for example, for ancient Greece see Parker, *MIASMA;* Stowers, "On the Comparison of Blood."

24. See Schwartz, "Israel's Holiness," 51; because Israel worshiped only one God and believed that the whole world is his kingdom, "Israel's status vis-à-vis the one God is analogous to that of the priests vis-à-vis the gods of each [other] people. They therefore make up, as it were, an entire 'kingdom of priests.'"

25. For a recent discussion see Klawans, *Impurity and Sin in Ancient Judaism.* Klawans, *Purity, Sacrifice, and the Temple*, 4, observes that "Ritual purity, by definition, is as-

sociated with those phenomena that are barred from the sanctuary." See also Sanders, *Judaism*, 70-71; Sapir, "Masada," 139-40, who lists the sources and degrees of impurity and people and objects that are susceptible to impurity. Neusner, *The Idea of Purity in Ancient Judaism*, 1, argues that the word "ritual" should not be used in association with purity as it implies a distinction with something that is real or moral (compare and contrast with Klawans, e.g.). I am persuaded by Neusner and try to avoid using the term "ritual" in connection with purity and impurity, except in cases where it seems necessary for purposes of clarity.

26. See Harrington, *The Purity Texts*, 10; Noam, "The Bounds of Non-Priestly Purity," 136-37 (for the rabbinic view); Klawans, *Purity, Sacrifice, and the Temple*, 54; *Impurity and Sin in Ancient Judaism*, 24; Himmelfarb, *A Kingdom of Priests*, 61, 89. For a dissenting view, see Kazen, *Jesus and Purity Halakhah*, 209-11.

27. See Harrington, *The Purity Texts*, 10, 21-23.

28. See Klawans, *Purity, Sacrifice, and the Temple*, 55; *Impurity and Sin in Ancient Judaism*, 34; Doering, "Purity and Impurity in the Book of Jubilees," 262; Werman, "The Concept of Holiness," 167; Himmelfarb, *A Kingdom of Priests*, 62, 90-91. Neusner, *The Idea of Purity in Ancient Judaism*, 86-87, says that the rabbis required the literal observance of purity laws as part of the divine will, and therefore "Impurity is not a metaphor for sin. It is a state to be avoided, and deliberate failure to avoid it is a sin in and of itself." On 119 Neusner describes impurity as a "metaphor" when it occurs in connection with immoral or unethical behavior. For a critique of this view, see Kazen, *Jesus and Purity Halakhah*, 204-7, who argues that the distinction between "ritual" and "moral" is a modern construct; see also Milgrom, "Systemic Differences in the Priestly Corpus," 327.

29. For the interpretation of this passage in the book of *Jubilees*, see Werman, "The Concept of Holiness," 169-70.

30. Neusner, *The Idea of Purity in Ancient Judaism*, 113. There is no evidence that even Jesus and Paul disputed this, as they seem to have purified themselves before entering the temple. As Sanders, *Judaism: Practice and Belief*, 238 puts it, "However they interpreted the law, Jews were zealous in keeping it." For arrangements segregating people at various degrees of purity in the temple compound see Oppenheimer, *The 'Am Ha-aretz*, 85-86; Yadin, *The Temple Scroll*, 1:192, 278.

31. See Noam, "The Bounds of Non-Priestly Purity," 132; Klawans, *Purity, Sacrifice, and the Temple*, 169; Schiffman, "Qumran and Rabbinic Halakhah," 139. According to Alon, *Jews, Judaism and the Classical World*, 191, the expansion applied to three areas: sacred objects, the eating of unconsecrated food, and the intrinsic obligation of purity (cleanness) and prohibition against impurity (uncleanness). Neusner, *The Idea of Purity in Ancient Judaism*, 65, singles out the eating of unconsecrated food and tithing; he notes that whereas the Pharisees and Qumran sect extended purity observance outside the temple cult, "Other Jews, following the plain sense of Leviticus, supposed that purity laws were to be kept only in the Temple." Neusner, "The Pharisaic Agenda," 322, observes that the observance of purity laws "became practically important in the lives of Pharisees in regard to the daily preparation of food, in the lives of all Jews only in connection with visiting the Temple, and of the priests in the cult itself."

32. As Bokser, "Approaching Sacred Space," 279, puts it, "if people believe that the divine may manifest itself in the world without being restricted to a single area, how should they treat this extended zone of the sacred?" In my opinion, this is a major point that Poirier, "Purity beyond the Temple," misses, setting up the "minimalists" as a straw man. For an ex-

cellent discussion see Shemesh, "The Holiness according to the *Temple Scroll*," 370, who distinguishes between two concepts: (1) whether God himself or his "name" dwells in a specific place (such as the tabernacle or temple); and (2) whether God dwells only in the sanctuary/temple or is present everywhere.

33. For *imitatio Dei*, see Klawans, *Purity, Sacrifice, and the Temple*, 112-23; Shemesh, "The Holiness according to the *Temple Scroll*," 371; Milgrom, *Leviticus 1–16*, 730-33. Harrington, "Holiness and Law," 129, defines purity as "a state of being . . . the absence of impurity," whereas holiness is "divine energy." Schwartz, "Israel's Holiness," 56-57, notes that the point of *imitatio Dei* is not that Israel is supposed to be holy like God but rather they are to be holy because God is holy.

34. For an excellent summary of this subject, see Werman, "The Concept of Holiness," 163-65. Regev, "Reconstructing Qumranic and Rabbinic Worldviews," defines the Qumranic attitude towards holiness as "dynamic," which means that any violation can desecrate God's holiness and cause it to disappear. He defines the rabbis' attitude towards holiness as "static" because in their view holiness is a status, not an entity, and therefore is not as vulnerable to desecration. According to Regev, for the rabbis "Desecration is only an unwelcome change in this status and not a cosmic or natural event . . . the whole cultic system of priests-Temple-sacrifices is a construction that follows God's orders but lacks an *inner meaning*" (102-3). He traces the "dynamic concept of holiness" to the Priestly Code and the "static concept" to Deuteronomy (106).

35. See Werman, "The Concept of Holiness," 168, who notes a shift in attitude beginning with the Babylonian exile (or earlier), when God's presence is extended to the entire world instead of just the Land of Israel; for the rabbinic notion of holiness see 175-79. See also Kazen, *Jesus and Purity Halakhah*, 74; Milgrom, "Systemic Differences in the Priestly Corpus," 326; Schwartz, "Israel's Holiness"; Himmelfarb, *A Kingdom of Priests*, 63. Shemesh, "The Holiness according to the *Temple Scroll*," 370, makes a similar observation, noting that the tendency to view God's presence as limited to the temple is associated with the book of Leviticus and the Priestly tradition, whereas the notion that God is everywhere (extends to all Israel) derives from Deuteronomy.

36. Harrington, "Holiness and Law in the Dead Sea Scrolls," 130. For the connection between holiness and moral behavior see Douglas, *Purity and Danger*, 53-54. I agree with the view that the Qumran sect considered sin to be a source of impurity; see Neusner, *The Idea of Purity in Ancient Judaism*, 54, 81: "nor did anyone except the *yaḥad* in the period of the Second Temple claim that sin causes impurity, though many, like Jesus, supposed that impurity might serve as an analogy for sin." As Broshi, "Qumran and the Essenes," 474, puts it, "for the Essenes sin is not a metaphor for impurity but its source." See also Regev, "Abominated Temple and a Holy Community," 257; Klawans, *Impurity and Sin*, 67-91, 138-50; *Purity, Sacrifice, and the Temple*, 55; Baumgarten, "Tohorot," 84; van de Sandt, "'Do Not Give What Is Holy to the Dogs,'" 244; Kazen, *Jesus and Purity Halakhah*, 201-11; Harrington, *The Purity Texts*, 27-30; "Holiness and Law," 130. In contrast to Pharisaic tradition, the sectarians sometimes recited a confession while undergoing purification from ritual impurity; see Eshel, "4Q414 Fragment 2," 6. For a different view, see Himmelfarb, "Impurity and Sin," who concludes that the sectarians considered impurity an indication of human imperfection but separate from sin. Himmelfarb identifies different attitudes towards impurity and sin in the biblical sources, noting that "For P impurity is an objective, ritual state, not a moral one," whereas "H understands certain moral sins as defiling" (11). See also Himmel-

farb, *A Kingdom of Priests*, 61-63, 87-92, 109, 132. For a recent study of sin (including its connection with impurity) in the Hebrew Bible's priestly literature, see Sklar, *Sin, Impurity, Sacrifice, Atonement*.

37. See Henschke, "The Sanctity of Jerusalem," 17, 19, who contrasts this with the rabbinic view (derived from Deuteronomy) that Jerusalem is holy because God chose it. According to the rabbis, God's choice of Jerusalem created a new reality that rendered obsolete the old model of a mobile desert camp. Shemesh, "The Holiness according to the *Temple Scroll*," notes that the author of the *Temple Scroll* was careful to describe God's **name** or **glory** as dwelling in the temple, as opposed to God's presence, which dwells among all Israel (see 375-77). A prayer from Qumran (4Q504 1-2 iv lines 3-4) refers to God's name dwelling in Jerusalem: "in Jerusal[em, the city that you ch]ose from all the earth, that your [nam]e should be there forever . . ."; see Eshel, "Three New Fragments from Qumran Cave 11," 7. Regev, "Abominated Temple and a Holy Community," 270, suggests that the sectarians believed that God's presence had been eliminated from the temple due to sin and constituted themselves as a holy community where the divine presence could dwell. See also Noam, "The Bounds of Non-Priestly Purity," 159.

38. As Chilton, *The Temple of Jesus*, 83 puts it, "The scrolls of Qumran make it abundantly clear that the Essenes saw themselves as the new camp in the wilderness, awaiting their rise to power and control of the Temple." VanderKam, "The Judean Desert and the Community," 162-63, 171, observes that whereas the notion of a desert community derives from Isa 40:3-5, the location by the Dead Sea comes from Ezek 47:8-12.

39. Translation from Baumgarten and Schwartz, "Damascus Document," 53.

40. See Yadin, *The Temple Scroll*, 2:199, who notes that, in the *Temple Scroll*, "the Temple city parallels the pentateuchal מחנה [camp] with all its halakhic implications." As García Martínez, *Qumranica Minora*, 2:216, remarks, "The aim of the Community established in the desert is, evidently, to make it possible for members to live the 'covenant' by perfect conduct." Holiness was required in the war camp in order to maintain God's presence; see Douglas, *Purity and Danger*, 51; Bokser, "Approaching Sacred Space," 282-83; Harrington, "Holiness and Law," 132; Wright, *The Disposal of Impurity*, 171.

41. See Hultgren, *From the Damascus Covenant to the Covenant of the Community*, 308-14; Harrington, *The Purity Texts*, 38; "Holiness and Law," 128, 132-33; Davidson, *Angels at Qumran*; García Martínez, *Qumranica Minora*, 2:216-17; Beall, *Josephus' Description of the Essenes*, 87-89; Schiffman, "Community Without Temple," 272-73 ("the life of the sect was conducted as if the community were a virtual Temple"); Wassen, *Women in the Damascus Document*, 149-50. Klawans, *Purity, Sacrifice, and the Temple*, 166, argues that the sectarians did not believe the divine presence dwelled among them in the present age. For the connection between the temple as *imitatio Dei* and purity requirements, see Klawans, *Purity, Sacrifice, and the Temple*, 58, 62. Klawans (113, 143) notes that purity is also required for priests because they often are understood as imitating angels.

42. From Vermes, *The Complete Dead Sea Scrolls in English*, 136-37. See also, e.g., 4Q511 frag. 35 (Songs of a Sage), discussed by Baumgarten, "Recent Qumran Discoveries and Halakhah," 157.

43. See Neusner, *The Idea of Purity in Ancient Judaism*, 69. Although it is not clear whether the Essenes participated in the sacrificial cult in the Jerusalem temple, they did not deny the importance of having a temple and animal sacrifices. For discussions, see Hultgren, *From the Damascus Covenant to the Covenant of the Community*, 309-11; Regev, "Abominated

Temple and a Holy Community," 260 n. 50; Beall, *Josephus' Description of the Essenes*, 115-19; Taylor, "Philo of Alexandria on the Essenes," 12-14; Baumgarten, "Josephus on Essene Sacrifice"; Magness, *Debating Qumran*, 94-95; Schiffman, "Community Without Temple"; Baumgarten, *Studies in Qumran Law*, 42, 52-53, who notes that "the community extended a form of priestly sanctity to all the members of the sect" (45). For a clever possible solution to Josephus's confused account of Essene offerings to the temple (*Ant.* 18.19), see Schwartz, *Studies in the Jewish Background of Christianity*, 107 ("On Sacrifice by Gentiles in the Temple of Jerusalem"), who suggests that the Essenes contributed gifts to the temple but did not offer sacrifices.

44. Noam, "The Bounds of Non-Priestly Purity"; see also Regev, "Reconstructing Qumranic and Rabbinic Worldviews." For the Qumran sect, see Shemesh, "The Holiness according to the *Temple Scroll*."

45. It was the view that God dwelled among all Israel and was not restricted to the Jerusalem temple (and that the divine could be experienced anywhere) which enabled Judaism to survive the disaster of 70; see Bokser, "Approaching Sacred Space," 287, who notes that the rabbis transformed the sacred with their view that God can be worshipped in everyday life without the temple, thereby emphasizing individual action. See also Regev, "Reconstructing Qumranic and Rabbinic Worldviews," who observes (93) that the rabbis held an "expansive" view of the locus of holiness with regard to people, time, and space. This is why the rabbis required purification before reciting the Shema' or studying Torah; see Poirier, "Purity beyond the Temple," 251, who criticizes Hyam Maccoby on this point. But Noam, "The Bounds of Non-Priestly Purity," 133 n. 20, points out that purification before reciting the Shema' or praying is necessary only for those who have had a seminal emission.

46. See Qimron, "The Controversy over the Holiness of Jerusalem."

47. See Regev, "Reconstructing Qumranic and Rabbinic Worldviews," 94-96; Qimron, "The Controversy over the Holiness of Jerusalem," who both cite the *Temple Scroll* and 4QMMT. For excrement, dogs, and chickens, see the relevant chapters below.

48. See Qimron, "The Controversy over the Holiness of Jerusalem," 73-74, who extrapolates the Pharisaic view from rabbinic sources and notes that the rabbis even ruled that corpses and those with corpse impurity may enter the Temple Mount. See also Schiffman, "The Impurity of the Dead," 136.

49. For an overview of the different ways in which modern scholars have treated Jesus' relationship to Jewish law and particularly his observance of purity requirements, see Kazen, *Jesus and Purity Halakhah*, 16-25, 49, who concludes that Jesus' behavior "must have been considered unacceptable in contexts where expansionist ideals were influential" (197). I agree with Fredriksen, *Jesus of Nazareth*, 203, that Jesus took purity observance for granted; see also Haber, "*They Shall Purify Themselves*," 181-206 ("Going Up to Jerusalem: Purity, Pilgrimage, and the Historical Jesus").

50. For a discussion of this episode in relation to purity laws, see Adler, "The Ritual Baths near the Temple Mount," 213. On the other hand, Joel Marcus notes, "Caution is necessary here. This is Luke's version of things, and he has a tendency to present Paul as a Torah-observant Jew in a way that many [scholars] doubt is historical" (personal communication, August 2009). However, in this case I do not think such caution is necessary since purification rituals were observed in connection with temples and sacred sites throughout the Greco-Roman world; see, e.g., Stowers, "On the Comparison of Blood," 184-87. Therefore, this statement need not be understood as Luke's concern with presenting Paul as a Torah-

observant Jew, but rather describes someone who underwent the required purification before entering a sacred compound (in this case, the Jerusalem temple).

51. See Furstenberg, "Defilement Penetrating the Body," 179 n. 5, who describes Jesus' position on some halakhic points as "conservative." Mason, "Pharisaic Dominance before 70 C.E.," 378, observes, "It is widely agreed that Jesus advocated Torah piety, for his disciples would eventually relax covenant obligations and endorse a mission to the gentiles only after strong initial opposition and intense debate." Mason notes that a Q passage attributes to Jesus a concern even for tithing herbs, which is not required by scripture (Matt 23:23; Luke 11:42).

52. See Wassen, *Women in the Damascus Document*, 114-18, 159-60, 162, who notes that the community behind the *Damascus Document* seems to have allowed for divorce. Brin, "Divorce at Qumran," 237, concludes that "the sect did not object to divorce in an absolute manner, but only under certain conditions, such as the possibility of remarriage after divorce." He suggests that a married member who was permanently expelled was forced to divorce his wife. See also Baumgarten, "The Qumran-Essene Restraints on Marriage," esp. 15; Crawford, "Not According to Rule," 133; Broshi, "Qumran and the Essenes," 467-68; Fredriksen, *Jesus of Nazareth*, 102; Schwartz, "Law and Truth," 230-31.

53. See Kazen, *Jesus and Purity Halakhah*, 261; Regev, "Abominated Temple and a Holy Community," 251; Fredriksen, *Jesus of Nazareth*, 103. This is why Jesus reportedly took a strict stand on issues such as adultery and divorce (see, e.g., Mark 7:20-23), but it does not mean that he was unconcerned with cultic matters or purity issues since moral offenses polluted the temple. As Pickup, "Matthew's and Mark's Pharisees," 85, puts it, "it becomes more plausible to understand Jesus to be emphasizing the point that moral purity is of greater importance to God than ritual purity — without trying to nullify the latter." Kister, "Law, Morality, and Rhetoric," 149, observes that Jesus' concern is moral but not antihalakhic. Jesus' emphasis on the polluting nature of immoral behavior recalls the view of the H source (Holiness Code) in the Hebrew Bible (see, e.g., Lev 18:26-28), according to which forbidden sexual relations, idolatry, and murder are the most severe offenses; see Himmelfarb, "Impurity and Sin," 11-12; Klawans, *Purity, Sacrifice, and the Temple*, 55, 58; Kazen, *Jesus and Purity Halakhah*, 214; Werman, "The Concept of Holiness," 174; Himmelfarb, *A Kingdom of Priests*, 61-63, 87-92, 131 (who notes that H does not use purity terminology to explain how the land will be purified from sinful behavior). The influence of the H source is also evident in Jesus' focus on the kingdom of God, for as Klawans observes, "the underpinning of the entire Holiness Code [is] *imitatio Dei*" (58; see also 62, 113, where he discusses the notion of *imitatio dei* in relation to earthly and heavenly temples). On the other hand, Sanders, *Judaism*, 71, remarks, "The purity laws, which were strictly observed and (when possible) enforced, were not primarily moral laws." He distinguishes between voluntary and involuntary transgressions (108, 192). In contrast, Sklar, *Sin, Impurity, Sacrifice, Atonement*, notes that the priestly literature of the Hebrew Bible considers even some unintentional sins as severe transgressions, concluding, "sacrificial atonement is a necessary aspect of addressing major ritual impurities as well as unintentional moral impurities" (149; see also 157).

54. Klawans, *Purity, Sacrifice, and the Temple*, 70-71, 176-77, 194-95, notes that in contrast to the Qumran sectarians, the rabbis compartmentalized their treatments of ritual and moral impurity and limited moral impurity to those sins explicitly listed in the Hebrew Bible (idolatry, sexual sin, and murder). See also Regev, "Abominated Temple and a Holy Community"; Werman, "The Concept of Holiness," 167. For the difference between defile-

ment resulting from bodily impurities and sin in priestly legislation, see Schwartz, "The Bearing of Sin in the Priestly Literature."

55. This saying is part of the putative Q source. For a discussion of both quotes, see Meier, *A Marginal Jew*, 1:515-20.

56. Davies, "Food, Drink and Sects," 155.

57. Ariel, "Imported Greek Stamped Amphora Handles," 279.

58. See Goodman, *The Ruling Class of Judaea*, 79.

59. See Baumgarten, *Studies in Qumran Law*, 21-22, who identifies the insistence on written laws as a conservative priestly tradition (27). The notion that laws become official and binding once they are written and posted in a public place was widespread in the Mediterranean world and ancient Near East, as exemplified by the Old Babylonian Hammurabi stela and the Royal Stoa in Athens, as Regev, *The Sadducees and Their Halakhah*, 126, also observes. For the possibility that the Sadducees had their own oral traditions see Wassen, "Sadducees and Halakah," 141-43, who notes that they seem to have created their own halakhah in matters not covered by the Torah; see also Regev, *The Sadducees and Their Halakhah*, 219-20. For the suggestion that the Qumran sect also used exegesis in the development of an oral law (but considered their exegesis as divinely-inspired truth revealed through the Torah), see Shemesh and Werman, "Hidden Things and Their Revelation." See also Schiffman, "Qumran and Rabbinic Halakhah," 143, who says that Sadducean exegesis adhered as closely as possible to the plain meaning of scripture.

60. For recent overviews, see Netzer, *The Palaces of the Hasmoneans and Herod the Great; The Architecture of Herod*.

61. Berlin, "Jewish Life before the Revolt," 448-50; Dunbabin, *The Roman Banquet*, 47.

62. Avigad, *Discovering Jerusalem*, 83. Regev, "Non-Priestly Purity and Its Religious Aspects," 231 n. 20, concurs that the inhabitants of these houses included Sadducees and chief priests.

63. Ostentatious architecture and interior decoration are attested in Galilee but on a much more limited scale, apparently reflecting the presence of local elites. For a survey, see Weiss, "Jewish Galilee in the First Century C.E.," esp. 53, who notes that no mosaic floors dating to before 70 have been discovered in the north.

64. See Avigad, *Discovering Jerusalem*, 83-192.

65. Avigad, *Discovering Jerusalem*, 139-42, 174-83.

66. See Avigad, *Discovering Jerusalem*, 129-31. For the possibility that the Kathros and Caiaphas families were related, see Reich, "Ossuary Inscriptions from the 'Caiaphas' Tomb"; "Caiaphas Name Inscribed on Bone Boxes."

67. See Broshi, "Excavations on Mount Zion," 83-85.

68. See Broshi, "Excavations on Mount Zion," 83-84; Rozenberg, "The Absence of Figurative Motifs."

69. Broshi, "Excavations on Mount Zion," 84.

70. Broshi, "Excavations on Mount Zion," 81; see also Regev, *The Sadducees and Their Halakhah*, 407. Of course, the Christian tradition does not mean this really was the site of Caiaphas's house, though it appears to have been an upper-class quarter.

71. See Mazar, *In the Shadow of the Temple*, 150-51; Geva, "The Temple Mount and Its Environs," 740; Fine, *Art and Judaism in the Greco-Roman World*, 78. One ossuary from the Akeldama tombs in Jerusalem has a bucranium (bull's head) carved in relief on one side; see Shadmi, "The Ossuaries and the Sarcophagus," 45 (Ossuary 17), including fig. 2.12. An exam-

ple of a figured scene dating to the reign of Herod has now been discovered at Herodium, in a room adjacent to a small theater on the lower slope of the mountain. The walls of the room (and probably the ceiling) were decorated with frescoes and stucco of the highest quality, including an open trompe l'oeil window framing a sacro-idyllic landscape. See Netzer et al., "Two Inscriptions from Herodium," 87, 90 (fig. 5).

72. For Jewish attitudes (and opposition) to wealth, see Goodman, *The Ruling Class of Judaea*, 125-32. But Sanders, *Judaism*, 338, cautions, "That rich people were wicked seems not to have been what average first-century Jews thought."

73. From Charles, *APOT*, 2:419-20. For a discussion of this work and its date, see Vriezen and van der Woude, *Ancient Israelite and Early Jewish Literature*, 605-9, who suggest that the author might have been from Jerusalem. For the consequences of the concentration of wealth in the hands of the Jerusalem elite, see Crossan, *The Historical Jesus*, 222-23.

74. Goodman, *The Ruling Class of Judaea*, 35-36.

75. Goodman, *The Ruling Class of Judaea*, 67. But see Hezser, *Jewish Slavery in Antiquity*, 125-27, for the suggestion that the tannaitic term *byt* ("house") is the Hebrew equivalent of the Roman *domus* and included slaves and other dependents.

76. Goodman, *The Ruling Class of Judaea*, 64-67.

77. Sanders, *Judaism: Practice and Belief*, 49-50.

78. Weiss, "Jewish Galilee in the First Century c.e.," 54, remarks on the absence of manor houses in Galilee. Terrenato, "The Auditorium Site in Rome," 27, observes that in Italy, "[rural] villas were rather an architectural fashion adopted by a moneyed élite that had acquired its prosperity elsewhere [and through other means]. . . . Landownership allowed aristocrats of old or of recently-acquired standing to project personas characterized by traditionalism and morality." Terrenato notes that classic villas are a consequence rather than a cause of social and economic processes and therefore represent a phenomenon that should be understood within the Italian context.

79. For rural villas in early Roman Palestine, see Hirschfeld, *Ramat Hanadiv Excavations*, 712-20; "Early Roman Manor Houses in Judea." I reject Hirschfeld's identification of Qumran as a manor house; see Magness, Review of *Qumran in Context; Debating Qumran*, 33-37. An elaborate (non-Jewish) Hellenistic period rural villa is located in Israel's Upper Galilee; see Herbert, *Tel Anafa*. For a recent discussion of "classic villas" in Italy with bibliog., see Terrenato, "The Auditorium Site in Rome."

80. For the final report on the excavations at Ḥorvat ʿEleq, see Hirschfeld, *Ramat Hanadiv Excavations*, 235-580. For Khirbet el-Muraq, see Damati, "Hilkiah's Palace"; "The Palace of Ḥilkiya."

81. See Hirschfeld, *Ramat Hanadiv Excavations*, 235-580. For the altar (identified as a "pillar-leg of stone table or washbowl"), see 266, 485. For the pig bones (which comprise only 2 percent of the Early Roman sample), see 512, 515, 517-18.

82. See Hirschfeld, *Ramat Hanadiv Excavations*, 658-59, 707-9. One small fragment of a chiseled stone vessel was found at Ḥorvat ʿEleq, apparently belonging to an uncommon type of tub or basin; see Hirschfeld, *Ramat Hanadiv Excavations*, 480, 482 pl. IV:11, for which the only parallel cited is Cahill, "Chalk Vessel Assemblages," 255 fig. 20:15-16. The presence of wheel-made (Herodian) oil lamps at Ḥorvat ʿEleq does not indicate Jewish presence, as these lamps are also found at non-Jewish sites (see the discussion of wheel-made lamps below). In contrast, the presence of a miqveh at Ḥorvat ʿAqav, a contemporary farm house just a couple of kilometers from Ḥorvat ʿEleq, indicates Jewish presence. Interestingly, the ce-

ramic assemblage from Horvat ʿAqav includes Eastern and Cypriote Sigillata and decorated discus lamps but no amphoras, imported cooking wares, or Western Terra Sigillata; see Hirschfeld, *Ramat Hanadiv Excavations*, 13-231 (for the miqveh, see 23-25). It is therefore unlikely that Horvat ʿEleq and Horvat ʿAqav "were the property of one person," as Hirschfeld, *Ramat Hanadiv Excavations*, 718, suggested. Stone vessels and a Greek inscription mentioning Hilkiah son of Simeon indicate that the owner of the villa at Khirbet el-Muraq was Jewish (perhaps an Idumaean Jew?); see Damati, "Hilkiah's Palace," 107-8.

83. See Hirschfeld, *Ramat Hanadiv Excavations*, 712-20 (esp. 719 fig. 40), a list that was expanded from Hirschfeld, "Early Roman Manor Houses in Judea"; see also Magness, *Debating Qumran*, 17-39. Hirschfeld, *Ramat Hanadiv Excavations*, 712, admitted that no agricultural installations are attested at most of the sites he identified as "manor houses." For Tel Goded, see Gibson, "The Tell el-Judeideh (Tel Goded) Excavations," 213-15, where a Hellenistic fortified tower was expanded in the early Roman period by a modest-sized structure to the east with rooms around a central court (perhaps colonnaded), which Gibson describes as part of a "rural estate." For the farm house at Ein Boqeq, see Magness, Review of ʿEn Boqeq; Berlin, "Business at the Bottom of the World." Magness's and Berlin's suggestion that the inhabitants of Ein Boqeq were Nabataeans rather than Judeans may be supported by the presence of pig bones; see Sade, "Animal Bones." No pigs are represented in late Second Temple–period contexts in the City of David in Jerusalem; see Horwitz, "Faunal Remains," 313. A major methodological problem affecting Hirschfeld's work is that his identification of these sites as manor houses was based on selected formal elements of architecture and layout alone, without taking into account other evidence such as interior decoration, ceramic corpora, and small finds; see Magness, *Debating Qumran*, 36-37.

84. See Hirschfeld, *Ramat Hanadiv Excavations*, 713-14 (with bibliog.); "Early Roman Manor Houses in Judea," 168; Shatzman, *The Armies of the Hasmonaeans and Herod*, 226-27. The evidence reviewed here contradicts Hirschfeld, *Ramat Hanadiv Excavations*, 718: "the manor houses of Judea were not unusual but rather part of a wider phenomenon of wealthy landowners throughout the Hellenistic and Early Roman world."

85. See Magen, "Qalandiya." Magen's conclusion that the site ceased to function as a farm during Herod's reign and became a stable for animals working at a nearby quarry (74) is contradicted by the finds, which come from various excavation areas and include coins, pottery (including amphoras; see below), and wheel-made oil lamps dating to the first century C.E. as well as dozens of stone vessels (as Magen, 93, remarks, "Their [stone vessels] presence in such quantities is exceptional because they began to appear when the farm was past its apex").

86. See Magen, "Qalandiya," 86, who correctly identifies the amphora illustrated on 116, pl. 3:9, as Peacock and Williams, *Amphorae and the Roman Economy*, Class 10 (105-6), dated later first century B.C.E. to mid–second century C.E. The amphoras in Magen, "Qalandiya," 118, pl. 4:20-22, might be local imitations of Dressel 2-4; see Bar-Nathan, *Masada VII*, 340-41, nos. 51-56, dated either to the reign of Herod or the time of the First Jewish Revolt.

87. See Magness, *The Archaeology of Qumran*, 69-70.

88. See Hultgren, *From the Damascus Covenant to the Covenant of the Community*, 314-15: "Since the idea of the community as the temple is derived at least in part from Ezek 20, which speaks of God taking Israel back into the wilderness, there purifying the nation, and then bringing Israel back into its land, it is natural that the community would look to Is-

rael's first years in the wilderness, when they were being constituted as a nation, for guidance in how they should be organized." See also VanderKam, "The Judean Desert and the Community." For the sacred status of the wilderness camp, see Milgrom, "First Day Ablutions in Qumran," 562.

89. For Qumran, see Magness, *The Archaeology of Qumran*, 47-48; compare with the description of Capernaum in Reed, *Archaeology and the Galilean Jesus*, 151-52, 157-59.

90. The archaeological remains at Qumran reflect a sectarian hierarchy that was not based on wealth and social status. Reed, *Archaeology and the Galilean Jesus*, 157, 159, notes the absence at Capernaum of any architectural or decorative features associated with elites.

91. Saldarini, *Pharisees, Scribes and Sadducees*, 36-37; see also Crossan, *The Historical Jesus*, 44-46, 67. I substitute "non-elite" and "lower-class" for Saldarini's term "peasant."

92. Saldarini, *Pharisees, Scribes and Sadducees*, 37.

93. Saldarini, *Pharisees, Scribes and Sadducees*, 40-41.

94. Saldarini, *Pharisees, Scribes and Sadducees*, 51.

95. Saldarini, *Pharisees, Scribes and Sadducees*, 44.

96. Meier, *A Marginal Jew*, 1:279-80, who concludes that Mark's (6:3) reference to Jesus as a "woodworker" *(tektōn)* is probably accurate and describes someone with a broad range of wood-making skills.

97. Reed, *Archaeology and the Galilean Jesus*, 136, agrees that "Jesus was certainly from the lower classes and [was] their advocate as well as that of the poor."

98. Meier, *A Marginal Jew*, 1:282; see 283-84 for a convincing response to the claim that Jesus was a prosperous master builder who traveled extensively and worked in cities like Sepphoris and Jerusalem. See also Fredriksen, *Jesus of Nazareth*, 164, who describes Jesus' family as "low-level craftsmen." Reed, *Archaeology and the Galilean Jesus*, 131, notes that the modest remains at Nazareth provide a "stark contrast" with Sepphoris.

99. Saldarini, *Pharisees, Scribes and Sadducees*, 46-47.

100. For the same conclusion, see Meier, *A Marginal Jew*, 1:284. Kazen, *Jesus and Purity Halakhah*, 294, concludes that Jesus had more influence in rural areas of Galilee than in the towns; see also Fredriksen, *Jesus of Nazareth*, 164. Reed, *Archaeology and the Galilean Jesus*, 133, concurs but cautions against reading too much into the omission of Sepphoris.

101. See Lenski, *Power and Privilege*. Crossan, *The Historical Jesus*, 43-46, presents a similar picture of ancient Palestinian society based on Lenski. However, in my opinion Crossan overstates Jesus' similarity and relationship to the Cynics.

102. Scheidel, "Stratification, Deprivation, and Quality of Life," 54; Morley, "The Poor in the City of Rome," 32.

103. Scheidel, "Stratification, Deprivation, and Quality of Life," 54.

104. For the disparities between rich and poor in Roman Palestine, see Goodman, *The Ruling Class of Judaea*, 51-75, who notes (124-27) that in contrast to Roman society, Jewish tradition does not equate wealth with prestige, which is why the Judean elite did not practice the euergetism that was so common among the Greeks and Romans. Goodman concludes, "In practice, therefore, much of the ostentatious expenditure of the rich was directed towards the interiors of their earthly and eternal dwellings, where only family and friends could admire the evidence of wealth. There was just no point in showing off to the poorer citizens" (129).

105. Nevertheless, Sanders, *Judaism*, 157-68, is right in pointing out that the lower-

class population of first-century Palestine was no worse off than most of their counterparts elsewhere in the Roman world.

106. See Meier, *A Marginal Jew,* 1:279. For patched clothing in antiquity, see Sheffer and Granger-Taylor, "Textiles," 238.

107. Reed, *Archaeology and the Galilean Jesus,* 137, points to wealthy members of Jesus' audience.

Notes to Chapter 2

1. Adler, "Second Temple Period Ritual Baths," 62; see n. 1 for bibliog. on miqva'ot. Zissu and Amit, "Common Judaism, Common Purity," 49, mention 220 miqva'ot documented by Zissu at 130 sites in the Judean hills and foothills and in the Land of Benjamin. Berlin, "Jewish Life before the Revolt," 452-53, notes that the earliest miqva'ot (in the Hasmonean palaces at Jericho, Jerusalem's Jewish Quarter, Qumran, and the villages at Gezer and Gamla) date to the first half of the first century B.C.E. See also Gibson, "The Pool of Bethesda in Jerusalem," 278-79, who dates the earliest miqva'ot to the late second or early first century B.C.E. For the possibility that Hasmonean period miqva'ot are characterized by narrow sets of steps, see Grossberg, "The *Miqva'ot* (Ritual Baths) at Masada," 101, who notes that some of the miqva'ot improvised by the rebels at the time of the First Jewish Revolt also had narrow steps (123). See also Reich, "Miqva'ot in the Second Temple Period," 57-58.

2. See Zissu and Amit, "Common Judaism, Common Purity."

3. For overviews, see Neusner, *A History of the Mishnaic Law of Purities,* 81-87, 93-94 (who notes that the arrival of sunset, not immersion in water, effects purification); Gibson, "The Pool of Bethesda," 271-75; Adler, "The Ritual Baths near the Temple Mount," 210-13; Sanders, *Judaism,* 222-29; Grossberg, "The *Miqva'ot* (Ritual Baths) at Masada," 95-98; Harrington, *The Purity Texts,* 10, 21-23. Wright, *The Disposal of Impurity,* 185 n. 38, remarks, "Bathing or washing appears to be a basic prerequisite for purification from all impurities." Baumgarten, "Tohorot," 80, 91-92, notes that at Qumran the biblical term *rḥṣ* was sometimes understood as meaning washing, whereas in rabbinic halakhah it always denotes immersion for purification. Reich, "Miqva'ot in the Second Temple Period," 83-84, observes that the Jerusalem temple is the only place mentioned in the Hebrew Bible as provided with water installations for purification, although not necessarily immersion (with interesting expansions by the author of the *Temple Scroll*).

4. See Magness, *The Archaeology of Qumran,* 151; Zissu and Amit, "Common Judaism, Common Purity," 47; Regev, *The Sadducees and Their Halakhah,* 407-9; Lawrence, *Washing in Water,* 165-67; Grossberg, "The *Miqva'ot* (Ritual Baths) at Masada," 97-98; Reich, "Miqva'ot in the Second Temple Period," 12-33.

5. Regev ("Ritual Baths"; "More on Ritual Baths") connects miqva'ot with double entrances or divided staircases to priestly groups and miqva'ot with an *'otsar* to the Pharisees. For dissenting views, see Grossberg, "Ritual Baths in Second Temple Period Jerusalem"; Zissu and Amit, "Common Judaism, Common Purity," 238 n. 12, who note that miqva'ot with an *'otsar* are rare.

6. Yonatan Adler informs me that 164 miqva'ot of the late Second Temple period have been discovered to date in Jerusalem (personal communication, April 2009); see also Reich, "Miqva'ot in the Second Temple Period," 87-101. For public miqva'ot by the Temple Mount,

see Adler, "The Ritual Baths near the Temple Mount." For Jericho, see Netzer, *Hasmonean and Herodian Palaces at Jericho.* For Qumran, see Galor, "Plastered Pools"; Magness, *The Archaeology of Qumran,* 134-62. For miqva'ot in the Hebron Hills, see Amit, "Ritual Baths"; "A *Miqveh* Complex near Alon Shevut"; Zissu and Amit, "Common Judaism, Common Purity," 57-58. Gibson, "The Pool of Bethesda in Jerusalem," 280-81, proposes *(pace* Amit) that the miqva'ot in the Hebron hills were used in connection with the production of oil and wine instead of by pilgrims en route to Jerusalem.

7. See Reich and Shukrun, "The Siloam Pool"; Zissu and Amit, "Common Judaism, Common Purity," 57. For the Pool of Bethesda, see Gibson, "The Pool of Bethesda in Jerusalem."

8. For discussions of the Sepphoris miqva'ot (some of which postdate 70), see Galor, "The Stepped Water Installations"; Amit and Adler, "The Observance of Ritual Purity after 70 C.E.," 127-30; Weiss, "Jewish Galilee in the First Century C.E.," 43-45; Reed, *Archaeology and the Galilean Jesus,* 127; Hoglund and Meyers, "The Residential Quarter on the Western Summit," 39-40. Miller, "Stepped Pools and the Non-Existent Monolithic 'Miqveh,'" 221, rejects a connection between priests and miqva'ot at Sepphoris; see also Miller, "Priests, Purities, and the Jews of Galilee," especially 391.

9. Zissu and Amit, "Common Judaism, Common Purity," 49. Grossberg, "The *Miqva'ot* (Ritual Baths) at Masada," identifies twenty-one miqva'ot at Masada and thirty basins for hand immersion. For miqva'ot in Samaria, see Itah, "Ritual Baths in the Hill Country of the Benjamin Region"; Magen, "Qalandiya"; Magen et al., "Khirbet Badd 'Isa."

10. See Adler, "Second Temple Period Ritual Baths," esp. 64-65; and "The Observance of Ritual Purity in Agricultural Industry," esp. 72-73, for miqva'ot adjacent to agricultural installations. Adler suggests that because an impure person who had immersed in a miqveh was at a lesser degree of impurity until sunset *(tebul yom),* the produce handled by workers who had immersed in these miqva'ot had the status of *ḥullin* (ordinary food). See also Zissu and Amit, "Common Judaism, Common Purity," 54-57; Zissu, Tepper, and Amit, "*Miqwa'ot* at Kefar 'Othnai," 61-63.

11. Zissu and Amit, "Common Judaism, Common Purity," 51-52, note that in rural areas few miqva'ot are located inside houses and suggest that public miqva'ot in villages were used for emergency situations when the water supply dwindled.

12. See Magen et al., "Khirbet Badd 'Isa," 182-85, 188-90, 195-96, 198, 217. But the village at Modi'in has only one miqveh, located in a building near the "synagogue"; see Onn et al., "Khirbet Umm el-'Umdan," 67*.

13. See Magen, "Qalandiya," 35, 39, 62-63.

14. See Seligman, "Jerusalem, Khirbat Ka'akul (Pisgat Ze'ev H)," 3-13, with references to miqva'ot at other villages and farms (5).

15. Amit, Torgü, and Gendelman, "Horvat Burnat," 104-5.

16. Adan-Bayewitz and Aviam, "Iotapata, Josephus, and the Siege of 67," 149-52, 163. For a distribution map of miqva'ot at Galilean sites, see Aviam, "Distribution Maps of Archaeological Data from Galilee," 118. I locate Gamla in Galilee instead of the Golan, following Danny Syon, who is publishing the final excavation report on Shmaryahu Guttman's excavations at Gamla.

17. Berlin, "Jewish Life before the Revolt," 453. Berlin, *Gamla I,* 150, suggests that the residents of Area R used the single communal miqveh in front of the synagogue. However,

Yonatan Adler thinks it is likely that there were additional miqva'ot in the unexcavated area between Area R and the synagogue (personal communication, April 2009).

18. As noted by Reed, *Archaeology and the Galilean Jesus*, 157-58.

19. For the translation of the the gloss in Mark 7:4, see Baumgarten, "Finding Oneself in a Sectarian Context," 136-37, who understands this as referring to full body immersion rather than hand washing.

20. For discussions of these passages, see Marcus, *Mark 1–8*, 439-54; Pickup, "Matthew's and Mark's Pharisees," 80-87; Kazen, *Jesus and Purity Halakhah*, 60-88; Booth, *Jesus and the Laws of Purity* (who believes that Mark exaggerates the extent of the practice of hand washing; see 70); Lambrecht, "Jesus and the Law"; Kister, "Law, Morality, and Rhetoric," 150-54. Neusner, *The Idea of Purity in Ancient Judaism*, 61-62, notes that Matthew ignores Mark's (correct) distinction between hand washing as a Pharisaic custom and the cleanness of foods as a biblical injunction.

21. For a passage about hand washing from Seder Eliyahu Rabba 16, see Milgrom, "The Scriptural Foundations and Deviations," 87-88. For examples of rabbinic legislation about hand washing, see *t. Ber.* 4:8; 5:6; 5:13.

22. Doering, "Purity and Impurity in the Book of Jubilees," 265, who notes that this legislation is included also in the *Aramaic Levi Document* and the *Testament of Levi*.

23. For useful surveys, see Marcus, *Mark 1–8*, 520-22; Kazen, *Jesus and Purity Halakhah*, 67-72, 81-85. See also Deines, *Jüdische Steingefäße*, 268-74; Poirier, "Why Did the Pharisees Wash Their Hands?"; Harrington, "Did the Pharisees Eat Ordinary Food"; Alon, *Jews, Judaism and the Classical World*, 205-23; Oppenheimer, *The 'Am Ha-aretz*, 220. According to Sanders, *Judaism*, 422, the New Testament discussions demonstrate that hand washing was practiced before 70. Regev, *The Sadducees and Their Halakhah*, 191, notes that the Pharisees disagreed among themselves about the need for hand washing. For different opinions on whether the practice of hand washing derives from Exod 30:17-21, see Lawrence, *Washing in Water*, 30-31, 55; Booth, *Jesus and the Laws of Purity*, 156-58; Furstenberg, "Defilement Penetrating the Body," 191. Furstenberg suggests that the Pharisees required hand washing before meals because they believed that the consumption (or ingestion) of contaminated food causes impurity, a position that is not based on biblical law. Instead, Furstenberg proposes that the Jewish custom of hand washing derives from Greco-Roman practice.

24. Grossberg, "The *Miqva'ot* (Ritual Baths) at Masada," 118-21. This suggestion was made previously by Elitzur, "Ritual Pools for Immersion of Hands," who notes that some miqva'ot are too shallow for full bodily immersion. According to rabbinic halakhah miqva'ot for immersing hands must contain at least 40 seahs of water and conform to the other requirements for miqva'ot for full immersion. Booth, *Jesus and the Laws of Purity*, 185-86, observes that washing purifies only the hands, not the entire body.

25. Yadin and Naveh, "The Hebrew and Aramaic Ostraca and Jar Inscriptions," 32-33. A cylindrical jar from Cave 8 at Qumran was incised twice with the letter *tet* (ט); see Baillet, Milik, and de Vaux, *Les 'Petites Grottes' de Qumrân*, pl. 7:2. Lange, "The Meaning of Dema'," 125-26, argues that since (in contrast to the Masada examples) the Qumran jar was incised before firing, it probably did not contain priestly tithes, as the Mishnah stipulates that single letters are to be used only in case of emergency.

26. Yadin and Naveh, "The Hebrew and Aramaic Ostraca and Jar Inscriptions," 33-34. Avemarie, "'Tohorat ha-Rabbim' and 'Mashqeh ha-Rabbim'," 220, notes that these inscrip-

tions provide evidence for the use of the word *ṭhrh* to designate pure food already in the Second Temple period.

27. Yadin and Naveh, "The Hebrew and Aramaic Ostraca and Jar Inscriptions," 36; one of these mentions a man named Yeshua, written in Palaeo-Hebrew script. Yadin and Naveh identified the letter *qof* (ק) on one ostracon as an abbreviation of *qodesh* or *qorban;* see also Sapir, "Masada: Evidence of Observing Jewish Laws of Purity," 144, who prefers *qodesh.*

28. Yadin and Naveh, "The Hebrew and Aramaic Ostraca and Jar Inscriptions," 35.

29. Yadin and Naveh, "The Hebrew and Aramaic Ostraca and Jar Inscriptions," 35-36.

30. Yadin and Naveh, "The Hebrew and Aramaic Ostraca and Jar Inscriptions," 37-38. Another ostracon from the same casemate room was inscribed with the word *lqdwš*.

31. Yadin and Naveh, "The Hebrew and Aramaic Ostraca and Jar Inscriptions," 37-38.

32. Yadin and Naveh, "The Hebrew and Aramaic Ostraca and Jar Inscriptions," 38-39.

33. See Grossberg, "The *Miqva'ot* (Ritual Baths) at Masada," 118-19; Elitzur, "Ritual Pools for Immersion of Hands," 172; Sapir, "Masada: Evidence of Observing Jewish Laws of Purity," 143-45. Sapir (138) objects to Yadin and Naveh's interpretation on the grounds that priests and others are forbidden to eat *qodashim* outside of Jerusalem, and there would be no point in collecting these goods on top of Masada, especially after the destruction of the temple. Furthermore, it is highly unlikely that the rebels atop Masada produced wine and oil.

34. For a discussion see Sapir, "Masada: Evidence of Observing Jewish Laws of Purity," 142.

35. Grossberg, "The *Miqva'ot* (Ritual Baths) at Masada," 118.

36. Elitzur, "Ritual Pools for Immersion of Hands."

37. For the early date of these traditions, see Instone-Brewer, *Prayer and Agriculture,* 85-86; Sanders, *Jewish Law,* 31.

38. See Instone-Brewer, *Prayer and Agriculture,* 86; Kazen, *Jesus and Purity Halakhah,* 82. For the connection between washing hands and eating, see Alon, *Jews, Judaism and the Classical World,* 219-21.

39. According to the Tosefta's version (*t. Ber.* 5:26), the house of Hillel assumed that the outer surface of the cup is always unclean anyway. For a discussion of the debate between the houses, see Booth, *Jesus and the Laws of Purity,* 172-73.

40. According to Alon, *Jews, Judaism and the Classical World,* 220, this halakhah antedates the time of the sages.

41. From Branham and Kinney, *Petronius Satyrica,* 30. See Clarke, "Jewish Table Manners in the *Cena Trimalchionis*," 260-61.

42. Neusner, *The Idea of Purity in Ancient Judaism,* 60, notes that the Synoptic Gospels deal with three aspects of purity: bodily afflictions, impure hands and food, and ethics, with the first emphasized in the stories about Jesus and the latter two emphasized in sayings attributed to him.

43. For a discussion including the corresponding passage in the *Gospel of Thomas,* see Kazen, *Jesus and Purity Halakhah,* 223-31, who concludes, "it is reasonable to suggest that Jesus (and hence his disciples) were criticized for not always washing or immersing before a meal, in a way expected by the expansionist current of the first century C.E. It is also reasonable to suggest that Jesus did discuss purity and impurity with other religious leaders, using categories of 'inside' and 'outside', making comparisons between vessels and people" (230-

31). See also Tomson, "Jewish Purity Laws as Viewed by the Church Fathers," 86; Pickup, "Matthew's and Mark's Pharisees," 107-8, who notes that most scholars attribute this material to Q. According to Furstenberg, "Defilement Penetrating the Body," 198, Jesus' sayings often reflect halakhic and moral points.

44. See Neusner, *The Idea of Purity in Ancient Judaism,* 62-63, who observes that although the distinction between inside and outside in rabbinic literature suggests that it was early, we do not know what use was made of it in early periods. Contemporary early Christian works continue to contrast external beauty and purity with internal sin; see, e.g., Oxyrhynchus papyrus fragment 840: "You have washed yourself in these running waters where dogs and pigs have wallowed night and day, and you have cleansed and wiped the outside skin which the prostitutes and flute-girls anoint, which they wash, and wipe, and make beautiful for human desire; but inwardly these women are full of scorpions and every wickedness" (2.7-8); from Bovon, *"Fragment Oxyrhynchus 840,"* 715.

45. Poirier, "Why Did the Pharisees Wash Their Hands?" 227-29, suggests that there was a Pharisaic tradition distinguishing between the insides and outsides of objects and the human body. This view might also be expressed in the rabbis' (literal) internalization of external bodily punishments such as burning, which might be due to their concept of *imago Dei* (the human form should not be mutilated because it is in God's image); see Berkowitz, *Execution and Invention,* 8-9, 166.

46. See Marcus, *Mark 1–8,* 454-55, 459-61; Pickup, "Matthew's and Mark's Pharisees," 85; Kazen, *Jesus and Purity Halakhah,* 261; Klawans, *Impurity and Sin in Ancient Judaism,* 148-49. But Furstenberg, "Defilement Penetrating the Body," argues that Jesus' position is halakhic (based on biblical law), as opposed to the rabbinic/Pharisaic view that consuming food contaminated by defiled hands makes a person impure.

47. See Neusner, *The Idea of Purity in Ancient Judaism,* 62; Poirier, "Why Did the Pharisees Wash Their Hands?" 227.

48. I agree with Kazen, *Jesus and Purity Halakhah,* 65, 67, that the discussion about inside versus outside refers to washing rather than clean and unclean foods. Luke's use of the verb "immerse" *(ebaptisthē)* rather than *niptō* (Luke 11:38) leaves open the question of whether full immersion is meant as opposed to hand washing (or perhaps hand immersion).

49. See also *Gos. Thom.* 89: "Jesus said, 'Why do you wash the outside of the cup? Do you not realize that he who made the inside is the same one who made the outside?'" (Lambdin translation online at http://www.gnosis.org/naghamm/gthlamb.html)

50. Marcus, *Mark 1–8,* 461 remarks, "The Markan Jesus, then, turns the whole notion of pollution upside down. . . ." See Poirier, "Why Did the Pharisees Wash Their Hands?" 227, for the suggestion that the Pharisees required hand washing before meals because they believed that impurity could be ingested and therefore make a person impure from within. Furstenberg, "Defilement Penetrating the Body," develops this argument and notes (196) that the rabbis present a process of contamination which is opposite that of the levitical system. Whereas in Lev 11 food can be contaminated by an impure vessel, according to rabbinic law a vessel as well as people can be contaminated by impure food and liquids.

51. See Marcus, *Mark 1–8,* 451-52. As Instone-Brewer, *Prayer and Agriculture,* 86, notes, Jesus' "disagreement with the Pharisees on this matter concerned not so much the fact that they did something which was not commanded in Scripture, but that they criticized others for not following their rules." See also Furstenberg, "Defilement Penetrating the Body";

Tomson, "Jewish Purity Laws as Viewed by the Church Fathers," 85; Baumgarten, "The Name of the Pharisees," 422 n. 47.

52. Sanders, *Judaism,* 438, believes that although such passages could have led the Pharisees and others to wash their hands frequently, this does not appear to have been their starting point.

53. For this text, see Brooke, *The Dead Sea Scrolls and the New Testament,* 225; Puech, "The Collection of Beatitudes in Hebrew and in Greek." See also Himmelfarb, *A Kingdom of Priests,* 133.

54. Baumgarten, *Studies in Qumran Law,* 32 n. 77. Klawans, *Impurity and Sin in Ancient Judaism,* 141, notes another difference: "the Gospel accounts of John the Baptist punctuate the verse in accordance with the Septuagint, whereas the Community Rule's version is in accordance with a (proto-) Masoretic text."

55. See Poirier, "Why Did the Pharisees Wash Their Hands?" 230-31, who suggests that the "morning bathers" rejected the Pharisaic belief in the ritual divisibility of the body. Baumgarten, "The Purification Rituals in *DJD 7,*" 203, proposes that this group required immersion before morning prayer because sleep was considered a source of defilement. Burns, "Essene Sectarianism and Social Differentiation," 264-65 n. 40, cites this passage as "a clear example of the continued occurrence of characteristically Essenic behavior among Jews after 70 C.E."

56. Cecilia Wassen (personal communication, August 2009) notes that the declaration of all foods as clean is missing from the parallel passage in Matthew (15:10-20), which instead might reflect a debate about hand washing (see Matt 15:20). For a recent discussion of this passage, see Furstenberg, "Defilement Penetrating the Body." Davies, "Food, Drink and Sects," 161, suggests that perhaps Jesus was criticizing the dining practices and regulations of groups such as the Essenes/Qumran sect.

57. Wassen (personal communication, August 2009) also points to the example of Jesus' command to the healed leper in Mark 1:44 to show himself to the priest and give an offering (following Lev 14:2-20). Mason, "Pharisaic Dominance before 70 C.E.," 378, notes that Jesus seems generally to have advocated Torah observance and may have observed some traditions such as tithing even more strictly than scripture requires. See also Furstenberg, "Defilement Penetrating the Body," 178 n. 5; Booth, *Jesus and the Laws of Purity,* 109, who describes Jesus as having been raised in "an orthodox Jewish home" (!)

58. See Neusner, *The Idea of Purity in Ancient Judaism,* 61-62; Marcus, *Mark 1-8,* 450-51; Lambrecht, "Jesus and the Law," 50-52, 56; Furstenberg, "Defilement Penetrating the Body."

59. See Regev, "Pure Individualism," 200 including nn. 75-76. Tomson, "Jewish Purity Laws as Viewed by the Church Fathers," 86, suggests that Jesus rejected the idea that impurity is transferred by food, but in my opinion the issue is the status of the food.

60. Neusner, *The Idea of Purity in Ancient Judaism,* 17.

61. As Kister, "Law, Morality, and Rhetoric," 149, observes, Jesus' concern was moral but not anti-halakhic. See also Pickup, "Matthew's and Mark's Pharisees," 79 (discussing Mk 2:23-28): "It is important to recognize that Mark's gospel never portrays Jesus as rejecting Sabbath observance per se, but only a very particular application of Sabbath observance that came from the Pharisees. Neusner, *The Idea of Purity in Ancient Judaism,* 114, observes that the unclean animals of Leviticus 11 play almost no role in purity debates among the Jewish

groups of the late Second Temple period. On 119 Neusner expresses the common view that Jesus "declared it unnecessary to observe the purity laws concerning foods."

62. As Kister, "Law, Morality, and Rhetoric," 154, concludes, "Transmitted in a different, nonhalakhic and sometimes antinomistic context, this saying came to be the most radical antinomistic saying in the Synoptic Gospels." See also Marcus, *Mark 1–8,* 453-54, 458: "The explicit revocation of the OT kosher laws ascribed to Jesus by Mark in 7:19b probably goes beyond what the historical Jesus actually did." Poirier, "Why Did the Pharisees Wash Their Hands?" 226, notes that the gloss "Thus he declared all foods clean" is at odds with what the pre-Markan Jesus intended. See also Lambrecht, "Jesus and the Law," 62-66, who describes the gloss as "disruptive." Fredriksen, *Jesus of Nazareth,* 108, remarks that, "If Jesus during his mission had already nullified the laws of kashrut, this argument never could have happened." Mason, "Pharisaic Dominance before 70 C.E.," 381, suggests that Jesus' original charge of hypocrisy against the Pharisees was later misconstrued by groups within the church.

63. For a recent discussion with references, see Milikowsky, "Reflections on Hand-Washing," 154-59. Lim, "The Defilement of Hands," appeared in print after this book went to press. For hand washing before prayer, see Lawrence, *Washing in Water,* 57-59.

64. All of the relevant passages are collected and discussed in Leiman, *The Canonization of Hebrew Scripture,* 102-20.

65. Goodman, "Sacred Scripture and 'Defiling the Hands,'" 102.

66. Goodman, "Sacred Scripture and 'Defiling the Hands,'" 105, observes that the religious texts at Qumran were written on parchment, whereas papyrus, which was less expensive, generally was used for secular documents at other sites around the Dead Sea. However, although the majority of the Qumran scrolls are written on parchment, a small number are written on papyrus. Most of these are nonbiblical works, but some biblical books are represented; see Tov, "The Papyrus Fragments Found in the Judean Desert."

67. Sanders, *Jewish Law,* 31, notes that the rabbinic passages discussing handling sacred scriptures go back to the earliest, presumably Pharisaic layer. But Neusner, *A History of the Mishnaic Law of Purities,* 152-53, states that the rite of purifying the hands is not defined in the time of Yavneh.

68. See Leiman, *The Canonization of Hebrew Scripture,* 102-20.

69. Broyde, "Defilement of the Hands," 66.

70. For the purposes of this discussion it is immaterial whether the "Sadducees" named in this passage are the historical Sadducees, or a later group of opponents so designated by the rabbis, or another group such as the Essenes. For a discussion, see Regev, *The Sadducees and Their Halakhah,* 190-92.

71. Magness, *Debating Qumran,* 151-68: "I believe that not only were the cylindrical and ovoid jars preferred because of the sect's unique halakhic concerns, but because their distinctive shape came to signify contents having a high degree of purity. In other words, because their shape was easily identifiable, these jars served as markers to those who were allowed or denied contact with the pure food or drink (or other pure goods) of the sect" (162).

72. Sanders, *Judaism,* 438, suggests that perhaps scrolls defile the hands because of their great holiness; see also Cohn, *Tangled Up in Text,* 140, who proposes that ancient tefillin comprised leather casings that were sewn shut in order to protect the parchment texts from impurity.

73. For discussions of the debate over the *niṣoq,* see Baumgarten, "The Pharisaic-

Sadducean Controversies about Purity," 163-64; Schwartz, "Law and Truth," 232; Selkin Wise, "*Miqwā'ôt* and Second Temple Sectarianism," 181-84; Elman, "Some Remarks on 4QMMT." For similarities between the sectarian position and that of the house of Shammai, see Noam, "Beit Shammai and the Sectarian Halakhah," 51-54.

74. I owe this suggestion to Eli Goldschmidt (personal communication, December 2005).

75. But see Elman, "Some Remarks on 4QMMT," 99-105, who questions the assumption that Qumran law was more stringent than Pharisaic halakhah. Furstenberg, "Defilement Penetrating the Body," 190, notes that defiled hands are not a source of impurity in the Hebrew Bible except as part of an impure person such as a *zab*.

76. Noam, "The Bounds of Non-Priestly Purity," 145 n. 71, notes that Eliezer b. Hanokh probably rejected the notion of hand impurity because he believed that full body immersion was required. Milikowsky, "Reflections on Hand-Washing," 151, points out that the correct name of this rabbi seems to be Eleazar ben Ha-Ner.

77. See the Scottenstein Daf Yomi Edition of the Babylonian Talmud, commentary on tractate *Ḥag.* 18b2.

78. See Magness, *Debating Qumran*, 161-66. Even if my suggestion is correct, it remains unclear whether the sectarians considered touching all scrolls or only Torah scrolls as defiling. On the one hand, the Qumran caves yielded various kinds of literature. On the other hand, we do not know which scrolls (if any) originally were stored in jars. Yadin, *The Temple Scroll*, 1:311, noted the parallels between the term *ṭhrt hmqdš* in the *Temple Scroll* (referring to liquids and solids) and the use of *ṭhrh* in other sectarian literature from Qumran to denote the pure meals of the community *(ṭhrt hrbym)*, and concluded that this "is clear testimony that the sect considered its meals taken when they dwelt in the desert as a definite substitute for the Temple worship."

79. For a discussion, see Leiman, *The Canonization of Hebrew Scripture*, 115-18.

80. Milgrom, "First Day Ablutions in Qumran," 568: "instead of terumot Qumran employed the term tahara by which they meant that their food should be maintained in a state of purity."

81. Milikowsky, "Reflections on Hand-Washing," 162, suggests that hand washing and hand impurity have something to do with the priestly service in the Jerusalem temple.

82. See Crowfoot, "The Linen Textiles," 18-19; Magness, *Debating Qumran*, 142.

83. Yadin, *The Temple Scroll*, 1:198-200.

84. From Baumgarten, *Studies in Qumran Law*, 21. However, Baumgarten, "Recent Qumran Discoveries and Halakhah," 153, translates the same passage as reading "Behold, it is written and **placed** in a corner."

85. From Baumgarten, *Studies in Qumran Law*, 22. For the scholion, see Noam, "From Philology to History." The Pharisees' claim that the Sadducees are unable to provide any proof from the Torah suggests the possibility that the Book of Decrees incorporated nonbiblical expansions of law, recalling Qumran legal tradition. However, Fraade, "Literary Composition and Oral Performance," 40 n. 20, believes that the scholion "is of too uncertain provenience to be of any historical value for pre-Rabbinic times."

86. For the rabbinic view, see Goodman, "Sacred Scripture and 'Defiling the Hands,'" 105; Cohn, *Tangled Up in Text*, 140-41. Schiffman, "Review of *Qumran Grotte 4*," 171, suggests that due to their sanctity old phylactery straps were used to fasten and bind scrolls at Qumran.

87. See Moore, "Review of *Kleine Schriften*," 104-5; Witke, "Propertianum Manuale," 108-9.

Notes to Chapter 3

1. Jesus seems to be criticizing his opponents for being more concerned with minor points of law than with the more important issues of morality; see Instone-Brewer, *Prayer and Agriculture*, 292. Kister, "Law, Morality, and Rhetoric," 148-49, notes that Jesus uses the woes as a rhetorical device to turn a halakhic issue into a moral point.

2. See Milgrom, *Leviticus 1–16*, 656, 682; "Two Biblical Hebrew Priestly Terms," 107-9; Maccoby, *Ritual and Morality*, 69; Douglas, "Impurity of Land Animals," 35; on 42 Douglas notes that the word *ṭame'* ("impure") occurs mostly in Leviticus and is rare elsewhere in the Hebrew Bible.

3. See Milgrom, "Two Biblical Hebrew Priestly Terms," 108-10, who notes that these differences are due to the various sources of these biblical passages; see also *Leviticus 1–16*, 683-87. Douglas, *Purity and Danger*, 56, observes that the movements of creeping, crawling, and swarming creatures are contrary to God's order (holiness).

4. Yadin, *The Temple Scroll*, 2:385, tentatively restored the relevant line in the *Temple Scroll* (48:1-2), which is missing, as reading "All winged insects that go upon all fours are an abomination to you (?)."

5. For the relationship between these passages in Leviticus and Deuteronomy, see Milgrom, *Leviticus 1–16*, 698-704; "Two Biblical Hebrew Priestly Terms," 114; Kelhoffer, "Did John the Baptist Eat Like a Former Essene?" 304. *Sheqetz* is used in 11QT 2:10 to denote idolatry.

6. See Milgrom, "Two Biblical Hebrew Priestly Terms," 110-14; Maccoby, *Ritual and Morality*, 70-71; Douglas, "Impurity of Land Animals," 35. Milgrom, "Two Biblical Hebrew Priestly Terms," 108-9, points out that according to the Priestly source a person is not punished for eating *sheqetz* accidentally or deliberately.

7. From Baumgarten and Schwartz, "The Damascus Document," 51-53; see Harrington, *The Purity Texts*, 23. *Sheqetz* is used elsewhere in the *Damascus Document* (7:3-4) to denote the defilement of an individual's spirit; see Himmelfarb, "Impurity and Sin," 13.

8. The sectarian view apparently stems from the susceptibility of wetted foods to impurity from swarming creatures; see Baumgarten, "Liquids and Susceptibility to Defilement," 91-92.

9. Milgrom, "Two Biblical Hebrew Priestly Terms," 109, does not mention that this prohibition is directed specifically at priests, in contrast to the legislation in Leviticus 11. But Milgrom, *Leviticus 1–16*, 654, notes that Leviticus prohibits only priests from eating or touching all animal carcasses.

10. I am indebted to Hannan Birenboim for bringing this to my attention.

11. See Kislev and Simchoni, "Hygiene and Insect Damage," 133-70, who note that dates and figs became "severely infested" during the siege (166).

12. See Kister, "Law, Morality, and Rhetoric," 148; Werrett, *Ritual Purity and the Dead Sea Scrolls*, 34-35.

13. See Hammett, "Camel."

14. See de Vaux, "Fouilles au Khirbet Qumrân," 227, fig. 6:8, with a drinking spout on the shoulder.

15. See Bar-Nathan, *Masada VII*, 110-12 (Group F), with parallels (including later variants from Galilee), and a painted variant (257-60, Type M-PJG3); *Hasmonean and Herodian Palaces at Jericho*, 159-60 (Type J-JG9); Rahmani, "Jason's Tomb," 81, Fig. 12:2; Tushingham, *Excavations in Jerusalem*, 54; 377, fig. 25:1 (found together with the Pompeian Red Ware pan in fig. 25:36). Bar-Nathan identifies the strainer jugs with the *tzartzur* mentioned in rabbinic literature; see *Masada VII*, 385; *Hasmonean and Herodian Palaces at Jericho*, 160.

16. Nabataean cream ware strainer jugs are common at sites around the Dead Sea and in the Negev; see Bar-Nathan, *Masada VII*, 112, 284-87, with parallels including unpublished examples from Qumran.

17. As noted by Bar-Nathan, *Hasmonean and Herodian Palaces at Jericho*, 160.

18. Werrett, *Ritual Purity and the Dead Sea Scrolls*, 32-33, notes that Leviticus 11, which is the basis for this legislation, does not require locusts to be alive or cooked before being consumed. Yadin, *The Temple Scroll*, 1:320, observed that the author of the *Temple Scroll* emphasized that only locusts that have already sprouted wings may be eaten, in contrast to rabbinic law.

19. For a recent discussion of this passage, see Werrett, *Ritual Purity and the Dead Sea Scrolls*, 124-26. Whether or not it was a sectarian composition (which is debated), the *Temple Scroll* seems to have been considered authoritative at Qumran; see, e.g., Milgrom, "The Scriptural Foundations and Deviations," 95 (who describes the *Temple Scroll* as "truly Qumranic"). For the relationship and parallels between the *Temple Scroll* and CD, see Schiffman, *The Courtyards of the House of the Lord*, 149-74; Crawford, *The Temple Scroll and Related Texts*, 80-82, who concludes that "both compositions originated in the same levitical priestly circles."

20. Werrett, *Ritual Purity and the Dead Sea Scrolls*, 32-33, notes that the author of the *Damascus Document* seems to suggest that an individual could become impure by eating an uncooked locust. The Karaites also prohibited the consumption of locusts that died naturally; see Baumgarten and Schwartz, "The Damascus Document," 53 n. 187.

21. Harrington, *The Purity Texts*, 23; Werrett, *Ritual Purity and the Dead Sea Scrolls*, 32-34.

22. See Irshai, "Yaakov of Naburaya," 164-67, who discusses the strict observance of the blood prohibition among other groups, including the Samaritans, Karaites, and Ebionites.

23. Broshi, "Anti-Qumranic Polemics in the Talmud," 599.

24. Translation from Slotki, *Midrash Rabbah*, 752-53. For discussions of this passage, see Irshai, "Yaakov of Naburaya," 163-67; Fine, "Nabratein in the Ancient Literary Sources."

25. This prohibition is also mentioned in 4Q251; see Larson et al., "4QHalakha A," 40.

26. See Yadin, *The Temple Scroll*, 1:321; Milgrom, *Leviticus 1–16*, 654; Eisenman, *The New Testament Code*, 127; Schwartz, "Law and Truth," 231.

27. For kosher fish sauces, see Cotton, Lernau, and Goren, "Fish Sauces from Masada," 236-27.

28. See Cotton, Lernau, and Goren, "Fish Sauces from Masada," 230-31; Grainger, *Cooking Apicius*, 27-28.

29. Cotton, Lernau, and Goren, "Fish Sauces from Masada"; Bar-Nathan, *Masada VII*, 314, 336-39, Types M-AM 12-14 (with a reference on 338 to an unpublished example from Cypros); *Hasmonean and Herodian Palaces at Jericho*, 132-33, 136-37, Types J-AM 4-6; "Pottery and Stone Vessels of the Herodian Period," 66; 117, Pl. 4:4-6; 127, Pl. 10:2.

30. See Tushingham, *Excavations in Jerusalem 1961-1967*, 55; 373 fig. 21:42; 374 fig. 22:1; see also Bar-Nathan, *Masada VII*, 337.

31. Finkielsztejn, "Imported Amphoras," 175.

32. Avigad, *Discovering Jerusalem*, 202-3, no. 249 (stamped *ex figlin[is] Caesaris* ["from the Imperial potteries"]).

33. See Cotton, Lernau, and Goren, "Fish Sauces from Masada," 237.

34. See Cotton, Lernau, and Goren, "Fish Sauces from Masada," 237.

35. For a discussion of John's diet, see Meier, *A Marginal Jew*, 1:48-49.

36. For other differences between the practices of John and the Qumran sect, see Klawans, *Impurity and Sin in Ancient Judaism*, 141-43.

37. See Baumgarten, "Finding Oneself in a Sectarian Context," 131; Fredriksen, *Jesus of Nazareth*, 186. Scholars have noted similarities with Josephus's description of Bannus's diet (*Life* 11); for discussions, see Lichtenberger, "The Dead Sea Scrolls and John the Baptist"; Baumgarten, "Finding Oneself in a Sectarian Context," 131. Kelhoffer, "Did John the Baptist Eat Like a Former Essene?" argues that the Gospel accounts do not describe John eating specific types of locusts (in contrast to Qumran law) and that they therefore "were not intended primarily for an audience that was concerned with the finer details of kashrut."

38. For a discussion, see Meier, *A Marginal Jew*, 1:950-67.

39. Bread and fish remained dietary staples for the lower classes in this region through the Middle Ages; see Ashtor, "The Diet of the Salaried Classes." In areas where fish was not cheap or easily obtainable, such as parts of Upper Egypt, the (non-Jewish) poor consumed field mice, snakes, donkeys, and camels (12). See also Booth, *Jesus and the Laws of Purity*, 175-76; Donahue, *The Roman Community at Table*, 19.

40. For a discussion, see Milgrom, *Leviticus 1–16*, 737-42.

41. For a discussion, see Kelhoffer, "Did John the Baptist Eat Like a Former Essene?" 309.

42. Sanders, *Judaism*, 217.

43. See Marcus, *Mark 1–8*, 513-14, including a review of other interpretations.

44. Yadin, *The Temple Scroll*, 1:139, who concluded that "The passage on the 'Herodians' in Mark would therefore be the sole allusion to the Essenes in the New Testament." The festival of the ordination of the priests was an innovation of the *Temple Scroll;* see Crawford, *The Temple Scroll*, 50-51.

45. Meier, "Matthew, Gospel of," 626, attributes the substitution of "Sadducees" for "Herodians" to Matthew's ignorance of the doctrines of the Sadducees.

46. For a discussion, see Magness, *Debating Qumran*, 92-104. The bones were analyzed by Zeuner, "Notes on Qumrân," 28-30, who examined about 500 specimens from 39 jars. Similar deposits with bones belonging to the same species were discovered in more recent excavations at Qumran; see Magen and Peleg, "Back to Qumran," 94-96.

47. De Vaux, *Archaeology and the Dead Sea Scrolls*, 14.

48. For the suggestion that the bones were buried to keep them from scavengers, see Magen and Peleg, "Back to Qumran," 96; Schiffman, *Reclaiming the Dead Sea Scrolls*, 338. Taylor, "'Roots, Remedies and Properties of Stones,'" 243, suggests that the bones were deposited for hygienic reasons, "to prevent flies and animals [from] being attracted to the leftovers."

49. For a discussion, see Magness, *Debating Qumran*, 92-106; see also "Qumran: The Site of the Dead Sea Scrolls," 650.

50. Schiffman, *Reclaiming the Dead Sea Scrolls,* 338; see also Magness, *Debating Qumran,* 96. Goodfriend, *"Keleb* in Deuteronomy 23:19," 395-96, observes "That canines were associated in the Israelite mind with the indiscriminate consumption of blood (a forbidden substance even if its source was a permitted animal) seems to have been the main element that led to their expulsion from anything related to sacrifice and sancta."

51. Noam, "Qumran and the Rabbis on Corpse-Impurity," 398, has a different translation, based on consultations with Elisha Qimron: "And concerning [the impurity] of the human [bone]: we say that every bone that is [incomplete should be treated as whole] and complete, according to the law of the dead or the slain." Noam notes that according to the author of 4QMMT, bones convey impurity like a corpse. See Werrett, *Ritual Purity and the Dead Sea Scrolls,* 196-97, for a critique of Qimron's reconstruction of this passage.

52. Yadin, *The Temple Scroll,* 1:340-41; 2:226. See also Qimron and Strugnell, *Qumran Cave 4, V: Miqṣat Maʿaśe ha-Torah,* 155; Werrett, *Ritual Purity and the Dead Sea Scrolls,* 128-29; Schwartz, "Law and Truth," 232; Sussman, "History of the 'Halakha,'" 31-32.

53. See Milgrom, *Leviticus 1–16,* 682.

54. From Yadin, *The Temple Scroll,* 1:341.

55. Whatever the identity of the "Sadducees" mentioned here, the evidence from Qumran indicates that this debate goes back to the period before 70. Baumgarten, "The Pharisaic-Sadducean Controversies about Purity," 162-63, assumes they are Sadducees who shared with the Qumran sectarians the same view on this point of law; see also his discussion on 166-68. See also Regev, *The Sadducees and Their Halakhah,* 192-94.

56. For the disposal of sacrificial remains from the Jerusalem temple (primarily the ḥaṭṭʾat), see Wright, *The Disposal of Impurity,* 134, 144, who notes that these remains were treated differently from other refuse because they were considered holy. The absence of fowl from the animal bone deposits at Qumran is interesting since ʿola bird parts were disposed of together with the remains of the ḥaṭṭʾat in the dump that served the Jerusalem temple (see Wright, *The Disposal of Impurity,* 134, 144). If my proposed analogy between the animal bone deposits at Qumran and the disposal of sacrificial remains in the Jerusalem temple is correct, it is interesting to consider Wright's observation (145-46) that leftover portions of sacrifices were disposed of to avoid profanation, not because they had become impure due to spoilage. It is also worth considering this phenomenon in light of an observation by Crown, "Qumran, Samaritan *Halakha* and Theology," 441, that for some groups "slaughter did not necessarily involve any formal sacrifice but was done ritually on behalf of the people by a priest." Crown is referring to the Samaritans, but could it apply to the Qumran sect as well? Crown also raises the question of whether some groups understood the ban on ḥullin (eating meat that has not been sacrificed) as limited only to the desert period or as existing in perpetuity.

57. Firmage, "Zoology," 1120.

58. See Magness, *Debating Qumran,* 98; perhaps this phenomenon partly accounts for the need for so many ceramic vessels at Qumran. However, I am not suggesting that the sectarians offered the ḥaṭṭʾat at Qumran. De Vaux, *Archaeology and the Dead Sea Scrolls,* 12-13, describes as follows the pottery associated with the animal bone deposits: "In the free spaces between the buildings or round them the excavations have laid bare animal bones deposited between large sherds of pitchers or pots, or sometimes placed in jars left intact with their lids on. In one instance such bones have been found covered simply by a plate. In the majority of

these cases the sherds come from several jars or pots to which fragments from one or more bowls, lids, or plates have been added."

59. See Magness, *Debating Qumran*, 92-112. 4QMMT makes it clear that the sectarians considered Jerusalem the sacred camp; see Sussman, "History of the 'Halakha,'" 34.

60. Flusser, "Pharisees, Sadducees and Essenes," 153-57.

61. See Henschke, "The Sanctity of Jerusalem," 18-27.

62. Henschke, "The Sanctity of Jerusalem," 18; see also Schiffman, "Sacral and Non-Sacral Slaughter," 74-76.

63. Henschke, "The Sanctity of Jerusalem," 18, 23; Shemesh, "A New Reading of 11QT^a," 404. Milgrom, *Leviticus 1–16*, 713, remarks on the "far-reaching amendment introduced by Deuteronomy," which allows Israel to slaughter meat profanely.

64. Henschke, "The Sanctity of Jerusalem," 18-19; Shemesh, "A New Reading of 11QT^a," who points out (*pace* the usual understanding) that the *Temple Scroll* and 4QMMT ban nonsacral slaughter only in Jerusalem and its environs (a distance of 30 stadia) rather than from a distance of three days' journey. For the suggestion that the authors of the *Temple Scroll* and 4QMMT used a version of Leviticus 17 that omitted a permanent ban on profane slaughter (which was in effect only in the wilderness), see Eshel, "4QLev^d." See also Schiffman, "Sacral and Non-Sacral Slaughter"; Werman, "The Rules of Consuming and Covering the Blood," 630-31; Shemesh and Werman, "Halakhah at Qumran," 121-22. Werrett, *Ritual Purity and the Dead Sea Scrolls*, 135, considers this legislation "utopian."

65. Henschke, "The Sanctity of Jerusalem," 20-22. See also Qimron, "The Controversy over the Holiness of Jerusalem," 74; Crawford, "The Meaning of the Phrase עיר המקדש."
. 248.

66. Henschke, "The Sanctity of Jerusalem," 24; Shemesh, "A New Reading of 11QT^a," 403-4; Qimron and Strugnell, *Qumran Cave 4*, 156; Schiffman, "Sacral and Non-Sacral Slaughter," 82. Werrett, *Ritual Purity and the Dead Sea Scrolls*, 191, notes that this passage appears to be a paraphrase of Lev 17:3. For the relationship and parallels between the *Temple Scroll* and 4QMMT, see Schiffman, *The Courtyards of the House of the Lord*, 123-47; Crawford, *The Temple Scroll and Related Texts*, 78-80, who concludes that it is "extremely likely that the two compositions were written in the same milieu."

67. Henschke, "The Sanctity of Jerusalem," 25; Shemesh, "A New Reading of 11QT^a," 404.

68. Henschke, "The Sanctity of Jerusalem," 25-26.

69. Henschke, "The Sanctity of Jerusalem," 27; Qimron and Strugnell, *Qumran Cave 4*, 163 n. 144. Furthermore, rabbinic purity requirements sometimes are more lenient for Jerusalem than for other cities; see Qimron, "The Controversy over the Holiness of Jerusalem." Fink, "Why Did *yrh* Play the Dog?" 55, suggests that a Mishnaic injunction against rearing a dog unless it is tied up by a chain originated among the Pharisees in response to the concerns raised in 4QMMT.

70. For 'Ein Gedi, see Sadeh, "Archaeozoological Finds from En-Gedi," 604-6, where nearly all of the animal bones come from Byzantine contexts. For 'Ein Boqeq, see Lernau, "Geflügel- und Fischknochen," 149-68, which include specimens from the *officina* (late Second Temple period) and the fort (Late Roman-Byzantine).

71. See, e.g., 11QT 60:4-10, where birds are included among tithes.

72. From Yadin, *The Temple Scroll*, 1:272.

73. See also the discussion in Werrett, *Ritual Purity and the Dead Sea Scrolls*, 121-23.

74. From García Martínez and Tigchelaar, *The Dead Sea Scrolls Study Edition*, 2:1307. Qimron, "Chickens in the Temple Scroll," notes that this fragment was erroneously assigned to the book of *Jubilees* but belongs to the *Temple Scroll*.

75. Qimron, "Chickens in the Temple Scroll," 473.

76. See Qimron, "Chickens in the Temple Scroll," 474-75, who notes that the rabbis and later commentators did not know the reasons for the ban on chickens in Jerusalem and attributed it to a desecration of "Holy Things."

77. See Henschke, "The Sanctity of Jerusalem," 27.

78. See Horwitz and Tchernov, "Bird Remains"; "Subsistence Patterns in Ancient Jerusalem"; Bouchnik et al., "Animal Bone Remains," 73, 76 (comprising 4.6 percent of the sample from a dump on the eastern slope of the City of David).

79. See Qimron, "Chickens in the Temple Scroll," 474 n. 8.

80. I am grateful to Randall Price for sharing with me this unpublished information and for his permission to cite it here. For a preliminary report on the 2002 excavation season, see Price, "Qumran Plateau."

81. For the wall, see de Vaux, *Archaeology and the Dead Sea Scrolls*, 59. Price's discoveries suggest that the wall dates to the period of the sectarian settlement, not the Iron Age as de Vaux thought.

82. See Magness, *The Archaeology of Qumran*, 121-26; *Debating Qumran*, 98-106.

83. In L22 (southwest corner of the courtyard of the main building), de Vaux reported finding a jar containing bird bones *(ossements d'oiseaux)*. However, since this jar is described as having been buried under the latest (uppermost) floor in this room, and since L22 existed only in Period III, the deposit appears to postdate the sectarian settlement. See Humbert and Chambon, *Fouilles de Khirbet Qumrân*, 300.

84. See Magness, *The Archaeology of Qumran*, 129; *Debating Qumran*, 112.

85. Yadin, *The Temple Scroll*, 1:318-20; see also Werman, "The Rules of Consuming and Covering the Blood," 631.

86. No gazelle bones were found in the early Roman stratum in Shiloh's excavations in the City of David, but deer comprised 1 percent of the sample; see Horwitz, "Faunal Remains," 313 (Table 3). No gazelle or deer bones are represented in the relatively small sample of the late Second Temple period published from Benjamin Mazar's excavations south of the Temple Mount; see Horwitz and Tchernov, "Subsistence Patterns in Ancient Jerusalem," 145. There are also no gazelle or deer bones from a dump on the eastern slope of the City of David; see Bouchnik et al., "Animal Bone Remains." Gazelle comprises 1.1 percent of the animal bones recovered in recent excavations outside the Temple Mount (near Robinson's Arch); I am indebted to Ronny Reich for sharing with me this unpublished information.

87. Schiffman, "Sacral and Non-Sacral Slaughter," 82.

88. Yadin, *The Temple Scroll*, 3:308-11.

89. From Baumgarten, "Finding Oneself in a Sectarian Context," 142.

90. Yadin, *The Temple Scroll*, 1:310-11. The possibility that the *Temple Scroll* was composed at about the same time as Antiochus III's decree raises interesting questions about the author's polemical tone. Does this tone reflect the existence of internal opposition to the ban in Jerusalem, or is it due to the author's extension of the ban to all nonsacrificial animals? For the date of the *Temple Scroll*, see Crawford, *The Temple Scroll*, 24-26.

91. Baumgarten, "Finding Oneself in a Sectarian Context," 142-43, describes this ban

as part of "an unwritten tradition imposed by priestly fiat" that is "among the oldest post-Biblical *halakhot* known."

92. For discussions, see Werman, "The Rules of Consuming and Covering the Blood"; Schiffman, "Sacral and Non-Sacral Slaughter."

93. Yadin, *The Temple Scroll*, 1:314-15; 2:234, 238; Shemesh and Werman, "Halakhah at Qumran," 110; Schiffman, "Sacral and Non-Sacral Slaughter," 75, 81; Werman, "The Rules of Consuming and Covering the Blood," 623. *Jubilees* 21:17 also requires that blood be covered with dust.

94. Fink, "Why Did *yrh* Play the Dog?" 55 n. 87, also concludes that "If indeed 4QMMT applied to Qumran, as Baumgarten and Schiffman suggest, then dogs were not allowed there." For dog bones in late Second Temple period contexts in Jerusalem, see Horwitz, "Faunal Remains," 313.

95. See Qimron, "Chickens in the Temple Scroll," 474-75; Qimron and Strugnell, *Qumran Cave 4*, 163. See also Sussman, "History of the 'Halakha,'" 34; Milgrom, *Leviticus 1-16*, 653.

96. Lambdin translation online at http://www.gnosis.org/naghamm/gthlamb.html.

97. Translation from van de Sandt, "'Do Not Give What Is Holy to the Dogs,'" 224. For a discussion, see Draper, "Christian Self-Definition," 239-41, who says that here "dogs" are the unbaptized.

98. See Draper, "Christian Self-Definition," 239-41.

99. Van de Sandt, "'Do Not Give What Is Holy to the Dogs,'" 230-31, 235.

100. See Fink, "Why Did *yrh* Play the Dog?"

101. From the Hittite "Instructions to Priests and Temple Officials" (1.83); from Fink, "Why Did *yrh* Play the Dog?" 49-50.

102. See Miller, "Attitudes toward Dogs in Ancient Israel," 497; Klawans, *Purity, Sacrifice, and the Temple*, 274-75 n. 57; Goodfriend, "*Keleb* in Deuteronomy 23:19"; Fink, "Why Did *yrh* Play the Dog?" 50 n. 58.

103. Qimron and Strugnell, *Qumran Cave 4*, 163.

104. See also 2 Pet 2:22; Bovon, "*Fragment Oxyrhynchus 840*," 715, understands the references to dogs and pigs in both works as "allegorical."

105. See Schwartz, "Dogs in Jewish Society," 265, 269 including n. 125, who remarks on "the patent connection" between dogs and pigs. However, the Hebrew Bible does not always portray dogs in a negative light; see Miller, "Attitudes towards Dogs in Ancient Israel."

Notes to Chapter 4

1. From Goldin, *The Fathers According to Rabbi Nathan*, 39.

2. For a recent discussion of the source of ESA, see Slane, "The Fine Wares," 272, who believes the evidence points to northern Syria; see also Slane et al., "Compositional Analysis of Eastern Sigillata A."

3. Bar-Nathan, *Hasmonean and Herodian Palaces at Jericho*, 198.

4. For a critique of Bar-Nathan's proposal on other grounds, see Rosenthal-Heginbottom, "Ceramics from Jericho and Masada," 95.

5. For imported stamped and unstamped amphoras of the Hasmonean period from the Jewish Quarter excavations, see Finkielsztejn, "Imported Amphoras" (Stratum 4), who

notes that all of the complete amphoras from Stratum 4 are illustrated in Avigad, *Discovering Jerusalem*, 87 fig. 69; Ariel, "Imported Greek Stamped Amphora Handles," who observes (268) that although the City of David yielded a much larger number of well-dated amphora handles than the Jewish Quarter, imports of Greek amphoras cease in the City of David ca. 150 B.C.E., whereas they continue in the Jewish Quarter (see also *Excavations at the City of David*, 25). Finkielsztejn, "Hellenistic Jerusalem," 24*, states that out of fifty-six Rhodian stamps from the various excavations on the western hill, fifteen (27 percent) date to the Hasmonean period. For amphoras of the Hasmonean period from the Armenian Garden excavations, see Tushingham, *Excavations in Jerusalem 1961-1967*, 370 fig. 18:19; 374 fig. 22:3-4 (see 39 for discussion); 419 fig. 67:28. Whereas Ariel and Finkielsztejn have each proposed that the importation of Greek wine declined dramatically or ceased after the destruction of the Akra fortress in 141 B.C.E. (perhaps reflecting a rise in purity concerns among the Jewish population), the stamped handles from Kathleen M. Kenyon's excavations peak in the Ptolemaic period and decline already during the Seleucid period; see Snow and Prag, "The Stamped Amphora Handles," 407.

6. Bar-Nathan, *Hasmonean and Herodian Palaces at Jericho*, 131, including n. 7.

7. One "Late Hellenistic" amphora is illustrated from the Jewish village at Qiryat Sefer (north of Modi'in); see Magen et al., "Khirbet Badd 'Isa," 220-21, pl. 2:4. Two complete amphoras and several fragments were discovered in the Jewish farm house at Qalandiya northwest of Jerusalem; see Magen, "Qalandiya."

8. Finkielsztejn, "Hellenistic Jerusalem," 27*-28*, who notes that most of the few Rhodian amphoras found in Jerusalem after the beginning of the Hasmonean period reached the city during the reigns of Alexander Jannaeus and Herod the Great. He attributes the reduction in numbers of imported amphoras after the mid-second century B.C.E. to purity observance, in contrast to Ariel and Strikovsky, "Appendix," who are more cautious (see discussion below).

9. Ariel and Finkielsztejn, "Stamped Amphora Handles," 183, 187 (see also the histogram on 17).

10. See Netzer, *Hasmonean and Herodian Palaces at Jericho*, 18, 35-37, 50-108 (see 89 for the Doric columns and triglyph and metope frieze), 157-59, 170.

11. Magness, *Debating Qumran*, 9.

12. Berlin, "Jewish Life before the Revolt," 444, 446-47. For imported pottery from the farmhouses at Horvat 'Aqav and Horvat 'Eleq, see Calderon, "Roman and Byzantine Pottery," 98-101; Silberstein, "Hellenistic and Roman Pottery," 436-37 (imported cooking wares including Pompeian Red Ware), 442-44 (amphoras), 454-62 (imported fine wares including Western Terra Sigillata).

13. The changes in the lifestyle of the Jerusalem elite in the middle of Herod's reign might have impacted social structures in other ways. For example, around this time the Pharisees seem to have been transformed from a political party to a nonpolitical group concerned with purity observance; see Neusner, "The Rabbinic Traditions about the Pharisees," 301.

14. Berlin, "Jewish Life before the Revolt," 451; Rozenberg, "Wall Painting Fragments from Area A," 302, discussing Hellenistic-Roman-style wall painting fragments from a fill with a terminus post quem in the early first century C.E.

15. See Avigad, *Discovering Jerusalem*, 83; Berlin, *Gamla I*, 140; "Jewish Life before the Revolt," 448, 450.

16. See Avigad, *Discovering Jerusalem*, 83-192.

17. Avigad, *Discovering Jerusalem*, 139-42, 174-83. Avigad's observations have been confirmed by more recent studies of the material from the Jewish Quarter excavations; see Rozenberg, "Wall Painting Fragments from Area A," 302; "The Absence of Figurative Motifs in Herodian Wall Painting." The same is true of Jewish elite dwellings in Galilee; see Weiss, "Jewish Galilee in the First Century C.E.," 54.

18. Rosenthal-Heginbottom, "Hellenistic and Early Roman Fine Ware," 220.

19. For ESA from Jerusalem's Jewish Quarter, see Avigad, *Discovering Jerusalem*, 88. Rosenthal-Heginbottom, "Hellenistic and Early Roman Fine Ware," 214, notes that ESA may have already been imported to Jerusalem beginning in the mid-first century B.C.E. Even so, most of it dates from the reign of Herod on. Imported wares also make their first appearance in the palaces at Jericho in the middle of Herod's reign; see Bar-Nathan, *Hasmonean and Herodian Palaces at Jericho*, 197.

20. Hershkovitz, "Jerusalemite Painted Pottery," 31*; Rosenthal-Heginbottom, "Hellenistic and Early Roman Fine Ware," 212; Perlman et al., "Pseudo-Nabataean Ware and Pottery of Jerusalem"; Avigad, *Discovering Jerusalem*, 185.

21. Rosenthal-Heginbottom, "Hellenistic and Early Roman Fine Ware," 209, 214-17. Some of the stone vessels manufactured in the Jerusalem area imitated the shapes of these fine wares; see Magen, *The Stone Vessel Industry in the Second Temple Period*, 65, 66, 68, 70, 72; Cahill, "Chalk Vessel Assemblages," 202, 204. Monopodial stone tables from the Jewish Quarter also imitated Roman prototypes; see Cahill, "Chalk Vessel Assemblages," 217; Berlin, *Gamla I*, 151-52.

22. Rosenthal-Heginbottom, "Hellenistic and Early Roman Fine Ware," 217; see also Berlin, *Gamla I*, 151.

23. Berlin, "Italian Cooking Vessels and Cuisine from Tel Anafa," 43-44. Berlin, *Gamla I*, 151-52, notes that the appearance of locally-produced versions of Italian pans in Galilee (the so-called Galilean bowls) beginning in the late first century B.C.E. shows that the preparation of Roman-type cuisine spread from the elite to the general population. For examples of Roman recipes, see Flower and Rosenbaum, *The Roman Cookery Book*.

24. Berlin, "Jewish Life before the Revolt," 442.

25. See Finkielsztejn, "Imported Amphoras" (Stratum 3); "Hellenistic Jerusalem," 28* ("Unstamped amphorae, found in the latter's [Herod's] palaces and in the Jewish Quarter, are evidence for the common practice of importing foreign wine to Judaea in the second half of the Ist c. BCE"); Tushingham, *Excavations in Jerusalem 1961-1967*, 55, referring to figs. 21:42-43, 22:1, 23:37.

26. Avigad, *Discovering Jerusalem*, 88.

27. Ariel, "Imported Greek Stamped Amphora Handles," 277; *Excavations at the City of David*, 24-25; Ariel and Strikovsky, "Appendix."

28. Even Alon, *Jews, Judaism and the Classical World*, 157, conceded that prohibitions against consuming Gentile oil, wine, and bread were not universally accepted in the Second Temple period. For a recent study, see Hayes, *Gentile Impurities and Jewish Identities*, who notes that "the decree of Gentile ritual impurity was . . . a volley in the internal cultural wars of first-century Judaism" (196). Contrary to Alon, Hayes believes that these prohibitions arose not because Gentiles were considered inherently impure but because of other factors, such as a concern that Gentiles are not careful to guard against impurity and their products might have been used in connection with idolatrous practices (see 66). The latter concern is

expressed in the *Damascus Document:* "Let no man sell clean animals or birds to Gentiles in order that they may not sacrifice them" (CD 12:8-9; from Baumgarten and Schwartz, "The Damascus Document," 51). For the sectarian position, see Schiffman, "Non-Jews in the Dead Sea Scrolls." See also Sanders, *Judaism: Practice and Belief,* 76.

29. Berlin, "Jewish Life before the Revolt," 450; see Damati, "Ḥilkiah's Palace"; "The Palace of Ḥilkiya."

30. Berlin, "Jewish Life before the Revolt," 449-50; *Gamla I,* 152; Hoglund and Meyers, "The Residential Quarter on the Western Summit," 40; Reed, *Archaeology and the Galilean Jesus,* 126 (with possible evidence of a mosaic floor). See also Weiss, "Jewish Galilee in the First Century C.E.," 22-23, 25 (a reference to eleven upper-class residences on the western side of the settlement at Gamla), 40 (fresco fragments under the House of Dionysos), 53. According to Weiss, Tiberias was the only *polis* in the classical sense of the word in Galilee before 70.

31. Berlin, *Gamla I,* 152, 156 n. 28, from Areas R and S.

32. Berlin, "Jewish Life before the Revolt," 441; "Romanization and Anti-Romanization," 63. For a pan from the Jewish village at Qiryat Sefer north of Modi'in, see Magen et al., "Khirbet Badd 'Isa," 224, pl. 5:2 (it is unclear whether it is an import or a local imitation). Pans are unattested at Qumran.

33. Berlin, "Jewish Life before the Revolt," 451. The non-Jewish inhabitants of the fortified villa at Ḥorvat 'Eleq near Caesarea consumed imported wine and prepared Roman style cuisine using imported cooking wares, but there are no amphoras and imported cooking wares at the contemporary farmhouse at Ḥorvat 'Aqav just a couple of kilometers away, which, judging by the presence of a miqveh, was inhabited by Jews; see Hirschfeld, *Ramat Hanadiv Excavations.*

34. Reed, *Archaeology and the Galilean Jesus,* 126, remarks that despite the relative affluence of the inhabitants of the Sepphoris house decorated with frescoes, "the inhabitants were not extravagantly wealthy. . . . Only a very few fine wares were present, and the more expensive terra sigillata serving bowls or plates were absent, as were imported wine amphora[s] with stamped handles." He concludes that, although some of the architectural elements at Sepphoris reflect Roman influence, "the implements of the social elite were not adopted in full or were not affordable" (126).

35. Berlin, "Jewish Life before the Revolt," 431.

36. I see no evidence that the Sadducees adopted the Pharisaic practice of eating nonsacrificial food in purity, as Regev, *The Sadducees and Their Halakhah,* 412, suggests.

37. For the chronology of stone vessels, see Magen, *The Stone Vessel Industry,* 162; Cahill, "Chalk Vessel Assemblages," 231-32; Gibson, "Stone Vessels of the Early Roman Period," 301-2, who suggests (304) that the majority of stone vessels date to 50-70 C.E.

38. Bar-Nathan, "Qumran and the Hasmonean and Herodian Winter Palaces," 266-72; *Hasmonean and Herodian Palaces at Jericho,* 86, 198; Netzer, *Hasmonean and Herodian Palaces at Jericho,* 42-44; Reich, "Area A — Stratigraphy and Architecture," 89-90; Avigad, *Discovering Jerusalem,* 74-75. Seligman, "Jerusalem, Khirbat Ka'kul (Pisgat Ze'ev H)," 18, suggests that the same phenomenon might be attested in a miqveh in the village at Pisgat Ze'ev.

39. Bar-Nathan, *Hasmonean and Herodian Palaces at Jericho,* 198; see also Reich, "Area A — Stratigraphy and Architecture," 90.

40. See also Miller, "Stepped Pools and the Non-Existent Monolithic 'Miqveh,'" 228 n. 19.

41. Bar-Nathan, "Qumran and the Hasmonean and Herodian Winter Palaces," 272,

cites a pottery deposit from a miqveh (L58) at Qumran as another example of this phenomenon. Several factors contradict her claim: (1) Although the deposit from L58 at Qumran included some *("quelques")* cups, bowls, and plates, jars, cooking pots, and juglets predomi-
nated. In contrast, the deposits from miqva'ot in Jericho and Jerusalem consisted mostly of
plates, bowls, and cups. (2) The deposit from L58 at Qumran is much smaller (about 30 re-
storable vessels) than those in Jericho and Jerusalem (and much smaller than the numbers
of dishes stored in L86 and L114 at Qumran). (3) Whereas the deposits in Jericho and Jerusalem date to the Hasmonean period (as Bar-Nathan, "Qumran and the Hasmonean and
Herodian Winter Palaces," 274, notes), the deposit from L58 at Qumran dates to Period II
(first century C.E.). For L58 at Qumran, see Humbert and Chambon, *Fouilles de Khirbet
Qumrân,* 311 and 90 photo 188; de Vaux suggested that the vessels were thrown into the pool
at the time of the site's destruction in 68 C.E. See Magness, *The Archaeology of Qumran,* 123,
for the possibility that the pottery was tossed from the second-story level of L77 (where the
communal dining room seems to have been located in Period II) into the pool below.

42. I owe this observation to Hannah Harrington.

43. Yadin, *The Temple Scroll,* 2:224, notes the polemical tone of this passage.
Crawford, *The Temple Scroll,* 26, dates the composition of the *Temple Scroll* to 350-175 B.C.E.
and the final redaction to ca. 200-175.

44. See Baruch and Avni, "Archaeological Evidence for the Bezetha Quarter," 59-60,
who mention that pierced cooking pots have been found in the City of David. They note
that the accumulated debris containing the cooking pots attests to a prolonged period of de-
position and not a one-time event. For these excavations, see also Avni et al., "Jerusalem, the
Old City," 77*-78* (but without a reference to the pierced holes).

45. Ben-Dov, *In the Shadow of the Temple,* 156-57, who proposes that sacrificial offerings had been cooked in these pots and therefore they could not be reused for cooking; in his
view the holes were made so that the pots could be utilized for growing plant seedlings.

46. See Avigad, *Discovering Jerusalem,* 119 and fig. 111; Goodman, *The Ruling Class of
Judaea,* 103 n. 27.

47. Grossberg, "Cooking Pots with Holes," 61, argues that the pierced cooking pots
have no connection with purity observance as *hullin* does not have to be consumed in a state
of purity (although some groups such as the *haverim* did this). Instead, he suggests that
these cooking pots were pierced because they had been used to cook sacrificial meat and
therefore could not be reused.

48. See, e.g., Seligman, "Jerusalem, Khirbat Ka'kul (Pisgat Ze'ev)"; Magen et al.,
"Khirbet Badd 'Isa"; Onn et al., "Khirbet Umm el-'Umdan," 65*-68*. Public buildings at
Modi'in (Kh. Umm el-'Umdan), Qiryat Sefer (Kh. Badd 'Isa), and Gamla have been identified
by the excavators as synagogues. For house types, see Hirschfeld, *The Palestinian Dwelling.*

49. Neusner, *The Idea of Purity in Ancient Judaism,* 65.

50. Marcus, *Mark 1–8,* 521, describes this passage as early, i.e., "at least pre-Markan."

51. Berlin, *Gamla I,* 140.

52. Berlin, *Gamla I,* 140; the number of casseroles per household increased in the first
century C.E., suggesting that the inhabitants ate more meat (stewed and braised) than before. Cooking pots with round bodies and small mouths were used for cooking soups and
bean dishes; casseroles were used for cooking stews with large chunks of meat and vegetables; and pans were used for baking; see Berlin, "Jewish Life before the Revolt," 437-39.

53. Berlin, *Gamla I,* 140-51; she suggests that group meals were held in synagogues in-

stead of in private houses. Although statistics are lacking, Berlin notes that published reports on excavations at Bethsaida, Capernaum, and Yodefat reflect the same changes as at Gamla; see "Jewish Life before the Revolt," 445.

54. Berlin, *Gamla I*, 151. Nevertheless, Berlin notes Roman influence (by way of the local Jewish elites) on Jewish villagers, including a few houses with Pompeian style wall paintings (for those who could afford it), and the widespread adoption of locally-produced pottery types that imitate Roman forms or are associated with the preparation of nonnative cuisines (see *Gamla I*, 152; "Jewish Life before the Revolt," 439-40).

55. For Pisgat Ze'ev, see Seligman, "Jerusalem, Khirbat Ka'kul (Pisgat Ze'ev)," 15-16, who observes that "The local or even rural nature of the ceramic assemblage is noteworthy. The vessels represent basic, subsistence types, and almost no fine or luxury wares were discovered. This is somewhat surprising, considering the proximity of the site to the contemporary and affluent urban center in Jerusalem. It clearly illustrates the hierarchical structure of the settlements, with Jerusalem ranking first." The only fine wares from the village at Pisgat Ze'ev, where occupation apparently ended in the early first century C.E., are two fragments of "pseudo-Terra Sigillata" (Seligman, "Jerusalem, Khirbat Ka'kul (Pisgat Ze'ev)," 18; 25, fig. 19:4). The only imports from Qiryat Sefer are an amphora and a pan (perhaps a local imitation); see Magen et al., "Khirbet Badd 'Isa," 220, pl. 2:4; 224, pl. 5:2. For 'Ein Gedi see de Vincenz, "The Pottery," 236 and pl. 1:25 (Terra Sigillata, possibly western); 272 and pl. 57:15 (amphora toe); 297 and pl. 78:9 (ESA fragment); 293-94 (ten fragments of Nabataean painted bowls). De Vincenz concludes (301): "The ceramic finds dated to the Roman period seem to suggest that long-distance trade with En-Gedi was nonexistent at that time. This is indicated by the lack of imported pottery."

56. Even in the first century B.C.E. ESA is attested in relatively small quantities, with only about 5-6 dishes and 2-3 bowls per household over the course of three generations, and it is usually the only imported ware found; see Berlin, "Jewish Life before the Revolt," 444-45. On 442, Berlin notes that ESA is found in much larger quantities at sites along the eastern Mediterranean littoral and in Cyprus, where it seems to have been used for serving and individual place settings. In contrast, at Gamla ESA apparently was reserved for table service only.

57. Berlin, *Gamla I*, 151.

58. Berlin, "Romanization and anti-Romanization," 69.

59. See Adan-Bayewitz and Aviam, "Iotapata, Josephus, and the Siege of 67," 165, who connect the absence of imported wares with purity concerns. Weiss, "Jewish Galilee in the First Century C.E.," 46, 53, suggests that economic factors might have played a role in the distribution and use of ESA and other imported wares. For the pans and lids at Gamla, see Berlin, *Gamla I*, 152, 156 n. 28.

60. Berlin, *Gamla I*, 151.

61. For discussions of the purity of pottery vessels and their contents, see Ariel, "Imported Greek Stamped Amphora Handles"; *Excavations at the City of David*, 24-25; Ariel and Strikovsky, "Appendix." Finkielsztejn, "Hellenistic Jerusalem," 31*-32*, argues (*pace* Ariel) that archaeological evidence attests to purity observance among Jerusalem's Jews already in the second century B.C.E.

62. Avshalom-Gorni and Getzov, "Phoenicians and Jews," 81, citing *m. Parah* 1:5.

63. Berlin, *Gamla I*, 153. Similarly, I have suggested that cylindrical jars were used at Qumran as distinctively-shaped containers for the pure goods of the sect; see Magness, *Debating Qumran*, 162; *The Archaeology of Qumran*, 84-85. In *Gamla I*, 156 n. 24, Berlin seems to

modify her earlier position suggesting that the disappearance of ESA was a form of social protest against the Romans among the Jewish population of the north.

64. Berlin, "Pottery and Pottery Production," 53-54; she notes that the potters' workshop at Qumran was established at about the same time; see also "Jewish Life before the Revolt," 425; *Gamla I*, 142. For Kfar Hananya, see Adan-Bayewitz, *Common Pottery in Roman Galilee*. For a potters' kiln at Yodefat, see Adan-Bayewitz and Aviam, "Iotapata, Josephus, and the Siege of 67," 162.

65. See Alon, *Jews, Judaism and the Classical World*, 180-82; Hayes, *Gentile Impurities and Jewish Identities*, 66, 205-7; Sanders, *Judaism*, 74-75; Ariel and Strikovsky, "Appendix"; Adler, "The Observance of Ritual Purity in Agricultural Industry," 63, 77. Doering, "Purity and Impurity in the Book of Jubilees," 272, suggests that "'ritual' impurity of Gentiles was not a total innovation of Tannaitic literature." Neusner, *The Idea of Purity in Ancient Judaism*, 111, notes that the language of cultic purity and impurity usually was not used in connection with Gentiles profaning the temple, but instead was used within the "Jewish sectarian environment." For sectarian disagreements concerning whether it was permissible to accept sacrificial offerings from Gentiles, see Noam, "Traces of Sectarian Halakhah in the Rabbinic World," 80-81.

66. Goodman, *The Ruling Class of Judaea*, 81, observed that the Qumran community produced their own pottery to ensure its purity; at the time he accepted the identification of the Qumran community with the Essenes but later changed his mind.

67. See Yellin et al., "Pottery of Qumran and Ein Ghuweir." For a discussion, see Magness, *The Archaeology of Qumran*, 74-75.

68. See Michniewicz and Krzysko, "The Provenance of Scroll Jars."

69. Michniewicz and Krzysko, "The Provenance of Scroll Jars," 76.

70. See Gunneweg and Balla, "Neutron Activation Analysis."

71. To the contrary, Gunneweg and Balla, "Neutron Activation Analysis," 8-9, note that there were no statistical matches between the kiln and stucco samples from the site on the one hand and the pottery on the other.

72. Magness, *The Archaeology of Qumran*, 74; "Qumran: The Site of the Dead Sea Scrolls," 652-53. Berlin, *Gamla I*, 142, suggests that the Qumran community imported clay from Jerusalem because they considered it pure. Analyses by Adan-Bayewitz et al., "Preferential Distribution of Lamps," have demonstrated that large numbers of Herodian oil lamps found at northern sites are made of Motza clay (the majority at Gamla, Jotapata, and Sepphoris, and significant numbers at Beth Shean and Dor). Herodian lamps made of local (non-Jerusalem) clay are also found at Beth Shean and Dor, whose populations were largely non-Jewish. Therefore, purity considerations do not seem to have been a factor, since, as Adan-Bayewitz et al. point out, Jewish potters in Galilee could have produced the same type of lamp locally (74 n. 76). I wonder whether the lamps (finished products) found at these northern sites were indeed manufactured in Jerusalem or whether instead the raw material (Motza clay) was exported to Galilee. For a discussion of Herodian lamps, see below. For one cylindrical jar and a few additional possible specimens from Qalandiya, eight kms northwest of Jerusalem, see Magen, "Qalandiya," 85; Magness, "Qumran: The Site of the Dead Sea Scrolls," 663. For the rim of a possible ovoid jar from Pisgat Ze'ev, see Seligman, "Jerusalem, Khirbat Ka'akul (Pisgat Ze'ev H)," 20; 21, fig. 17:3.

73. Regev, "Abominated Temple and a Holy Community," 247; Shemesh, "The Origins of the Laws of Separatism"; Schremer, "Seclusion and Exclusion," 133-34. Himmelfarb, *A King-*

dom of Priests, 123, notes that "Gentile" was an irrelevant category for the sectarians as they probably had few dealings with Gentiles and categorized them with the other sons of darkness.

74. Shemesh, "The Origins of the Laws of Separatism," 225-27, with a different translation of Nah 1:2.

75. Shemesh, "The Origins of the Laws of Separatism," 227-30; the rabbis excluded Jews who incite others to idolatry from the positive commandment of Lev 19:16-18.

76. *b. Šabbat* 31a relates a story in which Hillel tells a Gentile that the entire Torah is, "What is hateful to you, do not to your neighbor," and the rest is commentary. See also Matt 7:12, according to which Jesus enjoined his followers to "do to others as you would have them do to you; for this is the law and the prophets."

77. See Shemesh, "The Origins of the Laws of Separatism," 226.

78. These lamps are called by various names, including "wheel-made lamps," "knife-pared lamps," "wheel-made knife-pared lamps," and "Herodian lamps." Berlin, "Jewish Life before the Revolt," 434, suggests that these lamps were created by Jerusalem potters. For a comprehensive study of this type, see Barag and Hershkovitz, "Lamps," 24-58. For the beginning date of this type, see Berlin, "Jewish Life before the Revolt," 434; Geva and Hershkovitz, "Pottery of the Local Hellenistic and Early Roman Periods," 115.

79. Berlin, "Jewish Life before the Revolt," 434-36.

80. See the finds illustrated in Avigad, *Discovering Jerusalem*, 64-204. This observation is strengthened, not weakened, by the following exceptions: (1) A fresco from a house on Mount Zion with birds (see Broshi, "Excavations on Mount Zion," 84-85; pl. 19). The chamber of a rock-cut tomb in Jericho was also painted with vines and birds; see Hachlili, "The Wall Painting"; Hachlili and Killebrew, "Jewish Funerary Customs," 113; Hachlili, "The Goliath Family in Jericho." (2) Molded stucco with an animal frieze from a residential quarter to the south and west of the Temple Mount; see Mazar, *In the Shadow of the Temple*, 150-51; Geva, "The Temple Mount and Its Environs," 740; Fine, *Art and Judaism in the Greco-Roman World*, 78. (3) A clay fulcrum medallion decorated with the bust of a woman, apparently belonging to a bed or couch frame. This object, which is unparalleled in Palestine, comes from the Jewish Quarter excavations and dates to the first century B.C.E.; see Rosenthal-Heginbottom, "Late Hellenistic and Early Roman Lamps and Fine Ware," 156-59 and pl. 5.5. (4) Avigad, *Discovering Jerusalem*, 204, fig. 252, illustrates a locally-produced version of a Roman oil lamp with decorated discus that is labeled "first century A.D." However, the lamp's context is not indicated (the other finds illustrated on this page are from the period of Aelia Capitolina), and this type dates mainly to the late first century to third century; see Rosenthal and Sivan, *Ancient Lamps in the Schloessinger Collection*, 85-90; Bailey, "Imported Lamps and Local Copies," 99. For a newly-discovered figured fresco at Herodium, see Netzer et al., "Two Inscriptions from Herodium," 87, 90 (fig. 5). For an ossuary with a bucranium from the Akeldama tombs, see p. 247 n. 30 below.

81. Although the final reports on the finds from the Jewish Quarter mansions have not been published, Avigad illustrates some objects in his popular book, and the final reports on Areas A and E have appeared in print. For wheel-made and imported oil lamps, see Avigad, *Discovering Jerusalem*, 79, fig. 58; 88, fig. 70; 199 fig. 237; Rosenthal-Heginbottom, "Fine Ware and Lamps from Area A," 247, pl. 6.8:1-5; 249, pl. 6.9:43-44; 251, pl. 6.10:21; 255, pl. 6.12:1-18 (no. 19 [a mask] does not have a stratigraphic context; see p. 213); Geva and Hershkovitz, "Local Hellenistic and Early Roman Pottery," 143, pl. 4.13:19-20; Rosenthal-Heginbottom, "Late Hellenistic and Early Roman Fine Ware," 163, pl. 5.1.

82. Bar-Nathan, *Hasmonean and Herodian Palaces at Jericho*, 102, 267-68.

83. Bar-Nathan, *Hasmonean and Herodian Palaces at Jericho*, 190-91, 278 nos. 543-552.

84. See Bailey, "Imported Lamps and Local Copies," 94-98.

85. See Berlin, "Jewish Life before the Revolt," 434; Rosenthal-Heginbottom, "Fine Ware and Lamps from Area A," 219; Adan-Bayewitz et al., "Preferential Distribution of Lamps." Wheel-made lamps are also found at Horvat 'Eleq; see Silberstein, "Hellenistic and Roman Pottery," 448, pl. XIII: 2-6.

86. See Calderon, "Roman and Byzantine Pottery," 102-3.

87. See Magen, *The Stone Vessel Industry*, 145-46; Goodman, *The Ruling Class of Judaea*, 102.

88. On this passage, see Grossmark, "'And He Declared Impurity on Glass Vessels,'" 40-41.

89. See Grossmark, "'And He Declared Impurity on Glass Vessels.'"

90. Avigad, *Discovering Jerusalem*, 107-8, 127-28 (fig. 124). For the final publication of the glass from Areas A, E, and J, see Gorin-Rosen, "Glass Vessels"; "Glass Vessels from Area A"; Gorin-Rosen and Katsnelson, "Refuse of a Glass Workshop."

91. Gorin-Rosen, "Glass Vessels," 257. For the impurity of imported glass vessels, see Grossmark, "'And He Declared Impurity on Glass Vessels,'" 38.

92. Avigad, *Discovering Jerusalem*, 85, 88, 186-91. For the final publication of this glass, see Gorin-Rosen and Katsnelson, "Refuse of a Glass Workshop."

93. Avigad, *Discovering Jerusalem*, 186-91; Gorin-Rosen and Katsnelson, "Refuse of a Glass Workshop."

94. Gorin-Rosen and Katsnelson, "Refuse of a Glass Workshop," 413, 430.

95. Avigad, *Discovering Jerusalem*, 191. However, Gorin-Rosen and Katsnelson, "Refuse of a Glass Workshop," 430, note that glass production usually took place in two stages, with the raw glass transferred from areas close to sources of sand and fuel to workshops.

96. Berlin, "Pottery and Pottery Production," 53-54; she notes that the potters' workshops at Qumran and Kfar Hananya in Galilee were established at about the same time.

97. See Katsnelson, "Early Roman Glass Vessels from Judea," 6*.

98. For the excavations, see Bar-Nathan and Sklar-Parnes, "A Jewish Settlement in Orine"; Sklar-Parnes et al., "Excavations in Northeast Jerusalem."

99. Katsnelson, "Early Roman Glass Vessels from Judea," 9*.

100. Donceel and Donceel-Voûte, "The Archaeology of Khirbet Qumran," 7-9; Donceel-Voûte, "Les ruines de Qumran réinterprétées," 26, 28-29; Wouters et al., "Antique Glass from Khirbet Qumrân," 9-19.

101. Hirschfeld, *Qumran in Context*, 145, citing Wouters et al., "Antique Glass from Khirbet Qumrân," 10. See also Magen and Peleg, "Back to Qumran," 71, who report finding "numerous glass fragments," including mold-blown lamps, bottles, and "Sidon ware" with Greek inscriptions. However, most of the glass was found in the eastern dump.

102. See Katsnelson, "Early Roman Glass Vessels from Judea," 6*, who remarks, "Despite the short duration of the settlement, the salvage excavation yielded a surprisingly large number of glass fragments."

103. I am grateful to Mizzi for providing me with a prepublication copy of his paper, "The Glass from Khirbet Qumran." Mizzi demonstrates (120) that there is no evidence of glass production at Qumran.

104. Mizzi, "The Glass from Khirbet Qumran," 115-16, who also notes a fragment of a goblet of purple glass (a rare find), which lacks a datable context.

105. Mizzi, "The Glass from Khirbet Qumran," 111,

106. Mizzi, "The Glass from Khirbet Qumran," 113-15, notes that Magen and Peleg claim to have found a large number of "Sidonian" glass wares with several fragments bearing Greek inscriptions but they do not provide more specific information on the numbers. Furthermore, Magen and Peleg's fragments come from a dump. The one or two fragments of "Sidonian" glass from de Vaux's excavations come from a dump and from an unclear context in L46, respectively. It is unclear how many vessels the fragments of "Sidonian" glass represent; it is possible, e.g., that these fragments belonged to the same vessel.

107. Mizzi, "The Glass from Khirbet Qumran," 122.

108. See Mizzi, "The Glass from Khirbet Qumran," 118-23; Magness, *Debating Qumran*, 14-15: "the high cost of overland transport put the acquisition of imported wine and fine pottery beyond their reach [of the inhabitants of Ein ez-Zara]. It is possible that the absence of imported pottery (including Eastern Sigillata A) at Qumran reflects a deliberate rejection of these products by the inhabitants. However, even if the community at Qumran had wanted to acquire these products, it is doubtful they could have afforded them."

109. But the sectarians did distinguish between intentional and unintentional sin; see Shemesh, "Expulsion and Exclusion."

110. See Berlin, "Jewish Life before the Revolt," 429; Deines, *Jüdische Steingefäße*, 244-46. I discuss only hand-carved and lathe-turned vessels made of soft chalk or limestone of the late first century B.C.E. and first century C.E., not earlier vessels made of harder limestone.

111. Berlin, "Jewish Life before the Revolt," 430, 433; Deines, *Jüdische Steingefäße*, 161. Weiss, "Jewish Galilee in the First Century C.E.," 47, notes that stone vessels and miqva'ot are found at the same sites. Stone vessels are attested at the farmhouse at Qalandiya (northwest of Jerusalem) and the village at Qiryat Sefer (north of Modi'in), both of which were inhabited by a Jewish population; see Magen, "Qalandiya," 93-94; Magen et al., "Khirbet Badd 'Isa," 214-15. For miqva'ot at Samaritan sites, see Magen, "The Land of Benjamin in the Second Temple Period," 22; "The Ritual Baths *(Miqva'ot)* at Qedumim."

112. For the distribution of stone vessels and workshops with bibliog., see Magen, *The Stone Vessel Industry*, 148-62; "Jerusalem as a Center of the Stone Vessel Industry"; Berlin, "Jewish Life before the Revolt," 430; Deines, *Jüdische Steingefäße*, 71-165; Cahill, "Chalk Vessel Assemblages," 227-31; Gibson, "Stone Vessels of the Early Roman Period"; Aviam, "Distribution Maps of Archaeological Data," 119 Map 4. For stone vessels from Qumran, see Donceel and Donceel-Voûte, "The Archaeology of Qumran," 10-13; Magen and Peleg, "Back to Qumran," 71. For workshops in Galilee, see Weiss, "Jewish Galilee in the First Century C.E.," 47; Gal, "A Stone-Vessel Manufacturing Site." For a stone vessel workshop at Reina in Galilee, see Amit and Adler, "The Observance of Ritual Purity after 70 C.E.," 139-41.

113. Gibson, "Stone Vessels of the Early Roman Period," 302. Cahill, "Chalk Vessel Assemblages," 233, similarly remarks, "If the use of stone vessels was a Pharisaic tradition, why are they commonly found furnishing the homes of the wealthy?" Gibson, "The Pool of Bethesda," 289, makes the same observation with regard to miqva'ot. Regev, "Non-Priestly Purity and its Religious Aspects," 232, argues that stone vessels are too widespread to have been used only for handling terumah.

114. Amit et al., "Stone Vessel Workshops"; Deines, *Jüdische Steingefäße*, 161; Magen,

The Stone Vessel Industry, 4-17; Gibson, "Stone Vessels of the Early Roman Period," 289-91; "The Stone Vessel Industry at Hizma," 187; Cahill, "Chalk Vessel Assemblages," 227-28.

115. Magen, *The Stone Vessel Industry,* 163, distinguishes three main groups (hand-carved vessels, small lathe-turned vessels, and large lathe-turned vessels). For typologies, see Deines, *Jüdische Steingefäße,* 49-60; Magen, *The Stone Vessel Industry,* 63-115; Cahill, "Chalk Vessel Assemblages," 200-18; Gibson, "Stone Vessels of the Early Roman Period," 291-94. The small lathe-turned stone dishes have parallels in wood from the Cave of Letters; see Yadin, *The Finds from the Bar-Kokhba Period,* 128-29, fig. 50. See also Gibson, "The Stone Vessel Industry at Hizma," 182, who notes that one type of stone lid is close in shape to the ceramic bowl-shaped lids that are common at Qumran.

116. Reich, "Stone Vessels, Weights and Architectural Fragments," 268; Berlin, "Jewish Life before the Revolt," 430-31; Gibson, "The Stone Vessel Industry at Hizma," 184-85.

117. Berlin, "Jewish Life before the Revolt," 431; Avigad, *Discovering Jerusalem,* 127, fig. 125; 132, fig. 131; 136, fig. 141; 173-83. Deines, *Jüdische Steingefäße,* 243-46, believes that stone vessels were used mainly for serving food and dining. He suggests that they may also have been used for bringing consecrated food to the temple or outside the temple by people in a state of impurity. Magen, *The Stone Vessel Industry,* 146, proposes that stone vessels were used as substitutes for vessels made of materials that were susceptible to impurity.

118. See Berlin, "Jewish Life before the Revolt," 429; Deines, *Jüdische Steingefäße,* 24-38, 245-75; Meier, *A Marginal Jew,* 1:934-49; Gibson, "Stone Vessels of the Early Roman Period," 303. For the identification of these large vases with the *qalal* mentioned in rabbinic sources see Avigad, *Discovering Jerusalem,* 174; Gibson, "The Stone Vessel Industry at Hizma," 181; Magen, *The Stone Vessel Industry in the Second Temple Period,* 88; Gibson, "Stone Vessels of the Early Roman Period," 294; Reich, "Stone Vessels, Weights and Architectural Fragments," 267.

119. For the suggestion that mugs were used for hand washing, see Berlin, "Jewish Life before the Revolt," 431; Regev, "Pure Individualism," 182; Gibson, "Stone Vessels of the Early Roman Period," 303. Reich, "Stone Mugs from Masada," 201-6, demonstrates that mugs were not used as measuring cups; see also Gibson, "Stone Vessels of the Early Roman Period," 292-93.

120. For discussions of this passage, see Magen, *The Stone Vessel Industry,* 142-43; Deines, *Jüdische Steingefäße,* 206-9. Baumgarten, "Tohorot," 82, notes that the Qumran sect insisted that the sprinkling be done by a priest instead of young boys (4Q277). For *m. Parah* 3:3 and *t. Parah* 3:3 (a parallel passage that mentions *minim* instead of Sadducees), see Regev, *The Sadducees and Their Halakhah,* 411; Burns, "Essene Sectarianism and Social Differentiation," 264 n. 39 (who suggests that the point of disagreement in the passage in *t. Parah* concerned avoiding contact with impure waters such as those from which animals might drink).

121. Berlin, "Jewish Life before the Revolt," 431. Furstenberg, "Defilement Penetrating the Body," 190-91, observes that biblical law contains no legislation for purifying the hands alone, in contrast to rabbinic law. However, even if Furstenberg is correct in drawing analogies with Greco-Roman hand washing, among the Jews the custom differed in its association with ritual purity as opposed to table etiquette.

122. Berlin, *Gamla I,* 150.

123. Berlin, *Gamla I,* 19. Gibson, "Stone Vessels of the Early Roman Period," 304-5, mentions a total of 487 stone vessel fragments from Gamla, the majority of which are hand carved (as opposed to lathe turned), and include one inkwell. Gibson remarks on the absence of large *qalal*-type jars at Gamla.

124. See Adan-Bayewitz and Aviam, "Iotapata, Josephus, and the Siege of 67," 164.

125. See Y. Magen et al., "Khirbet Badd 'Isa," 214-15, 230 (Qiryat Sefer); Sidi, "Stone Utensils," 544-46 ('Ein Gedi).

126. For a discussion of these passages, see Deines, *Jüdische Steingefäße*, 213-16.

127. See Baumgarten, "The Pharisaic-Sadducean Controversies about Purity," 160; see also Magness, *The Archaeology of Qumran*, 83, 87, for the bowl-shaped lids associated with the cylindrical jars at Qumran.

128. Approximately 200 stone vessel fragments, "a good number" of which belong to mugs, are reported from de Vaux's excavations at Qumran; see Donceel and Donceel-Voûte, "The Archaeology of Qumran," 10-13. Magen and Peleg, "Back to Qumran," 71, mention finding "stone vessels of many types" in most parts of the site. See also Eshel, "CD 12:15-17 and the Stone Vessels," 45; Baumgarten, "The Essene Avoidance of Oil." In an unpublished seminar paper, Rivka Elitzur-Leiman suggests that according to sectarian law, stone vessels were susceptible to impurity but could be purified through immersion in water (in contrast to pottery and glass vessels), which might explain the presence of stone vessels at Qumran. I am grateful to Elitzur-Leiman for sharing her paper with me and for her permission to cite it here.

129. Lawrence, *Washing in Water*, 106-7, notes that although the washing of hands and feet by priests is mentioned in the *Testament of Levi* and the book of *Jubilees*, hand washing is not referred to in sectarian literature, including the *Temple Scroll* (which probably is not a sectarian work). See also Doering, "Purity and Impurity in the Book of Jubilees," 265.

130. For a similar conclusion, see Neusner, *A History of the Mishnaic Law of Purities*, 89; Booth, *Jesus and the Laws of Purity*, 161. Alon, *Jews, Judaism and the Classical World*, 202-3, distinguished between Jews who purified themselves before prayer by washing the hands and those who immersed the whole body. See also Harrington, *The Purity Texts*, 24-25, who observes (38) that the Qumran sect required "even hopelessly impure persons to wash before eating their profane food." The matter is further complicated by the fact that at Qumran the term *rḥṣ* was sometimes used for washing instead of immersion; see Baumgarten, "Tohorot," 91.

131. See Sanders, *Judaism*, 438: "Handwashing, however, is not a priestly rule; it is not even biblical. Priests, before eating holy food, immersed." See also Milikowsky, "Reflections on Hand-Washing," 151; Booth, *Jesus and the Laws of Purity*, 180-81; Regev, *The Sadducees and Their Halakhah*, 190; Harrington, "Holiness and Law in the Dead Sea Scrolls," 125, 133 (holiness brings both physical and moral power). Similarly, the sectarians do not seem to have shared the Pharisaic/rabbinic notion that touching holy scrolls defiles the hands.

132. See Baumgarten, "Tohorot," 84; Regev, "Abominated Temple and a Holy Community," 268. Werrett, *Ritual Purity and the Dead Sea Scrolls*, 303, notes that the Qumran community seems to have become more stringent in its observance of purity over time, and that in earlier texts (such as the *Temple Scroll* and 4QMMT) the connection between ritual and moral impurity is absent.

133. See the discussion in Kister, "Law, Morality, and Rhetoric," 149 n. 12.

134. See Birenboim, "*Tevul Yom* and the Red Heifer," 255-58.

135. On the basis of this passage, Harrington, "Did the Pharisees Eat Ordinary Food?" 52, concludes that "the sectarians of Qumran bathed before eating."

136. See Milikowsky, "Reflections on Hand-Washing," 152.

137. See Gibson, "Stone Vessels of the Early Roman Period," 300.

138. See Fischer et al., *'En Boqeq,* 69-71; Magness, "Review of *'En Boqeq.*" For small numbers of stone vessels found at Gentile sites that border on Jewish areas in other regions, see Weiss, "Jewish Galilee in the First Century C.E.," 47.

139. Bar-Nathan, *Masada VII,* 238-43.

140. In fact, Bar-Nathan's observation that similar vessels are still used in some Palestinian villages today indicates that they are not always used in connection with Jewish purity laws; see *Masada VII,* 239.

141. See Eshel, "CD 12: 15-17 and the Stone Vessels."

142. See Yadin, *The Temple Scroll,* 2:216 n. 15. Eshel, "CD 12: 15-17 and the Stone Vessels," 47, 51, observes that the *Temple Scroll* was probably composed before the development of the Jewish stone vessel industry in the late first century B.C.E. as its legislation does not refer to stone vessels, an omission that is also noted by Deines, *Jüdische Steingefäße,* 190-91. Magen, *The Stone Vessel Industry,* 145, attributes this omission to the development of halakhah over time instead of sectarian differences.

143. Sanders, *Judaism,* 428; see also 465.

Notes to Chapter 5

1. For inclusive and exclusionary commensality in the definition of group identities, with bibliog., see Blake, "The Material Expression of Cult, Ritual, and Feasting," 106-7. For the importance of commensality in the lives of sects and closed communities, see Baumgarten, "Finding Oneself in a Sectarian Context"; Kugler, "Making All Experience Religious," 137-38; Newman, *Proximity to Power,* 126-27.

2. See Donahue, *The Roman Community at Table,* 67, 83; Dunbabin, *The Roman Banquet,* 13, 39; Roller, *Dining Posture in Ancient Rome,* 1.

3. Crossan, *The Historical Jesus,* 344.

4. For a discussion, see Instone-Brewer, *Prayer and Agriculture,* 158-61.

5. As Flusser, "The Social Message from Qumran," 109, noted, "What Jesus wanted from his close group of adherents was not economic communism, but almost absolute poverty." This situation changed after Jesus' death, when shared property was introduced among the community of his followers in Jerusalem.

6. For discussions, see Pickup, "Matthew's and Mark's Pharisees," 77-80; Instone-Brewer, *Prayer and Agriculture,* 131; Goldenberg, "The Jewish Sabbath in the Roman World," 425-26; Kazen, *Jesus and Purity Halakhah,* 55-60, who concludes that reconstructions of Jesus' attitude are complicated by the church's presentation of this episode as a conflict story. Baumgarten, *Studies in Qumran Law,* 142, observes that Luke's version (6:1), which refers to this incident taking place on the "second first Sabbath," might have entailed a violation of the law of *hadash,* which required the setting aside of a sample offering before the firstfruits (the new harvest) could be consumed.

7. See Instone-Brewer, *Prayer and Agriculture,* 121-67; Sanders, *Judaism,* 230-31. For sectarian legislation relating to Pe'ah, see Shemesh, "The History of the Creation of Measurements."

8. See Berlin et al., "Ptolemaic Agriculture."

9. Davies, "Food, Drink and Sects," 161.

10. Baumgarten, "Finding Oneself in a Sectarian Context," 133. See also Davies,

"Food, Drink and Sects," 157: "eating and drinking are integrated into the physical boundary maintenance of the *Yaḥad.*"

11. See Magness, *Debating Qumran*, 89; Baumgarten, *Studies in Qumran Law,* 45-46, 48. Harrington, "Holiness and Law in the Dead Sea Scrolls," 126, observes that "Although the Torah requires only holy food to be eaten in a state of purity (Lev 7:19-20), the sectarians require even hopelessly impure persons to wash before eating their profane food (4Q274)." For a discussion of terms denoting the pure food and drink of the sect, see Avemarie, "'Tohorat ha-Rabbim' and 'Mashqeh ha-Rabbim.'"

12. See Shemesh, "The Origins of the Laws of Separatism," 237. Baumgarten, "Liquids and Susceptibility to Defilement," 94, notes that access to communal liquids was restricted even for those who were allowed to touch the other pure goods of the sect.

13. Translation from Milgrom, "First Day Ablutions in Qumran," 565, with commentary.

14. For a discussion, see Magness, *Debating Qumran*, 86-87.

15. Magness, *Debating Qumran*, 87.

16. See Beall, *Josephus' Description of the Essenes*, 57-58.

17. See Magness, *Debating Qumran*, 108; Beall, *Josephus' Description of the Essenes*, 55-57.

18. See Magness, *The Archaeology of Qumran*, 193.

19. See Magness, *Debating Qumran*, 106; *The Archaeology of Qumran*, 126; Roller, *Dining Posture in Ancient Rome*, 1.

20. Schiffman, *Sectarian Law in the Dead Sea Scrolls*, 199.

21. Berlin, *Gamla I*, 150.

22. Goodman, *The Ruling Class of Judaea*, 132, suggests that tax collectors are singled out because their position was due to Roman patronage alone, without the evidence of good birth or Torah knowledge required for status in Jewish tradition.

23. See Roller, *Dining Posture in Ancient Rome*, 12 n. 15.

24. See Magness, *Debating Qumran*, 89; see also Beall, *Josephus' Description of the Essenes*, 60-62.

25. Yadin, *Temple Scroll*, 1:140-42, suggested that the sectarians drank wine on the Feast of the First Fruit of Wine and Grain.

26. For discussions, see Magness, *Debating Qumran*, 88-89 including n. 36; Beall, *Josephus' Description of the Essenes*, 60-61.

27. Beall, *Josephus' Description of the Essenes*, 59.

28. See Magness, *Debating Qumran*, 99-106.

29. See Baumgarten, "Liquids and Susceptibility to Defilement," 91; Oppenheimer, *The 'Am Ha-aretz*, 60-61: "Food which comes in contact with a source of impurity, including other impure food, is rendered impure if it is susceptible to impurity." Liquids "are marked by an even greater degree of severity. . . . If a man eats impure food he himself becomes impure." Of course, the concern that impurity could be transmitted through food and drink was not limited to the sectarians and is apparently the reason that washing hands before eating even nonsacral food *(hullin)* became common among the Pharisees and perhaps other Jews; see Furstenberg, "Defilement Penetrating the Body," 184-85. Kazen, *Jesus and Purity Halakhah*, 82, notes that impurity could be spread by "dipping bread in a common dish." For the connection between food and moral values, see Goody, *Cooking, Cuisine, and Class*, 112-14.

30. See Magness, *Debating Qumran*, 91, 161-62. Since the sectarians did not recognize the principle of *ṭebul yom* (in contrast to the rabbis), an impure person who had purified himself (through immersion and other required methods) still had to wait until sundown before coming into contact with pure food and drink; see Schiffman, "Pharisaic and Sadducean Halakhah," 294, 297.

31. Berlin, *Gamla I*, 144.

32. For the pottery from the pantries at Qumran, see Magness, *Debating Qumran*, 99-106; the assemblage from L86 dates to 31 B.C.E. and the assemblage from L114 dates to ca. 9/8 B.C.E.

33. Berlin, *Gamla I*, 150-54, notes the change in dining habits at Gamla; see also Bar-Nathan, *Masada VII*, 128. Baumgarten, *The Flourishing of Jewish Sects*, 94, observes that Josephus's description suggests that the dining habits of the Essenes were "archaic" and represented a protest against new customs. For pottery that is apparently associated with the Period II phase of the dining room in L77 at Qumran, see Magness, *Debating Qumran*, 101.

34. Milgrom, "First Day Ablutions in Qumran," 568. See also Davies, "Food, Drink and Sects," 160.

35. Baumgarten, "Halakhic Polemics," 391, discussing 4Q513 and 4Q159 (Ordinances). See also the punishment in Ezek 4:16: "they shall eat bread by weight and with fearfulness; and they shall drink water by measure and in dismay." Sectarian halakhah displays a concern with setting measurements for other obligations as well; see Shemesh, "The History of the Creation of Measurements."

36. See also Avemarie, "'Tohorat ha-Rabbim' and 'Mashqeh ha-Rabbim,'" 200, who suggests that the use of the word טהרה indicates that the sectarians considered their pure food and drink at the level of purity required for the temple. But Himmelfarb, *A Kingdom of Priests*, 132, 221 n. 50, doubts that the sect considered its pure food as consecrated in status, on the grounds that the *Community Rule* (1QS) does not legislate for members in good standing who should be denied access because of occasional inevitable physical impurities.

Notes to Chapter 6

1. See Beall, *Josephus' Description of the Essenes*, 96-97.

2. Schiffman, *The Halakhah at Qumran*, 99.

3. From García Martínez and Tigchelaar, *The Dead Sea Scrolls Study Edition*, 2:885. This reading has been emended from an earlier reading; see Tigchelaar, "Sabbath Halakha and Worship," 364, 368; Noam, "Beit Shammai and the Sectarian Halakhah," 65-66. For a recent discussion, see Noam and Qimron, "A Qumran Composition of Sabbath Laws," 57-60, 88-96, who reconstruct the passage: *['l y'r 'yš] ghly 'š [lpny hšbt]*.

4. Noam and Qimron, "A Qumran Composition of Sabbath Laws," 90.

5. Similarly, the Karaites and Samaritans prohibited leaving fires burning on the Sabbath; see Noam and Qimron, "A Qumran Composition of Sabbath Laws," 90-94. Noam and Qimron suggest (following Avraham Geiger) that the importance placed by the Pharisees/rabbis on Sabbath candle-lighting was a response to this stringent position, which they associate not only with the Qumran sect but also with the Sadducees.

6. See Noam and Qimron, "A Qumran Composition of Sabbath Laws," 93, 95; Noam, "Beit Shammai and the Sectarian Halakhah," 65-66.

7. Fonrobert, "From Separatism to Urbanism," 47-49, traces the development of this legislation, beginning with Exod 16:29: "The Lord has given you the Sabbath, therefore on the sixth day he gives you food for two days; each of you stay where you are; do not leave your place on the seventh day." She notes that biblical law does not explicitly prohibit carrying items out of one's house on the Sabbath.

8. See Doering, "New Aspects of Qumran Sabbath Law," 258-64; Schürer, *The History of the Jewish People,* 2:470-71. Fonrobert, "From Separatism to Urbanism," 51, notes that most Jewish groups of the late Second Temple period acknowledged the prohibition against carrying on the Sabbath (even if they did not necessarily observe it).

9. See Fonrobert, "From Separatism to Urbanism," 49-56, including a discussion of CD 11:4-5, which she suggests refers to (and rejects) the mingling of property through the use of an 'eruv. For a similar conclusion with regard to the principle of the *niṣoq,* see Selkin Wise, "*Miqwā'ôt* and Second Temple Sectarianism," 190.

10. See Doering, "New Aspects of Qumran Sabbath Law," 261-63; Regev, *The Sadducees and Their Halakhah,* 59-66; both also consider the Sadducees' opposition. But for a more cautious view, see Fonrobert, "From Separatism to Urbanism," 59-63, who argues that this passage tells us more about "rabbinic halakhic self-perception" than about the "halakhic identity" of their opponents.

11. Baumgarten, "The Laws of the Damascus Document," 22; "Miscellaneous Rules," 77.

12. This prohibition also appears in 4Q265 and 4Q251; see Doering, "New Aspects of Qumran Sabbath Law," 256-58; Larson et al., "4QHalakha A," 28-29; Baumgarten, "Miscellaneous Rules," 68-69, 74. Baumgarten (74) notes that the prohibition in 4Q251 is a reformulation of the injunction in Exod 16:29. The same prohibition seems to be preserved in another scroll fragment (4Q421a frag. 11); see Noam and Qimron, "A Qumran Composition of Sabbath Laws," 63-64.

13. As Werman, "The Concept of Holiness," 169, notes, the book of *Jubilees* is "a work closely related to the Qumran sectarians if not actually a sectarian work." Himmelfarb, *A Kingdom of Priests,* 53-84, agrees that the book of Jubilees had an authoritative status at Qumran, but concludes that the author was opposed to the strongly sectarian outlook expressed in some of the Dead Sea Scrolls.

14. From *APOT,* 2:81-82. See Doering, "New Aspects of Qumran Sabbath Law," 260-61, who notes that the sectarian legislation is very close to *Jubilees;* see also Doering, "The Concept of the Sabbath."

15. Baumgarten, "The Laws of the Damascus Document," 22; *Qumran Cave 4,* 77. For strict Sabbath observance among the Dositheans, see Crown, "Qumran, Samaritan Halakha and Theology," 433-36.

16. For this phenomenon, see Magness, *Debating Qumran,* 160.

17. I am indebted to Professor Ranon Katzoff of Bar-Ilan University for sharing with me an unpublished article on fasting by the Jews of ancient Rome and for bibliographical assistance on this topic.

18. See also *Gos. Thom.* 6:1, where Jesus' disciples ask if he wants them to fast, and 14:1, where Jesus responds that fasting will "give rise to sin."

19. For this passage, see Levine, "Luke's Pharisees," 128.

20. Translation from Niederwimmer, *The Didache,* 131.

21. See, e.g., Niederwimmer, *The Didache*, 131-32; Draper, "Christian Self-Definition," 231-33; van de Sandt and Flusser, *The Didache*, 291-92; Audet, *La Didaché*, 368.

22. A minority view among scholars attributes the choice of Wednesdays and Fridays as fast days to the use of a solar calendar among some early Christian groups. This might suggest a connection with the sectarians' solar calendar, in which Wednesdays and Fridays are prominent, and thereby support the claim of Zias et al. See van de Sandt and Flusser, *The Didache*, 293; del Verme, *Didache and Judaism*, 178-80.

23. Zias et al., "Toilets at Qumran," 632; Zias, "Qumran Toilet Practices," 479.

24. See Kottek, "The Essenes and Medicine," 90-92; Kottek, *Medicine and Hygiene*, 166-67.

25. Hacham, "Communal Fasts in the Judean Desert Scrolls." For the importance of Yom Kippur at Qumran, see Baumgarten, "Miscellaneous Rules," 71. For the exclusion of individuals from the sect's communal meals, see Kugler, "Making All Experience Religious," 139.

26. As Hacham, "Communal Fasts in the Judean Desert Scrolls," remarks (139-40), "This silence appears to speak volumes. One would expect other occurrences of public fasts in the sectarian literature, since the sect was ascetic and centralized; that is to say, this group would logically accept upon itself communal fasts or mark them in some form. Additionally, sources from the same period or proximate to it mention public fasts instituted for war, mourning, and other purposes. The Qumran literature, in contrast, completely ignores this phenomenon."

27. See Gilat, *Studies in the Development of the Halakha*, 109, 115.

28. I thank Hanan Eshel z"l for this observation. See also Baumgarten, "Miscellaneous Rules," 69.

29. See Gilat, *Studies in the Development of the Halakha*, 109-22.

30. Levine, *Communal Fasts in Talmudic Literature*, ix, 187-204, shows that Babylonian traditions concerning communal fasts differ from Palestinian tannaitic and amoraic traditions in depicting these fasts as events limited largely to rabbinic circles.

31. See Gilat, *Studies in the Development of the Halakha*, 118-19.

32. Gilat, *Studies in the Development of the Halakha*, 115.

33. Translation from Rabbinowitz, *Midrash Rabbath*, 135. Williams, "Being a Jew in Rome," 11 n. 20, notes that this ruling is attributed to a third-to-fourth-century rabbi.

34. The same phrase from Isaiah also influenced Sabbath observance at Qumran; see Noam and Qimron, "A Qumran Composition of Sabbath Laws," 71.

35. Gilat, *Studies in the Development of the Halakha*, 115.

36. See Gilat, *Studies in the Development of the Halakha*, 110-11; Goldenberg, "The Jewish Sabbath in the Roman World," 430-42.

37. Stern, *Greek and Latin Authors*.

38. See Williams, "Being a Jew in Rome"; Goldenberg, "The Jewish Sabbath in the Roman World," 439-41 (who cites evidence of Sabbath fasting among medieval Jews). Scholars who dismiss the classical sources as confused suggest that the Jewish practice of not cooking on the Sabbath was perceived by non-Jews as meaning they did not eat.

39. Williams, "Being a Jew in Rome," 16-17.

40. See Gilat, *Studies in the Development of the Halakha*, 116-17.

41. Baumgarten, "4QHalakha B," 54-55, who notes that the prohibition concerns checking a scroll for errors. Noam and Qimron, "A Qumran Composition of Sabbath Laws,"

80-88, discuss two other scroll fragments (4Q264a 1 4-5 and 4Q251 1-2), which contain similar laws. They conclude that the prohibition concerns individual reading of biblical scrolls in private (as opposed to public reading and study).

42. Himmelfarb, *A Kingdom of Priests,* 53; Haber, *"They Shall Purify Themselves,"* 49-50.

43. See Doering, "The Concept of the Sabbath," 196, 200. Goldenberg, "The Jewish Sabbath in the Roman World," 424, notes that rabbinic law merely discourages fasting on the Sabbath and prescribes no penalty.

44. See also Baumgarten, "4QHalakha B," 54-55; Doering, "New Aspects of Qumran Sabbath Law from Cave 4 Fragments," 255-56; Noam and Qimron, "A Qumran Composition of Sabbath Laws," 59.

45. Yom Kippur is the only fast day mandated by biblical law; see Sanders, *Judaism,* 141. For the possibility that a fast commemorating the end of a severe drought and food shortage in Judea in 65 B.C.E. is mentioned in pesharim from Qumran, see Eshel, *The Dead Sea Scrolls and the Hasmonean State,* 144-50; but Hacham, "Communal Fasts in the Judean Desert Scrolls," 130-31, believes that the fast(s) refer to Yom Kippur.

46. Berlin, "Qumran Laments and the Study of Lament Literature," 11 n. 21. A passage in the Sabbath code of the *Damascus Document* reads: *'l yt'rb 'yš mrṣwnw bšbt* (CD 11:4-5). *yt'rb* usually is translated as "intermingle." For example, Schiffman translates this passage "No one shall enter partnership by his own volition on the Sabbath"; *The Halakhah at Qumran,* 109. García Martínez and Tigchelaar translate it "No-one should intermingle voluntarily on the sabbath." Some scholars have emended *yt'rb* to *ytr'b* or *yt'nh,* in which case this passage would mean "Let no one starve himself voluntarily on the Sabbath"; see Schiffman, *The Halakhah at Qumran,* 110-11. As Schiffman notes, the order of regulations in the *Damascus Document* favors this reading, which would provide an explicit prohibition against fasting on the Sabbath. However, other copies of the *Damascus Document* from Qumran confirm the reading of *yt'rb,* making it unlikely that the text was corrupted; see Doering, "New Aspects of Qumran Sabbath Law from Cave 4 Fragments," 256 n. 24. Fonrobert, "From Separatism to Urbanism," 52-56, proposes that *yt'rb* refers to the mingling of goods through the use of an *'eruv,* which the sectarians rejected.

47. Hacham, "Communal Fasts in the Judean Desert Scrolls," 141-44, suggests a connection between the rejection of fasting and the sacrificial cult in the Jerusalem temple. The sectarians might also have rejected the practice of individual fasting.

Notes to Chapter 7

1. De Vaux, *Archaeology and the Dead Sea Scrolls,* 129-30.

2. For Philo on the pooling of possessions, see Taylor, "Philo of Alexandria on the Essenes," 20-21.

3. For discussions, see Beall, *Josephus' Description of the Essenes,* 44-45; Baumgarten, *The Flourishing of Jewish Sects,* 105-7; Regev, *Sectarianism in Qumran,* 335-50.

4. From Baumgarten, "The 'Sons of Dawn' in *CDC* 13:14-15," 83, who identifies the "Sons of Dawn" as members of the sect.

5. Beall, *Josephus' Description of the Essenes,* 44-45; Murphy, *Wealth in the Dead Sea Scrolls,* 430.

6. For an account of the discovery, see Strange, "The 1996 Excavations at Qumran."

7. See Cross and Eshel, "Ostraca from Khirbet Qumrân"; Puech, "L'ostracon de *Khirbet* Qumrân (KHQ1996/1)"; Vermes, *The Complete Dead Sea Scrolls in English*, 596-97. For the reading of line 8, see Yardeni, "A Draft of a Deed on an Ostracon."

8. See Beall, *Josephus' Description of the Essenes*, 43. For the ideal of poverty at Qumran, see Flusser, "The Social Message from Qumran," 109-10.

9. See Beall, *Josephus' Description of the Essenes*, 83; on 45 he notes that differences between the *Damascus Document* and the *Community Rule* in the matter of possessions may reflect different stages in the community's development. Philo, *Contemplative Life* 66, seems to indicate that the Therapeutae considered ill-gained wealth as defiling.

10. Beall, *Josephus' Description of the Essenes*, 45.

11. Murphy, *Wealth in the Dead Sea Scrolls*, 309, 316.

12. See Bijovsky, "The Coin Finds from the Shu'afat (Giv'at Shaul) Excavations."

13. Ariel, "Coins from Excavations at Qumran" (on the 1999-2004 excavations of Yitzhak Magen and Yuval Peleg). Lönnqvuist and Lönnqvuist, "The Numismatic Chronology of Qumran," 128-29, also argue that coins are plentiful at Qumran. For a critique of the Lönnqvuists' dating of the deposit of the hoard from Qumran, see Ariel, "Coins from the Excavations at Qumran," n. 1. I am grateful to Donald Tsvi Ariel for permission to cite his forthcoming publication.

14. Ariel, "The Coins from Qalandiya," 147.

15. De Vaux, *Archaeology and the Dead Sea Scrolls*, 129.

16. See Broshi and Eshel, "Residential Caves at Qumran"; "Three Seasons of Excavations at Qumran"; "How Did the Qumranites Live?" However, Broshi and Eshel discovered coins associated with a tent encampment on the plateau to the north of the settlement and on paths leading to the caves around Qumran. Coins were also found in their Area B, which might be a collapsed cave in the marl terrace.

17. See Yadin, *The Finds from the Bar-Kokhba Period*, 30 (G.10), 41 (64.1); Kindler, "Coins from the Cave of Letters"; Avigad, "Expedition A," 179 (Cave of the Pool); Eshel and Amit, *Refuge Caves of the Bar Kokhba Revolt*, 77-78 ('Araq en-Na'saneh Cave), 89-90 (Makukh Cave), 98-102 (el-Jai Cave), 128-36 (Cave of the Sandal), 199-200 (Sela Cave), 231 (discussion).

18. See Kloner and Tepper, *The Hiding Complexes in the Judean Shephelah*, 333-37; Weksler-Bdolah, "'Yad Benjamin' — A Hiding Complex Site," 47; Zissu, Ganor, and Farhi, "Finds from the Hiding Complex at 'Moran 1' Site," 63-69; Kloner and Zissu, "Hiding Complexes in the Lydda Area," 78, 80, 82. For surveys of Bar Kokhba coins, see Zissu and Eshel, "The Geographical Distribution of the Bar Kokhba Coins"; Bijovsky, "The Coins from Khirbet Badd 'Isa," 249-51. For a general survey, see Ariel, "The Coins from the Surveys and Excavations of Caves," esp. 294-96.

19. See Hirschfeld, *En-Gedi Excavations II*, 132-56; Bijovsky, "The Coins," 160 (coin no. 501). For the rejection of Hirschfeld's identification of an "Essene" settlement at 'Ein Gedi, see Amit and Magness, "Not a Settlement of Hermits or Essenes."

20. For four coins from two rock-cut tombs at Jericho, see Hachlili, "The Coins." For a Bar Kokhba revolt coin from Tomb 8 at 'Ein Gedi, see Hadas, *Nine Tombs of the Second Temple Period at 'En Gedi*, 42.

21. See Magness, *The Archaeology of Qumran*, 70. For the finds from Caves 8 and 10, see de Vaux, "Archéologie," 30-31.

22. See Klawans, *Purity, Sacrifice, and the Temple*, 222-41, including an overview of scholarship on this episode.

23. Klawans, *Purity, Sacrifice, and the Temple*, 239-40.

24. Klawans, *Purity, Sacrifice, and the Temple*, 237.

25. See Liver, "The Half-Shekel Offering"; Schürer, *The History of the Jewish People*, 2:271-72; Broshi, "Anti-Qumranic Polemics in the Talmud," 593; Regev, *The Sadducees and Their Halakhah*, 135-36.

26. See Meshorer, "One Hundred Ninety Years of Tyrian Shekels," 171.

27. Klawans, *Purity, Sacrifice, and the Temple*, 239.

28. Klawans, *Purity, Sacrifice, and the Temple*, 239.

29. I have omitted Matt 17:24-27, which the *HarperCollins Study Bible* says was "probably composed by the author to address the question of Christ-believing Israelites' obligations to the temple (and to Rome?)." See also Chancey, *Greco-Roman Culture and the Galilee of Jesus*, 175-76, who points out that Matthew refers to a denomination of the Attic standard rather than to the Phoenician half-shekel that was required for the tax. For possible evidence of Sadducean opposition to the institution of an annual temple tax, see Regev, *The Sadducees and Their Halakhah*, 132-39, who proposes that the disagreements were based on different interpretations of Num 28:2 and Exod 29:38-40, in which God commands the Israelites to sacrifice a daily burnt offering *(tmyd)*. Regev attributes possible Sadducean opposition to conservatism and discomfort with the democratization of the temple cult.

30. See Liver, "The Half-Shekel Offering," 191; Broshi, "Anti-Qumranic Polemics in the Talmud," 593; Regev, *The Sadducees and Their Halakhah*, 138-39; Baumgarten, "Rabbinic Literature as a Source," 20-21.

31. Magness, *Debating Qumran*, 73-79. Recently two more Tyrian half-shekels were found to the west of Qumran, between the site and the caves; see Broshi and Eshel, "Residential Caves at Qumran," 345.

32. Eshel and Broshi, "Excavations at Qumran," 70-72, report finding a defaced Tyrian half-shekel in de Vaux's dumps at Qumran. They suggest that when the hoard from L120 was deposited (ca. 9/8 B.C.E. or shortly thereafter), Jews had not yet begun to deface pagan symbols on coins, but that the practice developed by the time of the First Jewish Revolt.

33. Meshorer, "The Coins of Masada," 76; see also Broshi and Eshel, "Residential Caves at Qumran," 345.

34. Eshel and Broshi, "Excavations at Qumran," 72.

35. For 'Ein Gedi, see Bijovsky, "The Coins." Half of the coins were unidentifiable, and approximately 150 of the identifiable coins antedate the end of the Bar Kokhba Revolt. For Herodian Jericho, see Meshorer, "The Coins."

36. For 'Ein Feshkha, see de Vaux, *Archaeology and the Dead Sea Scrolls*, 66, 70-71; Hirschfeld, "Excavations at 'Ein Feshkha," 44. For Ein el-Ghuweir, see Bar-Adon, "Another Settlement of the Judean Desert Sect." For 'Ein Boqeq, see Kindler, "Coins." For 'Ein ez-Zara, see Clamer, *Fouilles archéologiques de 'Aïn ez-Zâra/Callirrhoé*, 91-93; Strobel and Wimmer, *Kallirrhoë ('Ēn ez-Zāra)*, 47-50 (coin identifications by Christoph von Mosch). Four Tyrian shekels and half shekels were found at the Qalandiya farmhouse; see Ariel, "The Coins from Qalandiya," 146. On the other hand, there are no examples from the Jewish village at Qiryat Sefer; see Bijovsky, "The Coins from Khirbet Badd 'Isa."

37. Regev, *The Sadducees and Their Halakhah*, 138-39.

38. See Bar-Adon, *Excavations in the Judean Desert;* Hirschfeld and Ariel, "Coin Assemblage."

39. See Bar-Adon, *Excavations in the Judean Desert,* 28 fig. 21c, especially nos. 9-10 (incurved rim bowls); 13 (casserole); 14 (cooking pot); 25 (Judean radial oil lamp). For these types, see Bar-Nathan, *Hasmonean and Herodian Palaces at Jericho,* 83-87 (J-BL3); 68-69 (J-CP1); 73-74 (J-CS1); Barag and Hershkovitz, "Lamps," 14-24 (who date this type to the reign of Herod).

40. Bar-Adon, *Excavations in the Judean Desert,* 27 (my translation).

41. See Bar-Adon, *Excavations in the Judean Desert,* 27, 28 fig. 21c nos. 21-22 (amphora toes), 23 (stamped handle). The stamped handle seems to fall into the category described by Ariel, "Imported Greek Stamped Amphora Handles," 268, as late in the Rhodian series.

42. Hirschfeld and Ariel, "Coin Assemblage," 66.

43. Hirschfeld and Ariel, "Coin Assemblage," 69.

44. Eshel and Zissu, "A Note on the Rabbinic Phrase," 92.

45. Hirschfeld and Ariel, "Coin Assemblage," 69.

46. Hirschfeld and Ariel, "Coin Assemblage," 85.

47. Hirschfeld and Ariel, "Coin Assemblage," 81.

48. Hirschfeld and Ariel, "Coin Assemblage," 72, 78. They suggest that the dock may have gone out of use because the level of the Dead Sea dropped.

49. Hirschfeld and Ariel, "Coin Assemblage," 69 n. 5.

50. Hirschfeld and Ariel, "Coin Assemblage," 69 n. 5; Eshel and Zissu, "A Note on the Rabbinic Phrase," 92-94.

51. Eshel and Zissu, "A Note on the Rabbinic Phrase," especially 94-95.

52. Objects associated with idolatry were also cast into the Dead Sea; see *m. ʿAbod. Zar.* 3:3 and 3:9. For possible evidence (dating to the Late Roman period) at Meiron of the disposal of objects dedicated to the temple, see Goodman, "The Purpose of Room F."

53. Eshel and Zissu, "A Note on the Rabbinic Phrase," 92.

54. Eshel and Zissu, "A Note on the Rabbinic Phrase," 95.

55. Hirschfeld and Ariel, "Coin Assemblage," 72 n. 7.

56. Hirschfeld and Ariel, "Coin Assemblage," 72 n. 7.

57. Hirschfeld and Ariel, "Coin Assemblage," 72 n. 7.

Notes to Chapter 8

1. For nudity in classical antiquity, see Bonfante, "Nudity as a Costume in Classical Art"; Rykwert, "Privacy in Antiquity," 35-36.

2. For a discussion of this halakhah, see Ehrlich, *The Nonverbal Language of Prayer,* 137.

3. For nudity in Roman bathhouses, see Rykwert, "Privacy in Antiquity," 35-36.

4. See Ehrlich, *The Nonverbal Language of Prayer,* 136-38.

5. For rabbinic legislation dealing with the public nudity of criminals about to be executed, see Berkowitz, *Execution and Invention,* 172-73.

6. From O'Collins, "Crucifixion," 1210.

7. See Magness, *Debating Qumran,* 147; Baumgarten, "Tohorot," 95; Lawrence, *Washing in Water,* 143. Crown, "Qumran, Samaritan *Halakha* and Theology," 430-31, notes

that the Samaritans might have immersed themselves while clothed as well. For a response to Mason's claim that Josephus invented the married type of Essenes, see Taylor, "Philo of Alexandria on the Essenes," 22 n. 76, who notes, "Details such as the exact type of wrap the women wore in the purification bath (*War* 2.161) could hardly be expected in a fantasy."

8. Translation from *APOT*, 2:17. For the influence of *Jubilees* at Qumran, see Haber, *"They Shall Purify Themselves,"* 49-50.

9. See Magness, *Debating Qumran*, 137; Beall, *Josephus' Description of the Essenes*, 98.

10. This depends on the translation of *skepasmasin linois* in *War* 2.129, which Vermes and Goodman (*The Essenes According to the Classical Sources*) render as "linen loin-cloths" but can simply mean a linen covering. Elsewhere Josephus uses the term *perizōma* for the loincloth.

11. See also Schwartz, "Material Culture in the Land of Israel," 133-34.

12. See Beall, *Josephus' Description of the Essenes*, 46, 75.

13. See Tigchelaar, "The White Clothing of the Essenes," 308.

14. See Baumgarten, "The Purification Rituals," 202; Lawrence, *Washing in Water*, 143.

15. See Magness, *Debating Qumran*, 135-49. Burns, "Essene Sectarianism and Social Differentiation," 266 including n. 45, notes a parallel with *m. Meg.* 4:8 in which the rabbis condemn as heretical anyone who dresses in white and refuses to wear colored clothing. However, Nahum Ben-Yehuda (personal communication, August 2009) informs me that this halakhah merely refers to someone who refuses to be a *shaliah tsibur* (prayer leader on behalf of the congregation) while wearing dyed garments also being forbidden to do so while wearing white clothing.

16. Tigchelaar, "The White Clothing of the Essenes," 311 n. 48. Similarly Sanders, *Judaism*, 97-98, concludes that linen is not always white and that the white clothing worn by the Essenes was not an imitation of the priesthood.

17. See Yadin, *The Finds from the Bar-Kokhba Period*, 252: "Linen is characteristically difficult to dye; this is especially so for the colours of decorative patterns." See also Sanders, *Judaism*, 95. But see Shamir, "Textiles, Cordage, and Threads from En-Gedi," 590, for a reference to linen textiles dyed with indigo.

18. See Sheffer and Granger-Taylor, "Textiles," 160; Yadin, *The Finds from the Bar-Kokhba Period*, 252.

19. See Sheffer and Granger-Taylor, "Textiles," 160-61; Yadin, *The Finds from the Bar-Kokhba Period*, 204-40.

20. See Magness, *Debating Qumran*, 139-40.

21. Yadin, *The Finds from the Bar-Kokhba Period*, 254.

22. The linen mantle is illustrated on the website of the Israel Antiquities Authority at http://www.antiquities.org.il/scroll_eng.asp (08/09/2007).

23. Tigchelaar, "The White Clothing of the Essenes," 311 n. 48, in response to my understanding of Essene clothing as being made of linen.

24. This included the mantle, *pace* Tigchelaar, "The White Clothing of the Essenes." For discussions with references, see Magness, *Debating Qumran*, 146-48; Sanders, *Judaism*, 94-101; Schürer, *The History of the Jewish People*, 2:293.

25. Oppenheimer, *The ʿAm Ha-aretz*, 125, in relation to *ḥaverim*, and citing as an example *m. Ḥag.* 2:7, which is concerned with clothing that has *midras* impurity. See also Baumgarten, *The Flourishing of Jewish Sects*, 100-102.

26. The fact that Josephus and Philo describe the clothing of the Essenes in a manner that glorifies their lifestyle as ascetic does not mean that the information is incorrect.

27. Cohen, *The Beginnings of Jewishness*, 33-34, concluded that the majority of Jews were not distinguished in their everyday dress from non-Jews by the wearing of tefillin or *tzitzit*. For a general discussion, see Schürer, *The History of the Jewish People*, 2:479-81. For rabbinic sources criticizing ordinary Jews ('*ammei ha'aretz*) for not observing these commandments, see Cohen, *The Beginnings of Jewishness*, 34; Oppenheimer, *The 'Am Ha-aretz*, 224-27; for a different understanding of these sources, see Cohn, *Tangled Up in Text*, 112-13.

28. See Cohn, *Tangled Up in Text*, 56-60, with references. For possible phylacteries from Cave 11, see Eshel, "Three New Fragments from Qumran Cave 11," 1 n. 3; see also Cohn, *Tangled Up in Text*, 58 (who does not cite Eshel).

29. Yadin, *The Finds from the Bar-Kokhba Period*, 182-87. Although a couple of colleagues have told me that in later years Yadin retracted his identification of this wool bundle as *tzitzit*, I have not been able to find a retraction in print.

30. Yadin, *The Finds from the Bar-Kokhba Period*, 221; see also 171. The only reference to *tzitzit* in this *sugya* is: "R. Hiyya and R. Jonathan were once walking about in a cemetery, and the blue fringe of R. Jonathan was trailing on the ground. Said R. Hiyya to him: Lift it up, so that they [the dead] should not say: Tomorrow they are coming to join us and now they are insulting us!" For a discussion, see Lichtenstein, *Consecrating the Profane*, 114.

31. See Lichtenstein, *Consecrating the Profane*, 124, 169-70, who discusses the evidence presented by Yadin, and suggests that the blue threads were removed (to be reused) because of their scarcity and preciousness at the time of the First and Second Jewish Revolts.

32. Sheffer and Granger-Taylor, "Textiles," 241.

33. See Yadin, *The Temple Scroll*, 2:292, 423.

34. For the textiles from the Qumran caves, see Bélis, "Des textiles." For the clothing of the Essenes, see Magness, *The Archaeology of Qumran*, 193-202; Tigchelaar, "The White Clothing of the Essenes."

35. See Magness, *The Archaeology of Qumran*, 196. Clothing discovered in caves along the western shore of the Dead Sea suggests that the law of *sha'atnez* was observed by the local Jewish population in the first and second centuries C.E.

36. Instone-Brewer, *Prayer and Agriculture*, 217-18.

37. Yadin, *The Finds from the Bar-Kokhba Period*, 186.

38. From Yadin, *The Finds from the Bar-Kokhba Period*, 186.

39. From Yadin, *The Finds from the Bar-Kokhba Period*, 187. Yadin seems to understand the "mingled stuff" in this passage as referring to attachment of woolen *tzitzit* to the priestly garments of linen, whereas the commentary in the Schottenstein edition of the Babylonian Talmud cites Rashi's reference to the wool and linen belt worn by the priests. See also Sanders, *Judaism*, 95-96.

40. For the relationship between sectarian halakhah and the positions of the house of Shammai, see Shremer, "'[T]he[y] Did Not Read in the Sealed Book," 118 n. 41, with references.

41. The *Temple Scroll* emphasizes that two different animals may not be yoked together to a plow; see Yadin, *The Temple Scroll*, 2:234-35 (11QT 52:13).

42. In the cases of both the wool bundle from the Cave of Letters and the linen threads from Cave 1 at Qumran, the blue color was produced from indigo dye instead of murex (authentic Tyrian purple), which was more expensive and difficult to obtain; see Yadin, *The Finds from the Bar-Kokhba Period*, 182-86; Magness, *The Archaeology of Qumran*,

197-98. Yadin noted that the rabbis discussed whether it was permissible to use indigo dye for the blue color (see *b. Menaḥ.* 41b).

43. See also Sanders, *Judaism,* 95-96.

44. Yadin, *The Scroll of the War of the Sons of Light,* 219, 292. This echoes the emphasis on linen in Lev 16:4 and Ezek 44:17-18.

45. Some of the figures in the wall paintings of the third century C.E. synagogue at Dura Europos might be depicted with *tzitzit* attached to their mantles; see Kraeling, *The Excavations at Dura-Europos,* 81-82, including n. 239.

46. For some of the relevant passages, see Oppenheimer, *The 'Am Ha-aretz,* 224-27; Cohn, *Tangled Up in Text,* esp. 111-38.

47. For a comprehensive study of tefillin, see Cohn, *Tangled Up in Text,* who reaches the same conclusion (107).

48. For discussions of this passage, see Pickup, "Matthew's and Mark's Pharisees," 102-8; Cohn, *Tangled Up in Text,* 109-11, 128. The corresponding passages in Mark 12:38-39 and Luke 11:46; 20:45-46 omit the references to tefillin and *tzitzit.* The Greek term *kraspedon* usually denotes the hem or edge of a garment, but the reference to *tzitzit* in the Gospel accounts is clear from Matt 23:5, which otherwise makes no sense. That this attack should be understood as reflecting opposition (Jesus' or Matthew's?) to external displays of piety is supported by the context of the passage, which includes a condemnation of Jews who wear long robes (in Mark and Luke) and choose for themselves the best seats in synagogues. For the long robes *(stolai)* mentioned in these passages, see Deines, *Jüdische Steingefäße,* 11-15.

49. From Dods et al., *The Writings of Justin Martyr and Athenagoras,* 146. For the date and setting of *The Dialogue with Trypho,* see Falls, *St. Justin Martyr,* xii. Cohn, *Tangled Up in Text,* 122 n. 80, observes that Justin Martyr's reference to *tzitzit* is "far from clear-cut" as it mentions scarlet rather than blue dye, and Emil Schürer emended the Greek from *bamma* ("dye") to *ramma* ("seam" or "hem"); see Schürer, *The History of the Jewish People,* 2:2, 479 n. 80. However, Cohn believes that Justin displays an accurate knowledge of tefillin.

50. For a recent discussion focusing on Mark's version, see Haber, *"They Shall Purify Themselves,"* 125-41, who concurs with a majority of scholars that the woman's impurity stemmed from vaginal bleeding, though this is not specified. For a different view, see Levine, "Discharging Responsibility."

51. According to Kazen, *Jesus and Purity Halakhah,* 134-35, here Mark generalizes Jesus' behavior, with the reference to the *himation* being "Markan embroidery."

52. Cohen, *The Beginnings of Jewishness,* 34, notes that Josephus and Philo do not mention *tzitzit.*

53. That this seems to be the case is suggested by the references to fringe in all of the Synoptic Gospels, and therefore my conclusion is not affected by arguments that one or more of the authors of the synoptic accounts originally was Jewish or wrote for a law-observant Jewish community, as recently argued with regard to Matthew, e.g.; see Runesson, "From Where? To What?" Pickup, "Matthew's and Mark's Pharisees," 111, concludes that the halakhic debates presented in the Gospels were unlikely to have been invented by the early church, which had no such controversies. See also Fredriksen, *Jesus of Nazareth,* 109; Booth, *Jesus and the Laws of Purity,* 31, 109-10; Haber, *"They Shall Purify Themselves,"* 133 n. 33.

54. But Joel Marcus (personal communication, July 2009) notes that *himation* in the New Testament usually is just a generic term for a piece of clothing, citing Danker, *A Greek-English Lexicon of the New Testament,* s.v. ἱμάτιον. However, according to this source

himation not only is used to denote a generic article of clothing but can describe the cloak or mantle worn over a tunic. In my opinion, the usages in the Gospel accounts and especially Matthew are consistent with the latter meaning.

55. In other words, these articles of dress were not unusual; see Baumgarten, *The Flourishing of Jewish Sects*, 102; Cohn, *Tangled Up in Text*, 111.

56. See Sanders, *Judaism*, 229. For secondary impurity, see Wright, *The Disposal of Impurity*, 179-228. I thank Yonatan Adler for clarifying for me this type of impurity.

57. See Neusner, *A History of the Mishnaic Law of Purities*, 60-61; see 70-71 for *madaf* impurity (impurity caused to an object not used for sitting or lying that is located above a *zab*). See Wright, *The Disposal of Impurity*, 183 n. 34, for the possibility that clothing was equated with flesh.

58. For a discussion of these passages relative to rabbinic halakhah, see Neusner, *A History of the Mishnaic Law of Purities*, 60-71; Milgrom, *Leviticus 1–16*, 902-19, 1004-9. See also Haber, *"They Shall Purify Themselves,"* 128-29, who discusses the stricter priestly legislation of Num 5:1-4 (expanded upon by the author of the *Temple Scroll*), which excludes everyone with severe impurities from the camp.

59. Kazen, *Jesus and Purity Halakhah*, 164, suggests that clothing was considered a medium of defilement in the Second Temple period based on the assumption that the rabbis tended towards increased leniency, especially restricting the transmission of impurity to people.

60. See also *t. Kelim B. Bat.* 1:2-3.

61. See Yadin, *The Temple Scroll*, 1:339-40; Wright, *The Disposal of Impurity*, 204 n. 66. The *Damascus Document* forbids wearing clothing soiled with excrement on the Sabbath: "No one is to wear dirty clothes *(begadim tso'im)* . . ." (CD 11.3; see discussion below). Lawrence, *Washing in Water*, 84, notes that the term "launder" *(kbs)* occurs alone (without an object) much more frequently in the Dead Sea Scrolls than in the Hebrew Bible. Even sectarian law made some allowances; see Baumgarten, "Tohorot," 104-5 (4Q274). According to this legislation, a person who owns only one set of clothes may eat ordinary (nonsacred) food without laundering but must not allow the clothing to come into contact with the food.

62. From Daise, "Ritual Density in Qumran Practice."

63. From Yadin, *The Temple Scroll*, 1:340.

64. Kazen, *Jesus and Purity Halakhah*, 162. In support he cites *t. Zabim* 4:3, but there are two problems with Kazen's understanding of this passage: first, *tzitzit* is usually rendered here as "hair," not "fringes," and second, it refers to hair (or fringes) touching hair (or fringes), not clothing. A passage in *Hekhalot Rabbati* (225-28) provides (later) evidence for the view that clothing becomes impure when touched by an impure person. In this episode, Rabbi Nehuniah is rendered impure (according to a minority view) by coming into contact with a cloth that was touched by a menstruating woman; see Swartz, "Ritual and Purity in Early Jewish Mysticism," 162-64.

65. See Newman, *Proximity to Power*, 143-44, who identifies the *haverim* in this passage as Pharisees.

66. See Neusner, *The Idea of Purity in Ancient Judaism*, 60; Levine, "Discharging Responsibility," 78-79; Haber, *"They Shall Purify Themselves,"* 134 n. 35. Furthermore, the rabbinic principle of degrees or removes of impurity apparently was not accepted by all Jews; see Marcus, *Mark 1–8*, 446; Elman, "Some Remarks on 4QMMT," 100, who notes that it does not seem to be attested in Qumran law.

67. Sanders, *Judaism*, 440. On 521 n. 28 he remarks, "The existence of public immersion pools indicates that many people did not observe rules of garment-purity. Several impurities render the clothes impure. How can one walk to a public pool in impure clothes, immerse, and not touch one's impure clothes again?"

68. There were apparently different views concerning the defilement of clothing, due to the lack of clarity of the relevant biblical laws. See Wright, *The Disposal of Impurity*, 186 n. 39, who concludes that "The reason for the requirement of laundering [clothes] cannot simply be that the clothes have cont[r]acted the impurity"; see also 248-74; Milgrom, *Leviticus 1–16*, 953-57. Neusner, *The Idea of Purity in Ancient Judaism*, 116, suggests that purification was a means of exorcising evil demons or spirits, although in Jesus' healings the issue of purity is not made explicit.

69. For a similar suggestion, see Haber, *"They Shall Purify Themselves,"* 133-34.

Notes to Chapter 9

1. See Eshel, "CD 12:15-17 and the Stone Vessels"; Baumgarten, "The Essene Avoidance of Oil."

2. See Noam, "Qumran and the Rabbis on Corpse-Impurity," 424-25. Eshel, "CD 12: 15-17 and the Stone Vessels," 47, 51, observes that the *Temple Scroll* was probably composed before the development of the Jewish stone vessel industry in the late first century B.C.E. as its legislation does not refer to stone vessels.

3. See Beall, *Josephus' Description of the Essenes*, 45-46.

4. See Tigchelaar, "The White Clothing of the Essenes," 314.

5. Yadin, *The Temple Scroll*, 1:113-14, 142 (11QT 23:15). Yadin explained Josephus's observation by suggesting that even at this festival no oil was used because purified oil was not available at Qumran; see also Beall, *Josephus' Description of the Essenes*, 46. In my opinion, Josephus's observation is still valid even if oil was used once a year at this festival, as Josephus says that the Essenes refrain from being anointed without their consent but he does not say they refrain from oil altogether. In addition, Josephus's remark should be understood in light of the widespread custom of offering hospitality by anointing someone with oil. Bar-Ilan, "The Reasons for Sectarianism," 599, argues that the Essenes considered newly-pressed oil pure but refrained from using oil during the rest of the year because its purity could not be guaranteed, and that this is the basis for Josephus's observation. Eshel, "CD 12:15-17 and the Stone Vessels," 50, suggests that the sectarians considered oil more susceptible to defilement than other liquids.

6. See Tigchelaar, "The White Clothing of the Essenes," 314; Beall, *Josephus' Description of the Essenes*, 45-46.

7. Baumgarten, *The Flourishing of Jewish Sects*, 3, 58-60, notes that Josephus and Philo used terminology that was intended to make the beliefs and practices of the Jewish groups comprehensible to their (non-Jewish) readers.

8. From Deferrari, *Eusebius Pamphili*, 126.

9. See Chilton, "Paul and the Pharisees," 165, who connects these practices (and James' reported vegetarianism) with a Nazarite regime. For James' ascetic habits, see also Eisenman, *The New Testament Code*, 127.

10. From Bovon, *"Fragment Oxyrhynchus 840,"* 715, who places this work in "a Christian setting in the second or third century" (705).

11. Instone-Brewer, *Prayer and Agriculture*, 387, notes that in this episode Jesus appears to be unconcerned with impurity transmitted by the woman applying oil to his feet.

12. See, e.g., John 13:1-20; for a discussion, see Kazen, *Jesus and Purity Halakhah*, 251-55.

13. From Branham and Kinney, *Petronius Satyrica*, 64. See Clarke, "Jewish Table Manners," 262.

14. See Instone-Brewer, *Prayer and Agriculture*, 89-91.

15. See Clarke, "Jewish Table Manners," 257-58.

16. From Branham and Kinney, *Petronius Satyrica*, 24.

17. See Magness, *Debating Qumran*, 27.

18. See de Vaux, "Fouille au Khirbet Qumrân," 99, fig. 3:10; "Fouilles au Khirbet Qumrân," 223, fig. 4:4; "Fouilles de Khirbet Qumrân," 561, fig. 5:10.

19. See Bar-Nathan, *Hasmonean and Herodian Palaces at Jericho*, 57. For a juglet from a cave near Qumran that might have contained balsam oil, see Patrich and Arubas, "A Juglet Containing Balsam Oil (?)."

20. See de Vaux, "Fouilles de Feshkha," 241, fig. 2: 1, 2, 4; Bar-Adon, "Another Settlement of the Judean Desert Sect," 11, fig. 12:7-12. For the chronology of 'Ein Feshkha and 'Ein el-Ghuweir, see Magness, *Debating Qumran*, 49-61.

21. See Bar-Nathan, *Masada VII*, 198-207.

22. See Bar-Nathan, *Hasmonean and Herodian Palaces at Jericho*, 57-61, 165-67.

23. See Bar-Nathan, *Hasmonean and Herodian Palaces at Jericho*, 61-64.

24. See Geva and Rosenthal-Heginbottom, "Local Pottery from Area A," 185-86; Geva and Hershkovitz, "Local Pottery of the Hellenistic and Early Roman Periods," 104-5, 107-8.

25. See Jackson-Tal, "Glass Vessels from En-Gedi" (glass bottles).

26. See Hadas, *Nine Tombs of the Second Temple Period at 'En Gedi*, 10, fig. 15:25; 16, fig. 22:5-6; 22, fig. 32:8-9; 44, fig. 69:2-3.

27. Berlin, *Gamla I*, 142, 144, 146, 152, 154.

28. See Beall, *Josephus' Description of the Essenes*, 96.

29. See Kottek, "The Essenes and Medicine," 97-98 n. 15.

30. See Bokser, "Approaching Sacred Space," 290-91; Instone-Brewer, *Prayer and Agriculture*, 93.

31. From Gill and Hard, *The Discourses of Epictetus*, 281. I thank Professor Will Deming of the University of Portland for bringing this passage to my attention.

32. Oppenheimer, *The 'Am Ha-aretz*, 65, notes that the impurity of a Gentile is similar to that of a *zab*. See also Lightstone, "The Pharisees and Sadducees," 292-93. According to Hayes, *Gentile Impurities and Jewish Identities*, 195, "Early rabbis chose to stigmatize intimate relations with unconverted gentiles by attributing to them an ability to defile Israelites by means of their spittle and urine."

33. Alon, *Jews, Judaism and the Classical World*, 152, says that this is because according to the Palestinian Talmud the fuller of the Gentiles was in the Upper Market.

34. See Kottek, "The Essenes and Medicine," 90-91; Wise, "Review of *The Qumran Community*," 202; Sanders, *Jewish Law*, 349 n. 10.

35. Whereas rabbinic halakhah requires the widow to spit on the ground, the scholion to the *Megillat Ta'anit* suggests that some groups observed this injunction literally; see Noam, "From Philology to History," 61.

Notes to Chapter 10

1. From Hobson, *Latrinae et Foricae*, 145.

2. I wish to thank Adele Reinhartz, Achim Lichtenberger, and Albert Baumgarten for bringing to my attention some recent publications on toilets.

3. See Neudecker, *Die Pracht der Latrine;* Hodge, *Roman Aqueducts*, 270-71. For a discussion with references, see Magness, *Debating Qumran*, 63.

4. See Hobson, *Latrinae et Foricae*, 20. For latrines of this type in Palestine, see Baruch and Amar, "The *Latrina* in Eretz-Israel," 28-32.

5. See Rykwert, "Privacy in Antiquity," 36, who remarks that in the Roman world "there was nothing especially private about latrines or defecation." However, he also notes (37) that there seems to be a nearly universal sense of shame that causes people even in preliterate societies to withdraw from view while defecating (although public defecation was taken for granted in Roman latrines). It is unclear whether the sexes were segregated in Roman latrines. See also Hobson, *Latrinae et Foricae*, 79-83; Bouet, *Les latrines dans les provinces gauloises*, 175-80 (and see 98-99 for wooden latrine seats); Yegül, *Baths and Bathing in Classical Antiquity*, 32-33, 411-12. For a lack of concern with toilet privacy in some parts of the world today, see George, *The Big Necessity*, 174-97, who describes the practice of "open defecation" in India.

6. From Hobson, *Latrinae et Foricae*, 80.

7. See Hobson, *Latrinae et Foricae*, 69, 134-36; Bouet, *Les latrines dans les provinces gauloises*, 64-78; Horan, *The Porcelain God*, 14. Baruch and Amar, "The *Latrina* in Eretz-Israel," 33, note that only the well-to-do could afford to have private toilets in their homes; see 35 for the use of the outdoors.

8. From Hobson, *Latrinae et Foricae*, 136.

9. For references and a discussion, see Baruch and Amar, "The *Latrina* in Eretz-Israel," 41-43. In these passages it is the Gentile source of the urine that raises purity concerns. Unlike excrement, urine itself was not considered impure by Jews, not even by the Qumran sect.

10. From Hobson, *Latrinae et Foricae*, 96. See also Horan, *The Porcelain God*, 15.

11. Hodge, *Roman Aqueducts*, 335; Hobson, *Latrinae et Foricae*, 114 (describing the streets of Florence in the early seventeenth century).

12. Hobson, *Latrinae et Foricae*, 129-30.

13. Hobson, *Latrinae et Foricae*, 105, 143-46; Horan, *The Porcelain God*, 16; Hodge, *Roman Aqueducts*, 337. For analogous practices in some parts of the world today, see George, *The Big Necessity*, 174-204.

14. From Hobson, *Latrinae et Foricae*, 143.

15. From Hobson, *Latrinae et Foricae*, 144.

16. From Hobson, *Latrinae et Foricae*, 144-45.

17. See Hobson, *Latrinae et Foricae*, 5, 41 (a wooden toilet), 45-77; Bouet, *Les latrines dans les provinces gauloises*, 21-33. The cesspits of toilets usually were not connected with the central drainage or sewer system (if one existed), which instead was designed to carry overflow or runoff water in the streets and, with it, the accumulated waste; see Hobson, *Latrinae et Foricae*, 2, 46 (discussing Pompeii). George, *The Big Necessity*, 24, notes that "most ancient societies did not think of using water to transport waste because they didn't need to. . . . Even after toilets became popular, it remained illegal for London's citizens to connect their waste pipes to the sewers."

18. See Bouet, *Les latrines dans les provinces gauloises,* 169; Hobson, *Latrinae et Foricae,* 46-47, 90.

19. Hodge, *Roman Aqueducts,* 336; Scobie, "Slums, Sanitation, and Mortality," 409-17; Bodel, "Graveyards and Groves," 32; Hobson, *Latrinae et Foricae,* 99-100. For the use of night soil as fertilizer in China, see George, *The Big Necessity,* 110.

20. Cahill et al., "Scientists Examine Remains of Ancient Bathroom." For other examples of toilets of this type, see Magness, *Debating Qumran,* 64-65.

21. Humbert and Chambon, *Fouilles de Khirbet Qumrân,* 309; Photos 148-51. The caption to Photo 150 erroneously describes the (dried) mud-lining of the pit as a *"jarre receptacle."* Perhaps the terracotta pipe was intended to carry waste "flushed" down by pouring in water (although as is typical of ancient toilets/cesspits, there was no outlet).

22. Humbert and Chambon, *Fouilles de Khirbet Qumrân,* 307; see also Magness, *Debating Qumran,* 65. I have not seen the stone block and know of no published photographs.

23. Yadin, *The Temple Scroll,* 1:294-95; 2:199. Werrett, *Ritual Purity and the Dead Sea Scrolls,* 158 n. 121, notes that although Deut 23:12 uses the term *yad,* the phrase *maqom yad* is unattested in the Hebrew Bible.

24. See Qimron and Charlesworth, "Rule of the Community," 33.

25. As noted by Yadin, *The Temple Scroll,* 2:199.

26. See Beall, *Josephus' Description of the Essenes,* 97-98.

27. *Pace* Baumgarten, "The Temple Scroll, Toilet Practices, and the Essenes," who concluded that because the *Temple Scroll* and Josephus describe such different toilet habits, the groups they represent could not be the same.

28. See Magness, *Debating Qumran,* 65, 68, 111-12.

29. In *The Archaeology of Qumran,* 110, and *Debating Qumran,* 69, I discussed a fragmentary halakhic scroll (4Q472 or 4QHalakha C) that seems to refer to the covering or burial of excrement. I have removed this document from my discussion as new evidence suggests this reading is incorrect; see Elgvin and Werrett, "4Q472a in Infrared Light." For an argument that the fragment refers to covering excrement, see Baumgarten, "Tannaitic Halakhah and Qumran," 3; see also Harrington, *The Purity Texts,* 106.

30. Scobie, "Slums, Sanitation, and Mortality," 409.

31. Yadin, *The Temple Scroll,* 2:199, noted that the wording emphasizes "houses which are roofed."

32. See Scobie, "Slums, Sanitation, and Mortality," 429; Bodel, "Graveyards and Groves," 33; Magness, *Debating Qumran,* 67.

33. See Yadin, *The Temple Scroll,* 1:298-99.

34. Yadin, *The Temple Scroll,* 1:298. For the sectarians the Sabbath limit was 1000 cubits for walking and 2000 cubits for pasturing cattle (CD 10:21 and 11:5-6), double the rabbinic and probably Pharisaic limits; see Broshi and Eshel, "Residential Caves at Qumran," 334. See also Doering, "New Aspects of Qumran Sabbath Law from Cave 4 Fragments," 257; "Purity Regulations Concerning the Sabbath," 608.

35. Schürer, *The History of the Jewish People,* 2:472-73. For a discussion relating to the Qumran sect, see Crown, "Qumran, Samaritan *Halakha* and Theology," 435-36.

36. See Doering, "Purity Regulations Concerning the Sabbath," 608, who notes that the prohibition against defecation on the Sabbath stems from purity concerns. In contrast, the suggestion by Beall, *Josephus' Description of the Essenes,* 97, that the Essenes refrained

from defecating on the Sabbath because digging a pit would have violated the prohibition against working, fails to explain why they did not use built toilet facilities.

37. Cuffel, *Gendering Disgust*, 39, notes that "human waste was incompatible with divine or angelic presence."

38. See Sanders, *Jewish Law*, 349 n. 10.

39. See Magness, *Debating Qumran*, 70, 111. For the claim that remains associated with sectarian toilet facilities were found to the northwest of Qumran, see Zias et al., "Toilets at Qumran"; Zias, "Qumran Toilet Practices." I do not find this evidence convincing; see Magness, "Toilet Practices at Qumran."

40. See Magness, *Debating Qumran*, 71, with references; see also Cuffel, *Gendering Disgust*, 39.

41. See also Baruch and Amar, "The *Latrina* in Eretz-Israel," 36 n. 13.

42. As Yadin, *The Temple Scroll*, 1:297 noted, rabbinic discussions focus on an attitude of proper respect. See also Cuffel, *Gendering Disgust*, 39.

43. From Bokser, "Approaching Sacred Space," 292.

44. For a discussion, see Bokser, "Approaching Sacred Space," 294-96. See also Cuffel, *Gendering Disgust*, 39. Apparently, for similar reasons the rabbis prohibited reciting the Shema' in the vicinity of graves; see tractate *Semaḥot* 13:1-4.

45. See also *y. Ber.* 3:5. However, dog dung was used for tanning hides, and according to a late rabbinic tradition it could even be used for tanning Torah scrolls, tefillin, and mezuzot; see Schwartz, "Dogs in Jewish Society," 262, including n. 93.

46. See also Baruch and Amar, "The *Latrina* in Eretz-Israel," 38-39. However, Yael Wilfand has noted that there is no evidence to support Baruch and Amar's conclusion that the Palestinian rabbis mandated toilet privacy as a norm. Instead, a concern for toilet privacy and modesty seems to be associated mainly with Babylonian rabbis, a phenomenon which Wilfand attributes to possible Zoroastrian influence; see Wilfand, "Did the Rabbis Reject the Roman Public Latrine?"

47. It is interesting that this legislation applies to the event of an optional war, recalling the *War Scroll*. Perhaps the idea is that under these conditions there would be no access to permanent toilet facilities.

48. As Davies, "Food, Drink and Sects," 152, notes, Leviticus 15 does not consider urinating or defecating as unclean emissions, and although Deut 23:12-14 seems to regard excrement as unclean, "nowhere in the Bible is either urinating or defecating a cause of uncleanness to the person."

49. For Ezekiel texts and references at Qumran, see García Martínez, *Qumranica Minora II*, 1-12; Brooke, "Ezekiel in Some Qumran and New Testament Texts." Wacholder, "Historiography of Qumran"; "Ezekiel and Ezekielianism," discusses the sect's use of Ezekiel in their polemics and the importance of this work for the history of the sons of Zadok. See also Klawans, *Purity, Sacrifice, and the Temple*, 94-97.

50. See Harrington, *The Purity Texts*, 19.

51. See Baumgarten, "The Laws of the Damascus Document," 25: "the scriptural basis of Qumran law . . . unlike talmudic halakha, also included the Prophets."

52. Doering, "The Concept of the Sabbath," 196.

53. Doering, "The Concept of the Sabbath," 196. For a scroll fragment that might provide evidence of a similar prohibition at Qumran, see Doering, "Purity Regulations Concerning the Sabbath," 604.

54. See Doering, "The Concept of the Sabbath," 202, who suggests that Jubilee's concept of the sabbath is "priestly." This is interesting in light of Cuffel's observation that human waste was considered incompatible with divine or angelic presence; *Gendering Disgust*, 39.

55. For a discussion of this passage, see Reich, "Miqva'ot in the Second Temple Period," 156-57, who understands this legislation as meaning that the sectarians did not tolerate any changes to the color or odor of water used for immersion, even if they were due to natural causes such as silting. Selkin Wise, "*Miqwā'ôt* and Second Temple Sectarianism," 185, contrasts the rabbinic and sectarian views.

56. See also Baumgarten et al., *Qumran Cave 4*, 68-69, 76 (4Q265); Doering, "New Aspects of Qumran Sabbath Law," 266; "Purity Regulations Concerning the Sabbath," 603; Harrington, *The Purity Texts*, 106. For a dissenting view, see Werrett, *Ritual Purity and the Dead Sea Scrolls*, 239, 278, whose objection on the grounds that this means clothing soiled with excrement was worn on other days reflects an unrealistic, sanitized view of the ancient world. Scholars have had difficulty making sense of the next words in this passage of the *Damascus Document*. Schiffman's translation reads: "No one shall put on filthy garments or (those) put in storage *(bgz)* unless they have been washed with water or are rubbed with frankincense" (CD 11:3); *The Halakhah at Qumran*, 106. Baumgarten and Schwartz, "The Damascus Document," 47, translate: "Let no man put on soiled clothes or those brought with lint (?) unless they were washed with water or rubbed with frankincense." Louis Ginzberg translated: "No one shall put on filthy garments *(begadim tso'im)* or (those) soiled with excrement," reading the last word as *bgl* (from the word for animal dung; see Schiffman, *The Halakhah at Qumran*, 108). In this case the prohibition would be against wearing clothes soiled with human excrement or animal dung on the Sabbath, which makes more sense than the other suggested readings in light of the sectarian view associating excrement with impurity and prohibiting defecation on the Sabbath. However, Schiffman, *The Halakah at Qumran*, 106 n. 147, states that "the *zayin* [of *bgz*] is quite clear in the MS." A similar law in 4Q265 (frag. 6:3) says "Let no man [wea]r garments wh[ich] have dust *('pr)* or [*gz*]."; see Baumgarten, "Miscellaneous Rules," 68-69, who restores *gz* on the basis of CD 11:3 and translates it as "lint." For a different translation, see Doering, "Purity Regulations Concerning the Sabbath," 603 n. 22.

57. Grossberg, "The *Miqva'ot* (Ritual Baths) at Masada," 97, notes that according to rabbinic law silt or sludge that enters a miqveh through use does not render it invalid, but the miqveh is disqualified if a foreign body falls into it and changes the appearance of the water. Reich, "Miqva'ot in the Second Temple Period," 157, understands this as meaning that the rabbis did not allow changes to the color or odor of water in a miqveh caused by neglect or human intervention but did tolerate changes due to natural causes. See also Miller, "Stepped Pools and the Non-Existent Monolithic 'Miqveh,'" 228 n. 20: "The rabbis were primarily concerned with the discoloration of the water used for ritual purification, not necessarily how clean it was."

58. Translation from Goldin, *The Fathers According to Rabbi Nathan*, 62. Schwartz, "Material Culture in the Land of Israel," 135, translates as follows this passage: "If one degrades himself for the sake of Torah and eats dates and carobs and wears clothing soiled with excrement and sits and guards the entranceway of the Sages, every passer-by will wonder whether this is a fool, but in the end you will find all the Torah with him." Schwartz also cites another example from *Pesiq. Rab.* 23.

59. Furstenberg, "Defilement Penetrating the Body," 194-95, understands Jesus' response as halakhic — i.e., according to biblical law impurity is caused not by ingesting con-

taminated food, but by substances that come out of the body such as blood, saliva, and seminal emissions.

60. Marcus, *Mark 1–8,* 455, 459, notes the scatological associations raised by this statement. Lambrecht, "Jesus and the Law," 60, believes that the statement about defilement is based on a "pre-Markan logion." For a different conclusion, see Booth, *Jesus and the Laws of Purity,* 72-73.

61. According to 4Q274 1i:1-2 (a halakhic text), *zabim* must be segregated to the northwest of all dwellings at a distance of 12 cubits; see Baumgarten et al., *Qumran Cave 4,* 100-2.

62. See Magness, *Debating Qumran,* 70.

63. See Humbert and Chambon, *Fouilles de Khirbet Qumrân,* 309.

64. Broshi, "Anti-Qumranic Polemics in the Talmud," 595-96.

65. For the rabbinic sources, see Baruch and Amar, "The *Latrina* in Eretz-Israel."

66. For a discussion of this passage, see Wilfand, "Did the Rabbis Reject the Roman Public Latrine?" 189-90, although she does not address the matter of the north-south orientation.

Notes to Chapter 11

1. The "James ossuary" is in the possession of a private collector named Oded Golan and has no archaeological provenience. See Lemaire, "Burial Box of James the Brother of Jesus"; Shanks and Witherington, *The Brother of Jesus.*

2. See Jacobovici and Pellegrino, *The Jesus Family Tomb;* http://dsc.discovery.com/news/2007/02/25/tomb_arc_zoomo.html?category=archaeology&guid=20070225073000. The tomb and ossuaries are not new discoveries, having been excavated in 1980 and published in 1996 (see Kloner, "A Tomb with Inscribed Ossuaries"); what is new is the claim that this is the tomb of Jesus' family.

3. For foreign influences on Jewish burial customs in Galilee after 70, see Weiss, "Foreign Influences on Jewish Burial."

4. A comprehensive discussion of First Temple–period tombs lies outside the scope of this study. For general information including the tombs mentioned here, see Faust and Bunimovitz, "The Judahite Rock-Cut Tomb"; Bloch-Smith, *Judahite Burial Practices;* Barkay, "Burial Caves and Burial Practices"; "The Necropoli of Jerusalem in the First Temple Period"; Barkay and Kloner, "Jerusalem Tombs from the Days of the First Temple"; Barkay et al., "The Northern Cemetery of Jerusalem in First Temple Times"; Ussishkin, *The Village of Silwan;* Avigad, *Ancient Monuments in the Kidron Valley.*

5. See Barkay, "The Divine Name Found in Jerusalem."

6. See Magness, "A Near Eastern Ethnic Element?"

7. Phoenician influence is also evident in the Proto-Aeolic capitals, carved ivories, and other objects and decorative elements found in the Israelite and Judahite palaces; see Mazar, *Archaeology of the Land of the Bible.*

8. See Berlin, "Power and Its Afterlife"; Fedak, *Monumental Tombs of the Hellenistic Age.*

9. All translations of Josephus in this chapter are from Whiston.

10. Berlin, "Power and Its Afterlife," 145.

11. The Aramaic inscription in Jason's Tomb refers to a tomb and a *nefesh;* see Yardeni, *Textbook of Aramaic, Hebrew, and Nabataean Documentary Texts,* 224 (A); 78 (B); and the inscription on the façade of the tomb of Bene Ḥezir reads: "This is the grave and *nefesh* of Eleazar Ḥonia Joezer Joudah Simeon Johanan sons of Joseph son of Obed Joseph and Eleazar sons of Ḥonia priests of the sons of Ḥezir" (from Stern, "Aspects of Jewish Society: The Priesthood and Other Classes," 594). For monumental grave markers, see Triebel, *Jenseitshoffnung in Wort und Stein;* Kloner and Zissu, *The Necropolis of Jerusalem,* 49-50; Rubin, *The End of Life,* 156; Rahmani, "Ancient Jerusalem's Funerary Customs and Tombs, Part Three."

12. The influence of Hellenistic culture on the Hasmoneans is also reflected by their adoption of Greek names and is evident in literary works composed in this period; see Levine, *Jerusalem,* 144-45.

13. For pro-Ptolemaic and pro-Seleucid factions in Jerusalem, see Jagersma, *A History of Israel,* 40-41. Jagersma suggests that Onias III had a pro-Ptolemaic stance, whereas Simon and the rest of the Tobiads were more pro-Seleucid.

14. Hengel, *Judaism and Hellenism,* 277.

15. Berlin, "Power and Its Afterlife," 145-47.

16. See Hengel, *Judaism and Hellenism,* 64.

17. Berlin, "Power and Its Afterlife," 142.

18. Rahmani, "Jason's Tomb"; for a recent discussion, see Berlin, "Power and Its Afterlife," 142-43.

19. See Avigad, "Aramaic Inscriptions in the Tomb of Jason"; Rahmani, "Ancient Jerusalem's Funerary Customs and Tombs, Part Three," 45. Avigad, "Aramaic Inscriptions in the Tomb of Jason," 103, noted that "the name Jason was common among hellenizing Jews as the equivalent for Joshua."

20. See Rahmani, "Jason's Tomb"; Rahmani, "Ancient Jerusalem's Funerary Customs and Tombs, Part Three," 45.

21. A single column is unusual in Jerusalem's rock-cut tombs, which typically have two columns in the porch (if there are columns at all).

22. See Venit, *Monumental Tombs of Ancient Alexandria,* 175-78; Kloner and Zissu, *The Necropolis of Jerusalem,* 77-79; Rahmani, "Ancient Jerusalem's Funerary Customs and Tombs, Part Three," 45; McCane, *Roll Back the Stone,* 7; Hachlili and Killebrew, "Jewish Funerary Customs during the Second Temple Period," 110. Berlin, "Power and Its Afterlife," 139-41, notes that the tombs at Marisa, which were used by the Sidonian population at the site, continue Phoenician traditions such as the lack of external display while incorporating new Hellenistic features such as loculi.

23. For other examples of late second century to first century B.C.E. loculus tombs in Jerusalem that antedate the introduction of ossuaries, see Rahmani, "Ancient Jerusalem's Funerary Customs and Tombs, Part Three," 46.

24. See Segal, "Herodium"; for a recent discussion with bibliog., see Magness, "The Mausolea of Augustus, Alexander, and Herod the Great." For the recent discovery of Herod's tomb at Herodium, see Netzer et al., "Herod's Tomb — Finally Revealed"; Netzer et al., "Two Inscriptions from Herodium." The shape of the mountain and placement of the funerary remains on a terrace cut into its side recall the *hierothesion* of Antiochus I at Nemrud Dagh in Asia Minor (an observation that was made long before Netzer's discovery). For Nemrud Dagh, see Sanders, *Nemrud Daği;* Pollitt, *Art in the Hellenistic Age,* 274-75.

25. For bibliog. on these tombs, see Kloner and Zissu, *The Necropolis of Jerusalem;* Rahmani, "Ancient Jerusalem's Funerary Customs and Tombs, Part Three"; Evans, *Jesus and the Ossuaries,* 17-19. For Nicanor's Tomb, see Avigad, "Jewish Rock-Cut Tombs."

26. Kloner and Zissu, *The Necropolis of Jerusalem,* 39-40.

27. Rahmani, *A Catalogue of Jewish Ossuaries,* 21, suggested the date of ca. 20-15 B.C.E. The absence of ossuaries from Jason's Tomb provides a *terminus post quem* in the thirties B.C.E. (by which time the tomb had been abandoned) for their appearance; see Rahmani, "Jason's Tomb," 94, 99. For discussions of the chronology of ossuaries, see Vitto, "Burial Caves from the Second Temple Period "; Magen, *The Stone Vessel Industry,* 135; Cahill, "Chalk Vessel Assemblages"; 218. Fanny Vitto's discovery of an undisturbed tomb dating to the reign of Herod into which ossuaries were introduced during the last phase of use confirms Rahmani's dating; see Vitto, "Burial Caves from the Second Temple Period," 103. Interestingly, all of the ossuaries from this tomb are undecorated. On 119 n. 3, Vitto correctly notes that Rachel Hachlili's *terminus post quem* of ca. 10 B.C.E. for the appearance of ossuaries, which is based on evidence from the Jericho cemetery, is too late for Jerusalem. Vitto's evidence also contradicts Cahill's proposed first-century C.E. date for the introduction of ossuaries; Cahill, "Chalk Vessel Assemblages," 233. On the other hand, Gideon Hadas's proposed early first-century B.C.E. date, based on the discovery of a single stone ossuary in Tomb 4 at 'Ein Gedi, is much too early and is unsupported by the archaeological evidence; see Hadas, *Nine Tombs of the Second Temple Period,* 7*: "In view of the suggested date of the tomb, the date for the introduction of ossilegium in stone chests may be moved up to the early first century BCE." The pottery from this tomb includes cooking pots, unguentaria, and a Judean radial oil lamp, all of which represent types characteristic of the Herodian period (i.e., the time of Herod the Great, and in some cases continuing later); compare Hadas, *Nine Tombs of the Second Temple Period,* 22, fig. 32: 8-9 (unguentaria), 10 (oil lamp), 12-13 (cooking pots) with Bar-Nathan, *Hasmonean and Herodian Palaces at Jericho,* 165-67 (unguentaria), 170-72 (cooking pots). Although Judean radial lamps date generally to the first century B.C.E., most if not all of the specimens from Masada date to the reign of Herod the Great; see Barag and Hershkovitz, "Lamps"; 22-24. In other words, although Tomb 4 at 'Ein Gedi might have been used before Herod's time, burials certainly continued during his reign. There is thus no basis for dating the stone ossuary from this tomb to the early first century B.C.E. Kloner and Zissu, *The Necropolis of Jerusalem,* 112-13, report that more than 3000 ossuaries are known, most of them from Jerusalem and more than 2000 of which are plain.

28. Kloner and Zissu, *The Necropolis of Jerusalem,* 120, note that ossuaries were not used in Jerusalem "much after the year 70." For post-70 examples of ossuaries, see Rahmani, *A Catalogue of Jewish Ossuaries,* 23-25; many of the later specimens from Galilee are made of clay.

29. Magen, *The Stone Vessel Industry,* 133; Rahmani, *A Catalogue of Jewish Ossuaries,* 3.

30. See Rahmani, *A Catalogue of Jewish Ossuaries,* 4-6; Magen, *The Stone Vessel Industry,* 133-35. For an ossuary with a bucranium (bull's head) carved in relief on one side from the Akeldama tombs, see Shadmi, "The Ossuaries and the Sarcophagus," 45 (Ossuary 17), including Fig. 2.12.

31. See Fine, "A Note on Ossuary Burial," 75.

32. Rahmani, *A Catalogue of Jewish Ossuaries,* 11-19; see also Fine, "A Note on Ossuary Burial," 74; Rubin, *The End of Life,* 156.

33. Rahmani, *A Catalogue of Jewish Ossuaries,* 11, notes that richly decorated ossuaries

were found together with the much simpler sarcophagus of Queen Helena: "While it is clear that only wealthy families would have been able to afford the costly varieties of ossuaries, the choice of cheaper types should not be regarded as a sign of comparative poverty or of parsimony." Of the seven ossuaries discovered in Nicanor's Tomb, three are plain; Avigad, "Jewish Rock-Cut Tombs in Jerusalem," 124. In Cave 1 of the Akeldama tombs, none of the ossuaries is inscribed, half are plain, and only three are painted; see Shadmi, "The Ossuaries and the Sarcophagus," 51. Similarly, there is no correlation between the status of the deceased and the quality of the inscriptions on ossuaries. For example, Hachlili and Smith, "The Genealogy of the Goliath Family," 70, noted that "the individuals interred in the ossuaries lacking inscriptions did not differ in age or sex from those in ossuaries with inscriptions." Therefore, contrary to Evans, *Jesus and the Ossuaries*, 107-8, the relative simplicity of the Caiaphas tomb and the poor quality of the inscriptions on the ossuaries found in it do not disprove its identification as the tomb of the well-known high priest and his family. Instead, the archaeological and literary evidence supports this identification, although it cannot be established with absolute certainty. Rahmani, *A Catalogue of Jewish Ossuaries*, 11, observes that the seemingly high proportion of inscribed ossuaries is misleading since many plain or uninscribed ossuaries were discarded by the excavators or are unpublished.

34. See Greenhut, "Burial Cave of the Caiaphas Family"; Levine, *Jerusalem*, 210; McCane, *Roll Back the Stone*, 35; Rahmani, *A Catalogue of Jewish Ossuaries*, 174. As McCane, *Roll Back the Stone*, 35, cautions, "A poorly constructed tomb might appear to be evidence of a family's lower social and economic status, but conclusions of this sort require careful review, since rich families may have had the means to build a splendid tomb but simply chose to use their wealth in other ways. In fact, there would have been little social incentive for Jewish families in this region and period to expend resources on the construction and ornamentation of a tomb's interior. . . . A roughly hewn burial chamber might therefore be evidence not of a family's poverty, but rather of their inclination to spend wealth in other ways."

35. For this tomb, see Kon, *The Tombs of the Kings*; Levine, *Jerusalem*, 211; Rahmani, "Ancient Jerusalem's Funerary Customs and Tombs, Part Three," 48-49. For the inscribed stone sarcophagus from this tomb, which apparently contained the queen's remains, see Frey, *Corpus Inscriptionum Iudaicarum*, 320-21 no. 1388.

36. Other unparalleled features include the use of stone masonry revetment along the interior walls of the tomb and the fact that the two square pillars or piers in the porch are constructed of ashlars instead of being hewn out of rock. See Avigad, "Jewish Rock-Cut Tombs in Jerusalem," 119-24, who describes Nicanor's Tomb as "one of the most monumental tombs in Jerusalem" (119; my translation). See also Evans, *Jesus and the Ossuaries*, 24, 92-93.

37. See Avni and Greenhut, "Resting Place of the Rich and Famous," 36-46; Avni and Greenhut, *The Akeldama Tombs*, 32-33 remark, "A possible clue to the occurrence of these decorative schemes and the high standard of workmanship evidenced in Chamber C of Cave 3 may be found in the identity of the cave owners — a wealthy Jewish family from Syria." For the Syrian place names mentioned on the ossuaries from this cave, see Ilan, "The Ossuary and Sarcophagus Inscriptions," 68, who notes the prominent positions attained by some Diaspora Jewish families in Herodian Jerusalem. In addition, only six of the forty ossuaries discovered in the Akeldama tombs lacked ornamentation or an inscription; see Shadmi, "The Ossuaries and the Sarcophagus," 50-51. Archaeological evidence supports the Gospel tradi-

tion (Matt 27:7-8) that Akeldama (Potter's Field) was a burial ground for foreigners. For a discussion of how this elite cemetery came to be associated with the poor, see Ritmeyer and Ritmeyer, "Potter's Field or High Priest's Tomb?"

38. Rahmani, "Ancient Jerusalem's Funerary Customs and Tombs, Part One," 175-76; *A Catalogue of Jewish Ossuaries*, 53-55. For a recent discussion of resurrection in biblical Israel see Levenson, *Resurrection and the Restoration of Israel*. See also Sanders, *Judaism*, 298-303.

39. Rahmani, "Ancient Jerusalem's Funerary Customs and Tombs, Part One," 175; *A Catalogue of Jewish Ossuaries*, 53-55. See also McCane, *Roll Back the Stone*, 43; Magen, *The Stone Vessel Industry*, 136-37.

40. See, e.g., McCane, *Roll Back the Stone*, 43; Evans, *Jesus and the Ossuaries*, 30; Levine, *Jerusalem*, 264; Fine, "A Note on Ossuary Burial," 70-72; Regev, "The Individualistic Meaning of Jewish Ossuaries," 40-42; Rubin, *The End of Life*, 145-53; Meyers, *Jewish Ossuaries*, 85-86.

41. See Magen, *The Stone Vessel Industry*, 137; Fine, "A Note on Ossuary Burial," 75. Kloner and Zissu, *The Necropolis of Jerusalem*, 118, note that "In [burial] caves discovered in recent decades, approximately half of the intact ossuaries contained the remains of two or more people." The Caiaphas ossuary contained the remains of six individuals: two infants, a child between the ages of two and five, a youth aged thirteen to eighteen, an adult female, and a man about sixty years of age; see Greenhut, "Burial Cave of the Caiaphas Family," 34. The ossuary with the remains of Yohanan, the crucified man from Giv'at ha-Mivtar, contained the partial remains of a second adult as well as a child; see Zias and Sekeles, "The Crucified Man from Giv'at ha-Mivtar," 23-24. Several ossuaries from the Goliath family tomb in Jericho contained the remains of more than one individual; see Hachlili and Killebrew, *Jericho*, 170; Hachlili and Smith, "The Genealogy of the Goliath Family," 67, 69. See also the Akeldama tombs (Avni and Greenhut, *The Akeldama Tombs*, 51-52), where nearly every ossuary contained the remains of more than one individual. As Ilan, "The Ossuary and Sarcophagus Inscriptions," 66, observed, "Usually, bones that were collected into ossuaries included remains of more than one individual, at Akeldama and elsewhere." At the Princeton Theological Seminary's 2008 Jerusalem Symposium on Afterlife and Burial Practices in Second Temple Judaism, Amos Kloner distributed a handout which states that ossuaries from Jerusalem's rock-cut tombs contained an average of 1.7 individuals each. For ossuaries containing the bones of dogs and other animals together with human remains, see Rahmani, *A Catalogue of Jewish Ossuaries*, 124 no. 200.

42. See, e.g., Avni and Greenhut, *The Akeldama Tombs*, 34; see also Hadas, *Nine Tombs of the Second Temple Period at 'En Gedi*, 7*, who notes that the 'Ein Gedi caves provide evidence for the contemporaneous employment of different burial methods.

43. See Regev, "The Individualistic Meaning of Jewish Ossuaries," 41. Almost four decades ago Meyers, *Jewish Ossuaries*, 86, cautioned "It would seem hazardous, therefore, to try to relate either ossuaries or sarcophagi to a particular Jewish sect or segment of society in earlier Temple times." On the other hand, there is no doubt that rock-cut tombs belonged to members of Jerusalem's upper class, at least some of whom were Sadducees.

44. For the former, see Avigad, *Ancient Monuments in the Kidron Valley*, 37-78; Rahmani, "Ancient Jerusalem's Funerary Customs and Tombs, Part Three," 47; for the latter, see Reich, "Caiaphas Name Inscribed on Bone Boxes." For ossuaries inscribed with names of deceased identified as priests, see Evans, *Jesus and the Ossuaries*, 53-54, who lists seven speci-

mens, with additional examples on 104-11; Frey, *Corpus Inscriptionum Iudaicarum*, 250, no. 1221; Rahmani, *A Catalogue of Jewish Ossuaries*, 85 no. 41 (perhaps belonging to the priestly family Boethos); 250-51 no. 829 (inscribed with the names Ananias and Ananas, perhaps the well-known high priests); 259 no. 871 (perhaps containing the remains of the granddaughter of the high priest Theophilos). For ossuaries inscribed with the names of deceased who are identified as scribes, see Evans, *Jesus and the Ossuaries*, 56 (three specimens); Rahmani, *A Catalogue of Jewish Ossuaries*, 262-63 no. 893 (inscribed "Yehosef, son of Hananya, the scribe"). The wall of a tomb in Jerusalem's Giv'at ha-Mivtar neighborhood bears a large panel with an Aramaic inscription in paleo-Hebrew script which mentions "Abba son of the priest Eleazar," who was born in Jerusalem, exiled to Babylonia, and returned to Jerusalem; see Tzaferis, "The 'Abba' Burial Cave in Jerusalem"; Naveh, "An Aramaic Tomb Inscription."

45. See Regev, *The Sadducees and Their Halakhah*, 405. Cahill, "Chalk Vessel Assemblages," 233, made a similar observation about stone vessels: "If the use of stone vessels was a Pharisaic tradition, why are they commonly found furnishing the homes of the wealthy?"

46. See Murphy-O'Connor, Review of *The Necropolis of Jerusalem*, 450. Regev, *The Sadducees and Their Halakhah*, 404-5, notes that three of the priests named on ossuaries can be identified with confidence as Sadducees: Joseph son of Caiaphas; Simeon Boton (Boethos); and Yehohanah daughter of Yehonatan son of Theophilos the High Priest.

47. See Hachlili and Killebrew, *Jericho*; "Jewish Funerary Customs." Rahmani, *A Catalogue of Jewish Ossuaries*, 23, documents ossuaries up to 25 km away from Jerusalem (to Tell en-Nasbeh and 'Ai to the north; Ramat Raḥel and Beth Nattif to the south and southwest; and Beth Zayit to the west). Another group of ossuaries is associated with the rock-cut loculus tombs at Jericho (see Hachlili, "Ossuaries"; Hachlili and Killebrew, "Jewish Funerary Customs "), and there is a single stone ossuary from a loculus tomb at 'Ein Gedi (see Hadas, *Nine Tombs of the Second Temple Period*, 21; this example comes from the only rock-cut tomb with loculi at 'Ein Gedi). For an ossuary from the Nabataean cemetery at Mampsis in the Negev, see below. The distribution of rock-cut loculus tombs containing ossuaries reflects the settlement sphere of Jerusalem's elite, as well as rural elite families who adopted the same burial practices. Although ossuaries are usually found in loculus tombs, they can occur in rock-cut tombs without loculi. For example, four ossuaries were discovered on a burial bench in a rock-cut tomb of the late First Temple period in Bethlehem that was reused in the late Second Temple period; see Dadon, "Burial Caves at Bethlehem." When the Jewish elite relocated to Galilee in the aftermath of the two Jewish revolts, they displayed their wealth and status by interring their dead in the catacombs at Beth She'arim.

48. Rahmani, *A Catalogue of Jewish Ossuaries*, 54.

49. Levine, *Jerusalem*, 264-65; Foerster, "Ossilegium and Ossuaries."

50. The basic source is still Toynbee, *Death and Burial in the Roman World*; see 40. See also Patterson, "Living and Dying in the City of Rome," 273.

51. Toynbee, *Death and Burial in the Roman World*, 255-56.

52. For photos, see Davies, *Death, Burial and Rebirth*, 124, Fig. 14; Spanu, "Burial in Asia Minor," 172, fig. 17.5. Roller, *Dining Posture in Ancient Rome*, 24-45, discusses cinerary urns decorated with images of reclining figures.

53. These cinerary urns are unpublished. I saw them during a visit to the museum in July 2003 but was not allowed to photograph them.

54. Spanu, "Burial in Asia Minor," 172, who notes that these containers are poorly understood and inadequately published. Some may have contained cremations. For examples

from Ephesus, see Erdemgil, *Ephesus Museum,* 78: "In the corner just to the right of the Klazomenai sarcophagus is a series of ossuaries found in the cave of the Seven Sleepers."

55. Spanu, "Burial in Asia Minor," 172.

56. Negev and Gibson, *Archaeological Encyclopedia of the Holy Land,* 99; Negev, "Kurnub," 892. I thank Tali Erickson-Gini for pointing out to me this ossuary, which is on display at Mampsis (Mamshit), and for providing me with the published references.

57. See Rahmani, *A Catalogue of Jewish Ossuaries,* 3. Magen, *The Stone Vessel Industry,* 134, comes close when he observes that "even the name *gluskoma,* derived from the Greek word meaning a wooden coffin, implies that the form of the chalk ossuary was not original and that it was an exact replica of a wooden casket." For the reasons given here, Regev's objections to the suggestion that Roman cinerary urns were the source of inspiration for Judean ossuaries are not valid; see Regev, "The Individualistic Meaning of Jewish Ossuaries," 48, n. 15.

58. Rahmani, *A Catalogue of Jewish Ossuaries,* 58-59.

59. As Levine, *Jerusalem,* 261, notes, "The tombs that dotted the Jerusalem landscape are invariably of Hellenistic design but without figural depictions. The *tholos* of Absalom's tomb and the pyramid of Zechariah's tomb are classic Hellenistic architectural components."

60. Venit, *Monumental Tombs of Ancient Alexandria,* 175-80; McCane, *Roll Back the Stone,* 7.

61. As McCane, *Roll Back the Stone,* 45 notes (discussing the appearance of loculi in Judean tombs and the placement of coins on the mouths of the deceased), "All of these burial customs are of Hellenistic origin, so the ossuary would certainly not have been the first aspect of Jewish death ritual to be touched by the interaction of Judaism with Hellenism." Similarly, Roman cinerary urns were placed in loculi (niches) that were sealed by stone slabs; see Roller, *Dining Posture in Ancient Rome,* 25-26.

62. See McCane, *Roll Back the Stone,* 14, 46.

63. The names were apparently inscribed on the spot by the relatives of the deceased and are usually executed carelessly and clumsily. This is true even among prominent and high priestly families; see Rahmani, *A Catalogue of Jewish Ossuaries,* 11-12. Richardson, *Herod,* 241, observed that "the high priests were a natural part of the religious elite — indeed at the center of it — by virtue of family associations." Regev, "The Individualistic Meaning of Jewish Ossuaries," 43, notes the social importance of the inscriptions. Similar concerns are evident among the Roman aristocracy, as seen in the late Republican portrait busts depicting very aged men. These may be connected with the wax ancestral masks that were carried in funerary processions and then displayed in the household shrines of aristocratic families; see Kleiner, *Roman Sculpture,* 35-38.

64. See Rahmani, *A Catalogue of Jewish Ossuaries,* 173-74 no. 430; Evans, *Jesus and the Ossuaries,* 103-4.

65. See Levine, *Jerusalem,* 264. Rahmani, *A Catalogue of Jewish Ossuaries,* 55, responds to this objection by arguing that "the increased mobility of families and individuals in this period may have rendered *ossilegium* of relatives impossible."

66. Aviam, *Jews, Pagans and Christians in the Galilee,* 311, dates the use of ossuaries in Galilee to the second to fourth centuries. But Weiss, "Jewish Galilee in the First Century C.E.," 52, suggests that ossuaries might have been used in Galilee even before 70 and points to methodological problems in dating. For other Galilean cemeteries of this period, see Aviam,

Jews, Pagans and Christians in the Galilee, 257-311 ("Regionalism of Tombs and Burial Customs in the Galilee During the Hellenistic, Roman and Byzantine Periods"); Weiss, "The Location of Jewish Cemeteries," 234-35.

67. Rahmani, *A Catalogue of Jewish Ossuaries*, 21.

68. Although some ossilegium was still practiced; see Mazar, *Beth She'arim*, 135; Weiss, "Foreign Influences on Jewish Burial," 356. Avigad, *Beth She'arim*, 267, notes that in tombs dating to the mid-third century and later at Beth She'arim "the small niches (bone depositories), so common in the earlier catacombs, are almost completely absent."

69. For the stone and marble sarcophagi from Beth She'arim, as well as a small number of lead, clay, and wood specimens, see Avigad, *Beth She'arim*, 136-83.

70. See Mazar, *Beth She'arim*, 132-33; Avigad, *Beth She'arim*, 262-65 (compare and contrast Catacombs 14 and 20).

71. See Toynbee, *Death and Burial in the Roman World*, 40; Weiss, "Foreign Influences on Jewish Burial." 358. McCane, *Roll Back the Stone*, 7, noting the Hellenistic and Roman elements in the Beth She'arim tombs, describes this cemetery as "a case study in the ancient conversation between Judaism and Hellenism."

72. See Fine, "A Note on Ossuary Burial," 74; Magen, *The Stone Vessel Industry*, 132-35. Cahill, "Chalk Vessel Assemblages," 231-32, notes that the stone vessels and ossuaries are contemporary, although she seems to favor a first-century C.E. (instead of late-first-century B.C.E.) date for their appearance.

73. See Avigad, *Discovering Jerusalem*, 83-203; for the wall paintings, see Rozenberg, "Wall Painting Fragments from Area A," 302-28.

74. See Fine, "A Note on Ossuary Burial," 72. Although construction on and around the Temple Mount continued for decades (and was completed only in 64 C.E.), much of the work on the temple building (the sanctuary) was apparently carried out between ca. 23 and 15 B.C.E.; see Richardson, *Herod*, 197, 238, 245. For a discussion of the contradictory dates provided by Josephus and the suggestion that construction commenced in 20/19 B.C.E., see Levine, *Jerusalem*, 224-26.

75. Josephus, *Ant.* 15.268-71; see Richardson, *Herod*, 223; Levine, *Jerusalem*, 201.

76. Richardson, *Herod*, 230.

77. Josephus, *Ant.* 15.342.

78. Our sources mention that Augustus visited Syria, but it is not clear whether this included Judea; see Richardson, *Herod*, 234.

79. Josephus, *Ant.* 16.6.

80. Josephus, *Ant.* 16.12-15 (referred to in Nicolaus's speech); see Richardson, *Herod*, 232-33, 263-64.

81. Morris, *Burial and Ancient Society*, 105.

82. Fantalkin, "The Appearance of Rock-Cut Bench Tombs," 20-21; and Faust and Bunimovitz, "The Judahite Rock-Cut Tomb," 151, 156, 160, point to the same phenomenon in the late First Temple period, when elite families interred their dead in rock-cut tombs and the lower classes practiced "simple inhumation." Davies, *Death, Burial and Rebirth*, 82, discussing a rock-cut tomb of the late Second Temple period in Jerusalem, notes that "the cost of constructing the grave [tomb] itself indicated wealthy ownership." Zias, "A Rock-Cut Tomb in Jerusalem," 54, observes in his discussion of a tomb of the late Second Temple period which was poor in finds that "the family was apparently wealthy enough to afford a rock-hewn tomb." Regarding the Akeldama tombs, Zias, "Anthropological Analysis of Hu-

man Skeletal Remains," 118, remarks on "the relative wealth of the families buried here, manifested by tomb architecture and the ossuaries." Goodman, *The Ruling Class of Judaea*, 69, assumes that rock-cut tombs were expensive.

83. For the Jericho cemetery, see Hachlili and Killebrew, *Jericho;* "Jewish Funerary Customs "; Hachlili, "The Goliath Family in Jericho." For rock-cut tombs with loculi in the vicinity of the Jewish village at Qiryat Sefer (north of Modi'in), see Magen et al., "Khirbet Badd 'Isa," 179, 206. Berlin, "Jewish Life before the Revolt," 464-65, remarks on the absence of "display tombs" and ossuaries from Galilee before 70.

84. For the association of rock-cut bench tombs with the emergence of a Judahite elite in the eighth century, see Fantalkin, "The Appearance of Rock-Cut Bench Tombs." Magen, "Qalandiya," 82, wonders: "Where were the Jews and Samaritans buried from the time of the Babylonian Exile to the Hasmonean period?" (He suggests that they reused tombs of the First Temple period.)

85. Rock-cut tombs and ossuaries dating to after 70 are found at other Galilean and Golan sites including Dabburiyya, Gush Halav, Ibillin, Kafr Kanna, and Nazareth; see Berlin, "Jewish Life before the Revolt," 464; Aviam, *Jews, Pagans and Christians in the Galilee*, 257-311 ("Regionalism of Tombs and Burial Customs in the Galilee During the Hellenistic, Roman and Byzantine Periods").

86. See Kloner and Zissu, *The Necropolis of Jerusalem*, 11, 28-30; another 100 rock-cut tombs are located in a more distant strip within a radius of 3.5-5 km from the city and belonged to settlements in Jerusalem's "hinterland." For examples of the latter, see Seligman, "Jerusalem, Khirbat Ka'kul (Pisgat Ze'ev H)," 55-59, which Seligman notes are the simplest type of rock-cut tomb. For rock-cut tombs associated with the farmhouse at Qalandiya (eight km northwest of Jerusalem), see Magen, "Qalandiya," 74-80. At the Princeton Symposium on Afterlife and Burial Practices, Kloner distributed a handout stating that 850 rock-cut tombs of the Second Temple period have been discovered in the Jerusalem necropolis, over 70 percent of which have loculi, and with a statistical average of 24 burials per tomb.

87. Regev, "Family Structure in Jerusalem." This observation was first made by Goodman, *The Ruling Class of Judaea*, 68-69, who connected the relatively small number of burial spaces in rock-cut tombs with the break-up of extended families into nuclear units. For the relationship between rock-cut tombs of the late First Temple period and family structure, see Faust and Bunimovitz, "The Judahite Rock-Cut Tomb."

88. This estimate is inflated, as not only would each tomb not have held the maximum number of possible burials, but many tombs were in use for less than a century.

89. Levine, *Jerusalem*, 340-43. Sanders, *Judaism*, 136-38, gives a figure of three hundred thousand in Jerusalem during the Passover festival, when many pilgrims stayed for the entire two-week period.

90. Similar estimates for the late Iron Age have demonstrated that only a small proportion (perhaps 1.5 percent) of Jerusalem's population was interred in rock-cut tombs; see Fantalkin, "The Appearance of Rock-Cut Bench Tombs," 20. John Bodel estimates that the known tombs and burials account for only 1.5 percent of ancient Rome's population; see Bodel, "From *Columbaria* to Catacombs," 241.

91. Until now no rock-cut tombs or ossuaries that can be firmly dated before 70 have been found in Galilee. It is not clear whether this is because they were introduced to Galilee only after 70 by the displaced Judean elite or because they were in continuous use from the first century on; see Weiss, "Jewish Galilee in the First Century c.e.," 50-52.

92. Paper presented at the Annual Meeting of the Archaeological Institute of America, 3-6 January 2008, Chicago.

93. Morris, *Burial and Ancient Society*, 103. In contrast, archaeologists specializing in Iron Age Judah recognize the diversity of burial types and acknowledge that most of the population was buried in a manner that has left few traces; see, e.g., Fantalkin, "The Appearance of Rock-Cut Bench Tombs," 20-21.

94. See Morris, *Burial and Ancient Society*, 105, who comments (109), "There is certainly little incontrovertible evidence for archaeologically invisible burial, particularly from Attica; but then it is never easy to find positive evidence for a negative argument."

95. See, e.g., Faust and Bunimovitz, "The Judahite Rock-Cut Tomb," 151, 156, 160; Fantalkin, "The Appearance of Rock-Cut Bench Tombs," 20-21; Franklin, "The Tombs of the Kings of Israel," 1. I thank Franklin for giving me an offprint of her article.

96. See Fantalkin, "The Appearance of Rock-Cut Bench Tombs," 20-21.

97. Berlin, "Jewish Life before the Revolt," 463, sets up a straw man when she says that "these shafts cannot be dismissed as poor, casual burials, a simple covering of a body with earth. The excavation of each [shaft] tomb to a depth greater than the height of an average man would have taken some time and effort." Neither I nor anyone else of whom I am aware has suggested that shaft graves were casual burials consisting of a simple covering of the body with earth. This still does not change the fact that the effort and expense involved in hewing a rock-cut tomb were much greater than digging a shaft grave and therefore involved significant financial investment.

98. See Mazar, *Beth She'arim*; Avigad, *Beth She'arim* (125-30 for the burials outside the catacombs). See also Aviam, *Jews, Pagans and Christians in the Galilee*, 257-311 ("Regionalism of Tombs and Burial Customs in the Galilee During the Hellenistic, Roman and Byzantine Periods"), who notes elements of regionalism in tomb types. A diversity of burial customs characterized ancient Rome as well; see Patterson, "Living and Dying in the City of Rome," 264-70.

99. Quote from a handout that Kloner distributed at the conference.

100. Kloner and Zissu, *The Necropolis of Jerusalem*, 19, 98.

101. See Patrich, "Graves and Burial Practices in Talmudic Sources," 191-92; Kloner and Zissu, *The Necropolis of Jerusalem*, 95-97. For cist graves ("box burials") at Pisgat Ze'ev just north of Jerusalem, see Seligman, "Jerusalem, Khirbat Ka'kul (Pisgat Ze'ev H)," 58-59. At Princeton's Symposium on Afterlife and Burial Practices, Kloner reported finding 83 "shaft and field burials" of the Second Temple period in his survey of Jerusalem. For late Iron Age pit graves in Jerusalem, see Fantalkin, "The Appearance of Rock-Cut Bench Tombs," 20. In Rome the poor were buried in simple holes dug into the ground; see Davies, *Death, Burial and Rebirth*, 148. The corpses of paupers and criminals were disposed of in mass graves; see Bodel, "Graveyards and Groves," 38; "Dealing with the Dead," 131.

102. Millard, Review of *L'homme face à la mort au royaume de Juda*, 320.

103. Bodel, "From *Columbaria* to Catacombs," 241-42.

104. See Magness, *The Archaeology of Qumran*, 168-75, with bibliog. on 186-87; Schultz, "The Qumran Cemetery"; Patrich, "Graves and Burial Practices in Talmudic Sources," 192.

105. See Bar-Adon, "Another Settlement of the Judean Desert Sect," 12-17; Patrich, "Graves and Burial Practices in Talmudic Sources," 192 n. 10; Zissu, "'Qumran Type' Graves in Jerusalem"; "Odd Tomb Out"; Kloner and Zissu, *The Necropolis of Jerusalem*, 95-97. For

another cemetery of this type in the Judean desert, see Eshel and Greenhut, "Ḥiam el-Sagha." Bar-Adon, "Another Settlement of the Judean Desert Sect," 12, mentions large headstones at the southern end of each grave at ʿEin el-Ghuweir but does not describe the heaps of stones characteristic of Qumran. He also notes that large stones mark both ends (north and south) of each grave at Qumran.

106. See Magness, *The Archaeology of Qumran*, 220-23; Patrich, "Graves and Burial Practices in Talmudic Sources," 192 n. 10. Despite the small size of the sample at Qumran, the random distribution of the excavated graves suggests that male burials predominate, with only a handful of women attested. The complete absence of children seems to be meaningful as children are represented elsewhere in trench graves and rock-cut tombs around Judea and in light of the high rate of infant and child mortality. As Morris, *Burial and Ancient Society*, notes (62), "Nowhere in the world was a consistent mortality rate below one hundred per thousand even for infants (0-1 year) alone achieved until about 1900 AD."

107. See Shanks, "Who Lies Here?"; Politis, "The Nabataean Cemetery at Khirbet Qazone," 128.

108. Shanks, "Who Lies Here?" 51.

109. See Kloner and Zissu, *The Necropolis of Jerusalem*, 97-99. Weiss, "The Location of Jewish Cemeteries," 231, notes that in rabbinic literature and inscriptions the word *qbr* can refer both to a rock-cut tomb (or burial cave) and to an individual grave or burial place and that the analogous Greek terms have similar double meanings.

110. This despite the fact that the wealthier (including high-priestly) residents of Jericho to the north and those at ʿEin Gedi to the south interred their dead in rock-cut tombs. For Jericho, see Hachlili and Killebrew, *Jericho*; "Jewish Funerary Customs during the Second Temple Period." For ʿEin Gedi, see Hadas, *Nine Tombs of the Second Temple Period*.

111. See Magness, *The Archaeology of Qumran*, 202-6; but for Hellenistic influence on the Essenes, see Levine, *Jerusalem*, 145.

112. Translation from Baumgarten and Schwartz, "The Damascus Document," 53.

113. Yadin, *The Temple Scroll*, 1:325-26. For a recent discussion, see Noam, "Qumran and the Rabbis on Corpse-Impurity," 398-407.

114. See Noam, "Qumran and the Rabbis on Corpse-Impurity," 418; Schiffman, "The Impurity of the Dead," 139-40; Sanders, *Jewish Law from Jesus to the Mishnah*, 33-34; Broshi, "Qumran and the Essenes," 469. For the concept of the tent in rabbinic Judaism, see Neusner, *A History of the Mishnaic Law of Purities*, 72-75, 90-91, 208-12.

115. Yadin, *The Temple Scroll*, 1:325-26, who notes that the Septuagint also has the word "house" *(oikia)*. See also Noam, "Qumran and the Rabbis on Corpse-Impurity," 416; Schiffman, "The Impurity of the Dead," 138-40; Swanson, *The Temple Scroll and the Bible*, 186-87; Werrett, *Ritual Purity and the Dead Sea Scrolls*, 36-38. In 4Q265 (a document about Sabbath observance), "tent" also seems to have been understood as "house"; see Doering, "New Aspects of Qumran Sabbath Law," 260-63.

116. Yadin, *The Temple Scroll*, 1:324.

117. This legislation has no parallel in the Hebrew Bible; see Yadin, *The Temple Scroll*, 1:336-38. But Noam, "Qumran and the Rabbis on Corpse-Impurity," 414, believes that an "implicit midrash can be discerned in the text of the Temple Scroll." See also Sussman, "History of the 'Halakha,'" 33; Broshi, "Anti-Qumranic Polemics in the Talmud," 595; Schiffman, "The Impurity of the Dead," 150-51.

118. For a discussion of this passage, which immediately precedes the legislation that

mandates that corpse impurity extends to the nails and pegs in a house, see Eshel, "CD 12: 15-17"; Noam, "Qumran and the Rabbis on Corpse-Impurity," 415-28.

119. Noam, "Qumran and the Rabbis on Corpse-Impurity," 427, concludes that according to sectarian law raw materials became susceptible to impurity once they were adapted and converted to human use, though I do not know whether she would include rock-cut tombs in this category. I agree with Werrett, *Ritual Purity and the Dead Sea Scrolls,* 40-41, that the *Damascus Document* assumes that an individual entering a tent or house in which someone has died contracts corpse impurity, though this is not explicitly stated (in contrast to the *Temple Scroll*).

120. See Green, "Sweet Spices in the Tomb," 161-63.

121. This possibility is supported by the rabbinic ruling that a woman carrying a still-born child is clean. See Yadin, *The Temple Scroll,* 1:336, who observed that "the likeness in language, on the one hand, and the contrast between the laws, on the other, attests a palpable controversy, and there is no doubt that the Tannaites knew of laws such as those in the [Temple] scroll." For a more recent discussion, see Noam, "Qumran and the Rabbis on Corpse-Impurity," 407-15. Sanders, *Jewish Law from Jesus to the Mishnah,* 34, remarks on the apparent Pharisaic and rabbinic lack of concern with corpse impurity. See also Neusner, *A History of the Mishnaic Law of Purities,* 208-9 (discussing the Ushans).

122. Eshel, "4Q414 Fragment 2"; "Ritual of Purification." For the sectarian legislation, see 11QT 49 and 4Q414; for a discussion, see Milgrom, "Deviations from Scripture."

123. Eshel, "4Q414 Fragment 2," 9; "Ritual of Purification," 138-39.

124. Eshel, "4Q414 Fragment 2," 9; "Ritual of Purification," 139; Kloner and Zissu, *The Necropolis of Jerusalem,* 44-45; Zissu and Amit, "Common Judaism, Common Purity," 59-61. For Jericho, see Hachlili and Killebrew, *Jericho,* 47. Regev, "Non-Priestly Purity and Its Religious Aspects," 235-36, connects this phenomenon with "non-priestly" purity.

125. Magness, *The Archaeology of Qumran,* 154.

126. Adler, "Ritual Baths Adjacent to Tombs." However, if this had been a widespread concern, miqva'ot adjacent to tombs should be much more common.

127. De Vaux, *Archaeology and the Dead Sea Scrolls,* 46; see also Zissu, "'Qumran Type' Graves in Jerusalem," 160; "Odd Tomb Out," 52.

128. See McCane, *Roll Back the Stone,* 68-70.

129. This legislation is reiterated in the *Temple Scroll* (11QT 50:4-6); see Yadin, *The Temple Scroll,* 1:334-36; Noam, "Qumran and the Rabbis on Corpse-Impurity," 397-407.

130. See Sanders, *Jewish Law from Jesus to the Mishnah,* 34; Schiffman, "The Impurity of the Dead," 143, who notes that according to the *Temple Scroll* corpse impurity contaminates even objects attached to the ground.

131. Sanders, *Jewish Law from Jesus to the Mishnah,* 34.

132. *m. Šeqal.* 1:1 and *m. Ma'aś. Š.* 5:1 describe marking off graves or areas of graves (in the latter reference using lime), apparently due to purity concerns.

133. See Kazen, *Jesus and Purity Halakhah,* 179.

134. Yadin, *The Temple Scroll,* 1:322-23; see also Wright, *The Disposal of Impurity,* 123-27. Schiffman, "The Impurity of the Dead," 137, expands on Yadin's observation, noting that whereas the tannaim and amoraim allowed burials everywhere except within walled cities and the boundaries of the Levitical cities (respectively), the *Temple Scroll* restricts burial to designated cemeteries. But Noam, "The Bounds of Non-Priestly Purity," 147-52, argues that Yadin misunderstood the rabbinic position, which in reality sought to ban burials from all

settlements, walled and unwalled alike. Nevertheless, the Mishnah and tractate *Semaḥot* indicate that the random disposal of bodies was common.

135. Bodel, "Graveyards and Groves," 34-35; see also "Dealing with the Dead," 129.

136. Bodel, "Dealing with the Dead," 131.

137. Bodel, "Graveyards and Groves," 38; "Dealing with the Dead," 133.

138. See Patterson, "Living and Dying in the City of Rome," 267; Bodel, "Dealing with the Dead," 129, estimates that some 1500 unclaimed and unwanted corpses turned up annually on the streets of ancient Rome.

139. See Scobie, "Slums, Sanitation, and Mortality," 418; Bodel, "Dealing with the Dead," 129; Hobson, *Latrinae et Foricae*, 97-98.

140. In a rare example of leniency compared with the rabbis, the Qumran sectarians apparently considered as defiling only severed limbs from a corpse and not those belonging to someone who was still alive; see Baumgarten, "The Pharisaic-Sadducean Controversies," 161 n. 17; "Halivni's *Midrash*," 61. This leniency might be an illusion, since according to sectarian law a bone could render a "tent" impure, whereas the early rabbis restricted this type of impurity to corpses; see Noam, "Qumran and the Rabbis on Corpse-Impurity," 397-407.

141. Fredriksen, *Jesus of Nazareth*, 11.

142. Matt 27:57-60, 28:1; Mark 15:33-34, 42-43; Luke 23:44, 50-54; John 19:31.

143. For a discussion of the differences in the Gospel accounts of this episode, see McCane, *Roll Back the Stone*, 101-2; for John's account, see Murphy-O'Connor, Review of *The Necropolis of Jerusalem*, 451-54. Here I focus on the accounts of Mark and Matthew. The differences between the two include describing Joseph as a member of the council/Sanhedrin (Mark) or as a rich man (Matthew) (which are complementary, not contradictory statements) and mentioning that this was Joseph's family tomb (Matthew) versus no such reference (Mark). Since rock-cut tombs belonged to families, I believe that Matthew is accurate in this detail.

144. See McCane, *Roll Back the Stone*, 94-95.

145. Hengel, *Crucifixion in the Ancient World*, 19, 83, 90.

146. See, e.g., Evans, *Jesus and the Ossuaries*, 101; McCane, *Roll Back the Stone*, 89; Crossan, *Who Killed Jesus?* 160-63; Brown, *The Death of the Messiah*, 2:947. But for an argument that Jesus did receive a proper burial, see Evans, "Jewish Burial Traditions and the Resurrection of Jesus."

147. Hengel, *Crucifixion in the Ancient World*, 34, 40, 46-47; Tzaferis, "Crucifixion — the Archaeological Evidence," 48; Chapman, *Ancient Jewish and Christian Perceptions of Crucifixion*, 44. Berkowitz, *Execution and Invention*, 174-77, notes that although the rabbinic execution system resembles the Roman one in some respects, the rabbis changed the equation between the methods of execution used and an individual's social status.

148. Hengel, *Crucifixion in the Ancient World*, 49.

149. McCane, *Roll Back the Stone*, 90, 105; Brown, *The Death of the Messiah*, 2:1207; *pace* Crossan, *Who Killed Jesus*, 160-61.

150. For discussions, see Shemesh, "The Dispute between the Pharisees and the Sadducees"; Regev, *The Sadducees and Their Halakhah*, 124, who concludes that the rabbinic system of execution is a late (and somewhat idealized) development.

151. For a discussion of this passage, see Chapman, *Ancient Jewish and Christian Perceptions of Crucifixion*, 117-20.

152. Berkowitz, *Execution and Invention*, 160-61; Berrin, *The Pesher Nahum Scroll from*

Qumran, 171; Eshel, *The Dead Sea Scrolls and the Hasmonean State,* 129 n. 34; Baumgarten, *Studies in Qumran Law,* 173-74; Vermes, *The Complete Dead Sea Scrolls in English,* 473. See also Bauckham, "For What Offence Was James Put to Death?" 221, who notes that according to Jewish law "hanging is not a method of execution but the exposure of an already dead corpse." Halperin, "Crucifixion, the Nahum Pesher, and Strangulation," 40-41, observes that the rabbis seem to have altered earlier methods of execution to shorten the process of dying and thereby lessen the victim's suffering.

153. See Yadin, *The Temple Scroll,* 2:289 n. 8; Berrin, *The Pesher Nahum Scroll from Qumran,* 172, 183 (with a reference to the interpretation of Deut 21:23 as reflecting a sectarian controversy); Halperin, "Crucifixion, the Nahum Pesher, and Strangulation," 43; Crown, "Qumran, Samaritan *Halakha* and Theology," 427; Bernstein, "*Midrash Halakhah* at Qumran?" 150, 154-55.

154. From Yadin, *The Temple Scroll,* 1:373-74; "Pesher Nahum Reconsidered," 9. See also Berrin, *The Pesher Nahum Scroll from Qumran,* 180-84; Baumgarten, *Studies in Qumran Law,* 173; Shemesh, "The Dispute between the Pharisees and the Sadducees," 19-20, who notes that the author of the *Temple Scroll* elaborated on the biblical injunction, which does not specify for which crimes the hanged criminal was executed. For a different reading of this passage in the *Temple Scroll,* see Schwartz, *Studies in the Jewish Background of Christianity,* 81-88 ("The Contemners of Judges and Men"). For a review of secondary literature on this passage, see Chapman, *Ancient Jewish and Christian Perceptions of Crucifixion,* 125-32.

155. Yadin, *The Temple Scroll,* 1:374; 2:289 n. 7; Baumgarten, *Studies in Qumran Law,* 175-76 n. 13. Shemesh, "The Dispute between the Pharisees and the Sadducees," 20-28, notes that the authors of the *Temple Scroll* and the *Damascus Document* added to the crimes punishable by death listed in the Hebrew Bible (whereas the rabbis added none) and changed the agent of execution for defilement of the temple from divine to human; see also Regev, *The Sadducees and Their Halakhah,* 127. Similarly Bernstein, "*Midrash Halakhah* at Qumran?" observes that the author of the *Temple Scroll* added a clause from Lev 19:16a to the legal material of Deut 21:22-23, and changed the meaning of *tlk rkyl* from being a slanderer or tale-bearer to committing treason. He suggests that 11QT 64:6-13 is an interpolation, perhaps replacing an earlier version which contained a closer paraphrase of Deut 21:22-23. Weinfeld, "High Treason in the Temple Scroll," demonstrates that the law of high treason found in the *Temple Scroll* had a long history in the ancient Near East.

156. See Baumgarten, *Studies in Qumran Law,* 173-74; Halperin, "Crucifixion, the Nahum Pesher, and Strangulation."

157. See Baumgarten, *Studies in Qumran Law,* 176 n. 13; "Halivni's *Midrash,*" 63; Shemesh, "The Dispute between the Pharisees and the Sadducees," 30-31; Regev, *The Sadducees and Their Halakhah,* 126. For a comprehensive study of the scholion, see Noam, "From Philology to History." According to the scholiast the Sadducees were unable to provide a scriptural basis for this practice, instead citing the fact that the book had been "written and deposited" (publicized) as a basis for its authority. For evidence of Jews executing criminals by hanging in the Second Temple period, see Yadin, *The Temple Scroll,* 1:375-76.

158. See Hengel, *Crucifixion in the Ancient World,* 85: "from the beginning of direct Roman rule crucifixion was taboo as a form of the Jewish death penalty." Baumgarten, *Studies in Qumran Law,* 179, notes that the rabbis viewed crucifixion as a Roman practice. See also Tzaferis, "Crucifixion — the Archaeological Evidence," 48: "Among the Jews crucifixion was an anathema. . . . The traditional method of execution among the Jews was ston-

ing. . . . At the end of the first century B.C., the Romans adopted crucifixion as an official punishment for non-Romans for certain legally limited transgressions."

159. Baumgarten, *Studies in Qumran Law*, 178-79; Eshel, *The Dead Sea Scrolls and the Hasmonean State*, 129. The prolonged process of dying would have made it difficult to ensure burial took place within twenty-four hours of death, something to which even executed criminals were entitled according to Jewish law. For the opposite view, see Berrin, *The Pesher Nahum Scroll from Qumran*, 190 n. 72.

160. See Halperin, "Crucifixion, the Nahum Pesher, and Strangulation," who notes that "tree" can denote a wooden pole; see also Eshel, *The Dead Sea Scrolls and the Hasmonean State*, 128-29 n. 33; Chapman, *Ancient Jewish and Christian Perceptions of Crucifixion*, 15-26, 112-14. But Berrin, *The Pesher Nahum Scroll from Qumran*, 167 n. 10, points out that *ṣlb* is simply Aramaic for *tlh*. She argues that the author of the *Temple Scroll* understood "hanging alive" as including crucifixion (188). In Acts 5:30; 10:39; and Gal 3:13 the Deuteronomic verse is applied to Jesus' crucifixion; see Schwartz, *Studies in the Jewish Background of Christianity*, 82 ("The Contemners of Judges and Men").

161. Berkowitz, *Execution and Invention*, 160-61, who notes that the reference to "the way that the kingdom does" makes it likely that crucifixion is intended. See also Chapman, *Ancient Jewish and Christian Perceptions of Crucifixion*, 143-44.

162. For comprehensive discussions of the terms hanging and strangulation, see Chapman, *Ancient Jewish and Christian Perceptions of Crucifixion*, esp. Part One (see 177 for his conclusion); Berrin, *The Pesher Nahum Scroll from Qumran*, 165-68, who concludes, "it is most likely that the range of the term תלה included, but was not limited to, sorts of hanging executions denoted by the word חנק. . . . Crucifixion could be called תליה though it would probably not be called חנק" (168). Berrin notes that the apologistic tendencies of modern scholars have influenced their views (178-79). Halperin, "Crucifixion, the Nahum Pesher, and Strangulation," esp. 40, argues that the Jews adopted crucifixion as a mode of execution from the Romans early on and that it was rejected by the rabbis. See also Yadin, "Pesher Nahum Reconsidered."

163. Josephus, *War* 1.97; *Ant.* 13.380; see also Hengel, *Crucifixion in the Ancient World*, 84, with references.

164. The reconstruction and interpretation of this passage have been the subject of much debate. For recent discussions with different opinions, see Chapman, *Ancient Jewish and Christian Perceptions of Crucifixion*, 14-15; Berrin, *The Pesher Nahum Scroll from Qumran*, 165-92; Eshel, *The Dead Sea Scrolls and the Hasmonean State*, 117-31. See also Baumgarten, *Studies in Qumran Law*, 178-80, who concludes that "hanging alive" refers to crucifixion whereas "hanging" describes hanging someone alive or dead from a tree. Yadin, "Pesher Nahum Reconsidered"; *The Temple Scroll*, 1:378 n. 11; and Halperin, "Crucifixion, the Nahum Pesher, and Strangulation," believe that the *Temple Scroll* and *Pesher Nahum* (and rabbinic sources) indicate that some Jewish groups in pre-70 Palestine sanctioned crucifixion as a legal mode of execution by equating it with hanging/strangulation.

165. Although the exact manner in which the body was affixed to the cross is debated; for two different reconstructions, see Tzaferis, "Crucifixion — the Archaeological Evidence," 49; Zias and Sekeles, "The Crucified Man from Giv'at ha-Mivtar," 27. Zias and Sekeles note (26) that death resulted from asphyxiation and not from the trauma caused by nailing the body to the cross.

166. In light of the relationship between Luke and Acts, it is interesting that in these

two books (but not in Mark and Matthew) the distinction between hanging and crucifixion is blurred, with the Greek terms being used interchangeably; see Luke 23:39: "One of the criminals who was hanging there *(kremasthentōn)* abused him"; Acts 5:30: "The God of our forefathers raised Jesus to life when you had hung him on a cross *(kremasantes epi xylou)* and killed him." I thank Bart Ehrman for bringing this to my attention. For a discussion, see Fitzmyer, "Crucifixion in Ancient Palestine," 509-10, who suggests that the Pauline and Lucan references to hanging on a tree may have been influenced by the LXX of Deut 21:22. See also Chapman, *Ancient Jewish and Christian Perceptions of Crucifixion*, 9-10, including n. 40; 211.

167. *Pace* Crossan, *Who Killed Jesus,* 166, 169. In my opinion, Josephus's rhetorical use of this episode to illustrate the impiety of the rebels (in this case, Idumaeans) does not affect the value of his testimony regarding the burial of crucifixion victims in accordance with Jewish law. For Josephus's condemnation of the rebels' lawless and impious behavior, see Cohen, *Josephus in Galilee and Rome,* 88, 97; Rajak, *Josephus,* 81.

168. From Watson, *The Digest of Justinian,* 864.

169. From Watson, *The Digest of Justinian,* 864. Evans, "Jewish Burial Traditions and the Resurrection of Jesus," 5-7, believes that the Romans usually prohibited burial during times of open rebellion and armed conflict, not when it was peaceful. Berkowitz, *Execution and Invention,* 137-38, suggests that perhaps the Roman authorities denied families the right to bury relatives executed for treason but not those guilty of other violations.

170. Baumgarten, *Studies in Qumran Law,* 178, notes that Jesus' quick death on the cross seems to have come as a surprise to Pilate (Mark 15:44), as crucifixion victims typically suffered longer before expiring.

171. As McCane, *Roll Back the Stone,* 100-1, notes, *pace* Crossan. See also Tzaferis, "Crucifixion — the Archaeological Evidence"; Rahmani, "Ancient Jerusalem's Funerary Customs and Tombs, Part Three," 51; 1994: 131 no. 218. McCane, *Roll Back the Stone,* 99, remarks, "Dishonorable burial was reserved for those who had been condemned by *the people of Israel*" (McCane's emphasis). Nevertheless, McCane concurs that Jesus was buried in shame. The prominence of Yoḥanan's family is indicated by the fact that another ossuary from this tomb was inscribed "Simon, the builder of the temple," apparently someone who had participated in the reconstruction of the temple under Herod; see Tzaferis, "Crucifixion — the Archaeological Evidence," 47, 50; Brown, *The Death of the Messiah,* 2:1210.

172. Crossan, *Who Killed Jesus,* 168; Crossan, *The Historical Jesus,* 391.

173. See Chapman, *Ancient Jewish and Christian Perceptions of Crucifixion,* 202; see also Brown, *The Death of the Messiah,* 2:1210, although on 1243 he presents the opposite conclusion. According to Josephus, *Ant.* 4.202, blasphemers who were stoned and then hanged were "buried in an ignominious and obscure manner." However, Jesus was not condemned by the Sanhedrin for violating Jewish law and was not executed by stoning. Therefore, it is erroneous to apply this passage to Jesus' execution and burial. On the other hand, this halakhah would have applied to James, who was apparently executed by stoning for violating Jewish law and therefore would have been ineligible for burial in a rock-cut family tomb (see the discussion of James's burial below).

174. According to tractate *Semaḥot* 2:6, "For those executed by the [Jewish] court, no [mourning] rites whatsoever should be observed." For a discussion, see Berkowitz, *Execution and Invention,* 133-34, 136.

175. Crossan, *The Historical Jesus,* 391.

176. For the intact repository at Ketef Hinnom, see Barkay, "The Divine Name Found in Jerusalem."

177. As Crossan, *Who Killed Jesus*, 169, notes.

178. Tzaferis, "Crucifixion — the Archaeological Evidence," 50 (my emphasis). In their reexamination of this skeleton, Zias and Sekeles, "The Crucified Man from Giv'at ha-Mivtar," 24, found no evidence for amputation but confirmed that the nail could not be removed from the heel bone because it was bent: "Once the body was removed from the cross, albeit with some difficulty in removing the right leg, the condemned man's family would now find it impossible to remove the bent nail without completely destroying the heel bone" (27).

179. Tzaferis, "Crucifixion — the Archaeological Evidence," 49; see also Crossan, *Who Killed Jesus*, 135, for a description from the *Acts of Andrew*.

180. From Brown, *The Death of the Messiah*, 2:1319.

181. Of course, had Jesus' family owned a rock-cut tomb, it presumably would have been located near their home in Nazareth. But in light of what we know of Jesus' family and his background, there is no reason to assume they could afford a rock-cut tomb.

182. The Jewish concern that the deceased be buried on the same day is scripturally based (Deut 21:22; *m. Sanh.* 6:5; for a discussion, see Davies, *Death, Burial and Rebirth*, 102). This explains the haste to bury Jesus, since the onset of the Sabbath would have meant delaying the burial for more than twenty-four hours. The Mishnah provides guidelines for quick burials when death occurs during a festival: "They do not hew out a tomb niche or tombs on the intermediate days of a festival. But they refashion tomb niches on the intermediate days of a festival. They dig a grave on the intermediate days of a festival, and make a coffin, and while the corpse is in the same courtyard. R. Judah prohibits, unless there were boards [already sawn and made ready in advance]" (*m. Mo'ed Qat.* 1:6). The reference to rock-cut tombs with loculi suggests that this halakhah might have originated in the late Second Temple period. Notice also the description of graves dug into the ground.

183. Mark 15:43 describes Joseph as "a highly respected member of the council," apparently the Sanhedrin; see Brown, *The Death of the Messiah*, 2:1213-14, 1223.

184. For discussions, see Brown, *The Death of the Messiah*, 2:1244-46, 1252.

185. For discussions of the type of stone that sealed the tomb in which Jesus' body was placed, see Kloner, "Did a Rolling Stone Close Jesus' Tomb?"; Kloner and Zissu, *The Necropolis of Jerusalem*, 54-56, who note that circular rolling stones (as opposed to square or rectangular blocking stones) are rare in the Jerusalem necropolis. See also Brown, *The Death of the Messiah*, 2:1247-48.

186. For the suggestion that Joseph of Arimathea was not a follower of Jesus, see Brown, *The Death of the Messiah*, 2:1216-18, 1223-24, 1246. For the claim that he was a completely fictional character, see Crossan, *Who Killed Jesus*, 172-73, 176. See also Murphy-O'Connor, Review of *The Necropolis of Jerusalem*, 452-53.

187. *Pace* Brown, *The Death of the Messiah*, 2:1249-50.

188. *Pace* Kloner and Zissu, *The Necropolis of Jerusalem*, 122-23; Brown, *The Death of the Messiah*, 2:1249: "A distinguished member of the Sanhedrin, Joseph may have had access to tombs that served for those whom the Sanhedrin judged against. Into one of these tombs nearby the cross, then, the Marcan Joseph, acting quite consistently as a pious law-observant Jew, could have placed the corpse of Jesus."

189. See Ritmeyer and Ritmeyer, "Potter's Field or High Priest's Tomb?"

190. Brown, *The Death of the Messiah*, 2:1272; Evans, *Jesus and the Ossuaries*, 103; McCane, *Roll Back the Stone*, 103-4.

191. As noted also by Evans, *Jesus and the Ossuaries*, 15: "what the Gospels depict is consistent with what is known from archaeology and from literary and epigraphical sources."

192. For different possibilities, see Vermes, *The Resurrection*, 142-48.

193. Kloner, "A Tomb with Incised Ossuaries."

194. See Jacobovici and Pellegrino, *The Jesus Family Tomb*.

195. Kloner, "A Tomb with Incised Ossuaries," 17-19.

196. See Rahmani, *A Catalogue of Jewish Ossuaries*, 17.

197. See Rahmani, *A Catalogue of Jewish Ossuaries*, nos. 57, 18, 67.

198. See Rahmani, *A Catalogue of Jewish Ossuaries*, nos. 99, 139, 404. Literary sources (such as the Gospels, Flavius Josephus, etc.) often make the same distinctions between Judeans and non-Judeans (e.g., Galileans, Idumaeans, Mary Magdalene, Saul of Tarsus, Simon of Cyrene, etc.).

199. For a statement about the Talpiyot tomb by Eric Meyers and Jodi Magness, see http://dukereligion.blogspot.com/2008/01/talpiot-tomb-controversy-revisited.html.

200. See Aviam, "Magdala," 399, who describes Magdala as "a small town in the early Hellenistic to Byzantine periods" whose inhabitants engaged mainly in fishing.

201. For a review of the evidence for the use of Greek in Galilee in Jesus' time, see Chancey, *Greco-Roman Culture and the Galilee of Jesus*, 122-65.

202. The Gospel accounts suggest that John the Baptist was also buried in a trench grave: "When his disciples heard about it, they came and took his body, and laid it in a tomb *(en mnēmeiō)*" (Mark 6:29). That *mnēmeion* refers to a trench grave seems to be indicated by Luke 11:44, where this is certainly its meaning: "For you are like unmarked graves, and people walk over them without realizing it." I owe this observation to Joan Taylor.

203. Joan Taylor observed (personal communication 01/08): "The point is that there was only one tomb remembered as the *mnemeion* or *taphos* where Jesus' body lay after it was brought down from the cross, the tomb of Joseph of Arimathea, and that is the one now in the Church of the Holy Sepulcher. Nothing in early Christian literature, or any sources fiercely opposed to Christianity, indicates that Jesus was buried anywhere else, when that would have been so useful to counter the resurrection stories. Matt 28:13-15 reports what people were saying about the disappearance of Jesus' body: 'His disciples came by night and stole him away.' But given all the polemic, you'd think someone in Jerusalem would notice if his bones went into another place nearby [such as the Talpiyot tomb]. If Jesus' disciples stole him away, I agree they would have taken him much further afield, and put him anonymously in the ground, not in an ossuary with his name on it for anyone going into the tomb to see! Also, if Jesus' important family had a church-funded rock-cut tomb in Jerusalem it seems likely to me that it would have been remembered through the ages, rather than totally forgotten. Jerusalem was one rare place where there was some continuity of Christian tradition, because the Jewish church there — despite disruptions — survived and melded into the Gentile (orthodox) church, as it did also in Rome and Antioch."

204. I am not concerned with the question of whether James was related to Jesus by blood or not. For the sake of convenience I use the term "early Christian community" to describe the Jewish followers of Jesus in Jerusalem during the second and third quarters of the first century C.E., although of course they were a Jewish sect. For discussions of James's role

in this community with references, see Painter, *Just James*, 3-5; Witherington, "The Story of James," 121.

205. See Evans, "Jesus and James," 246-47; Moo, *The Letter of James*, 16; Painter, *Just James*, 125; Witherington, "The Story of James," 112. Hegesippus (in Eusebius, *Hist. eccl.* 2.23:4-18) relates that James was "holy from his birth; he drank no wine or intoxicating liquor and ate no animal food; no razor came near his head; he did not smear himself with oil, and he took no baths. He alone was permitted to enter the Holy Place, for his garments were not of wool but of linen. He used to enter the Sanctuary alone, and was often found on his knees beseeching forgiveness for the people, so that his knees grew hard like a camel's." Painter, *Just James*, 125, notes that other early (second-century) sources preserve the tradition of James' pious and ascetic lifestyle.

206. As Painter, *Just James*, 239, notes, "The vast majority of modern scholars question the authenticity of the letter, although its authorship by James is not without significant defenders." Witherington, "The Story of James," 144, 146, believes that James wrote the letter and dates it to around 52 C.E.; for a similar opinion, see Maynard-Reid, *Poverty and Wealth in James*, 7-8. For discussions of the arguments for and against James' authorship, see Edgar, *Has God Not Chosen the Poor?*, 11, 19-22, 223 (who believes it is likely a pseudepigraphical composition); Davids, "Palestinian Traditions in the Epistle of James," 33-57 (who notes on 34 that "the most one can demonstrate with a high level of probability is that the material in James appears to come from the environment in which James lived and functioned and thus *could well* stem from James"); Moo, *The Letter of James*, 9-22 (who favors authorship by James); Painter, *Just James*, 234-48 (who believes that the letter was written by a Greek-speaking, Diaspora Jew and that it was "intentionally attributed" to James). Even if the letter was not written by James, many scholars seem to agree that it accurately reflects his views on wealth; see, e.g., Painter, *Just James*, 13. Witherington, "The Story of James," 153, notes that James' wisdom is intended for the poor and oppressed versus the rich.

207. Painter, *Just James*, 249. For the theme of wealth and poverty in the Letter of James and the modest lifestyle of the early Christian community in Jerusalem, see Maynard-Reid, *Poverty and Wealth in James*; Edgar, *Has God Not Chosen the Poor*, 133; Moo, *The Letter of James*, 35-36.

208. See, e.g., Painter, *Just James*, 249: "The poverty of the early Jerusalem church is well attested by Paul and the author of Acts. . . . In Jerusalem the believers experimented with an early form of 'communism,' that is, of giving up the private ownership of land and resources to provide resources for all."

209. See Flusser, "The Social Message from Qumran," 109-11. Witherington, "The Story of James," 115, explicitly compares the early Christian community in Jerusalem with the Essenes. For the suggestion that the Essenes' negative attitude towards the accumulation of wealth and glorification of poverty influenced Jesus' movement, see Broshi, "Matrimony and Poverty," 632-34; "What Jesus Learned from the Essenes"; Eisenman, *James the Brother of Jesus*, 4. Flusser, *Judaism of the Second Temple Period*, 36-37, notes that the principle of shared property seems to have been adopted by the Jerusalem church only after Jesus' death.

210. For the question of whether the Sanhedrin actually carried out executions, see Vermes, *The Passion*, 17-27 (who answers in the affirmative); for bibliog., see Berkowitz, *Execution and Invention*, 220 n. 37. Berkowitz (4, 19-20) describes how the key Mishnaic passage (*Mak.* 1:10) has been used for apologetic purposes in modern times. Shemesh, "The Dispute between the Pharisees and the Sadducees," 33, argues that this passage reflects a general ten-

dency on the part of the tannaim to limit the imposition of the death penalty, whereas (earlier) sectarian law extended it.

211. See Painter, *Just James*, 251, 264. Bauckham, "For What Offence Was James Put to Death?" 229, suggests that James was executed for blasphemy or for leading astray the town. Regev, *The Sadducees and Their Halakhah*, 127, proposes that the Pharisees opposed James's execution because they did not consider his offense (whatever it was) deserving of capital punishment.

212. For a discussion of this passage, see McLaren, "Ananus, James, and Earliest Christianity," who notes that this is only one of two episodes in which Josephus labels an individual (Ananus) as a Sadducee. Unlike Josephus's more controversial reference to Jesus (*Ant.* 18.63), most scholars do not believe this passage was added or substantially altered by later Christian copyists; see Bauckham, "For What Offence Was James Put to Death?" 198; Witherington, "The Story of James," 168.

213. For a different view, see Eliav, "The Tomb of James Brother of Jesus."

214. Hegesippus's description of the stoning is consistent with the method described in rabbinic literature, according to which the victim was thrown off a precipice and only stoned if he was still alive. Halperin, "Crucifixion, the Nahum Pesher, and Strangulation," 41, suggests that the rabbinic version is a more humane modification of the original process whereby the victim was pelted to death by stones (see also Berkowitz, *Execution and Invention*, 72). In support Halperin cites John 8:7: "Let anyone among you who is without sin be the first to throw a stone at her." However, Hegesippus's account and John's Gospel are separated only by about seventy-five years. Why would Hegesippus choose to describe stoning as the rabbis prescribed rather than as it was performed before 70 and as seems to be described by John ca. 100? Hegesippus's testimony suggests that the "rabbinic" method was practiced even before 70, perhaps alongside the "traditional" method.

215. Witherington, "The Story of James," 187, 188, who incorrectly (and misleadingly) translates the Greek word *stele* here as "*inscribed* stone" (my emphasis). Painter, *Just James*, 123, renders it more accurately as "headstone."

216. For discussions of these terms, see Rahmani, *A Catalogue of Jewish Ossuaries*, 3; Evans, *Jesus and the Ossuaries*, 11. Σορός *(soros)* occurs on an ossuary from Jericho; see Hachlili, "The Inscriptions," 142-44; "The Goliath Family in Jericho," 33, 55. For an ossuary inscribed twice with the Greek word *osteophagos*, see Avigad, "Jewish Rock-Cut Tombs in Jerusalem," 141. For an ossuary referred to in Palmyrene as *kayka* ("amphora" in the sense of "urn"), see Frey, *Corpus Inscriptionum Iudaicarum*, 250 no. 1222; Rahmani, *A Catalogue of Jewish Ossuaries*, 3. For ossuaries inscribed with the word "tomb" (probably referring to the ossuary), see Rahmani, *A Catalogue of Jewish Ossuaries*, 109 no. 125 *(kibra)*; 198 no. 561 *(topou)*.

217. Even if the stele that Hegesippus mentions did not mark the authentic location of James's grave, his testimony indicates that Jerusalem's early Christian community preserved a tradition about the manner in which James had been buried. Jerome's testimony suggests that by the fourth century the stele was no longer visible; see Painter, *Just James*, 223; Eisenman, *James the Brother of Jesus*, 454-55.

218. According to Witherington, "The Story of Jesus," 101, Joseph would have passed the family trade of carpentry on to his sons: "While carpenters did not rank at the high end of the social structure of society, neither were they at the low end . . . even a woodworker

who simply built furniture might expect to make a living that could support the family." See also Crossan, *The Historical Jesus*, 29.

219. Assuming, of course, that the prohibition described in the Mishnah was in effect in the second half of the first century c.e. For the nature of James's offense, see McLaren, "Ananus, James, and Earliest Christianity," 17-18.

220. Painter, *Just James*, 140. I agree with McLaren, "Ananus, James, and Earliest Christianity," 17, that James likely was executed on a trumped-up charge, and that this episode should be understood within the context of political as well as religious rivalries.

221. See, e.g., Witherington, "The Story of James," 171: "The Jewish Christians who buried James evidently wanted to honor him in death, and they apparently expected some would come and visit the burial spot and see the inscription written on the side of the box." If the inscription on the "James ossuary" was authentic and referred to James the Just, we would expect his place of origin (Nazareth or Galilee) to be indicated, as on other ossuaries containing the remains of émigrés who settled or died in Jerusalem. As Rahmani, *A Catalogue of Jewish Ossuaries*, 17, noted, "In Jerusalem's tombs, the deceased's place of origin was noted [on ossuaries] when someone from outside Jerusalem and its environs was interred in a local tomb." For example, one ossuary from Nicanor's Tomb is inscribed "[these] bones of [the family] of Nicanor of Alexandria who made the gates. Nicanor, the Alexandrian" (see Frey, *Corpus Inscriptionum Iudaicarum*, 261-62 no. 1256). For other examples, see Rahmani, *A Catalogue of Jewish Ossuaries*, 17; Frey, *Corpus Inscriptionum Iudaicarum*, 273 no. 1283, which reads "Judah, son of Judah, of Bethel"; 273 no. 1284, which reads "Maria, wife of Alexander, of Capua"; 276 no. 1285, which reads "Joseph the Galilean"; 314-15, nos. 1372-74, on which "of Scythopolis" is added after the names of the deceased.

222. See Painter, *Just James*, 52.

223. Goodman, *The Ruling Class of Judaea*, 67. For Rome, see Patterson, "Living and Dying in the City of Rome," 272-77, who notes, however, that "in many ways . . . the relationship could be better characterized as one of family ties than one of patronage" (273).

224. Goodman, *The Ruling Class of Judaea*, 64-67.

225. Goodman, *The Ruling Class of Judaea*, 65-66. For example, biblical law mandates that unharvested parts of fields and crops be left to the poor; see also Instone-Brewer, *Prayer and Agriculture*, 160-61.

226. For evidence of the custom of Jewish family burials, see Rubin, *The End of Life*, 140-42. Perhaps the injunction against transferring human remains represents a rabbinic response to the rise of the Christian cult of relics. For references in rabbinic literature to other practices that honor the dead, see Green, "Sweet Spices in the Tomb," 165-67.

227. In a paper presented at Princeton Seminary's Symposium on Afterlife and Burial Practices, Amos Kloner emphasized that Jerusalem's ancient rock-cut tombs were family tombs.

228. Goodman, *The Ruling Class of Judaea*, 68-69; Regev, "Family Structure in Jerusalem."

229. See Nagar and Torgee, "Biological Characteristics of Jewish Burial."

230. From Stern, "Aspects of Jewish Society," 594.

231. See Reich, "Caiaphas Name Inscribed on Bone Boxes."

232. Hachlili, "The Inscriptions," 153; "The Goliath Family in Jericho," 56-57, who notes that "family tombs containing ossuaries with inscriptions hold no more than three generations of a family, and even these are rare."

233. Hachlili, "The Inscriptions," 153-54; "The Goliath Family in Jericho," 57-58. She suggests that the tomb's occupants might have been a priestly family and notes the presence of a miqveh attached to the tomb. If a married woman died without children, she was buried with her father's family, not her husband's; see Rubin, *The End of Life*, 142.

234. Hachlili and Smith, "The Genealogy of the Goliath Family," 68.

235. See Rubin, *The End of Life*, 140-42.

236. See Hachlili, "The Inscriptions," 142-45; "The Goliath Family in Jericho," 33, for an inscribed ossuary that contained the remains of a freedman named Theodotos who belonged to the second generation of the family that owned the tomb.

237. One exception might be an inscription from Beth She'arim which mentions a tomb dedicated by Procopius to a freedwoman named Calliope; see Hezser, *Jewish Slavery in Antiquity*, 165. Jewish funerary inscriptions set up by slaveowners for their slaves are more common in the Diaspora, reflecting Roman influence; see Hezser, *Jewish Slavery in Antiquity*, 162-64.

238. Berkowitz, *Execution and Invention*, 136, notes that the "practice of family burial is also reflected in rabbinic law." For the problem of the dating and provenience of the minor tractate *Semaḥot*, see Green, "Sweet Spices in the Tomb," 158, including n. 30.

239. Hezser, *Jewish Slavery in Antiquity*, 158; see also Stern, "Aspects of Jewish Society," 624-30. For slavery among the Essenes, see Beall, *Josephus' Description of the Essenes*, 120-21.

240. From Guggenheimer, *The Jerusalem Talmud*, 238-39, who notes that this is the Galilean attitude, which contrasts with the Babylonian attitude as expressed by Rabbi Yosé in the Babylonian Talmud. For a discussion of these passages, see Hezser, *Jewish Slavery in Antiquity*, 157-58, who notes that whereas R. Gamaliel is portrayed as the ideal master and Tevi is portrayed as a "disciple of sages" who is eager to learn Torah, R. Eliezer's behavior towards slaves represents the norm.

241. Zlotnick, *The Tractate "Mourning,"* 99. See also Hezser, *Jewish Slavery in Antiquity*, 158.

242. Although even at Beth She'arim the spaces in the catacombs were purchased by different families.

243. As suggested by Witherington, "The Story of James," 105, 170 (although on 170 he notes that "James was not likely buried in a graveyard specifically for Christians. He was buried with his fellow Jews").

244. As Instone-Brewer, *Prayer and Agriculture*, 51 notes, for Jews the need to bury one's close relatives overrides even the most important commandments; see also Sanders, *Judaism*, 72. For this reason, scholars have long puzzled over Jesus' command to one of his disciples: "Another of his disciples said to him, 'Lord, first let me go and bury my father.' But Jesus said to him, 'Follow me, and let the dead bury their own dead'" (Matt 8:21-22; Luke 9:59-60). For a discussion of this passage including references, see Kister, "'Leave the Dead to Bury Their Own Dead.'"

245. Painter, *Just James*, 129. See also Bauckham, "For What Offence Was James Put to Death?", 200, 206, who concludes that Hegesippus's testimony indicates that like Josephus, the Christian tradition about the stoning of James "had some access to historical fact" (206).

246. See Flesher, "The Story Thus Far . . . ," 64.

247. By the fourth and fifth centuries the figure of James had been marginalized in the Western church, whereas in Gnostic Christianity James enjoyed a prominent position; see Painter, *Just James*, 167, 178, 220, 271, 274. For the Nag Hammadi texts, see Robinson, *The*

Nag Hammadi Library. For the Byzantine Christian reuse of earlier tombs in Jerusalem, see Avni, "Christian Secondary Use of Jewish Burial Caves."

248. In other words, if the inscription is authentic (ancient), it must refer to one of the other twenty or so first-century C.E. Jews in Jerusalem who could have had this combination of names; see Lemaire, "Burial Box of James," 33.

249. Ossuaries were frequently placed inside loculi, sometimes alongside primary burials. For examples, see Vitto, "Burial Caves from the Second Temple Period," 68-71, figs. 3-11. See 114 for a rock-cut tomb with a burial chamber containing loculi and a second room that was used as a repository for ossuaries.

250. A possible exception to this scenario is suggested by *m. Sanh.* 6:5–6:6, which prescribes special burial grounds for those executed for transgressing Jewish law and allows their bones to be collected and reburied in family tombs after the flesh had decayed. Since we have no evidence that the Sanhedrin paid for and maintained rock-cut tombs for executed felons, the deceased presumably were inhumed in individual graves dug into the ground. Therefore, this passage presumably refers to cases where the deceased belonged to wealthy families with rock-cut tombs who dug up the remains after the flesh had decayed.

Notes to Chapter 12

1. The editors of the Mishnah and other rabbinic documents sought to represent Yavneh as the end of sectarianism; see Hezser, *The Social Structure of the Rabbinic Movement,* 64. For the claim that Essenes should be identified among those whom the early rabbis condemned as *minim,* see Burns, "Essene Sectarianism and Social Differentiation." Burns makes an argument from silence: "But just as the absence of the title 'Christian' in rabbinic texts does not mean that Christians were absent from the social world of the early rabbis, the lack of explicit testimony to the Essenes does not mean that the sect had ceased to exist" (268).

2. Instone-Brewer, *Prayer and Agriculture,* 4; on 4-5 he notes that "the defining characteristic of Yavneh became inclusiveness rather than sectarian exclusiveness, which explains why those who continued after 70 CE to call themselves 'Pharisee' (*'Perushim'* in rabbinic literature) were regarded as sectarians."

3. For the relationship between the Pharisees and [later] rabbis, see Burns, "Essene Sectarianism and Social Differentiation," 255-56, including n. 18, who observes that the early rabbis assumed the "ideological platform" and "religious tenets" of Pharisaism. For the rabbinic view that the divine presence is everywhere and not just in the Jerusalem temple, see Bokser, "*Ma'al* and Blessings over Food," 567-68.

4. As Himmelfarb, *A Kingdom of Priests,* 175, puts it, "even if the pre-70 sects did not survive long in the post-temple era, it would not necessarily mean the end of sectarianism."

5. See Poirier, "Purity beyond the Temple," 264-65.

6. Cohen, "The Significance of Yavneh," 29, 45, 48; Instone-Brewer, *Prayer and Agriculture,* 5. Milgrom, "The Scriptural Foundations and Deviations," 89, remarks that although the Qumran sect and the rabbis both were heirs to the Bible's minimalist and maximalist traditions, "Qumran rejected the principle that the Rabbis had derived from Scripture: that even divergent interpretations can be the word of the living God."

7. Baumgarten, *The Flourishing of Jewish Sects,* 134-35, suggests that sectarian divisive-

ness disappeared after 70 because of the "return to orality" in the era of the Mishnah, which enabled scholars to disagree.

8. Instone-Brewer, *Prayer and Agriculture*, 5. See also Cohen, "The Significance of Yavneh," 29. Noam, "Beit Shammai and the Sectarian Halakhah," 47, makes the important distinction that after 70 disagreements and differences of opinion are confined to individuals instead of between sects or "schools," and these disagreements are on specific points of law rather than systemic approaches and attitudes.

9. For a discussion of this passage, see Kister, "Law, Morality, and Rhetoric," 146-47.

10. Even Cohen, "The Significance of Yavneh," 49, acknowledges the limits of rabbinic tolerance.

11. Boyarin, *Border Lines*, 63, 65.

12. For rabbinic self-definition in opposition to sectarianism, see Burns, "Essene Sectarianism and Social Differentiation," esp. 253-57.

13. See Crown, "Redating the Schism," 42-50.

14. Boyarin, *Border Lines*, 63.

15. Amit and Adler, "The Observance of Ritual Purity after 70 C.E.," 124, note that there is no comprehensive study of the observance of ritual purity laws after 70.

16. See, e.g., Neusner, *The Idea of Purity in Ancient Judaism*, 130, who observes that in talmudic Judaism the concern for purity continued and purity laws were greatly developed.

17. Poirier, "Purity beyond the Temple," 264; see also Regev, "Non-Priestly Purity and Its Religious Aspects," 243.

18. Oppenheimer, *The 'Am Ha-aretz*, 66, observes that after the ashes of the red heifer ran out, purification from corpse impurity was no longer possible. See also Adler, "The Observance of Ritual Purity," 59 n. 3; Amit and Adler, "The Observance of Ritual Purity after 70 C.E.": "the ability to achieve and maintain ritual purity was not dependent on the presence of the Jerusalem temple but on the continued supply of red-heifer ash" (p. 123). Furthermore, Amit and Adler note that there is no indication in talmudic literature that purification using the ashes of a red heifer had been discontinued, and that the earliest evidence that purity observance had ceased dates to the Geonic period. Even then, menstruants and women who had given birth continued to immerse in miqva'ot for the purpose of maintaining marital relations. See also Miller, "Stepped Pools and the Non-Existent Monolithic 'Miqveh,'" 222-24, 231 n. 58. Elitzur, "Miqva'ot for the Immersion of Hands," 172, mentions that the observance of purification for the consumption of *ḥullin* relaxed in the centuries following the destruction of the temple.

19. Kazen, *Jesus and Purity Halakhah*, 350.

20. Adler, "The Observance of Ritual Purity," 71, notes that the demand for ritually pure agricultural produce (grain, wine, oil) declined dramatically after the temple's destruction.

21. Instone-Brewer, *Prayer and Agriculture*, 35-37. Yonatan Adler points out that the continuation of debates about certain practices does not mean that they were still observed (personal communication April 2009).

22. Bokser, "*Ma'al* and Blessings over Food," points out that the temple's destruction created special problems because Jews were obligated by biblical law to bring agricultural offerings and tithes to Jerusalem before the rest of the produce could be consumed. The rabbis adapted legal observance to the changed situation after 70 in various ways, including permitting the redemption of second tithes with money, allowing *terumah* to be given to any

priest, and requiring blessings before all meals. See also Amit and Adler, "The Observance of Ritual Purity after 70 c.e.," 122.

23. The same is true of ossilegium, although in my opinion the use of ossuaries is not connected with purity observance but instead reflects fashions that were adopted by the Jewish elite. This is demonstrated by the fact that by the third-fourth century stone sarcophagi largely replaced ossuaries in the catacombs at Beth She'arim, reflecting the influence of contemporary Roman funerary customs.

24. Amit and Adler, "The Observance of Ritual Purity after 70 c.e.," 137, suggest that the large numbers of post-70 miqva'ot found at Sepphoris and Susiya may be connected with priestly groups and therefore might not reflect purity observance among the general population. Miller, "Stepped Pools and the Non-Existent Monolithic 'Miqveh'," 221, rejects a connection between priests and miqva'ot at Sepphoris.

25. See Yadin, *The Finds from the Bar-Kokhba Period*, 117, fig. 43:A.7, 59.10.

26. The settlement is located four km north of Jerusalem, along the early Roman road to Nablus. The excavated remains consist of a ca. 500 m-long narrow strip. For preliminary reports, see Bar-Nathan and Sklar-Parnes, "A Jewish Settlement in Orine"; Sklar-Parnes, "Jerusalem, Shu'fat, Ramallah Road" (2005 and 2006); Sklar-Parnes et al., "Excavations in Northeast Jerusalem"; Bar-Nathan and Sklar-Parnes, "A Jewish Settlement Revealed in the Shu'afat Neighborhood of Jerusalem."

27. Bar-Nathan and Sklar-Parnes, "A Jewish Settlement in Orine," 59, 60 (including a miqveh in a bath house), 63; Bar-Nathan and Sklar-Parnes, "A Jewish Settlement Revealed in the Shu'afat Neighborhood."

28. Bar-Nathan and Sklar-Parnes, "A Jewish Settlement in Orine," 63; Sklar-Parnes et al., "Excavations in Northeast Jerusalem," 39*; Sklar-Parnes, "Jerusalem, Shu'fat, Ramallah Road" (2005).

29. Bar-Nathan and Sklar-Parnes, "A Jewish Settlement in Orine," 60; Sklar-Parnes et al., "Excavations in Northeast Jerusalem," 36*-37*; Sklar-Parnes, "Jerusalem, Shu'fat, Ramallah Road" (2005). For the pottery from the legionary kiln works in Jerusalem, see Magness, "The Roman Legionary Pottery." Perhaps pottery produced in the legionary kiln works is the "Hadrianic earthenware" prohibited by the rabbis among the "things belonging to Gentiles" (*m. 'Abod. Zar.* 2:3). In the Babylonian Talmud (*'Abod. Zar.* 32a), this prohibition was attributed to the possibility that Hadrianic earthenware could absorb wine and, when subsequently wetted, would release the wine, which was prohibited for Jewish consumption.

30. Bar-Nathan and Sklar-Parnes, "A Jewish Settlement in Orine," 60 (from Insula 8); Sklar-Parnes et al., "Excavations in Northeast Jerusalem," 39*; Sklar-Parnes, "Jerusalem, Shu'fat, Ramallah Road" (2005). For an inkwell of this type from the kiln works, see Magness, "The Roman Legionary Pottery," 156 fig. 33:3.

31. See Bar-Nathan and Sklar-Parnes, "A Jewish Settlement in Orine," 63, who suggest that the villagers were aristocratic Jewish refugees. The village at Shu'afat brings to mind Josephus's reference to a settlement called Gophna which Titus allotted to members of the Jewish elite (*War* 6.115). For Gophna, see Cotton, "The Administrative Background," 12*-14*.

32. For miqva'ot and stone vessels dating to after 70, see Amit and Adler, "The Observance of Ritual Purity after 70 c.e." Nearly all of the post-70 miqva'ot that they document are no later than the fourth century, and the "Byzantine" examples that they cite are unpublished or not securely dated. See also Weiss, "Jewish Galilee in the First Century c.e.," 47

n. 101; Gibson, "Stone Vessels of the Early Roman Period," 302; Reich, "Miqva'ot in the Second Temple Period," 142-44.

33. See Adan-Bayewitz, *Common Pottery in Roman Galilee*, 231-32, 239-43, who attributes the cessation of production at Kefar Ḥananyah to the decline of Jewish settlement in Galilee during the mid-fourth to early fifth centuries. For a pottery workshop at Shikhin, see Strange et al., "The Location and Identification of Shikhin, Part I"; Strange et al., "The Location and Identification of Shikhin, Part II."

34. Goodman, "Sadducees and Essenes after 70 c.e."; Goodman, "Religious Variety and the Temple," 211-13. See also Burns, "Essene Sectarianism and Social Differentiation," who places the final demise of Jewish sectarianism — and in particular the Essene movement — in the third to fourth centuries (272 n. 61).

35. See Goodman, "Religious Variety and the Temple," 212-13. For a similar argument with regard to the Essenes, see Burns, "Essene Sectarianism and Social Differentiation." It is not clear whether this evidence attests to the continued existence of sectarian groups (in any form) or only to isolated sectarian practices among individual members of the population. See Fine, "Nabratein in the Ancient Literary Sources," 12-13, for a discussion of the nature of Jacob of Kefar Nibburaya's *minut*.

36. Noam and Qimron, "A Qumran Composition of Sabbath Laws," 95.

37. Some scholars have suggested that the visibility of Pharisees versus other groups in the Gospels reflects the new reality after 70; see, e.g., Schürer, *The History of the Jewish People*, 2:400. Meier, *A Marginal Jew*, 3:412, deduces that Mark must be earlier than the other Gospels (around 70) because it alone preserves an account of a clash between Jesus and the Sadducees. For the dating of Mark to ca. 65-70, see Pickup, "Matthew's and Mark's Pharisees," 67.

38. Lawrence, *Washing in Water*, 168, notes that "there is no physical evidence for ritual bathing in the Diaspora during the Second Temple period"; but see 57-59 for the possibility that hand washing before prayer was practiced by the Jews of Egypt in the Second Temple period. I agree with Matassa, "Unravelling the Myth of the Synagogue on Delos," that the archaeological and inscriptional evidence does not support the identification of a Hellenistic-period building on Delos as a synagogue. New excavations at Ostia have indicated that the synagogue building was not erected until the third century c.e., as Michael White reported in a paper presented at the International Meeting of the Society of Biblical Literature in Rome in 2009 ("Revisioning the Ostia Synagogue and Its Neighborhood: Findings from the UT Excavations").

39. Neusner, *The Idea of Purity in Ancient Judaism*, 108-9. Douglas, "Critique and Commentary," 141, suggests that distance from membership in a sectarian group turns purity rules into metaphors of spiritual good instead of regulations for admission, exclusion, and rankings.

40. Neusner, *A History of the Mishnaic Law of Purities*, 254-56, who discusses changes in rabbinic purity laws after the Bar Kokhba Revolt, as hopes of a rebuilt temple faded.

41. Bokser, "*Ma'al* and Blessings over Food," 557, 570-71, notes that during the third and fourth centuries the rabbis distanced themselves from the temple and consciously accepted its loss.

42. See Dothan, *Hammath Tiberias*; Magness, "Heaven on Earth."

Bibliography

Adan-Bayewitz, David. *Common Pottery in Roman Galilee: A Study of Local Trade.* Ramat-Gan: Bar-Ilan University Press, 1993.

——, and Mordechai Aviam. "Iotapata, Josephus, and the Siege of 67: Preliminary Report on the 1992-94 Seasons." *JRA* 10 (1997) 131-65.

——, Frank Asaro, Moshe Wieder, and Robert D. Giauque. "Preferential Distribution of Lamps from the Jerusalem Area in the Late Second Temple Period (Late First Century B.C.E.–70 C.E.)." *BASOR* 350 (2008) 37-85.

Adler, Yonatan. "The Observance of Ritual Purity in Agricultural Industry during the Second Temple and Mishnah Periods." Yehuda Feliks Memorial Volume. *Jerusalem and Eretz-Israel* 4-5 (2007) 59-83. [Hebrew]

——. "Ritual Baths Adjacent to Tombs." *JSJ* 40 (2009) 55-73.

——. "The Ritual Baths near the Temple Mount and Extra-Purification before Entering the Temple Courts: A Reply to Eyal Regev." *IEJ* 56 (2006) 209-15.

——. "Second Temple Period Ritual Baths Adjacent to Agricultural Installations: The Archaeological Evidence in Light of the Halakhic Sources." *JSJ* 59 (2008) 62-72.

Alon, Gedalyahu. *Jews, Judaism and the Classical World: Studies in Jewish History in the Times of the Second Temple and Talmud.* Jerusalem: Magnes, 1977.

Amit, David. "A *Miqveh* Complex near Alon Shevut." *'Atiqot* 38 (1999) 75-84.

——. "Ritual Baths (Miqva'ot) from the Second Temple Period in the Hebron Mountains." In *Judea and Samaria Research Studies: Proceedings of the 3rd Annual Meeting-1993,* ed. Ze'ev H. Ehrlich and Ya'acov Eshel, 157-89. Kedumim-Ariel College of Judea and Samaria, 1994. [Hebrew]

——, and Yonatan Adler. "The Observance of Ritual Purity after 70 C.E." In *"Follow the Wise": Studies in Jewish History and Culture in Honor of Lee I. Levine,* ed. Oded Irshai, Jodi Magness, Seth Schwartz, and Ze'ev Weiss, 121-43. New York: Jewish Theological Seminary, 2010.

——, and Jodi Magness. "Not a Settlement of Hermits or Essenes: A Response to

Y. Hirschfeld, 'A Settlement of Essenes above 'En Gedi.'" *Tel Aviv* 27 (2000) 273-85.

———, Jon Seligman, and Irina Zilberbod. "Stone Vessel Workshops of the Second Temple Period East of Jerusalem." In Geva, *Ancient Jerusalem Revealed*, 353-58.

———, Hagit Torgü, and Peter Gendelman. "Horvat Burnat, a Jewish Village in the Lod Shephelah during the Hellenistic and Roman Periods." *Qad* 41 (2008) 96-107. [Hebrew]

Ariel, Donald T. "Coins from Excavations at Qumran." In *Excavations at Khirbet Qumran*, ed. Yitzhak Magen and Yuval Peleg. Jerusalem: Staff Officer of Archaeology — Civil Administration of Judea and Samaria, forthcoming.

———. "The Coins from Qalandiya." In Magen et al., *The Land of Benjamin*, 145-77.

———. "The Coins from the Surveys and Excavations of Caves in the Northern Judean Desert." *'Atiqot* 41 (2002) 281-304.

———. "Imported Greek Stamped Amphora Handles." In Geva, *Jewish Quarter Excavations*, 1:267-83.

———, and Gerald Finkielsztejn. "Stamped Amphora Handles." In Herbert, *Tel Anafa*, 1/1:183-240.

———, and Aryeh Strikovsky. "Appendix." In *Excavations at the City of David*, 2:25-28.

———, ed. *Excavations at the City of David Directed by Yigal Shiloh*. Vol. 2: *1978-1985: Imported Stamped Amphora Handles, Coins, Worked Bone and Ivory, and Glass*. Qedem 30. Jerusalem: Hebrew University, 1990.

———, and Alon de Groot, eds. *Excavations at the City of David Directed by Yigal Shiloh*. Vol. 4: *1978-1985: Various Reports*. Qedem 35. Jerusalem: Institute of Archaeology, Hebrew University, 1996.

Arubas, Benny, and Haim Goldfus, eds. *Excavations on the Site of the Jerusalem International Convention Center (Binyanei Ha'uma): A Settlement of the Late First to Second Temple Period, the Tenth Legion's Kilnworks, and a Byzantine Monastic Complex. The Pottery and Other Small Finds*. JRASup 60, Portsmouth: Journal of Roman Archaeology, 2005.

Ashtor, Eliyahu. "The Diet of the Salaried Classes in the Medieval Near East." *Journal of Asian History* 4 (1970) 1-24.

Atkins, Margaret, and Robin Osborne, eds. *Poverty in the Roman World*. Cambridge: Cambridge University Press, 2006.

Attridge, Harold W., ed. *The HarperCollins Study Bible*. Rev. ed. San Francisco: HarperSanFrancisco, 1989.

Audet, Jean-Paul. *La Didaché, Instructions des Apôtres*. Paris: Gabalda, 1958.

Avemarie, Friedrich. "'Tohorat ha-Rabbim' and 'Mashqeh ha-Rabbim': Jacob Licht Reconsidered." In Bernstein, García Martínez, and Kampen, *Legal Texts and Legal Issues*, 215-29.

Aviam, Mordechai. "Distribution Maps of Archaeological Data from the Galilee: An Attempt to Establish Zones Indicative of Ethnicity and Religious Affiliation." In Zangenberg, Attridge, and Martin, *Religion, Ethnicity, and Identity in Ancient Galilee*, 115-32.

———. *Jews, Pagans and Christians in the Galilee: 25 Years of Archaeological Excavations and Surveys, Hellenistic to Byzantine Periods.* Rochester: University of Rochester Press, 2004.

―――. "Magdala." In *The Oxford Encyclopedia of Archaeology in the Near East,* ed. Eric M. Meyers, 3:399-400. New York: Oxford University Press, 1997.

Avigad, Nahman. *Ancient Monuments in the Kidron Valley.* Jerusalem: Bialik Institute, 1954. [Hebrew]

―――. "Aramaic Inscriptions in the Tomb of Jason." *IEJ* 17 (1967) 101-11.

―――. *Beth She'arim.* Vol. 3: *The Excavations 1953-1958.* New Brunswick: Rutgers University Press, 1976.

―――. *Discovering Jerusalem.* Nashville: Nelson, 1983.

―――. "Expedition A — Nahal David." *IEJ* 12 (1962) 169-83.

―――. "Jewish Rock-Cut Tombs in Jerusalem and the Judaean Hill Country." *ErIsr* 8 (1967) 119-25. [Hebrew]

Aviram, Joseph, Gideon Foerster, and Ehud Netzer, eds. *Masada IV: The Yigael Yadin Excavations 1963-1965, Final Reports.* Vol. 4. Jerusalem: Israel Exploration Society, 1994.

Avni, Gideon. "Christian Secondary Use of Jewish Burial Caves in Jerusalem in the Light of New Excavations at the Aceldama Tombs." In Manns and Alliata, *Early Christianity in Context,* 265-76.

―――, and Zvi Greenhut. "Resting Place of the Rich and Famous." *BAR* 20/6 (1994) 36-46.

―――, Yuval Baruch, and Shlomit Weksler-Bdolah. "Jerusalem, the Old City — Herod's Gate." *Hadashot Arkheologiyot (Excavations and Surveys in Israel)* 113 (2001) 76*-79*.

―――, and Zvi Greenhut, eds. *The Akeldama Tombs: Three Burial Caves in the Kidron Valley, Jerusalem.* IAA Reports 1. Jerusalem: Israel Antiquities Authority, 1996.

Avshalom-Gorni, Dina, and Nimrod Getzov. "Phoenicians and Jews: A Ceramic Case-study." In Berlin and Overman, *The First Jewish Revolt,* 74-83.

Bailey, Donald M. "Imported Lamps and Local Copies." In Aviram, Foerster, and Netzer, *Masada IV,* 79-99.

Baillet, Maurice, Josef T. Milik, and Roland de Vaux. *Les 'Petites Grottes' de Qumrân.* DJD 3. Clarendon: Oxford University Press, 1962.

Bar-Adon, Pesach. "Another Settlement of the Judean Desert Sect at 'En el-Ghuweir on the Shores of the Dead Sea." *BASOR* 227 (1977) 1-25.

―――. *Excavations in the Judean Desert.* 'Atiqot 9. Jerusalem: Israel Department of Antiquities, 1989. [Hebrew with English summary]

Barag, Dan, and Malka Hershkovitz. "Lamps." In Aviram, Foerster, and Netzer, *Masada IV,* 7-147.

Bar-Ilan, Meir. "The Reasons for Sectarianism According to the Tannaim and Josephus's Allegation of the Impurity of Oil." In Schiffman, Tov, and Vander-Kam, *The Dead Sea Scrolls Fifty Years After Their Discovery,* 587-99.

Barkay, Gabriel. "Burial Caves and Burial Practices in Judah in the Iron Age." In Zinger, *Graves and Burial Practices in Israel in the Ancient Period,* 96-164. [Hebrew]

————. "News from the Field: The Divine Name Found in Jerusalem." *BAR* 9/2 (1983) 14-19.

————. "The Necropoli of Jerusalem in the First Temple Period." In *The History of Jerusalem: The Biblical Period*, ed. Shemuel Ahituv and Amihai Mazar, 233-70. Jerusalem: Yad Izhak Ben-Zvi, 2000. [Hebrew]

————, and Amos Kloner. "Jerusalem Tombs from the Days of the First Temple." *BAR* 12/2 (1986) 22-39.

————, Amihai Mazar, and Amos Kloner. "The Northern Cemetery of Jerusalem in First Temple Times." *Qad* 30-31 (1975) 71-76. [Hebrew]

Bar-Nathan, Rachel. *Masada VII: The Yigael Yadin Excavations 1963-1965, Final Reports.* Vol. 7: *The Pottery of Masada.* Jerusalem: Israel Exploration Society, 2006.

————. *The Pottery.* Vol. 3 of Netzer, *Hasmonean and Herodian Palaces at Jericho.* Jerusalem: Israel Exploration Society, 2002.

————. "Pottery and Stone Vessels of the Herodian Period (1st century B.C.–1st century A.D.)." In *Greater Herodium*, ed. Ehud Netzer, 54-70. Qedem 13. Jerusalem: Hebrew University, 1981.

————. "Qumran and the Hasmonean and Herodian Winter Palaces of Jericho: The Implication of the Pottery Finds on the Interpretation of the Settlement at Qumran." In Galor, Humbert, and Zangenberg, *Qumran, the Site of the Dead Sea Scrolls,* 263-77.

————, and Deborah A. Sklar-Parnes. "A Jewish Settlement in Orine between the Two Revolts." In Patrich and Amit, *New Studies in the Archaeology of Jerusalem and Its Region,* 57-64. [Hebrew]

————. "A Jewish Settlement Revealed in the Shuʿafat Neighborhood of Jerusalem." *American Schools of Oriental Research 2007 Annual Meeting Abstract Book* (2007) 13; at http://www.asor.org/AM/abstracts07(final).pdf

Barrera, Julio Trebolle, and Luis Montaner, eds. *The Madrid Qumran Congress: Proceedings of the International Congress on the Dead Sea Scrolls, Madrid 18-21 March, 1991.* 2 vols. STDJ 11. Leiden: Brill, 1992.

Baruch, Eyal, and Zohar Amar. "The *Latrina* in Eretz-Israel in the Roman-Byzantine Period." *Jerusalem and Eretz-Israel* 2 (2004) 27-50.

————, and Avraham Faust, eds. *New Studies on Jerusalem.* Vol. 10. Ramat-Gan: Ingeborg Rennert Center for Jerusalem Studies, Bar-Ilan University, 2004.

Baruch, Yuval, and Gideon Avni. "Archaeological Evidence for the Bezetha Quarter in the Second Temple Period." In *Ingeborg Rennert Center for Jerusalem Studies: New Studies on Jerusalem. Proceedings of the Sixth Conference, December 7th 2000,* ed. Avraham Faust and Eyal Baruch, 52-63. Ramat Gan: Bar-Ilan University Press, 2000. [Hebrew]

Bauckham, Richard. "For What Offence Was James Put to Death?" In Chilton and Evans, *James the Just and Christian Origins,* 199-232.

Baumbach, Günther. "The Sadducees in Josephus." In *Josephus, the Bible, and History,* ed. Louis H. Feldman and Gohei Hata, 173-95. Detroit: Wayne State University Press, 1989.

Baumgarten, Albert I. "Finding Oneself in a Sectarian Context: A Sectarian's Food and

Its Implications." In *Self, Soul and Body in Religious Experience*, ed. Baumgarten, Jan Assmann, Guy G. Stroumsa, 125-47. SHR 78. Leiden: Brill, 1998.

———. *The Flourishing of Jewish Sects in the Maccabean Era: An Interpretation*. JSJSup 55. Leiden: Brill, 1997.

———. "Josephus on Essene Sacrifice." *JJS* 45 (1994) 169-83.

———. "The Name of the Pharisees." *JBL* 102 (1983) 411-28.

———. "Rabbinic Literature as a Source for the History of Jewish Sectarianism in the Second Temple Period." *DSD* 2 (1995) 14-57.

———. "The Rule of the Martian as Applied to Qumran." *IOS* 14 (1994) 121-42.

———. "The Temple Scroll, Toilet Practices, and the Essenes." *Jewish History* 10 (1996) 9-20.

Baumgarten, Joseph M. "The Essene Avoidance of Oil and the Laws of Purity." *RevQ* 6 (1967) 183-93.

———. "4QHalakha B." In *Qumran Cave 4: XXV, Halakhic Texts*, 53-56.

———. "Halakhic Polemics in New Fragments from Cave 4." In *Biblical Archaeology Today: Proceedings of the International Congress on Biblical Archaeology, Jerusalem, April 1984*, 390-99. Jerusalem: Israel Exploration Society, 1985.

———. "Halivni's *Midrash, Mishnah, and Gemara*," *JQR* 77 (1986) 59-64.

———. "The Laws of the Damascus Document — Between Bible and Mishnah." In *The Damascus Document*, 17-26.

———. "Liquids and Susceptibility to Defilement in New 4Q Texts." *JQR* 85 (1994) 91-101.

———. "Miscellaneous Rules." In *Qumran Cave 4: XXV, Halakhic Texts*, 57-78.

———. "The Pharisaic-Sadducean Controversies about Purity and the Qumran Texts." *JJS* 31 (1980) 157-70.

———. "The Purification Rituals in *DJD 7*." In Dimant and Rappaport, *The Dead Sea Scrolls*, 199-209.

———. "The Qumran-Essene Restraints on Marriage." In Schiffman, *Archaeology and History in the Dead Sea Scrolls*, 13-24.

———. "Recent Qumran Discoveries and Halakhah in the Hellenistic-Roman Period." In Talmon, *Jewish Civilization in the Hellenistic-Roman Period*, 147-58.

———. "The 'Sons of Dawn' in *CDC* 13:14-15 and the Ban on Commerce among the Essenes." *IEJ* 33 (1983) 81-85.

———. *Studies in Qumran Law*. SJLA 24. Brill: Leiden, 1977.

———. "Tannaitic Halakhah and Qumran — A Re-evaluation." In Orion Center for the Study of the Dead Sea Scrolls, *Rabbinic Perspectives*, 1-11.

———. "Tohorot." In *Qumran Cave 4: XXV, Halakhic Texts*, 79-122.

——— et al. *Qumran Cave 4 XXV: Halakhic Texts*. DJD 35. Oxford: Clarendon, 1999.

———, Esther G. Chazon, and Avital Pinnick, eds. *The Damascus Document: A Centennial of Discovery. Proceedings of the Third International Symposium of the Orion Center for the Study of the Dead Sea Scrolls and Associated Literature, 4-8 February, 1998*. STDJ 34. Leiden: Brill, 2000.

———, and Daniel R. Schwartz. "Damascus Document (CD)." In *The Dead Sea Scrolls: Hebrew, Aramaic, and Greek Texts with English Translations*. Vol. 2: *Damascus*

Document, War Scroll, and Related Documents, ed. James H. Charlesworth, 4-57. PTSDSSP. Tübingen: Mohr Siebeck, and Louisville: Westminster John Knox, 1995.

Beall, Todd S. *Josephus' Description of the Essenes Illustrated by the Dead Sea Scrolls.* SNTSMS 58. Cambridge: Cambridge University Press, 1988.

Bélis, Mireille. "Des textiles, catalogues et commentaires." In Humbert and Gunneweg, *Khirbet Qumrân et 'Aïn Feshkha,* 2:207-76.

Ben-Dov, Meir. *In the Shadow of the Temple: The Discovery of Ancient Jerusalem.* New York: Harper & Row, 1985.

Bergsma, John S. "Qumran Self-Identity: 'Israel' or 'Judah'?" *DSD* 15 (2008) 172-89.

Berkowitz, Beth A. *Execution and Invention: Death Penalty Discourse in Early Rabbinic and Christian Cultures.* Oxford: Oxford University Press, 2006.

Berlin, Adele. "Qumran Laments and the Study of Lament Literature." In *Liturgical Perspectives: Prayer and Poetry in Light of the Dead Sea Scrolls. Proceedings of the Fifth International Symposium of the Orion Center for the Study of the Dead Sea Scrolls and Associated Literature, 19-23 January, 2000,* ed. Esther G. Chazon, 1-17. Leiden: Brill, 2003.

Berlin, Andrea. "Business at the Bottom of the World." *JRA* 15 (2002) 646-50.

———. *Gamla I: The Pottery of the Second Temple Period.* IAA Reports 29. Jerusalem: Israel Antiquities Authority, 2006.

———. "Italian Cooking Vessels and Cuisine from Tel Anafa." *IEJ* 43 (1993) 35-44.

———. "Jewish Life before the Revolt: The Archaeological Evidence." *JSJ* 36 (2005) 417-70.

———. "The Plain Wares." In Herbert, *Tel Anafa,* 2/2: 1-244.

———. "Pottery and Pottery Production in the Second Temple Period." In Arubas and Goldfus, *Excavations on the Site of the Jerusalem International Convention Center,* 29-60.

———. "Power and Its Afterlife, Tombs in Hellenistic Palestine." *NEA* 65 (2002) 138-48.

———. "Ptolemaic Agriculture, 'Syrian Wheat,' and *Triticum aestivum.*" *Journal of Archaeological Science* 30 (2003) 115-21.

———. "Romanization and Anti-Romanization in Pre-Revolt Galilee." In *The First Jewish Revolt,* 57-73.

———, and J. Andrew Overman, eds. *The First Jewish Revolt: Archaeology, History, and Ideology. Proceedings of the Conference Held at the University of Minnesota and Macalester College, April 21-23, 1999.* London: Routledge, 2002.

Bernstein, Moshe J. "4Q159 Fragment 5 and the 'Desert Theology' of the Qumran Sect." In Paul, Kraft, Schiffman, and Fields, *Emanuel,* 43-56.

———. "*Midrash Halakhah* at Qumran? 11Q Temple 64:6-13 and Deuteronomy 21:22-23." *Gesher* 7 (1979) 145-66.

———, Florentino García Martínez, and John Kampen, eds. *Legal Texts and Legal Issues: Proceedings of the Second Meeting of the International Organization for Qumran Studies, Cambridge 1995, Published in Honour of Joseph M. Baumgarten.* STDJ 23. Leiden: Brill, 1997.

Bibliography

Berrin, Shani L. *The Pesher Nahum Scroll from Qumran: An Exegetical Study of 4Q169*. STDJ 53. Leiden: Brill, 2004.

Bijovsky, Gabriela. "The Coin Finds from the Shuʿafat (Givʿat Shaul) Excavations: Preliminary Report)." In Patrich and Amit, *New Studies in the Archaeology of Jerusalem and its Region*, 65-72. [Hebrew]

———. "The Coins." In Hirschfeld, *En-Gedi Excavations II*, 157-233.

———. "The Coins from Khirbet Badd ʿIsa — Qiryat Sefer." In Magen et al., *The Land of Benjamin*, 243-300.

Birenboim, Hannan. "*Tevul Yom* and the Red Heifer: Pharisaic and Sadducean Halakah." *DSD* 16 (2009) 254-73.

Blake, Emma. "The Material Expression of Cult, Ritual, and Feasting." In *The Archaeology of Mediterranean Prehistory*, ed. Emma Blake and A. Bernard Knapp, 102-29. Malden: Blackwell, 2005.

Bloch-Smith, Elizabeth. *Judahite Burial Practices and Beliefs about the Dead*. JSOTSup 123. Sheffield: JSOT, 1992.

Bodel, John. "Dealing with the Dead: Undertakers, Executioners, and Potter's Fields in Ancient Rome." In *Death and Disease in the Ancient City*, ed. Valerie M. Hope and Eireann Marshall, 128-51. New York: Routledge, 2000.

———. "From *Columbaria* to Catacombs: Collective Burial in Pagan and Christian Rome." In Brink and Green, *Commemorating the Dead*, 177-242.

———. "Graveyards and Groves, A Study of the *Lex Lucerina*." *American Journal of Ancient History* 11 (1994) 1-133.

Bokser, Baruch M. "Approaching Sacred Space." *HTR* 78 (1985) 279-99.

———. "*Maʿal* and Blessings over Food: Rabbinic Transformation of Cultic Terminology and Alternative Modes of Piety." *JBL* 100 (1981) 557-74.

Bonfante, Larissa. "Nudity as a Costume in Classical Art." *AJA* 93 (1989) 543-70.

Booth, Roger P. *Jesus and the Laws of Purity: Tradition History and Legal History in Mark 7*. JSNTSup 13. Sheffield: Sheffield Academic, 1986.

Bouchnik, Ram, Guy Bar-Oz, and Ronny Reich. "Animal Bone Remains from the City Dump of Jerusalem from the Late Second Temple Period." In Baruch and Faust, *New Studies on Jerusalem*, 10:71-80.

Bouet, Alain. *Les latrines dans les provinces gauloises, germaniques et alpines*. GALLIA Sup 59e. Paris: CNRS, 2009.

Bovon, François. "*Fragment Oxyrhynchus 840*, Fragment of a Lost Gospel, Witness of an Early Christian Controversy over Purity." *JBL* 119 (2000) 705-28.

Boyarin, Daniel. *Border Lines: The Partition of Judaeo-Christianity*. Philadelphia: University of Pennsylvania Press, 2004.

Branham, R. Bracht, and Daniel Kinney, eds. and trans. *Petronius Satyrica*. Berkeley: University of California Press, 1996.

Bray, Tamara L. "The Commensal Politics of Early States and Empires." In *The Archaeology and Politics of Food and Feasting in Early States and Empires*, ed. Tamara L. Bray, 1-13. New York: Kluwer Academic/Plenum, 2003.

Brin, Gershon. "Divorce at Qumran." In Bernstein, García Martínez, and Kampen, *Legal Texts and Legal Issues*, 231-44.

Brink, Laurie, and Deborah Green, eds. *Commemorating the Dead: Texts and Artifacts in Context: Studies of Roman, Jewish, and Christian Burials.* Berlin: de Gruyter, 2008.

Brooke, George J. *The Dead Sea Scrolls and the New Testament.* Minneapolis: Fortress, 2005.

————. "Ezekiel in Some Qumran and New Testament Texts." In Barrera and Montaner, *The Madrid Qumran Congress,* 1:317-37.

Broshi, Magen. "Anti-Qumranic Polemics in the Talmud." In Barrera and Montaner, *The Madrid Qumran Congress,* 2:589-600.

————. "Excavations on Mount Zion, 1971-1972." *IEJ* 26 (1976) 81-88.

————. "Matrimony and Poverty: Jesus and the Essenes." *RevQ* 19 (2000) 632-34.

————. "Qumran and the Essenes: Purity and Pollution, Six Categories." *RevQ* 87[22] (2006) 463-74.

————. "What Jesus Learned from the Essenes." *BAR* 30/1 (2004) 32-37, 64.

————, and Hanan Eshel. "How and Where Did the Qumranites Live?" In *The Provo International Conference on the Dead Sea Scrolls: Technological Innovations, New Texts, and Reformulated Issues,* ed. Donald W. Parry and Eugene C. Ulrich, 266-73. STDJ 30. Leiden: Brill, 1999.

————. "Residential Caves at Qumran." *DSD* 6 (1999) 328-48.

————. "Three Seasons of Excavations at Qumran." *JRA* 17 (2004) 321-32.

Brown, Raymond E. *The Death of the Messiah from Gethsemane to the Grave: A Commentary on the Passion Narratives in the Four Gospels.* 2 vols. New York: Doubleday, 1994.

Broyde, Michael J. "Defilement of the Hands, Canonization of the Bible, and the Special Status of Esther, Ecclesiasticus, and Song of Songs." *Judaism* 44 (1995) 65-79.

Burns, Joshua Ezra. "Essene Sectarianism and Social Differentiation in Judea After 70 C.E." *HTR* 99 (2006) 247-74.

Cahill, Jane M. "The Chalk Vessel Assemblages of the Persian/Hellenistic and Early Roman Periods." In *Excavations at the City of David 1978-1985 Directed by Yigal Shiloh.* Vol. 3: *Stratigraphical, Environmental, and Other Reports,* ed. Alon de Groot and Donald T. Ariel, 190-274. Qedem 33. Jerusalem: Institute of Archaeology, Hebrew University, 1992.

————, Karl Reinhard, David Tarler, and Peter Warnock. "Scientists Examine Remains of Ancient Bathroom." *BAR* 17 (1991) 64-69.

Calderon, Rivka. "Roman and Byzantine Pottery." In Hirschfeld, *Ramat Hanadiv Excavations,* 91-165.

Chalcraft, David J., ed. *Sectarianism in Early Judaism: Sociological Advances.* London: Equinox, 2007.

Chancey, Mark A. *Greco-Roman Culture and the Galilee of Jesus.* New York: Cambridge University Press, 2005.

Chapman, David W. *Ancient Jewish and Christian Perceptions of Crucifixion.* WUNT 244. Tübingen: Mohr Siebeck, 2008.

Charles, R. H. *The Apocrypha and Pseudepigrapha of the Old Testament in English.* 2 vols. Oxford: Clarendon, 1913.

Bibliography

Chilton, Bruce. "Paul and the Pharisees." In Neusner and Chilton, *In Quest of the Historical Pharisees*, 149-174.

————. *The Temple of Jesus: His Sacrificial Program Within a Cultural History of Sacrifice.* University Park: Pennsylvania State University Press, 1992.

————, and Craig A. Evans, eds. *James the Just and Christian Origins.* NovTSup 98. Leiden: Brill, 1999.

Clamer, Christa. *Fouilles archéologiques de ʿAïn ez-Zâra/Callirrhoé, villégiature hérodienne.* Bibliothèque archéologique et historique 147. Beirut: Institut français d'archéologie du proche-orient, 1997.

Clarke, William M. "Jewish Table Manners in the *Cena Trimalchionis*." *CJ* 87 (1992) 257-63.

Cohen, Shaye J. D. *The Beginnings of Jewishness: Boundaries, Varieties, Uncertainties.* Berkeley: University of California Press, 1999.

————. *Josephus in Galilee and Rome.* Boston: Leiden, 2002.

————. "The Significance of Yavneh: Pharisees, Rabbis, and the End of Jewish Sectarianism." *HUCA* 55 (1985) 27-53.

Cohn, Yehudah B. *Tangled Up in Text: Tefillin and the Ancient World.* BJS 351. Providence: Brown Judaic Studies, 2008.

Cotton, Hannah M. "The Administrative Background to the New Settlement Recently Discovered near Givʿat Shaul, Ramallah-Shuʿafat Road." In Patrich and Amit, *New Studies in the Archaeology of Jerusalem and Its Region*, 12*-18*.

————, Omri Lernau, and Yuval Goren. "Fish Sauces from Herodian Masada." *JRA* 9 (1996) 223-38.

Crawford, Sidnie White. "The Meaning of the Phrase עיר המקדש in the Temple Scroll." *DSD* 8 (2001) 242-54.

————. "Not According to Rule: Women, the Dead Sea Scrolls, and Qumran." In Paul, Kraft, Schiffman, and Fields, *Emanuel*, 127-50.

————. *The Temple Scroll and Related Texts.* Companion to the Qumran Scrolls 2. Sheffield: Sheffield Academic, 2000.

Cross, Frank Moore, and Esther Eshel. "Ostraca from Khirbet Qumrân." *IEJ* 47 (1997) 17-28.

Crossan, John Dominic. *The Historical Jesus: The Life of a Mediterranean Jewish Peasant.* San Francisco: Harper & Row, 1991.

————. *Who Killed Jesus? Exposing the Roots of Anti-Semitism in the Gospel Story of the Death of Jesus.* San Francisco: HarperSanFrancisco, 1995.

Crowfoot, Grace M. "The Linen Textiles." In *Qumran Cave 1*, ed. Dominique Barthélemy and Josef T. Milik, 18-40. DJD 1. Oxford: Clarendon, 1956.

Crown, Alan D. "Qumran, Samaritan *Halakha* and Theology and Pre-Tannaitic Judaism." In *Boundaries of the Ancient Near Eastern World: A Tribute to Cyrus H. Gordon*, ed. Meir Lubetski, Claire Gottlieb, and Sharon Keller, 420-41. JSOTSup 273. Sheffield: Sheffield Academic, 1998.

————. "Redating the Schism between the Judaeans and the Samaritans." *JQR* 82 (1991) 17-50.

Cuffel, Alexandra. *Gendering Disgust in Medieval Religious Polemic.* Notre Dame: University of Notre Dame Press, 2007.

Dadon, Mikel. "Burial Caves at Bethlehem." *'Atiqot* 32 (1997) 199-201. [Hebrew]

Daise, Michael A. "Ritual Density in Qumran Practice: Ablutions in the Serekh Ha-Yahad." at http://orion.mscc.huji.ac.il/symposium/10th/papers/daise.htm

Damati, Emanuel. "Ḥilkiah's Palace." In *Between Hermon and Sinai: Memorial to Amnon,* ed. Magen Broshi, 93-113. Jerusalem: Yedidim, 1977. [Hebrew]

———. "The Palace of Ḥilkiya." *Qad* 60 (1982) 117-21. [Hebrew]

Danker, Frederick William, rev. and ed. *A Greek-English Lexicon of the New Testament and Other Early Christian Literature.* Chicago: University of Chicago Press, 2000.

Davids, Peter H. "Palestinian Traditions in the Epistle of James." In Chilton and Evans, *James the Just and Christian Origins,* 33-57.

Davidson, Maxwell J. *Angels at Qumran: A Comparative Study of 1 Enoch 1–36, 72–108 and Sectarian writings from Qumran.* JSPSup 11. Sheffield: Sheffield Academic, 1992.

Davies, Jon. *Death, Burial and Rebirth in the Religions of Antiquity.* New York: Routledge, 1999.

Davies, Philip R. "Food, Drink and Sects: The Question of Ingestion in the Qumran Texts." *Semeia* 86 (1999) 151-63.

Deferrari, Roy J. *Eusebius Pamphili, Ecclesiastical History.* New York: Fathers of the Church, 1953.

Deines, Roland. *Jüdische Steingefäße und pharisäische Frömmigkeit: Ein archäologisch-historischer Beitrag zum Verständnis von Joh 2,6 und der jüdischen Reinheitschalacha zur Zeit Jesu.* WUNT 52. Tübingen: Mohr, 1993.

Dimant, Devorah, and Uriel Rappaport, eds. *The Dead Sea Scrolls: Forty Years of Research.* STDJ 10. Leiden: Brill, 1992.

Dods, Marcus, George Reith, and B. P. Pratten. *The Writings of Justin Martyr and Athenagoras.* Edinburgh: T. & T. Clark, 1867.

Doering, Lutz. "The Concept of the Sabbath in the Book of Jubilees." In *Studies in the Book of Jubilees,* ed. Matthias Albani, Jörg Frey, and Armin Lange, 179-205. TSAJ 65. Tübingen: Mohr Siebeck, 1997.

———. "New Aspects of Qumran Sabbath Law from Cave 4 Fragments." In Bernstein, García Martínez, and Kampen, *Legal Texts and Legal Issues,* 251-74.

———. "Purity and Impurity in the Book of Jubilees." In *Enoch and the Mosaic Torah,* ed. Gabriele Boccaccini and Giovanni Ibba, 261-75. Grand Rapids: Wm. B. Eerdmans, 2009.

———. "Purity Regulations Concerning the Sabbath in the Dead Sea Scrolls and Related Literature." In Schiffman, Tov, and VanderKam, *The Dead Sea Scrolls Fifty Years After Their Discovery,* 600-9.

Donahue, John F. *The Roman Community at Table during the Principate.* Ann Arbor: University of Michigan Press, 2004.

Donceel, Robert, and Pauline Donceel-Voûte. "The Archaeology of Khirbet Qumran." In *Methods of Investigation of the Dead Sea Scrolls and the Khirbet Qumran Site: Present Realities and Future Prospects,* ed. Michael O. Wise, Norman Golb, John J.

Collins, and Dennis G. Pardee, 1-38. Annals of the New York Academy of Sciences 722. New York: New York Academy of Sciences, 1994.

Donceel-Voûte, Pauline. "Les ruines de Qumran réinterprétées." *Archeologia* 298 (1994) 24-35.

Dothan, Moshe. *Hammath Tiberias: Early Synagogue and the Hellenistic and Roman Remains.* Jerusalem: Israel Exploration Society, 1983.

Douglas, Mary. "Critique and Commentary." In Neusner, *The Idea of Purity in Ancient Judaism,* 137-42.

————. "Impurity of Land Animals." In Poorthuis and Schwartz, *Purity and Holiness,* 33-45.

————. *Purity and Danger: An Analysis of Concepts of Pollution and Taboo.* New York: Praeger, 1966.

Draper, Jonathan A. "Christian Self-Definition against the 'Hypocrites' in Didache VIII." In *The Didache in Modern Research,* 223-43. AGJU 37. Leiden: Brill, 1996.

Dunbabin, Katherine M. D. *The Roman Banquet: Images of Conviviality.* Cambridge: Cambridge University Press, 2003.

Edgar, David Hutchinson. *Has God Not Chosen the Poor? The Social Setting of the Epistle of James.* JSNTSup 206. Sheffield: Sheffield Academic, 2001.

Edwards, Douglas R., and C. Thomas McCollough, eds. *The Archaeology of Difference: Gender, Ethnicity, Class and the "Other" in Antiquity. Studies in Honor of Eric M. Meyers.* AASOR 60/61. Boston: American Schools of Oriental Research, 2007.

Ehrlich, Uri. *The Nonverbal Language of Prayer: A New Approach to Jewish Liturgy.* TSAJ 105. Tübingen: Mohr Siebeck, 2004.

Eisenman, Robert. *James the Brother of Jesus: The Key to Unlocking the Secrets of Early Chrisitianity and the Dead Sea Scrolls.* New York: Penguin, 1997.

————. *The New Testament Code: The Cup of the Lord, the Damascus Covenant, and the Blood of Christ.* London: Watkins, 2006.

Elgvin, Torleif, and Ian Werrett. "4Q472a in Infrared Light: Latrine Manual Down the Drain." *RevQ* 90 (2007) 261-68.

Eliav, Yaron Z. "The Tomb of James Brother of Jesus as *Locus Memoriae.*" *HTR* 97 (2004) 32-59.

Elitzur, Yoel. "Miqva'ot for the Immersion of Hands." *Cathedra* 91 (1991) 169-72. [Hebrew]

Elman, Yaakov. "Some Remarks on 4QMMT and the Rabbinic Tradition: or, When Is a Parallel Not a Parallel?" In *Reading 4QMMT: New Perspectives on Qumran Law and History,* ed. John Kampen and Moshe J. Bernstein, 99-128. SBLSymS 2. Atlanta: Scholars, 1996.

Epstein, Isidore. *The Babylonian Talmud: Seder Kodashim.* London: Soncino, 1948.

Erdemgil, Selahattin. *Ephesus Museum.* Istanbul: Do-gu, 1989.

Eshel, Esther. "4Q414 Fragment 2: Purification of a Corpse-Contaminated Person." In Bernstein, García Martínez, and Kampen, *Legal Texts and Legal Issues,* 3-10.

————. "4QLev^d: A Possible Source for the Temple Scroll and Miqsat Ma'aśe Ha-Torah." *DSD* 2 (1995) 1-13.

————. "Ritual of Purification." In Baumgarten et al., *Qumran Cave 4: XXV, Halakhic Texts*, 135-54.

Eshel, Hanan. "CD 12:15-17 and the Stone Vessels Found at Qumran." In Baumgarten, Chazon, and Pinnick, *The Damascus Document*, 45-52.

————. *The Dead Sea Scrolls and the Hasmonean State*. SDSSRL. Grand Rapids: Wm. B. Eerdmans, 2008.

————. "New Information from the Dead Sea Scrolls Regarding the Sects of the Second Temple Period." In *Judea and Samaria Research Studies: Proceedings of the 3rd Annual Meeting — 1993*, ed. Ze'ev H. Erlich and Ya'acov Eshel, 147-55. Kedumim-Ariel: College of Judea and Samaria, 1994. [Hebrew]

————. "Three New Fragments from Qumran Cave 11." *DSD* 8 (2001) 1-8.

————, and David Amit. *Refuge Caves of the Bar Kokhba Revolt*. Jerusalem: Israel Exploration Society, 1998. [Hebrew]

————, and Magen Broshi. "Excavations at Qumran, Summer of 2001." *IEJ* 53 (2003) 61-73.

————, and Zvi Greenhut. "Ḥiam el-Sagha, A Cemetery of the Qumran Type, Judaean Desert." *RB* 100 (1993) 252-59.

————, and Boaz Zissu. "A Note on the Rabbinic Phrase: 'Cast Them into the Dead Sea.'" In *Judea and Samaria Research Studies* 12, ed. Ya'acov Eshel, 91-96. Ariel: College of Judea and Samaria, 2003. [Hebrew]

————, eds. *New Studies on the Bar Kokhba Revolt: Dr. Leo Mildenberg — In Memoriam*. Ramat Gan: Bar-Ilan University Press, 2001.

Evans, Craig A. "Jesus and James, Martyrs of the Temple." In Chilton and Evans, *James the Just and Christian Origins*, 233-49.

————. *Jesus and the Ossuaries: What Jewish Burial Practices Reveal about the Beginning of Christianity*. Waco: Baylor University Press, 2003.

————. "Jewish Burial Customs and the Resurrection of Jesus." http://www.craigaevans.com/Burial_Traditions.pdf.

Falls, Thomas B., trans. *Saint Justin Martyr: Dialogue with Trypho*, ed. Michael Slusser. Washington: Catholic University of America Press, 2003.

Fantalkin, Alexander. "The Appearance of Rock-Cut Bench Tombs in Iron Age Judah as a Reflection of State Formation." In *Bene Israel: Studies in the Archaeology of Israel and the Levant during the Bronze and Iron Ages in Honour of Israel Finkelstein*, ed. Alexander Fantalkin and Assaf Yasur-Landau, 17-44. CHANE 31. Leiden: Brill, 2008.

Faust, Avraham, and Shlomo Bunimovitz. "The Judahite Rock-Cut Tomb: Family Response at a Time of Change." *IEJ* 58 (2008) 150-70.

Fedak, Janos. *Monumental Tombs of the Hellenistic Age*. Toronto: University of Toronto Press, 1990.

Fine, Steven. *Art and Judaism in the Greco-Roman World: Toward a New Jewish Archaeology*. Cambridge: Cambridge University Press, 2005.

————. "Nabratein in the Ancient Literary Sources." In *Excavations at Ancient Nabratein: Synagogue and Environs*. Eric M. Meyers and Carol L. Meyers, 3-14. Winona Lake: Eisenbrauns, 2009.

―――. "A Note on Ossuary Burial and the Resurrection of the Dead in First-Century Jerusalem." *JJS* 51 (2000) 69-76.

Fink, Amir S. "Why Did *yrh* Play the Dog? Dogs in RS 24.258 (= KTU 1.114) and 4QMMT." *AuOr* 21 (2003) 35-61.

Finkielsztejn, Gerald. "Hellenistic Jerusalem: The Evidence of the Rhodian Amphora Stamps." In *New Studies on Jerusalem: Proceedings of the Fifth Conference, December 23rd 1999*, ed. Avraham Faust and Eyal Baruch, 21*-36*. Ramat Gan: Bar-Ilan University Press, 1999.

―――. "Imported Amphoras." In Geva, *Jewish Quarter Excavations*, 3:168-83.

Firmage, Edwin. "Zoology." *ABD* 6:1109-67.

Fischer, Moshe, Mordechai Gichon, and Oren Tal. *'En Boqeq: Excavations in an Oasis on the Dead Sea*. Vol. 2: *The Officina: An Early Roman Building on the Dead Sea Shore*. Mainz: von Zabern, 2000.

Fitzmyer, Joseph A. "Crucifixion in Ancient Palestine, Qumran Literature, and the New Testament." *CBQ* 40 (1978) 493-513.

Flesher, Paul V. M. "The Story Thus Far . . . A Review Essay of *The Brother of Jesus: The Dramatic Story & Meaning of the First Archaeological Link to Jesus and His Family*, Hershel Shanks and Ben Witherington III, Harper San Francisco, New York, 2003." *Polish Journal of Biblical Research* 2/2(4) (2003) 61-80.

Flower, Barbara, and Elisabeth Rosenbaum. *The Roman Cookery Book: A Critical Translation of Cooking by Apicius for Use in the Study and the Kitchen*. London: Harrap, 1958.

Flusser, David G. *Judaism of the Second Temple Period*. Vol. 1: *Qumran and Apocalypticism*. Grand Rapids: Wm. B. Eerdmans, 2007.

―――. "Pharisees, Sadducees and Essenes in the Pesher Nahum." In *In Memory of Gedaliahu Alon: Essays in Jewish History and Philology*, ed. Menahem Dorman, Shemuel Safrai, and Menahem Stern, 133-68. Tel Aviv: Hakibbutz Hame'uchad, 1970. [Hebrew]

―――. "The Social Message from Qumran." *Journal of World History* 11 (1968) 107-15.

Foerster, Gideon. *Masada V: The Yigael Yadin Excavations 1963-1965, Final Reports*. Vol. 5: *Art and Architecture*. Jerusalem: Israel Exploration Society, 1996.

―――. "Ossilegium and Ossuaries: The Origins and Significance of a Jewish Burial Practice in the Last Decades of the 1st Century B.C. and the 1st Century A.D.." In *Abstracts of the XVth International Congress of Classical Archaeology*. Amsterdam: Allard Pierson Museum, 1998.

Fonrobert, Charlotte E. "From Separatism to Urbanism: The Dead Sea Scrolls and the Origins of the Rabbinic 'Eruv." *DSD* 11 (2004) 43-71.

Fraade, Steven D. "Interpretive Authority in the Studying Community at Qumran." *JJS* 44 (1993) 46-69.

―――. "Literary Composition and Oral Performance in Early Midrashim." *Oral Tradition* 14 (1999) 33-51.

Franklin, Norma. "The Tombs of the Kings of Israel: Two Recently Identified 9th-Century Tombs from Omride Samaria." *ZDPV* 119 (2003) 1-11.

Fredriksen, Paula. *Jesus of Nazareth, King of the Jews: A Jewish Life and the Emergence of Christianity.* New York: Knopf, 1999.

Frey, Jean-Baptiste. *Corpus Inscriptionum Iudaicarum.* Vol. 2: *Asie-Afrique.* Rome: Pontifico Istituto di Archeologia Cristiana, 1952.

Furstenberg, Yair. "Defilement Penetrating the Body: A New Understanding of Contamination in Mark 7.15." *NTS* 54 (2008) 176-200.

Gal, Zvi. "A Stone-Vessel Manufacturing Site in the Lower Galilee." *'Atiqot* 29 (1991) 25*-26*. [Hebrew]

Galor, Katharina. "Plastered Pools, A New Perspective." In Humbert and Gunneweg, *Khirbet Qumrân et 'Aïn Feskha,* 2:291-320.

————. "The Stepped Water Installations of the Sepphoris Acropolis." In Edwards and McCollough, *The Archaeology of Difference,* 201-13.

————, Jean-Baptiste Humbert, and Jürgen Zangenberg, eds. *Qumran, the Site of the Dead Sea Scrolls: Archaeological Interpretations and Debates. Proceedings of a Conference held at Brown University, November 17-19, 2002.* STDJ 57. Leiden: Brill, 2006.

García Martínez, Florentino. *Qumranica Minora.* Vol. 2: *Thematic Studies on the Dead Sea Scrolls,* ed. Eibert J. C. Tigchelaar. STDJ 64. Leiden: Brill, 2007.

————, and Eibert J. C. Tigchelaar. *The Dead Sea Scrolls Study Edition.* 2 vols. Leiden: Brill and Grand Rapids: Wm. B. Eerdmans, 1997-98.

George, Rose. *The Big Necessity: The Unmentionable World of Human Waste and Why It Matters.* New York: Metropolitan, 2008.

Geva, Hillel. "Jerusalem: The Temple Mount and Its Environs." In *NEAEHL,* 2:736-44.

————, ed. *Ancient Jerusalem Revealed.* Rev. ed. Jerusalem: Israel Exploration Society, 2000.

————. *Jewish Quarter Excavations in the Old City of Jerusalem Conducted by Nahman Avigad, 1969-1982.* Vol. 1: *Architecture and Stratigraphy: Areas A, W and X-2, Final Report.* Jerusalem: Israel Exploration Society, 2000.

————. *Jewish Quarter Excavations in the Old City of Jerusalem Conducted by Nahman Avigad, 1969-1982.* Vol. 2: *The Finds from Areas A, W and X-2, Final Report.* Jerusalem: Israel Exploration Society, 2003.

————. *Jewish Quarter Excavations in the Old City of Jerusalem Conducted by Nahman Avigad, 1969-1982.* Vol. 3: *Area E and Other Studies, Final Report.* Jerusalem: Israel Exploration Society, 2006.

————, and Malka Hershkovitz. "Local Pottery of the Hellenistic and Early Roman Periods." In *Jewish Quarter Excavations,* 3:94-143.

————, and Renate Rosenthal-Heginbottom. "Local Pottery from Area A." In Geva, *Jewish Quarter Excavations,* 2:176-91.

Gibson, Shimon. "The Pool of Bethesda in Jerusalem and Jewish Purification Practices of the Second Temple Period." *Proche-Orient Chrétien* 55 (2005) 270-93.

————. "The Stone Vessel Industry at Hizma." *IEJ* 33 (1983) 176-88.

————. "Stone Vessels of the Early Roman Period from Jerusalem and Palestine: A Reassessment." In *One Land — Many Cultures: Archaeological Studies in Honour of*

Bibliography

Stanislao Loffreda, ed. G. Claudio Bottini, Leah Di Segni, and L. Daniel Chrupcała, 287-308. Jerusalem: Franciscan, 2003.

————. "The Tell el-Judeideh (Tel Goded) Excavations: A Re-Appraisal Based on Archival Records in the Palestine Exploration Fund." *Tel Aviv* 21 (1994) 194-234.

Gilat, Yitzhak D. *Studies in the Development of the Halakha*. Ramat Gan: Bar-Ilan University Press, 1992. [Hebrew]

Gill, Christopher, ed., and Robin Hard, trans. *The Discourses of Epictetus*. Rutland: Tuttle, 1995.

Goldenberg, Robert. "The Jewish Sabbath in the Roman World up to the Time of Constantine the Great." In *Aufstieg und Niedergang der römischen Welt*. Vol. 2.19.1: *Principat, Religion (Judentum: Allgemeines; Palästinisches Judentum)*, ed. Wolfgang Haase, 414-47. Berlin: de Gruyter, 1979.

Goldin, Judah, trans. *The Fathers According to Rabbi Nathan*. Yale Judaica 10. New Haven: Yale University Press, 1955.

Goodblatt, David. "The Place of the Pharisees in First Century Judaism: The State of the Debate." *JSJ* 20 (1989) 12-30.

————, Avital Pinnick, and Daniel R. Schwartz, eds. *Historical Perspectives: From the Hasmoneans to Bar Kokhba in Light of the Dead Sea Scrolls*. Proceedings of the Fourth International Symposium of the Orion Center for the Study of the Dead Sea Scrolls and Associated Literature, 27-31 January, 1999. STDJ 37. Leiden: Brill, 2001.

Goodfriend, Elaine Adler. "Could *keleb* in Deuteronomy 23:19 Actually Refer to a Canine?" In Wright, Freedman, and Hurvitz, *Pomegranates and Golden Bells*, 381-97.

Goodman, Martin D. "A Note on the Qumran Sectarians, the Essenes and Josephus." *JJS* 46 (1995) 161-66.

————. "The Purpose of Room F." In *Excavations at Ancient Meiron, Upper Galilee, Israel, 1971-72, 1974-75, 1977*, ed. Eric M. Meyers, James F. Strange, and Carol L. Meyers, 71-72. Cambridge, MA: American Schools of Oriental Research, 1981.

————. "Religious Variety and the Temple in the Late Second Temple Period and Its Aftermath." *JJS* 60 (2009) 202-13.

————. *The Ruling Class of Judaea: The Origins of the Jewish Revolt against Rome, A.D. 66-70*. Cambridge: Cambridge University Press, 1987.

————. "Sacred Scripture and 'Defiling the Hands.'" *JTS* 41 (1990) 99-107.

————. "Sadducees and Essenes after 70 C.E.." In *Crossing the Boundaries: Essays in Biblical Interpretation in Honour of Michael D. Goulder*, ed. Stanley E. Porter, Paul Joyce, and David E. Orton, 347-56. Biblical Interpretation 8. Leiden: Brill, 1994.

————. "Texts, Scribes, and Power in Roman Judaea." In *Literacy and Power in the Ancient World*, ed. Alan K. Bowman and Greg D. Woolf, 99-108. Cambridge: Cambridge University Press, 1994.

Goody, Jack. *Cooking, Cuisine, and Class: A Study in Comparative Sociology*. Cambridge: Cambridge University Press, 1982.

Gorin-Rosen, Yael. "Glass Vessels." In Geva, *Jewish Quarter Excavations*, 3:239-65.

————. "Glass Vessels from Area A." In Geva, *Jewish Quarter Excavations,* 2:364-93.

————, and Natalya Katsnelson. "Refuse of a Glass Workshop of the Second Temple Period from Area J." In Geva, *Jewish Quarter Excavations,* 3:411-60.

Grainger, Sally. *Cooking Apicius: Roman Recipes for Today.* Devon: Prospect, 2006.

Green, Deborah. "Sweet Spices in the Tomb: An Initial Study on the Use of Perfume in Jewish Burials." In Brink and Green, *Commemorating the Dead,* 145-73.

Greenhut, Zvi. "Burial Cave of the Caiaphas Family." *BAR* 18/5 (1992) 28-36, 76.

Grossberg, Asher. "Cooking Pots with Holes Found in Jerusalem and the Customs of Haverim and Amei ha-Aretz." In *New Studies on Jerusalem,* ed. Eyal Baruch and Avraham Faust, 8:59-71. Ramat-Gan: Ingeborg Rennert Center for Jerusalem Studies, Bar-Ilan University, 2002. [Hebrew with English summary, 11*]

————. "The *Miqva'ot* (Ritual Baths) at Masada." In *Masada VIII,* 95-126.

————. "Ritual Baths in Second Temple Period Jerusalem and How They Were Ritually Prepared." *Jerusalem Cathedra* 83 (1996) 151-68. [Hebrew]

Grossmark, Ziona. "'And He Declared Impurity on Glass Vessels': A Reexamination of the Historical Background for the Beginning of Laws of Impurity and Purity of Glass Vessels." *Jerusalem Cathedra* 127 (2008) 33-54. [Hebrew]

Guggenheimer, Heinrich W. *The Jerusalem Talmud.* Berlin: de Gruyter, 2000.

Gunneweg, Jan, and Marta Balla. "Neutron Activation Analysis, Scroll Jars and Common Ware." In Humbert and Gunneweg, *Khirbet Qumrân et 'Aïn Feshkha* 2:3-53.

Haber, Susan. *"They Shall Purify Themselves": Essays on Purity in Early Judaism,* ed. Adele Reinhartz. SBLEJL 24. Atlanta: Society of Biblical Literature, 2008.

Hacham, Noah. "Communal Fasts in the Judean Desert Scrolls." In Goodblatt, Pinnick, and Schwartz, *Historical Perspectives,* 127-45.

Hachlili, Rachel. "The Coins." In *Jericho,* 135-36.

————. "The Goliath Family in Jericho: Funerary Inscriptions from a First Century A.D. Jewish Monumental Tomb." *BASOR* 235 (1979) 31-65.

————. "The Inscriptions." In *Jericho,* 142-58.

————. "Ossuaries." In *Jericho,* 93-114.

————. "The Wall Painting." In *Jericho,* 157-61.

————, and Ann E. Killebrew. *Jericho: The Jewish Cemetery of the Second Temple Period.* IAA Reports 7. Jerusalem: Israel Antiquities Authority, 1999.

————. "Jewish Funerary Customs during the Second Temple Period in the Light of the Excavations at the Jericho Necropolis." *PEQ* 115 (1983) 109-32.

————, and Patricia Smith. "The Genealogy of the Goliath Family." *BASOR* 235 (1979) 67-70.

Hadas, Gideon. *Nine Tombs of the Second Temple Period at 'En Gedi.* 'Atiqot 24. Jerusalem: Israel Antiquities Authority, 1994.

Halperin, David J. "Crucifixion, the Nahum Pesher, and the Rabbinic Penalty of Strangulation." *JJS* 32 (1981) 32-46.

Hammett, John S. "Camel." In *EDB,* 212.

Harrington, Hannah K. "Did the Pharisees Eat Ordinary Food in a State of Ritual Purity?" *JSJ* 26 (1995) 42-54.

————. "Holiness and Law in the Dead Sea Scrolls." *DSD* 8 (2001) 124-35.

Bibliography

————. *The Purity Texts*. London: T. & T. Clark, 2004.

Hayes, Christine E. *Gentile Impurities and Jewish Identities: Intermarriage and Conversion from the Bible to the Talmud*. Oxford: Oxford University Press, 2002.

Hempel, Charlotte, ed. *The Dead Sea Scrolls: Texts and Context*. STDJ 90. Leiden: Brill, 2010.

Hengel, Martin. *Crucifixion in the Ancient World and the Folly of the Message of the Cross*. Philadelphia: Fortress, 1977.

————. *Judaism and Hellenism*. 2 vols. Philadelphia: Fortress, 1974.

Henschke, David. "The Sanctity of Jerusalem: The Sages and Sectarian Halakhah." *Tarbiz* 66 (1997) 5-28. [Hebrew]

Herbert, Sharon C. *Tel Anafa*. Vol. 1/1-2: *Final Report on Ten Years of Excavation at a Hellenistic and Roman Settlement in Northern Israel*. JRASup 10. Ann Arbor: Kelsey Museum, University of Michigan, 1994.

————. *Tel Anafa*. Vol. 2/1-2: *The Hellenistic and Roman Pottery*. JRASup 10. Ann Arbor: Kelsey Museum, University of Michigan, 1998.

Hershkovitz, Malka. "Jerusalemite Painted Pottery from the Late Second Temple Period." In *The Nabataeans in the Negev*, ed. Renate Rosenthal-Heginbottom, 31*-34*. Haifa: Hecht Museum, 2003.

Hezser, Catherine. *Jewish Slavery in Antiquity*. Oxford: Oxford University Press, 2005.

————. *The Social Structure of the Rabbinic Movement in Roman Palestine*. TSAJ 66. Tübingen: Mohr Siebeck, 1997.

Himmelfarb, Martha. "Impurity and Sin in 4QD, 1QS, and 4Q512." *DSD* 8 (2001) 9-37.

————. *A Kingdom of Priests: Ancestry and Merit in Ancient Judaism*. Philadelphia: University of Pennsylvania Press, 2006.

Hirschfeld, Yizhar. "Early Roman Manor Houses in Judea and the Site of Khirbet Qumran." *JNES* 57 (1998) 161-89.

————. *En-Gedi Excavations II: Final Report (1996-2002)*. Jerusalem: Israel Exploration Society, 2007.

————. "Excavations at 'Ein Feshkha, 2001." *IEJ* 54 (2004) 37-74.

————. *The Palestinian Dwelling in the Roman-Byzantine Period*. Jerusalem: Franciscan, 1995.

————. *Qumran in Context: Reassessing the Archaeological Evidence*. Peabody: Hendrickson, 2004.

————, ed. *Ramat Hanadiv Excavations: Final Report of the 1984-1998 Seasons*. Jerusalem: Israel Exploration Society, 2000.

————, and Donald T. Ariel. "A Coin Assemblage from the Reign of Alexander Jannaeus Found on the Shore of the Dead Sea." *IEJ* 55 (2005) 66-89.

Hobson, Barry. *Latrinae et Foricae: Toilets in the Roman World*. London: Duckworth, 2009.

Hodge, A. Trevor. *Roman Aqueducts and Water Supply*. London: Duckworth, 1992.

Hoglund, Kenneth G., and Eric M. Meyers. "The Residential Quarter on the Western Summit." In *Sepphoris in Galilee: Crosscurrents of Culture*, ed. Rebecca Martin Nagy, Carol L. Meyers, Eric M. Meyers, and Zeev Weiss, 38-49. Raleigh: North Carolina Museum of Art, 1996.

Horan, Julie L. *The Porcelain God: A Social History of the Toilet.* Secaucus: Birch Lane, 1996.

Horwitz, Liora Kolska. "Faunal Remains from Areas A, B, D, H and K." In Ariel and de Groot, *Excavations at the City of David 1978-1985,* 4:302-17.

————, and Eitan Tchernov. "Bird Remains from Areas A, D, H and K." In Ariel and de Groot, *Excavations at the City of David 1978-1985,* 4:298-301.

————. "Subsistence Patterns in Ancient Jerusalem: A Study of Animal Remains." In *Excavations in the South of the Temple Mount: The Ophel of Biblical Jerusalem,* ed. Eilat Mazar and Benjamin Mazar, 144-54. Qedem 29. Jerusalem: Institute of Archaeology, Hebrew University, 1989.

Hultgren, Stephen. *From the Damascus Covenant to the Covenant of the Community: Literary, Historical, and Theological Studies in the Dead Sea Scrolls.* STDJ 66. Leiden: Brill, 2007.

Humbert, Jean-Baptiste, and Alain Chambon. *Fouilles de Khirbet Qumrân et de Aïn Feshkha.* Vol. 1: *Synthèse des notes de chantier du père Roland de Vaux, OP.* NTOA SA 3. Fribourg: Éditions universitaires and Göttingen: Vandenhoeck & Ruprecht, 1994.

————, and Jan Gunneweg. *Khirbet Qumrân et ʿAïn Feshkha.* Vol. 2: *Études d'anthropologie, de physique et de chimie.* NTOA SA 3. Fribourg: Academic and Göttingen: Vandenhoeck & Ruprecht, 2003.

Ilan, Tal. "The Ossuary and Sarcophagus Inscriptions." In Avni and Greenhut, *The Akeldama Tombs,* 57-72.

Instone-Brewer, David. *Prayer and Agriculture.* TRENT 1. Grand Rapids: Wm. B. Eerdmans, 2004.

Irshai, Oded. "Yaakov of Naburaya — A Sage who Erred in Heterodoxy." *Jerusalem Studies in Jewish Thought* 2/2 (1982/83) 153-68. [Hebrew]

Itah, Michel. "Ritual Baths in the Hill Country of the Benjamin Region." In *Judea and Samaria Research Studies* 11, ed. Yaʿacov Eshel, 81-90. Ariel: College of Judea and Samaria, 2002. [Hebrew]

Jackson-Tal, Ruth E. "Glass Vessels from En-Gedi." In Hirschfeld, *En-Gedi Excavations II,* 474-506.

Jacobovici, Simha, and Charles Pellegrino. *The Jesus Family Tomb: The Discovery, the Investigation, and the Evidence That Could Change History.* New York: HarperCollins, 2007.

Jagersma, Henk. *A History of Israel from Alexander the Great to Bar Kochba.* Philadelphia: Fortress, 1986.

Jastram, Nathan. "Hierarchy at Qumran." In Bernstein, García Martínez, and Kampen, *Legal Texts and Legal Issues,* 349-76.

Katsnelson, Natalya. "Early Roman Glass Vessels from Judea — Locally Produced Glass? Preliminary Report." In Patrich and Amit, *New Studies in the Archaeology of Jerusalem and Its Region,* 5*-11*.

Kazen, Thomas. *Jesus and Purity Halakhah: Was Jesus Indifferent to Impurity?* ConBNT 38. Stockholm: Almqvist & Wiksell, 2002.

Kelhoffer, James A. "Did John the Baptist Eat Like a Former Essene? Locust-Eating in the Ancient Near East and at Qumran." *DSD* 11 (2004) 293-314.

Kindler, Arie. "Coins." In Fischer, Gichon, and Tal, *'En Boqeq*, 2:85-92.

——. "Coins from the Cave of Letters (1999-2000 Seasons)." In Eshel and Zissu, *New Studies on the Bar Kokhba Revolt*, 11-15.

Kislev, Mordechai, and Orit Simchoni. "Hygiene and Insect Damage of Crops and Foods at Masada." In *Masada VIII*, 133-70.

Kister, Menahem. "Law, Morality, and Rhetoric in Some Sayings of Jesus." In Kugel, *Studies in Ancient Midrash*, 145-54.

——. " 'Leave the Dead to Bury Their Own Dead.' " In Kugel, *Studies in Ancient Midrash*, 43-56.

Klawans, Jonathan. *Impurity and Sin in Ancient Judaism*. Oxford: Oxford University Press, 2000.

——. *Purity, Sacrifice, and the Temple: Symbolism and Supersessionism in the Study of Ancient Judaism*. Oxford: Oxford University Press, 2006.

Kleiner, Diana E. E. *Roman Sculpture*. New Haven: Yale University Press, 1992.

Kloner, Amos. "Did a Rolling Stone Close Jesus' Tomb?" *BAR* 25/5 (1999) 22-29, 76.

——. "A Tomb with Inscribed Ossuaries in East Talpiyot, Jerusalem." *'Atiqot* 29 (1996) 15-22.

——, and Yigal Tepper. *The Hiding Complexes in the Judean Shephelah*. Tel Aviv: Hakibbutz Hameuchad, 1987. [Hebrew]

——, and Boaz Zissu. "Hiding Complexes in the Lydda Area and the Northern Border of the Bar Kokhba Administration." In Eshel and Zissu, *New Studies on the Bar Kokhba Revolt*, 73-85.

——. *The Necropolis of Jerusalem in the Second Temple Period*. Leuven: Peeters, 2007.

Kon, Maximilian. *The Tombs of the Kings*. Tel Aviv: Dvir, 1947. [Hebrew]

Kottek, Samuel S. "The Essenes and Medicine." *Clio medica* 18 (1983) 81-99.

——. *Medicine and Hygiene in the Works of Flavius Josephus*. Leiden: Brill, 1994.

Kraeling, Carl. *The Excavations at Dura-Europos: The Synagogue*. New Haven: Yale University Press, 1956.

Kugel, James L., ed. *Studies in Ancient Midrash*. Cambridge, MA: Harvard University Press, 2001.

Kugler, Rob. "Making All Experience Religious: The Hegemony of Ritual at Qumran." *JSJ* 33 (2002) 131-52.

Lambrecht, Jan. "Jesus and the Law, An Investigation of Mk 7,1-23." *ETL* 53 (1977) 24-82.

Lange, Armin. "The Meaning of Dema' in the Copper Scroll and Ancient Jewish Literature." In *Copper Scroll Studies*, ed. George J. Brooke and Philip R. Davies, 122-38. JSPSup 40. Sheffield: Sheffield Academic, 2002.

Larson, Erik, Manfred R. Lehmann, and Lawrence Schiffman. "4QHalakha A." In Baumgarten et al., *Qumran Cave 4: XXV, Halakhic Texts*, 25-51.

Lawrence, Jonathan David. *Washing in Water: Trajectories of Ritual Bathing in the Hebrew Bible and Second Temple Literature*. Atlanta: Society of Biblical Literature, 2006.

Leiman, Sid Z. *The Canonization of Hebrew Scripture: The Talmudic and Midrashic Evi-*

dence. Transactions of the Connecticut Academy of Arts and Sciences 47, 1-234. Hamden: Archon, 1976.

Lemaire, André. "Burial Box of James the Brother of Jesus." *BAR* 28/6 (2002) 24-33, 70.

Lenski, Gerhard E. *Power and Privilege: A Theory of Social Stratification.* New York: McGraw-Hill, 1966.

Lernau, Hanan. "Geflügel- und Fischknochen aus 'En Boqeq." In Fischer, Gichon, and Tal, *'En Boqeq,* 2:149-81.

Levenson, Jon D. *Resurrection and the Restoration of Israel: The Ultimate Victory of the God of Life.* New Haven: Yale University Press, 2006.

Levine, Amy-Jill. "Discharging Responsibility: Matthean Jesus, Biblical Law, and Hemorrhaging Woman." In *A Feminist Companion to Matthew,* 70-87. Sheffield: Sheffield Academic, 2001.

———. "Luke's Pharisees." In Neusner and Chilton, *In Quest of the Historical Pharisees,* 113-30.

Levine, David. "Communal Fasts in Talmudic Literature — Theory and Practice." Ph.D. diss. Jerusalem: Department of Talmud at the Hebrew University, 1998. [Hebrew]

Levine, Lee I. *Jerusalem: Portrait of the City in the Second Temple Period (538 B.C.E.–70 C.E.).* Philadelphia: Jewish Publication Society, 2002.

Lichtenberger, Hermann. "The Dead Sea Scrolls and John the Baptist: Reflections on Josephus' Account of John the Baptist." In Dimant and Rappaport, *The Dead Sea Scrolls,* 340-46.

Lichtenstein, Yechezkel S. *Consecrating the Profane: Rituals performed and prayers recited at cemeteries and burial sites of the pious.* Tel-Aviv: Hakibbutz Hameuchad, 2007. [Hebrew]

Lieberman, Saul. "The Discipline in the So-Called Dead Sea Manual of Discipline." *JBL* 71 (1952) 199-206.

Lightstone, Jack N. "Sadducees versus Pharisees." In *Christianity, Judaism, and Other Greco-Roman Cults: Studies for Morton Smith at Sixty,* ed. Jacob Neusner, 206-17. SJLA 12. Leiden: Brill, 1975.

Lim, Timothy H. "The Defilement of the Hands as a Principle Determining the Holiness of Scriptures." *JTS* 2010. Published online 24 June 2010.

———. "The Pharisees and the Sadducees in the Earliest Rabbinic Documents." In Neusner and Chilton, *In Quest of the Historical Pharisees,* 255-96.

Liver, Jacob. "The Half-Shekel Offering in Biblical and Post-Biblical Literature." *HTR* 56 (1963) 173-98.

Lönnqvuist, Kenneth, and Minna Lönnqvuist. "The Numismatic Chronology of Qumran: Fact and Fiction." *Numismatic Chronicle* 166 (2006) 121-65.

Maccoby, Hyam. *Ritual and Morality: The Ritual Purity System and Its Place in Judaism.* Cambridge: Cambridge University Press, 1999.

Magen, Yitzhak. "Jerusalem as a Center of the Stone Vessel Industry during the Second Temple Period." In Geva, *Ancient Jerusalem Revealed,* 244-56.

———. "The Land of Benjamin in the Second Temple Period." In *The Land of Benjamin,* 1-28.

———. "Qalandiya: A Second Temple-period Viticulture and Wine-manufacturing Agricultural Settlement." In *The Land of Benjamin*, 29-144.

———. "The Ritual Baths *(Miqva'ot)* at Qedumim and the Observance of Ritual Purity among the Samaritans." In Manns and Alliata, *Early Christianity in Context*, 181-92.

———. *The Stone Vessel Industry in the Second Temple Period: Excavations at Hizma and the Jerusalem Temple Mount.* Jerusalem: Israel Exploration Society, 2002.

———, and Yuval Peleg. "Back to Qumran: Ten Years of Excavation and Research." In Galor, Humbert, and Zangenberg, *Qumran, the Site of the Dead Sea Scrolls*, 55-113.

———, Yoav Tzionit, and Orna Sirkis. "Khirbet Badd 'Isa — Qiryat Sefer." In *The Land of Benjamin*, 179-241.

———, et al. *The Land of Benjamin.* Jerusalem: Israel Antiquities Authority, 2004.

Magness, Jodi. *The Archaeology of Qumran and the Dead Sea Scrolls.* SDSSRL. Grand Rapids: Wm. B. Eerdmans, 2002.

———. *Debating Qumran: Collected Essays on Its Archaeology.* Leuven: Peeters, 2004.

———. "Heaven on Earth: Helios and the Zodiac Cycle in Ancient Palestinian Synagogues." *Dumbarton Oaks Papers* 59 (2005) 1-52.

———. "The Mausolea of Augustus, Alexander, and Herod the Great." In *Hesed ve-Emet*, 313-39.

———. "A Near Eastern Ethnic Element among the Etruscan Elite?" *Etruscan Studies* 8 (2001) 79-117.

———. "Ossuaries and the Burials of Jesus and James." *JBL* 124 (2005) 121-54.

———. "Qumran: The Site of the Dead Sea Scrolls: A Review Article." *RevQ* 88 (2007) 641-64.

———. Review of Fischer, Gichon, and Tal, *'En Boqeq. AJA* 106 (2002) 346-47.

———. Review of Bar-Nathan, *The Pottery. DSD* 10 (2003) 420-28.

———. Review of Hirschfeld, *Qumran in Context. RBL* (August 2005): http://www.bookreviews.org/BookDetail.asp?TitleId=4500.

———. "The Roman Legionary Pottery." In Arubas and Goldfus, *Excavations on the Site of the Jerusalem International Convention Center*, 69-191.

———. "Toilet Practices at Qumran: A Response." *RevQ* 86 (2006) 277-78.

———. "A Villa at Khirbet Qumran?" *RevQ* 63 (2004) 397-419.

———, and Seymour Gitin, eds. *Hesed ve-Emet: Studies in Honor of Ernest S. Frerichs.* BJS 320. Atlanta: Scholars, 1998.

Manns, Frédéric, and Eugenio Alliata, eds. *Early Christianity in Context: Monuments and Documents.* SBFCM 38. Jerusalem: Franciscan, 1993.

Marcus, Joel. *Mark 1–8.* AB 27. New York: Doubleday, 1999.

Masada: The Yigael Yadin Excavations 1963-1965. Final Reports. 8 vols. Jerusalem: Israel Exploration Society, 1989-2007.

Mason, Steve. *Flavius Josephus on the Pharisees.* StPB 39. Leiden: Brill, 2001.

———. "Josephus' Pharisees: The Narratives." In Neusner and Chilton, *In Quest of the Historical Pharisees*, 3-40.

————. "Josephus' Pharisees: The Philosophy." In Neusner and Chilton, *In Quest of the Historical Pharisees*, 41-66.

————. "Pharisaic Dominance before 70 c.e. and the Gospels' Hypocrisy Charge (Matt 23:2-3)." *HTR* 83 (1990) 363-81.

Matassa, Lidia. "Unravelling the Myth of the Synagogue on Delos." *Bulletin of the Anglo-Israel Archaeological Society* 25 (2007) 81-115.

Maynard-Reid, Pedrito U. *Poverty and Wealth in James.* Maryknoll: Orbis, 1987.

Mazar, Amihai. *Archaeology of the Land of the Bible 10,000-586 b.c.e.* ABRL. New York: Doubleday, 1990.

Mazar, Benjamin. *Beth She'arim: Report on the Excavations during 1936-1940.* Vol. 1: *Catacombs 1-4.* New Brunswick: Rutgers University Press, 1973.

McCane, Byron R. *Roll Back the Stone: Death and Burial in the World of Jesus.* Harrisburg: Trinity, 2003.

McCready, Wayne O., and Adele Reinhartz, eds. *Common Judaism: Explorations in Second-Temple Judaism.* Minneapolis: Fortress, 2008.

McLaren, James S. "Ananus, James, and Earliest Christianity: Josephus' Account of the Death of James." *JTS* 52 (2001) 1-25.

Meier, John P. *A Marginal Jew: Rethinking the Historical Jesus.* 4 vols. ABRL. New York: Doubleday, 1991-2009.

————. "Matthew, Gospel of." *ABD* 4:622-41.

Meshorer, Ya'akov. "The Coins." In Netzer, *Hasmonean and Herodian Palaces* 2:289-312. Jerusalem: Israel Exploration Society, 2004.

————. "The Coins of Masada." In Yadin, Naveh, and Meshorer, *Masada I*, 71-132.

————. "One Hundred Ninety Years of Tyrian Shekels." In *Festschrift für/Studies in Honor of Leo Mildenberg: Numismatics, Art History, Archaeology*, ed. Arthur Houghton, Silvia Hurter, Patricia Erhart Mottahedeh, and Jane Ayer Scott, 171-79. Wetteren: Editions NR, 1984.

Meyers, Eric M. *Jewish Ossuaries: Rebirth and Birth.* BibOr 24. Rome: Biblical Institute Press, 1971.

Michniewicz, Jacek, and Miroslaw Krzysko. "The Provenance of Scroll Jars in the Light of Archaeometric Investigations." In Humbert and Gunneweg, *Khirbet Qumrân et 'Aïn Feshkha*, 2:59-99.

Milgrom, Jacob. "Deviations from Scripture in the Purity Laws of the *Temple Scroll*." In Talmon, *Jewish Civilization in the Hellenistic-Roman Period*, 159-67.

————. "First Day Ablutions in Qumran." In Barrera and Montaner, *The Madrid Qumran Congress*, 2:561-70.

————. *Leviticus 1–16.* AB 3. New York: Doubleday, 1991.

————. "The Scriptural Foundations and Deviations in the Laws of Purity of the *Temple Scroll*." In Schiffman, *Archaeology and History in the Dead Sea Scrolls*, 82-99.

————. "Systemic Differences in the Priestly Corpus: A Response to Jonathan Klawans." *RB* 112 (2005) 321-29.

————. "Two Biblical Hebrew Priestly Terms: Šeqes and Tame'." *Maarav* 8 (1992) 107-16.

Bibliography

Milikowsky, Chaim. "Reflections on Hand-Washing, Hand-Purity and Holy Scripture in Rabbinic Literature." In Poorthuis and Schwartz, *Purity and Holiness*, 149-62.

Millard, Alan. Review of Hélène Nutkowicz, *L'homme face à la mort au royaume de Juda: Rites pratiques et représentations*. Paris: Cerf, 2006. *JJS* 60 (2009) 320-23.

Miller, Geoffrey D. "Attitudes toward Dogs in Ancient Israel: A Reassessment." *JSOT* 32 (2008) 487-500.

Miller, Stuart S. "Priests, Purities, and the Jews of Galilee." In Zangenberg, Attridge, and Martin, *Religion, Ethnicity, and Identity in Ancient Galilee*, 375-402.

————. "Stepped Pools and the Non-Existent Monolithic 'Miqveh.'" In Edwards and McCollough, *The Archaeology of Difference*, 215-34.

Mizzi, Dennis J. "The Glass from Khirbet Qumran: What Does It Tell Us about the Qumran Community?" In Hempel, *The Dead Sea Scrolls*, 99-198.

Moo, Douglas J. *The Letter of James*. Pillar. Grand Rapids: Wm. B. Eerdmans, 2000.

Moore, Clifford H. Review of Albrecht Dieterich, *Kleine Schriften, mit einem Bildniss und zwei Tafeln*. *CP* 9 (1914) 103-7.

Morley, Neville. "The Poor in the City of Rome." In Atkins and Osborne, *Poverty in the Roman World*, 21-39.

Morris, Ian. *Burial and Ancient Society: The Rise of the Greek City-State*. Cambridge: Cambridge University Press, 1987.

Murphy, Catherine M. *Wealth in the Dead Sea Scrolls and in the Qumran Community*. STDJ 40. Leiden: Brill, 2002.

Murphy-O'Connor, Jerome. Review of Kloner and Zissu, *The Necropolis of Jerusalem in the Second Temple Period*. *RB* 115 (2008) 448-55.

Nagar, Yossi, and Hagit Torgee. "Biological Characteristics of Jewish Burial in the Hellenistic and Early Roman Period." *IEJ* 53 (2003) 164-71.

Naveh, Joseph. "An Aramaic Tomb Inscription Written in Paleo-Hebrew Script." *IEJ* 23 (1973) 82-91.

Negev, Avraham. "Kurnub." In *NEAEHL*, 3:882-93.

————, and Shimon Gibson, eds. *Archaeological Encyclopedia of the Holy Land*. New York: Continuum, 2001.

Netzer, Ehud. *The Architecture of Herod, the Great Builder*. TSAJ 117. Tübingen: Mohr Siebeck, 2006.

————. *Hasmonean and Herodian Palaces at Jericho*. Vol. 1: *Stratigraphy and Architecture*. Jerusalem: Israel Exploration Society, 2001.

————. *Masada III: The Yigael Yadin Excavations 1963-1965, Final Reports*. Vol. 3: *The Buildings, Stratigraphy and Architecture*. Jerusalem: Israel Exploration Society, 1991.

————. *The Palaces of the Hasmoneans and Herod the Great*. Jerusalem: Yad Ben-Zvi, 2001.

————, ed. *Hasmonean and Herodian Palaces at Jericho: Final Reports of the 1973-1987 Excavations*. 4 vols. Jerusalem: Israel Exploration Society, 2001-2008.

————, Yaakov Kalman, Roi Porath, and Rachel Chachy-Laureys. "Herod's Tomb — Finally Revealed." In *Judea and Samaria Research Studies* 17, ed. Ya'acov Eshel, 57-67. Ariel: College of Judea and Samaria, 2008. [Hebrew]

————, Yaakov Kalman, Roi Porath, Rachel Chachy, Leah DiSegni, and Esther Eshel. "Two Inscriptions from Herodium." In *Judea and Samaria Research* 18, ed. Ya'acov Eshel, 85-103. Ariel: College of Judea and Samaria, 2009. [Hebrew]

Neudecker, Richard. *Die Pracht der Latrine: Zum Wandel öffentlicher Bedürfnisanstalten in der kaiserzeitlichen Stadt.* Munich: Pfeil, 1994.

Neusner, Jacob. *A History of the Mishnaic Law of Purities.* Part 22: *The Mishnaic System of Uncleanness, Context and History.* SJLA 6. Leiden: Brill, 1977.

————. *The Idea of Purity in Ancient Judaism.* SJLA 1. Leiden: Brill, 1973.

————. *The Mishnah, A New Translation.* New Haven: Yale University Press, 1988.

————. "The Pharisaic Agenda: Laws Attributed in the Mishnah and the Tosefta to Pre-70 Pharisees." In Neusner and Chilton, *In Quest of the Historical Pharisees,* 313-28.

————. "The Rabbinic Traditions about the Pharisees before 70 c.e.: An Overview." In *In Quest of the Historical Pharisees,* 297-312.

————. *The Talmud of the Land of Israel: A Preliminary Translation and Explanation.* Chicago: University of Chicago Press, 1982-1993.

————. *The Tosefta: Translated from the Hebrew with a New Introduction.* 2 vols. Peabody: Hendrickson, 2002.

————, and Bruce D. Chilton, eds. *In Quest of the Historical Pharisees.* Waco: Baylor University Press, 2007.

Newman, Hillel. *Proximity to Power and Jewish Sectarian Groups of the Ancient Period: A Review of Lifestyle, Values, and Halakhah in the Pharisees, Sadducees, Essenes, and Qumran.* Ed. Ruth Ludlam. Leiden: Brill, 2006.

Niederwimmer, Kurt. *The Didache.* Minneapolis: Fortress, 1998.

Noam, Vered. "Beit Shammai and the Sectarian Halakhah." *Jewish Studies (World Union of Jewish Studies)* 41 (2002) 45-67. [Hebrew]

————. "The Bounds of Non-Priestly Purity: A Reassessment." *Zion* 72 (2007) 127-60. [Hebrew]

————. "From Philology to History: The Sectarian Dispute, as Portrayed in the Scholium to *Megillat Ta'anit.*" In *Recent Developments in Midrash Research: Proceedings of the 2002 and 2003 SBL Consultation on Midrash,* ed. Lieve M. Teugels and Rikva Ulmer, 53-95. Piscataway: Gorgias, 2005.

————. "Qumran and the Rabbis on Corpse-Impurity: Common Exegesis — Tacit Polemic." In Hempel, *The Dead Sea Scrolls,* 397-430.

————. "Traces of Sectarian Halakhah in the Rabbinic World." In Orion Center for the Study of the Dead Sea Scrolls, *Rabbinic Perspectives,* 67-85.

————, and Elisha Qimron. "A Qumran Composition of Sabbath Laws and Its Contribution to the Study of Early Halakah." *DSD* 16 (2009) 55-96.

O'Collins, Gerald. "Crucifixion." *ABD* 1:1207-10.

Onn, Alexander, Shlomit Wexler-Bdolah, Yehuda Rapuano, and Tzaḥ Kanias. "Khirbet Umm el-'Umdan." *Hadashot Arkheologiyot (Excavations and Surveys in Israel)* 114 (2002) 64*-68*.

Oppenheimer, Aharon. *The 'Am Ha-aretz: A Study in the Social History of the Jewish People in the Hellenistic-Roman Period.* ALGHJ 8. Leiden: Brill, 1977.

Bibliography

Orion Center for the Study of the Dead Sea Scrolls and Associated Literature. *Rabbinic Perspectives: Rabbinic Literature and the Dead Sea Scrolls.* Proceedings of the Eighth International Symposium, 7-9 January, 2003, ed. Steven D. Fraade, Aharon Shemesh, and Ruth A. Clements. STDJ 62. Leiden: Brill, 2006.

Painter, John. *Just James: The Brother of Jesus in History and Tradition.* Columbia: University of South Carolina Press, 1997.

Parker, Robert. *MIASMA: Pollution and Purification in Early Greek Religion.* Oxford: Clarendon, 1983.

Patrich, Joseph. "Graves and Burial Practices in Talmudic Sources." In Zinger, *Graves and Burial Practices in Israel in the Ancient Period,* 190-211. [Hebrew]

————, and David Amit, eds. *New Studies in the Archaeology of Jerusalem and Its Region.* Vol. 1. Jerusalem: Israel Antiquities Authority and Hebrew University, 2007. [Hebrew]

————, and Benny Arubas. "A Juglet Containing Balsam Oil (?) from a Cave near Qumran." *IEJ* 39 (1989) 43-59.

Patterson, John R. "Living and Dying in the City of Rome: Houses and Tombs." In *Ancient Rome: The Archaeology of the Eternal City,* ed. Jon Coulston and Hazel Dodge, 259-89. Oxford: Oxford University School of Archaeology, 2000.

Paul, Shalom M., Robert A. Kraft, Lawrence H. Schiffman, and Weston W. Fields, eds. *Emanuel: Studies in Hebrew Bible, Septuagint, and Dead Sea Scrolls in Honor of Emanuel Tov.* VTSup 94. Leiden: Brill, 2003.

Peacock, David P. S., and D. F. Williams. *Amphorae and the Roman Economy.* New York: Longman, 1986.

Perlman, Isadore, Jan Gunneweg, and Joseph Yellin. "Pseudo-Nabataean Ware and Pottery of Jerusalem." *BASOR* 262 (1986) 77-82.

Pickup, Martin. "Matthew's and Mark's Pharisees." In Neusner and Chilton, *In Quest of the Historical Pharisees,* 67-112.

Poirier, John C. "Purity beyond the Temple in the Second Temple Era." *JBL* 122 (2003) 247-65.

————. "Why Did the Pharisees Wash their Hands?" *JJS* 47 (1996) 217-33.

Politis, Konstantinos D. "The Nabataean Cemetery at Khirbet Qazone." *NEA* 62 (1999) 128.

Pollitt, J. J. *Art in the Hellenistic Age.* Cambridge: Cambridge University Press, 1986.

Poorthuis, M. J. H. M., and Joshua Schwartz, eds. *Purity and Holiness: The Heritage of Leviticus.* Leiden: Brill, 2000.

Price, Randall. "Qumran Plateau." In *Hadashot Arkheologiyot (Excavations and Surveys in Israel)* 117 (2005). http://www.hadashot-esi.org.il/report_detail_eng.asp?id =126&mag_id=110

Puech, Émile. "The Collection of Beatitudes in Hebrew and in Greek (4Q525 1-4 and Mt 5,3-12)." In Manns and Alliata, *Early Christianity in Context,* 353-68.

————. "L'ostracon de *Khirbet* Qumrân (KHQ1996/1) et une vente de terrain à Jéricho, témoin de l'occupation essénienne à Qumrân." In *Flores Florentino: Dead Sea Scrolls and Other Early Jewish Studies in Honour of Florentino García Martínez,* ed. Anthony Hilhorst, Emile Puech, and Eibert Tigchelaar, 1-29. JSJSup 122. Leiden: Brill, 2007.

Qimron, Elisha. "Chickens in the Temple Scroll (11QTc)." *Tarbiz* 54 (1995) 473-76. [Hebrew]

———. "The Controversy over the Holiness of Jerusalem in the Second Temple Period." In *Judea and Samaria Research Studies: Proceedings of the 6th Annual Meeting-1996*, ed. Ya'acov Eshel, 73-77. Kedumim-Ariel: College of Judea and Samaria, 1997. [Hebrew]

———, and James H. Charlesworth. "Rule of the Community." In *The Dead Sea Scrolls, Hebrew, Aramaic, and Greek Texts with English Translations*. Vol. 1: *Rule of the Community and Related Documents*, ed. Charlesworth, 1-103. PTSDSSP. Tübingen: Mohr Siebeck and Louisville: Westminster John Knox, 1994.

———, and John Strugnell. *Qumran Cave 4: V, Miqsat Ma'ase ha-Torah*. DJD 10. Oxford: Clarendon, 1994.

Rabbinowitz, J., trans. *Midrash Rabbah: Deuteronomy*. London: Soncino, 1983.

Rahmani, Levy Y. "Ancient Jerusalem's Funerary Customs and Tombs, Part One." *BA* 44 (1981) 171-77.

———. "Ancient Jerusalem's Funerary Customs and Tombs, Part Three." *BA* 45 (1982) 43-53.

———. *A Catalogue of Jewish Ossuaries in the Collections of the State of Israel*. Jerusalem: Israel Antiquities Authority, 1994.

———. "Jason's Tomb." *IEJ* 17 (1967) 61-100.

Rajak, Tessa. *Josephus: The Historian and His Society*. London: Duckworth, 1983.

Reed, Jonathan L. *Archaeology and the Galilean Jesus: A Re-examination of the Evidence*. Harrisburg: Trinity, 2000.

Regev, Eyal. "Abominated Temple and a Holy Community: The Formation of the Notions of Purity and Impurity in Qumran." *DSD* 10 (2003) 243-78.

———. "Family Structure in Jerusalem during the Herodian Period Based on the Archaeological Findings of Burial Caves." In *Judea and Samaria Research Studies* 12, ed. Ya'acov Eshel, 97-116. Ariel: College of Judea and Samaria, 2003. [Hebrew]

———. "The Individualistic Meaning of Jewish Ossuaries: A Socio-Anthropological Perspective on Burial Practice." *PEQ* 133 (2001) 39-49.

———. "More on Ritual Baths of Jewish Groups and Sects: On Research Methods and Archaeological Evidence — A Reply to A. Grossberg." *Jerusalem Cathedra* 83 (1996) 169-76. [Hebrew]

———. "Non-Priestly Purity and Its Religious Aspects According to Historical Sources and Archaeological Findings." In Poorthuis and Schwartz, *Purity and Holiness*, 223-44.

———. "Pure Individualism: The Idea of Non-Priestly Purity in Ancient Judaism." *JSJ* 31 (2000) 176-202.

———. "Reconstructing Qumranic and Rabbinic Worldviews: Dynamic Holiness vs. Static Holiness." In Orion Center for the Study of the Dead Sea Scrolls, *Rabbinic Perspectives*, 87-112.

————. "Ritual Baths of Jewish Groups and Sects in the Second Temple Period." *Jerusalem Cathedra* 79 (1996) 3-21. [Hebrew]

————. *The Sadducees and Their Halakhah.* Jerusalem: Yad Ben-Zvi, 2005. [Hebrew]

————. *Sectarianism in Qumran: A Cross-cultural Perspective.* Berlin: de Gruyter, 2007.

Reich, Ronny. "Area A — Stratigraphy and Architecture: Hellenistic to Medieval Strata 6-1." In Geva, *Jewish Quarter Excavations,* 1:83-110.

————. "Caiaphas Name Inscribed on Bone Boxes." *BAR* 18/5 (1992) 38-44, 76.

————. "Miqva'ot in the Second Temple Period and Period of the Mishnah and Talmud." Ph.D. diss. Jerusalem: Institute of Archaeology, Hebrew University, 1990. [Hebrew]

————. "Ossuary Inscriptions from the 'Caiaphas' Tomb." *'Atiqot* 21 (1992) 72-77.

————. "Stone Mugs from Masada." In *Masada VIII,* 195-206.

————. "Stone Vessels, Weights and Architectural Fragments." In Geva, *Jewish Quarter Excavations,* 2:263-91.

————, and Eli Shukrun. "The Siloam Pool in the Wake of Recent Discoveries." In Baruch and Faust, *New Studies on Jerusalem,* 10:137-40.

Richardson, Peter. *Herod: King of the Jews and Friend of the Romans.* Minneapolis: Fortress, 1999.

Ritmeyer, Leen, and Kathleen Ritmeyer. "Potter's Field or High Priest's Tomb?" *BAR* 20/6 (1994) 22-35, 76.

Robinson, James M., ed. *The Nag Hammadi Library.* Rev. ed. San Francisco: Harper and Row, 1988.

Roller, Matthew B. *Dining Posture in Ancient Rome: Bodies, Values, and Status.* Princeton: Princeton University Press, 2006.

Rosenthal-Heginbottom, Renate. "Ceramics from Jericho and Masada: Review Article." *IEJ* 59 (2009) 92-99.

————. "Hellenistic and Early Roman Fine Ware and Lamps from Area A." In Geva, *Jewish Quarter Excavations,* 2:192-223.

————. "Late Hellenistic and Early Roman Lamps and Fine Ware." In Geva, *Jewish Quarter Excavations,* 3:144-67.

————, and Renee Sivan. *Ancient Lamps in the Schloessinger Collection.* Qedem 8. Jerusalem: Hebrew University, 1978.

Rozenberg, Silvia. "The Absence of Figurative Motifs in Herodian Wall Painting." In *I Temi Figurativi nella Pittura Parietale Antica; IV sec. a.C.–IV sec. d.C. Atti del VI Convegno Internazionale sulla Pittura Parietale Antica,* ed. D. Scagliarini Corlàita, 283-85, 415-16. Imola: University Press Bologna, 1997.

————. "Wall Painting Fragments from Area A." In Geva, *Jewish Quarter Excavations,* 2:302-28.

Rubin, Nissan. *The End of Life: Rites of Burial and Mourning in the Talmud and Midrash.* Tel Aviv: Hakibbutz Hameuchad, 1997. [Hebrew]

Runesson, Anders. "From Where? To What? Common Judaism, Pharisees, and the Changing Socioreligious Location of the Matthean Community." In McCready and Reinhartz, *Common Judaism,* 97-113.

Rykwert, Joseph. "Privacy in Antiquity." *Social Research* 68 (2001) 29-40.

Sade(h), Moshe. "Animal Bones." In Fischer, Gichon, and Tal, '*En Boqeq*, 2:131-36.

————. "Archaeozoological Finds from En-Gedi." In Hirschfeld, *En-Gedi Excavations II*, 604-12.

Saldarini, Anthony J. *Pharisees, Scribes and Sadducees in Palestinian Society*. BRS. Grand Rapids: Wm. B. Eerdmans and Livonia: Dove, 2001.

Sanders, Donald H., ed. *Nemrud Daği: The Hierothesion of Antiochus I of Commagene: Results of the American Excavations Directed by Theresa B. Goell*. Winona Lake: Eisenbrauns, 1996.

Sanders, E. P. *Jesus and Judaism*. Philadelphia: Fortress, 1985.

————. *Jewish Law from Jesus to the Mishnah: Five Studies*. Philadelphia: Trinity, 1990.

————. *Judaism: Practice and Belief, 63 BCE–66 CE*. Philadelphia: Trinity, 1992.

van de Sandt, Huub. "'Do Not Give What Is Holy to the Dogs' (Did 9:5D and Matt 7:6A): The Eucharistic Food of the Didache in Its Jewish Purity Setting." *VC* 56 (2002) 223-46.

————, and David Flusser. *The Didache: Its Jewish Sources and Its Place in Early Judaism and Christianity*. Minneapolis: Fortress, 2002.

Sapir, Yitzchak. "Masada: Evidence of Observing Jewish Laws of Purity." In *Judea and Samaria Research Studies: Proceedings of the 3rd Annual Meeting — 1993*, ed. Ze'ev Erlich and Ya'acov Eshel, 137-46. Kedumim-Ariel: College of Judea and Samaria, 1994. [Hebrew]

Scheidel, Walter. "Stratification, Deprivation, and Quality of Life." In Atkins and Osborne, *Poverty in the Roman World*, 40-59.

Schiffman, Lawrence H. "Community Without Temple: The Qumran Community's Withdrawal from the Jerusalem Temple." In *Gemeinde ohne Tempel/Community without Temple: Zur Substituierung und Transformation des Jerusalemer Tempels und seines Kults im Alten Testament, antiken Judentum und frühen Christentum*, ed. Beate Ego, Armin Lange, and Peter Pilhofer, 267-84. WUNT 118. Tübingen: Mohr Siebeck, 1999.

————. *The Courtyards of the House of the Lord: Studies on the Temple Scroll*. Ed. Florentino García Martínez. STDJ 75. Leiden: Brill, 2008.

————. *The Halakhah at Qumran*. SJLA 16. Leiden: Brill, 1975.

————. "The Impurity of the Dead in the *Temple Scroll*." In *Archaeology and History in the Dead Sea Scrolls*, 135-56.

————. "Non-Jews in the Dead Sea Scrolls." In *The Quest for Context and Meaning: Studies in Biblical Intertextuality in Honor of James A. Sanders*, ed. Craig A. Evans and Shemaryahu Talmon, 153-71. Biblical Interpretation 28. Leiden: Brill, 1997.

————. "Pharisaic and Sadducean Halakhah in Light of the Dead Sea Scrolls." *DSD* 1 (1994) 285-99.

————. "Qumran and Rabbinic Halakhah." In Talmon, *Jewish Civilization in the Hellenistic-Roman Period*, 138-46.

————. *Reclaiming the Dead Sea Scrolls*. Philadelphia: Jewish Publication Society, 1994.

————. Review of Roland de Vaux, *Qumran Grotte 4: II, I. Archéologie*; Josef T. Milik, *II. Tefillin, Mezuzot et Targums (4Q128-4Q157)*. DJD 6. Oxford: Oxford University Press, 1977. *JAOS* 100 (1980) 170-72.

————. "Sacral and Non-Sacral Slaughter according to the *Temple Scroll*." In *Time to Prepare the Way in the Wilderness: Papers on the Qumran Scrolls by Fellows of the Institute for Advanced Studies of the Hebrew University, Jerusalem, 1989-1990,* ed. Devorah Dimant and Lawrence H. Schiffman, 69-84. STDJ 16. Leiden: Brill, 1995.

————. *Sectarian Law in the Dead Sea Scrolls: Courts, Testimony, and the Penal Code.* BJS 33. Chico: Scholars, 1983.

————, ed. *Archaeology and History in the Dead Sea Scrolls: The New York University Conference in Memory of Yigael Yadin.* JSPSup 8. Sheffield: JSOT, 1990.

————, Emanuel Tov, and James C. VanderKam, eds. *The Dead Sea Scrolls Fifty Years After Their Discovery: Proceedings of the Jerusalem Congress, July 20-25, 1997.* Jerusalem: Israel Exploration Society, 2000.

Schremer, Adiel. "Seclusion and Exclusion: The Rhetoric of Separation in Qumran and Tannaitic Literature." In Orion Center for the Study of the Dead Sea Scrolls, *Rabbinic Perspectives,* 127-45.

————. "'[T]he[y] Did Not Read in the Sealed Book': Qumran Halakhic Revolution and the Emergence of Torah Study in Second Temple Judaism." In Goodblatt, Pinnick, and Schwartz, *Historical Perspectives,* 105-26.

Schürer, Emil. *The History of the Jewish People in the Age of Jesus Christ (175 B.C.–A.D. 135).* Rev. and ed. Geza Vermes, Fergus Millar, and Matthew Black. 3 vols. Edinburgh: T. & T. Clark, 1973-1986.

Schultz, Brian. "The Qumran Cemetery: 150 Years of Research." *DSD* 13 (2006) 194-228.

Schwartz, Baruch. "The Bearing of Sin in the Priestly Literature." In Wright, Freedman, and Hurvitz, *Pomegranates and Golden Bells,* 3-21.

————. "Israel's Holiness: The Torah Traditions." In Poorthuis and Schwartz, *Purity and Holiness,* 47-59.

Schwartz, Daniel R. "Law and Truth: On Qumran-Sadducean and Rabbinic Views of Law." In Dimant and Rappaport, *The Dead Sea Scrolls,* 229-40.

————. *Studies in the Jewish Background of Christianity.* WUNT 60. Tübingen: Mohr, 1992.

Schwartz, Joshua. "Dogs in Jewish Society in the Second Temple Period and in the Time of the Mishnah and Talmud." *JJS* 55 (2004) 246-77.

————. "Material Culture in the Land of Israel: Monks and Rabbis on Clothing and Dress in the Byzantine Period." In *Saints and Role Models in Judaism and Christianity,* ed. Marcel Poorthuis and Schwartz, 121-38. Leiden: Brill, 2004.

Scobie, Alexander. "Slums, Sanitation, and Mortality in the Roman World." *Klio* 68 (1986) 399-433.

Segal, Arthur. "Herodium." *IEJ* 23 (1973) 27-29.

Seligman, Jon. "Jerusalem, Khirbat Ka'kul (Pisgat Ze'ev H): Early Roman Farmsteads and a Medieval Village." *'Atiqot* 54 (2006) 1-73.

Selkin Wise, Carol. "*Miqwā'ôt* and Second Temple Sectarianism." In Edwards and McCollough, *The Archaeology of Difference,* 181-200.

Shadmi, Tamar. "The Ossuaries and the Sarcophagus." In Avni and Greenhut, *The Akeldama Tombs,* 41-55.

Shamir, Orit. "Textiles, Cordage, and Threads from En-Gedi." In Hirschfeld, *En-Gedi Excavations II*, 587-603.

Shanks, Hershel. "Who Lies Here? Jordan Tombs Match Those at Qumran." *BAR* 25/5 (1999) 48-53, 76.

―――, and Ben Witherington III. *The Brother of Jesus: The Dramatic Story & Meaning of the First Archaeological Link to Jesus & His Family.* San Francisco: HarperSanFrancisco, 2003.

Shatzman, Israel. *The Armies of the Hasmonaeans and Herod: From Hellenistic to Roman Frameworks.* TSAJ 25. Tübingen: Mohr Siebeck, 1991.

Sheffer, Avigail, and Hero Granger-Taylor. "Textiles." In Aviram, Foerster, and Netzer, *Masada IV*, 153-243.

Shemesh, Aharon. "The Dispute between the Pharisees and the Sadducees on the Death Penalty." *Tarbiz* 70.1 (2000) 17-33. [Hebrew]

―――. "Expulsion and Exclusion in the Community Rule and the Damascus Document." *DSD* 9 (2002) 44-74.

―――. "The History of the Creation of Measurements: Between Qumran and the Mishnah." In Orion Center for the Study of the Dead Sea Scrolls, *Rabbinic Perspectives*, 147-73.

―――. "The Holiness according to the *Temple Scroll*," *RevQ* 19 (2000) 369-82.

―――. "A New Reading of 11QTᵃ 52:13-16." In Schiffman, Tov, and VanderKam, *The Dead Sea Scrolls Fifty Years After Their Discovery*, 400-10.

―――. "The Origins of the Laws of Separatism: Qumran Literature and Rabbinic Halacha." *RevQ* 18 (1997) 223-41.

―――. "Scriptural Interpretations in the Damascus Document and Their Parallels in Rabbinic Midrash." In Baumgarten, Chazon, and Pinnick, *The Damascus Document*, 161-75.

―――, and Cana Werman. "Halakhah at Qumran: Genre and Authority." *DSD* 10 (2003) 104-29.

―――. "Hidden Things and Their Revelation." *RevQ* 18 (1998) 409-27.

Sidi, Naomi. "Stone Utensils." In Hirschfeld, *En-Gedi Excavations II*, 544-73.

Silberstein, Naama. "Hellenistic and Roman Pottery." In Hirschfeld, *Ramat Hanadiv Excavations*, 420-69.

Sklar, Jay. *Sin, Impurity, Sacrifice, Atonement: The Priestly Conceptions.* Sheffield: Sheffield Phoenix, 2005.

Sklar-Parnes, Deborah A. "Jerusalem, Shu'fat, Ramallah Road." *Hadashot Arkheologiyot* 117 (2005). http://www.hadashot-esi.org.il/report_detail_eng.asp?id=179&mag_id=110

―――. "Jerusalem, Shu'fat, Ramallah Road." *Hadashot Arkheologiyot* 118 (2006). http://www.hadashot-esi.org.il/report_detail_eng.asp?id=347&mag_id=111

―――, Yehudah Rapuano, and Rachel Bar-Nathan. "Excavations in Northeast Jerusalem — A Jewish Site in between the Revolts." In Baruch and Faust, *New Studies on Jerusalem*, 10:35*-41*.

Slane, Kathleen W. "The Fine Wares." In Herbert, *Tel Anafa*, 2/1:252-418.

―――, J. Michael Elam, Michael D. Glascock, and Hector Neff. "Compositional Analysis of Eastern Sigillata A and Related Wares from Tel Anafa (Israel)." *Journal of Archaeological Science* 21 (1994) 51-64.

Slotki, Judah J. *Midrash Rabbah, Numbers.* Vol. 2. London: Soncino, 1983.

Snow, Deborah, and Kay Prag, with Andreas Dimoulinis, Carolyn G. Koehler, and Philippa M. W. Matheson. "The Stamped Amphora Handles." In *Excavations by K. M. Kenyon in Jerusalem 1961-1967.* Vol. 5: *Discoveries in Hellenistic to Ottoman Jerusalem. Centenary Volume: Kathleen M. Kenyon, 1906-1978,* ed. Kay Prag, 389-409. LevantSup 7. Oxford: Oxbow, 2008.

Spanu, Marcello. "Burial in Asia Minor during the Imperial Period, with a Particular Reference to Cilicia and Cappadocia." In *Burial, Society, and Context in the Roman World,* ed. John Pearce, J. Martin Millett, and Manuela Struck, 169-77. Oxford: Oxbow, 2000.

Stern, Ephraim, ed. *The New Encyclopedia of Archaeological Excavations in the Holy Land.* 4 vols. New York: Simon and Schuster, 1993.

Stern, Menahem. "Aspects of Jewish Society: The Priesthood and Other Classes." In *The Jewish People in the First Century: Historical Geography, Political History, Social, Cultural and Religious Life and Institutions,* ed. Shemuel Safrai and Stern, 2:561-630. CRINT 1/1. Philadelphia: Fortress, 1987.

―――. *Greek and Latin Authors on Jews and Judaism: Edited with Introductions, Translations, and Commentary.* Vols. 1-3. Jerusalem: Israel Academy of Sciences and Humanities, 1974.

Stowers, Stanley K. "On the Comparison of Blood in Greek and Israelite Ritual." In Magness and Gitin, *Hesed ve-Emet,* 179-94.

Strange, James F. "The 1996 Excavations at Qumran and the Context of the New Hebrew Ostracon." In Galor, Humbert, and Zangenberg, *Qumran, the Site of the Dead Sea Scrolls,* 41-54.

―――, Dennis E. Groh, and Thomas R. W. Longstaff. "Excavations at Sepphoris: The Location and Identification of Shikhin, Part I." *IEJ* 44 (1994) 216-27.

―――. "Excavations at Sepphoris: The Location and Identification of Shikhin, Part II." *IEJ* 45 (1995) 171-87.

Strobel, August, and Stefan Wimmer. *Kallirrhoë ('Ēn ez-Zāra): Dritte Grabungskampagne des Deutschen Evangelischen Instituts für Altertumswissenschaft des Heiligen Landes und Exkursionen in Süd-Peräa.* Wiesbaden: Harrassowitz, 2003.

Sussman, Ya'akov. "The History of the 'Halakha' and the Dead Sea Scrolls: Preliminary Talmudic Observations on Miqsat Ma'ase Ha-Torah (4QMMT)." *Tarbiz* 59 (1990) 11-76. [Hebrew]

Swanson, Dwight D. *The Temple Scroll and the Bible: The Methodology of 11QT.* STDJ 14. Leiden: Brill, 1995.

Swartz, Michael D. "Ritual and Purity in Early Jewish Mysticism." *AJS Review* 19 (1994) 135-67.

Talmon, Shemaryahu, ed. *Jewish Civilization in the Hellenistic-Roman Period.* Philadelphia: Trinity, 1991.

Taylor, Joan E. "Philo of Alexandria on the Essenes: A Case Study on the Use of Classical Sources in Discussions of the Qumran-Essene Hypothesis." *Studia Philonica Annual* 19 (2007) 1-28.

———. "'Roots, Remedies and Properties of Stones': The Essenes, Qumran and Dead Sea Pharmacology." *JJS* 60 (2009) 226-44.

Terrenato, Nicola. "The Auditorium Site in Rome and the Origins of the Villa." *JRA* 14 (2001) 5-32.

Tigchelaar, Eibert J. C. "Sabbath Halakha and Worship in *4QWays of Righteousness*: *4Q421* 11 and 13+2+8 par *4Q264a* 1-2." *RevQ* 18 (1998) 359-72.

———. "The White Clothing of the Essenes and the Pythagoreans." In *Jerusalem, Alexandria, Rome: Studies in Ancient Cultural Interaction in Honour of A. Hilhorst*, ed. Florentino García Martínez and Gerald P. Luttikhuizen, 301-22. JSJSup 82. Leiden: Brill, 2003.

Tomson, Peter J. "Jewish Purity Laws as Viewed by the Church Fathers and by the Early Followers of Jesus." In Poorthuis and Schwartz, *Purity and Holiness*, 73-91.

Tov, Emanuel. "The Papyrus Fragments Found in the Judean Desert." In *Lectures et Relectures de la Bible: Festschrift P.-M. Bogaert*, ed. Jean-Marie Auwers and André Wénin, 247-55. BETL 144, Leuven: Leuven University Press, 1999.

Toynbee, Jocelyn M. C. *Death and Burial in the Roman World.* Ithaca: Cornell University Press, 1971.

Triebel, Lothar. *Jenseitshoffnung in Wort und Stein: Nefesch und pyramidales Grabmal als Phänomene antiken jüdischen Bestattungswesens im Kontext der Nachbarkulturen.* AGJU 56. Brill: Leiden, 2004.

Tushingham, A. D. *Excavations in Jerusalem 1961-1967.* Vol. 1. Toronto: Royal Ontario Museum, 1985.

Tzaferis, Vassilios. "The 'Abba' Burial Cave in Jerusalem." *'Atiqot* 7 (1974) 61-64. [Hebrew]

———. "Crucifixion — The Archaeological Evidence." *BAR* 11/1 (1985) 44-53.

Ussishkin, David. *The Village of Silwan: The Necropolis from the Period of the Judean Kingdom.* Jerusalem: Israel Exploration Society, 1993.

VanderKam, James C. "The Judean Desert and the Community of the Dead Sea Scrolls." In *Antikes Judentum und frühes Christentum: Festschrift für Hartmut Stegemann zum 65. Geburtstag*, ed. Bernd Kollmann, Wolfgang Reinbold, and Annette Steudel, 159-71. BZNW 97. Berlin: de Gruyter, 1999.

de Vaux, Roland. *Archaeology and the Dead Sea Scrolls.* Rev. ed. London: Oxford University Press, 1973.

———. "Archéologie." In Baillet, Milik, and de Vaux, *Les 'Petites Grottes' de Qumrân*, 1-36.

———. "Fouille au Khirbet Qumrân: Rapport préliminaire." *RB* 60 (1953) 83-106.

———. "Fouilles au Khirbet Qumrân: Rapport préliminaire sur la deuxième campagne." *RB* 61 (1954) 206-36.

———. "Fouilles de Khirbet Qumrân: Rapport préliminaire sur les 3ᵉ, 4ᵉ, et 5ᵉ campagnes." *RB* 63 (1956) 533-77.

———. "Fouilles de Feshkha." *RB* 66 (1959) 225-55.

Bibliography

Venit, Marjorie S. *Monumental Tombs of Ancient Alexandria: The Theater of the Dead.* Cambridge: Cambridge University Press, 2002.

del Verme, Marcello. *Didache and Judaism, Jewish Roots of an Ancient Christian-Jewish Work.* New York: T&T Clark, 2004.

Vermes, Geza. *The Complete Dead Sea Scrolls in English.* New York: Penguin, 1998.

―――. *The Passion.* New York: Penguin, 2005.

―――. *The Resurrection.* New York: Doubleday, 2008.

―――, and Martin D. Goodman, eds. *The Essenes According to the Classical Sources.* Sheffield: JSOT, 1989.

de Vincenz, Anna. "The Pottery." In Hirschfeld, *En-Gedi Excavations II,* 234-427.

Vitto, Fanny. "Burial Caves from the Second Temple Period in Jerusalem (Mount Scopus, Giv'at Hamivtar, Neveh Ya'akov)." *'Atiqot* 40 (2000) 65-121.

Vriezen, Th. C., and A. S. van der Woude. *Ancient Israelite and Early Jewish Literature.* Leiden: Brill, 2005.

Wacholder, Ben Zion. "Ezekiel and Ezekielianism as Progenitors of Essenianism." In Dimant and Rappaport, *The Dead Sea Scrolls,* 186-96.

―――. "Historiography of Qumran: The Sons of Zadok and Their Enemies." In *Qumran Between the Old and New Testaments,* ed. Frederick H. Cryer and Thomas L. Thompson, 347-77. JSOTSup 290. Sheffield: Sheffield Academic, 1998.

Wassen, Cecilia. "Sadducees and Halakah." In *Law in Religious Communities in the Roman Period: The Debate over Torah and Nomos in Post-Biblical Judaism and Early Christianity,* ed. Peter Richardson and Stephen Westerholm, with Albert I. Baumgarten, Michael Pettem, and Wassen, 127-46. Waterloo: Wilfrid Laurier University Press, 1991.

―――. *Women in the Damascus Document.* Leiden: Brill and Atlanta: Society of Biblical Literature, 2005.

―――, and Jutta Jokiranta. "Groups in Tension: Sectarianism in the *Damascus Document* and the *Community Rule*." In Chalcraft, *Sectarianism in Early Judaism,* 205-45.

Watson, Alan, trans. *The Digest of Justinian.* Vol. 4. Philadelphia: University of Pennsylvania Press, 1985.

Weinfeld, Moshe. "High Treason in the Temple Scroll and in the Ancient Near Eastern Sources." In Paul, Kraft, Schiffman, and Fields, *Emanuel,* 827-31.

Weiss, Zeev. "Foreign Influences on Jewish Burial in Galilee in the Period of the Mishnah and Talmud." *ErIsr* 25, 356-64. Aviram Volume. Jerusalem: Israel Exploration Society, 1996. [Hebrew]

―――. "Jewish Galilee in the First Century C.E.: An Archaeological View." In *Flavius Josephus, Vita,* trans. Daniel R. Schwartz, 15-60. Jerusalem: Yad Ben-Zvi, 2007. [Hebrew]

―――. "The Location of Jewish Cemeteries in Galilee in the Period of the Mishnah and Talmud." In Zinger, *Graves and Burial Practices in Israel in the Ancient Period,* 230-40. [Hebrew]

Weksler-Bdolah, Shlomit. "'Yad Benjamin' — A Hiding-Complex Site in the Western

Judaean Foothills." In Eshel and Zissu, *New Studies on the Bar Kokhba Revolt,* 41-51.

Werman, Cana. "The Concept of Holiness and the Requirements of Purity in Second Temple and Tannaitic Literature." In Poorthuis and Schwartz, *Purity and Holiness,* 163-79.

————. "The Rules of Consuming and Covering the Blood in Priestly and Rabbinic Law." *RevQ* 16 (1995) 621-36.

Werrett, Ian C. *Ritual Purity and the Dead Sea Scrolls.* STDJ 72. Leiden: Brill, 2007.

Whiston, William, trans. *Josephus, Complete Works.* Grand Rapids: Kregel, 1984.

Wilfand, Yael. "Did the Rabbis Reject the Roman Public Latrine?" *Babesch* 84 (2009) 183-96.

Williams, Margaret. "Being a Jew in Rome: Sabbath Fasting as an Expression of Romano-Jewish Identity." In *Negotiating Diaspora: Jewish Strategies in the Roman Empire,* ed. John M. G. Barclay, 8-18. LSTS 45. London: T. & T. Clark, 2004.

Wise, Michael O. Review of Michael A. Knibb, *The Qumran Community.* New York: Cambridge University Press, 1987. *JNES* 49 (1990) 200-2.

Witherington, Ben, III. "The Story of James, Son of Joseph, Brother of Jesus." In Shanks and Witherington, *The Brother of Jesus,* 89-223.

Witke, Charles. "Propertianum Manuale." *CP* 64 (1969) 107-9.

Wouters, Helena, Chantal Fontaine-Hodiamont, Robert Donceel, Ann Aerts, and Koen Janssens. "Antique Glass from Khirbet Qumrân: Archaeological Context and Chemical Determination." *Bulletin de l'Institut Royal du Patrimoine Artistique/ Van het Koninklijk Instituut voor het Kunstpartimonium* 28 (1999/2000) 9-40.

Wright, David P. *The Disposal of Impurity: Elimination Rites in the Bible and in Hittite and Mesopotamian Literature.* SBLDS 101. Atlanta: Scholars, 1987.

————, David Noel Freedman, and Avi Hurvitz, eds. *Pomegranates and Golden Bells: Studies in Biblical, Jewish, and Near Eastern Ritual, Law, and Literature in Honor of Jacob Milgrom.* Winona Lake: Eisenbrauns, 1995.

Yadin, Yigael. *The Finds from the Bar-Kokhba Period in the Cave of Letters.* Jerusalem: Israel Exploration Society, 1963.

————. *Masada: Herod's Fortress and the Zealots' Last Stand.* New York: Random House, 1966.

————. "Pesher Nahum (4Q pNahum) Reconsidered." *IEJ* 24 (1971) 1-12.

————. *The Scroll of the War of the Sons of Light against the Sons of Darkness.* London: Oxford University Press, 1962.

————. *The Temple Scroll.* 3 vols. Jerusalem: Israel Exploration Society, 1971-1983.

————. *The Temple Scroll.* New York: Random House, 1985.

————, and Joseph Naveh. "The Aramaic and Hebrew Ostraca and Jar Inscriptions." In Yadin, Naveh, and Meshorer, *Masada I,* 6-68.

————, Joseph Naveh, and Yaacov Meshorer. *Masada I: The Yigael Yadin Excavations 1963-1965, Final Reports.* Vol. 1: *The Aramaic and Hebrew Ostraca and Jar Inscriptions.* Jerusalem: Israel Exploration Society, 1989.

Yardeni, Ada. "A Draft of a Deed on an Ostracon from Khirbet Qumrân." *IEJ* 47 (1997) 233-37.

Bibliography

————. *Textbook of Aramaic, Hebrew, and Nabataean Documentary Texts from the Judaean Desert and Related Material.* Vol. 1: *The Documents;* Vol. 2: *Translation, Palaeography, Concordance.* Jerusalem: Hebrew University, 2000.

Yegül, Fikret. *Baths and Bathing in Classical Antiquity.* Cambridge, MA: MIT Press, 1992.

Yellin, Joseph, Magen Broshi, and Hanan Eshel. "Pottery of Qumran and Ein Ghuweir: The First Chemical Exploration of Provenience." *BASOR* 321 (2001) 65-78.

Zangenberg, Jürgen, Harold W. Attridge, and Dale B. Martin, eds. *Religion, Ethnicity, and Identity in Ancient Galilee: A Region in Transition.* WUNT 210. Tübingen: Mohr Siebeck, 2007.

Zeuner, Frederick E. "Notes on Qumrân." *PEQ* 92 (1960) 27-36.

Zias, Joseph. "Anthropological Analysis of Human Skeletal Remains." In Avni and Greenhut, *The Akeldama Tombs,* 117-21.

————. "Qumran Toilet Practices: A Response to a Response." *RevQ* 87 (2006) 479-81.

————. "A Rock-Cut Tomb in Jerusalem." *BASOR* 245 (1982) 53-56.

————, and Eliezer Sekeles. "The Crucified Man from Giv'at ha-Mivtar: A Reappraisal." *IEJ* 35 (1985) 22-27.

————, James D. Tabor, and Stephanie Harter-Lailheugue. "Toilets at Qumran, the Essenes, and the Scrolls: New Anthropological Data and Old Theories." *RevQ* 88 (2006) 631-40.

Zinger, Itamar, ed. *Graves and Burial Practices in Israel in the Ancient Period.* Jerusalem: Yad Izhak Ben-Zvi, 1994. [Hebrew]

Zissu, Boaz. "Odd Tomb Out: Has Jerusalem's Essene Cemetery Been Found?" *BAR* 25/ 2 (1999) 50-55, 62.

————. "'Qumran Type' Graves in Jerusalem: Archaeological Evidence of an Essene Community?" *DSD* 5 (1998) 158-71.

————, and David Amit. "Common Judaism, Common Purity, and the Second Temple Period Judean *Miqwa'ot* (Ritual Immersion Baths)." In McCready and Reinhartz, *Common Judaism,* 47-62, 237-42.

————, and Hanan Eshel. "The Geographical Distribution of the Bar Kokhba Coins." In Eshel and Zissu, *New Studies on the Bar Kokhba Revolt,* 17-40.

————, Amir Ganor, and Yoav Farhi. "Finds from the Hiding Complex at 'Moran 1' Site in the Southern Judaean Foothills." In Eshel and Zissu, *New Studies on the Bar Kokhba Revolt,* 53-72.

————, Yotam Tepper, and David Amit. "*Miqwa'ot* at Kefar 'Othnai near Legio." *IEJ* 56 (2006) 57-66.

Zlotnick, Dov. *The Tractate "Mourning" (Semahot) (Regulations Relating to Death, Burial, and Mourning).* Yale Judaica Series 17. New Haven: Yale University Press, 1966.

Index of Modern Authors

Index of Modern Authors

Bokser, Baruch M., 191n.32, 194n.45, 268n.22, 270n.41
Boyarin, Daniel, 183-84
Bray, Tamara L., 77
Brin, Gershon, 195n.52
Broshi, Magen, 10, 100, 102-3, 143, 192n.36, 232n.16, 233n.32
Brown, Raymond E., 260n.173, 261n.188
Broyde, Michael, 26
Bunimovitz, Shlomo, 252n.82
Burns, Joshua Ezra, 205n.55, 224n.120, 235n.15, 267n.1, 267n.3, 270n.34

Cahill, Jane M., 223n.113, 247n.27, 250n.45, 252n.72
Chancey, Mark A., 233n.29
Chilton, Bruce, 189n.18, 193n.38, 239n.9
Cohen, Shaye J. D., 181, 236n.27, 237n.52, 267n.10
Cohn, Yehudah B., 206n.72, 236n.47, 237n.49
Crawford, Sidnie White, 208n.19, 212n.66, 218n.43
Crossan, John Dominic, 77-78, 169, 199n.101
Crown, Alan D., 211n.56, 234n.7
Cuffel, Alexandra, 243n.37, 244n.54

Davids, Peter H., 263n.206
Davies, Philip R., 205n.56, 226-27n.10, 243n.48, 252n.82
Deines, Roland, 224n.117
Doering, Lutz, 140, 202n.22, 220n.65, 229n.14, 242n.36, 244n.54
Donceel, Robert, 68
Donceel-Voûte, Pauline, 68
Dothan, Moshe, 104
Douglas, Mary, 208nn.2-3, 270n.39

Elitzur, Yoel, 20, 202n.24, 268n.18
Elitzur-Leiman, Rivka, 225n.128
Eshel, Esther, 161

Eshel, Hanan, 100, 102-3, 104-6, 189n.17, 226n.142, 231n.45, 232n.16, 233n.32, 239n.2, 239n.5
Evans, Craig A., 248n.33, 249n.44, 257n.146, 260n.169, 262n.191

Faust, Avraham, 252n.82
Fink, Amir S., 212n.69, 214n.94
Finkielsztejn, Gerald, 214n.5, 215n.8, 216n.25, 219n.61
Firmage, Edwin, 43-44
Fitzmyer, Joseph A., 260n.166
Flusser, David, 44, 226n.5, 263n.209
Foerster, Gideon, 152-53
Fonrobert, Charlotte E., 229nn.7-10, 231n.46
Fraade, Steven D., 207n.85
Fredriksen, Paula, 190n.20, 199n.98, 206n.62
Furstenberg, Yair, 195n.51, 202n.23, 204n.43, 204n.46, 204n.50, 205nn.56-57, 207n.75, 224n.121, 244n.59

García Martínez, Florentino, 193n.40, 231n.46
Gat, Joseph, 172
George, Rose, 241n.17
Getzov, Nimrod, 61-62
Gibson, Shimon, 70, 157, 198n.83, 200n.1, 201n.6, 217n.37, 223n.113, 224n.115, 224n.123
Gilat, Yitzhak, 91
Ginzberg, Louis, 244n.56
Goldenberg, Robert, 230n.38, 231n.43
Goodfriend, Elaine Adler, 211n.50
Goodman, Martin D., 11, 25-26, 177, 181, 185-86, 199n.104, 206n.66, 220n.66, 227n.22, 235n.10, 253n.82, 253n.87
Gorin-Rosen, Yael, 67, 222n.95
Greenhut, Zvi, 248n.37
Grossberg, Asher, 19, 20, 200n.1, 201n.9, 218n.47, 244n.57

Index of Subjects

Index of Scripture and Other Ancient Texts